Carolyn Steedman was born in 1947 and grew up in South London. She studied history at the University of Sussex and Newnham College, Cambridge from 1965–72. Her first book, *The Tidy House* (Virago, 1983), was the winner of the 1983 Fawcett Society Book Award. Her book *Policing the Victorian Community* was published in 1984, followed by *The Radical Soldier's Tale* (1988), *Childhood, Culture and Class in Britain: Margaret McMillan, 1860–1931* (Virago, 1990) and *Past Tenses* (1992). She has also edited *Language, Gender and Childhood* (1985) and contributed to *Truth, Dare or Promise* (Virago, 1985). Carolyn Steedman is a Reader in the Centre for Social History at the University of Warwick and lives in Leamington Spa.

STRANGE DISLOCATIONS

Childhood and the Idea of Human Interiority, 1780–1930

CAROLYN STEEDMAN

Published by VIRAGO PRESS Limited, 1995
20 Vauxhall Bridge Road, London SW1V 2SA

*A CIP catalogue record for this title
is available from the British Library*

Typeset by M Rules

Printed and bound in Great Britain by
Mackays of Chatham PLC, Chatham, Kent

Some children, whose bodies portrayed the strangest dislocations, aroused now astonishment and now horror, and Wilhelm could not refrain from feeling intense pity when he saw the child . . . performing the strange postures with some effort.
Goethe, *Wilhelm Meister*, Volume 1, Book 2, Chapter 4.

Rolamo: [starting up wildly] What! restored? restored? ha! ha! ha! . . .
Stand from about me – let me see my child! – my lost child found! – my child that I can own!
John Howard Payne, *Clari; or, the Maid of Milan: An Opera in Two Acts* (1823), Cumberland's British Theatre, 1829.

'Sir', she called out, 'if you are unhappy, what is to become of Mignon?' – 'Dear creature,' he said, taking her hands, 'you too are part of my sadness.'
Goethe, *Wilhelm Meister*, Volume 1, Book 2, Chapter 14.

Acknowledgements

Most of the work for this book was undertaken when I was a Senior Simon Research Fellow of the University of Manchester from 1990 to 1991. I would like to thank the Simon (Social Sciences) Committee for appointing me Fellow and allowing me not only research time but the opportunity for so much fruitful discussion with colleagues in the Sociology Department (where I held the Fellowship) and the Wellcome Unit for the History of Medicine. In the autumn of 1992, colleagues and graduate students in the History Department, the University of Michigan, Ann Arbor made me think hard about the work I had already done; I owe them a great deal. For his work of translation my debt to Richard Parker, Subject Specialist for History of the University of Warwick Library, is acknowledged in dozens of notes below. Many friends and colleagues have talked to me over the last six years about the contents of this book. John Churcher of the Psychology Department, the University of Manchester read the earliest version of the manuscript that it was possible for anyone to see. I am extremely grateful for his reading. I particularly thank John Stokes of the Department of English, the University of Warwick, whose discourse on the acrobat is the best. I found all of my anonymous readers' comments most helpful, one so much so that on two occasions, fragments of his or her remarks turn up in the rewritten text. Whoever that anonymous reader is should see this as cognizance, not plagiarism.

Some portions of Chapters 2 and 9 originally appeared as 'Mignon's Meanings' in John Stokes (ed.), *Fin-de-Siècle, Fin du Globe. Fears and Fantasies of the Late Nineteenth Century*, Macmillan, 1992, pp.102–16.

Note on the cover photograph:
El Nino Farini, performing on the trapeze. Of this early action photograph by Nandin, taken some time in the mid-1860s, Raymond Mander and Joe Mitchenson write: 'When he grew up, he was reintroduced by his father as Mlle Lulu . . . At the Royal Amphitheatre, Holborn in 1871 . . . "she" was shot out of a cannon. A visit by the Prince and Princess of Wales caused humanitarians and moralists to protest at the danger to the "young lady", only to be confounded when it was proved that she was "a lubly boy".' Raymond Mander and Joe Mitchenson, *Victorian and Edwardian Entertainment from Old Photographs*, Batsford, 1978, plate 52.

Contents

Preface

Once, some time ago now, I had a different title for this book. The idea for it – just a proposal, really – was called 'Finding the Child'. The long-abandoned working title suggested two searches. The first was the compulsive one, which has both shaped and been the subject of much literary and psychological endeavour of the last two hundred years: the search for the lost realm of the adult's past, for the far country of dreams and reverie that came to assume the shape of childhood from the end of the eighteenth century onwards. The second search (I thought briefly that it was uniquely my own, though it turned out to be a great many other people's as well) was for a child-figure of the late eighteenth century, for Goethe's Mignon, who was first published (though not first written) in his *Wilhelm Meister* of 1795–6. This strange, deformed and piercingly beautiful child-acrobat of Italian origins haunted the nineteenth century, as this book will relate. Constantly rewritten, reshaped, transmogrified, she was constantly rediscovered, reused, reformulated; it appears indeed, that she was found, again and again. My use of Mignon to structure this book is part of a long tradition of employing this particular child-figure to think by. Strange Dislocations is – and this is a point that I shall make again – part of the story it is trying to tell.

It was Mignon, and the search for her, that incited the change of title. The reader must discover, as I did in pursuing her, that Mignon and all she represents is really not to be found at all. The search is an impossible one, for a past that is lost and gone; for the child that has gone away. The social and psychic consequences of embodying what is lost and gone in the shape and form of a child became the concomitant topic of this book.

The strange dislocations of the title are several. There are – as the first epigraph tells the reader – the awkward movements, the bizarre alignment of limbs, and the weird postures that young Wilhelm Meister notes when he sees the little troupe of child acrobats perform for the first time. The acrobat has been shaped, her body dislocated, by adult hand. A great many nineteenth-century audiences appear to have conventionally understood the acrobat as a metaphor for adult–child relations. But I shall suggest that other dislocations are evoked in conventional uses of the Mignon-figure, in the century or so after its inception. The dislocation is the loss that provides the aetiology of the self; the imagined child embodies the loss and dislocation. Nineteenth-century physiology, which gave rise to growth studies, provided a detailed, material understanding of the processes that produce the adult body. Physiology gave an itemised account of the way in which a child grows up, and goes away, yet also remains to haunt the present. That is the reason why these pages dwell so very much on the uses that nineteenth-century people made of physiological concepts and images in thinking about the self.

And then there is the strangest dislocation of them all, which is that children are the bloody fragments of another body, little parcels of flesh and bone split off from another. That we are nervous when this aspect of our existence is articulated or explored – as for instance (in a book that figures absolutely nowhere in these pages) Mary Shelley explored it when she wrote Frankenstein's Monster as a child-figure – should not lead us to ignore quite strenuous investigations of the topic that took place within and without the literary realm during the course of the nineteenth century.[1]

Most societies have paid some imaginative and theoretical attention to the strange circumstance of our individual origin in parturition. Yet different knowledge is brought to bear upon the question, in different historical periods. I am particularly concerned to outline the implications of nineteenth-century physiology and biology for the place of childhood in the imaginative life of adults of the period. The most resonant connection made by nineteenth-century physiological inquiry was between growth and death. I accept, as many readers of this book in manuscript form have pointed out, that until infant mortality began to decline in the early years of this century, any adult contemplating a small child was sharply aware of the immanence of death in growth. But I am concerned to show what new knowledge was brought to bear on this old perception, so that death was no longer understood only as the immediate and very real threat to the child's existence, but understood also as the inevitable outcome of the very process the child embodied, which was growth itself.

The interest of the topic is, of course, that it is *not* transhistorical, that children have not always and everywhere been used as emblems of the adult human condition, though that is indeed the imaginative and cognitive legacy with which we operate in regard to children in the late twentieth century. Though it is always difficult to recall the genesis of a piece of work, I think that what prompted this book was the desire to understand modern uses of childhood, especially those attitudes of projection on to and identification and empathy with children that are a fairly recent historical development in Western societies. What I disinter are some of the means by which children have come to be closely identified with adult selfhood. These attitudes constitute a problem, particularly for human beings in the state of childhood, but for the adults performing acts of projection and identification as well. At one point in the book I raise serious doubts about the ability of historical accounts of phenomena to offer solutions to the dilemmas they outline and show coming into being. But it is evident that I do believe that the historical tale can tell of how we got to be the way we are. My conviction that events marshalled into chronology can *explain* something is a turn of thought connected to the very development of childhood in its modern sense, and one that I cannot escape, even should I want to. 'Childhood' and 'history' as ways of thinking are the topics of this book, and it is written under their propulsion.

What follows is a history, not some other form of narrative. It is a history because what I am about to describe happened in the world, in one way rather than another. To say this – which indeed, is not to say much more than that something didn't not happen – is to undertake to proceed in a particular manner. I shall proceed chronologically, on the understanding that some things happened before others, and after other happenings; I shall speculate about why these things took place when they did I shall discuss cause and agency, where I am able); and I shall take into account material circumstances, including 'natural and humanly fashioned elements, not exclusively linguistic in nature'.[2] There are bottom lines in the account that follows; things-that-are-the-way-they-are, which I attempt to deal with myself and which I observe a large number of people living in the past dealing with as well. They are: that human beings have bodies that grow through a process of development to full adult stature, and to an adult state; that the story starts with childhood, and at the end of it we die.

I labour these points in the manner of a primer in order to emphasise that in the following pages I do not take language as a metaphor for other kinds of social process, nor do I – can I – understand language as a force that shapes or forms people living in the past, or texts and narratives as productive of meaning or human identity. I write on the assumption that understanding language historically means paying attention to what people do with language and texts (and in the argument that follows, with ideas and images from texts, and with the broken fragment of language that 'mignon' and 'Mignon' represented) rather than paying attention to what language does with people, and how they might be made up or constructed by language. What follows is a history of a visceral sense of insideness, of an interiorised selfhood that the word Mignon and the cluster of ideas and beliefs embodied in 'child' allow us to retrieve; and of the how and why of its coming into being. It claims that Mignon *happened* (that all the beliefs about and conceptualisations of the self that she so conveniently helps us locate, happened in the world, in one way rather than another), so that there is nothing else to call this account of her but a history.

1

Introduction: Lost and Found

This book is about two things, not quite one and the same, but one anterior, and one illuminative. It is about the development of an idea or concept of the self, from the end of the eighteenth century onwards; and it is about a *figure* – a figure with its origins in the literary realm – that was often used to articulate an understanding of that idea, or concept. The account that follows could have been given without using the figure at all, but it is actually helpful to tell the story in this way, partly because the impulse to personify ideas of the self, to give them shape and form, which use of the figure reveals, is part of the story, as, indeed, are this book and the questions it embodies.

I first encountered Goethe's Mignon, the child-figure whose presence structures this book, in the mid-1980s, when I was working on Margaret McMillan (1860–1931). By then (I had been working on the topic for a very long time), my research was more or less guided by the need to understand how McMillan had been able to put childhood on to the political agenda of the Independent Labour Party (later the Labour Party) in the Edwardian years, and how the various theories of childhood she promulgated had been understood within her own circle of political allies, and beyond it. Between 1911 and 1912, the veteran socialist propagandist and journalist wrote a series of articles for the *Highway*, the journal of the Workers' Educational Association, under the general title, 'In Our Garden'. Here she described the setting up and early operation of the camp-school (open-air school) and health centre that she had recently opened in Deptford, a notoriously poor and 'derelict' part of south-east London.[1]

The series was nothing surprising: using the journalistic form she had made her own, the heart-wrenching socio-fiction of slum life, she described the operation of her new enterprise by means of striking vignettes – of children, in this case – that allowed her readers to 'see' the point of the administrative, medical and policy information she imparted. However, the third article in the series, published in September 1911, did hold many surprises, once the range of allusions McMillan fleetingly employed had been understood. She called this piece 'Marigold – An English Mignon', thereby making reference to the strange and disturbed child-figure of Goethe's *Wilhelm Meister* (1795–6), whose otherness and exoticism are indicated by her Italian origins, the mystery of her provenance, and her work as an acrobat with the troupe of rope-dancers that had abducted her. By using as a subtitle (or, in some reprints, as a colophon) the question 'Kennst du das Land?' McMillan not only gestured towards the song of yearning that Goethe's original sang, but also towards the eighty or so settings the song had been given by various composers, since the early years of the nineteenth century.[2]

What was startling in this usage was not, as I thought at the time, the very high literary and affective claims that McMillan made for the eponymous seven-year-old, a Deptford coster's child, for all of her efforts since the mid-1890s had been to bring outcast children within the framework of a childhood that had received attention from literature and art. Nor was it surprising that she used the figure of Mignon to discuss beauty in conjunction with deformity (or at least, thwarted development), in a child of the unrespectable, Edwardian poor, and at the same time to conveniently prefigure the doom of this child of the residuum. Two things that were always known about Mignon through all her nineteenth-century metamorphoses, was that adults had damaged her in order to turn her into an acrobat, and that death was properly her fate, no matter what popular plots of restoration might give her by way of futurity. What astonishes, in retrospect, was McMillan's calm assumption that her WEA readers would *get* all of this.

The *Highway*'s readership was made up of working- and lower-middle-class students of the WEA, pursuing a further education beyond the elementary level that they had experienced, and their tutors, some of them drawn from a similar class background and some, like McMillan herself, members of the professionally and politically engaged middle class. This last category might well have been expected to know their Goethe, but McMillan evidently believed that she needed to supply only minimal explanation of her references for all her readers. She simply remarked on Marigold's facial beauty, in particular on 'the nose, which like Goethe's Mignon's, is extremely lovely', and that was all. It remained for me to discover, as so many others have done before, that as the most referred-to, re-represented and transmogrified child-figure of the nineteenth century, Mignon's appearance in the most out of the way places should not provoke amazement at all but is, rather, to be expected.

There are very deep pleasures involved in pursuing a figure like this, across vast tracts of text, across continents, time and genre, and in finding more and more of Mignon's siblings, Mignon-figures, and Mignon-types. The pleasures are particularly delicious for the historian, for the pursuit is a kind of analogy of the historical enterprise itself, the adherents of which are doggedly determined to track down what is in fact lost and gone, so that with the barely sensible burden of the past in our arms, we might stagger on to the melodramatic stage and cry '"Found!"'; and in that moment before the body we are holding breathes its last, *know* that, as Christina Crosby says, 'what was lost is found, what was missing recovered', and that there really is 'such satisfaction, such a reconciliation, such a homecoming'. All fantasy; and indeed, by stricter analogy with the melodrama of 1856 that provides this picture, it is the historian carrying the burden who gasps his or her last with the cry 'Found!'

In describing history as 'the melodramatic fix', Crosby uses the third act of Wilkie Collins's 'The Frozen Deep' to suggest that the nineteenth-century melodramatic imagination was 'an extreme instance of the Victorian historical imagination, a conceptualising of history as home, as the recoverable origin of man, something lost which can be found.'[3] We can argue later on with Crosby's formulation of exactly what it is that has been lost. For the time being, the ineluctable connection of historical practice, in the modern form that was established in the middle years of the last century, to a search that is hopeless yet compulsive is useful for describing the allure of Mignon's many manifestations, and the deep satisfactions there would be in ferreting out all of them, of uttering 'Found!' again and again.

But the central topic of this book is not the strange, androgynous child that Goethe wrote, nor the many versions of her that continue to be reproduced. Rather, it concerns the ideas, beliefs and conceptualisations that were involved in remembering and reshaping a literary figure in the century and a half after it was first written in *Wilhelm Meister*. At the end of it all it should be clearer why the idea of childhood that Mignon embodied – as in the case of McMillan's use of her in the guise of Marigold – *meant* something – was an idea, an entity – to those who had not read Goethe, who had never purchased the sheet music for Schubert's most famous of all the settings of her most famous song, who had never seen a shoddy *sério-comique* version of Ambroise Thomas's opera *Mignon* (let alone a staging in its pristine form); meant something to those who did not know why child acrobats performing on the music-hall stage, and young women vaulting on horseback at the circus, were so frequently called Mignon.[4] At the end of it, it should be clearer why 'Mignon' meant something to those who had – perhaps – never even heard the word, and could not have called what it was they knew by that name. The proposition is that the complex of beliefs, feelings and sentiments that 'Mignon' frequently articulated were to do with childhood, and to do with the self, and the relationship between the two, in the period 1780–1930.

Mignon, being constantly found, is a feature of the following pages; but their principal concern is a form of subjectivity that came into being between the end of the eighteenth century and the beginning of the twentieth. By stating even this much, I make the claim that the various ways in which people in the past have felt, or perceived or known a self are to some extent historically retrievable. And I also make the conventional historical claims of specificity and alteration: a change took place in the way that people understood themselves – indeed, came to new understandings of what a self was, and how a self came into being – in Western societies, during the last century.

Particularly important for understanding this change is the part that Freudian psychoanalysis played, between about 1900 and 1920, in summarising and reformulating a great many nineteenth-century articulations of the idea that the core of an individual's psychic identity was his or her own lost past, or childhood. The account of infantile sexuality and the process of repression that emerged from Sigmund Freud's writing in this period *theorised* childhood in this sense, gave it another name as 'the unconscious', or 'the unconscious mind'.

The historical development outlined below is discussed in terms of British society, but with much reference to continental Europe as well – a perspective dictated by the social and figurative trajectory of the child-figure who also provides the time-span of this study. The year 1780 is a starting point, because it was in the very late 1770s that Mignon was born, in the pages of Goethe's first draft of *Wilhelm Meister*. The study ends in the 1920s, because by then some of what the Mignon-figure represented had been theorised, in the way just indicated, and that theory had been quite widely disseminated. By this time a certain understanding of selfhood had been formalised, most typically in the 'discovery' of the unconscious, and its connection as a formulation to the idea of the lost child within all of us.

'Interiority' is a term quite widely used in modern literary and cultural history, and in literary criticism, to describe an interiorised subjectivity, a sense of the self *within* – a quite richly detailed self. In discussing Gothic fiction of the late eighteenth century, Robert Miles says that when he uses the term 'interiority' he means 'something akin to, but not quite the same as, "subjectivity"'. In his account of the making of interiority – which he further discusses as 'inner space' – in the fiction of Ann Radcliffe he is clear that interiority is 'not . . . a universal, but . . . a creation and extension of the self's emotional terrain rooted in history'.[5] If we are to historicise interiority then it is important not only to consider the social and cultural circumstances of its creation in this way, but also – and Miles's case of Radcliffe's *Mysteries of Udolpho* (1794) is much to the point here – to consider the new uses of the historical past made by those writers who inscribed it.

Not only did 'history' help create the idea of interiority, but the individual and personal history that a child embodied came to be used to represent human 'insideness' in the period under discussion. This development is explored in two ways in this book: first by considering its conceptualisation over a period of time; and secondly, by arguing that it was the belief itself, that each individual self has a history, that promoted the development of an interiorised self. These developments are the focus of the first half of this book.

The interiorised self, understood to be the product of a personal history, was most clearly expressed in the idea of 'childhood', and the idea of 'the child'. The sum of technical knowledge about childhood increased dramatically in the middle years of the nineteenth century, and there was a veritable explosion of information about this period of physiological and cognitive development in human beings. It is the way in which that information was used that matters to the following argument, so this book is also a partial history of people's belief that there was such a thing as 'childhood'. It will suggest that the effect of this belief was twofold. First, new information about childhood was abstracted, or conceptualised into the figure of 'the child', or the idea of the child. Literary child-figures have a long history, and this is not a claim that a particular trope was a new phenomenon of the late eighteenth and early nineteenth centuries.[6] But the material used in making the figure *was* new, and the period sees an extension of this process (of ideation, or personification) beyond the literary realm, so that the child-figure becomes a central vehicle for expressing ideas about the self and its history. Second, the complex understanding that there was such a thing as childhood focused new forms of attention on actually living and real children, from the late eighteenth century onwards.

Real children (children observed, children described, children remembered by the adults they became) fuelled the imaginative constructs that in their turn interpreted and explained – for instance – the 'child-life' of industrial conurbations, the statistics of child labour, or the physiological bodies of children that were described in child-care manuals of the nineteenth century. It seems important to emphasise, very early on, that the imagination under discussion here is that of the adult, that this book concerns the adult beliefs, desires and fantasies that are expressed in the figure of a child, and that it does not attempt at all to describe childhood experiences, or to recapture the state of being a child through the words of those who recall it in fictional and other writing.

In the following pages I proceed on the assumption that it is helpful to make an analytic separation between real children, living in the time and space of particular societies, and the ideational and figurative force of their existence. However, this is a cognitive dislocation that is extremely difficult to perform. Wordsworth's babe leaps in his mother's arms, and we believe that we see there a figure that resists the processes of both history and symbolism – a child: a true thing.[7] Those familiar with literary-critical discussion of children in texts will recognise a common elision of literature and life, whereby writers feel compelled to determine to what extent child-figures 'reflect the reality of childhood experience'.[8] That writers and readers of widely varying degrees of sophistication find the separation of sociology and symbol difficult when they encounter fictional children (and the divorce of children and their meaning even harder outside the pages of literary texts) is a result of the historical development that this book seeks to describe. It has something (though not everything) to do with a particular legacy of nineteenth-century reforming Liberalism, especially in Britain, whereby individual and collective progress in civilisation is expressed by being kind to groups of the weak, feeble and disenfranchised in society – women, slaves, the insane and, above all others, children. Some readers will also be familiar with the peculiarities of much history of childhood, where the historian's propriety of response is expressed through a kindness to long-dead children, and a dramatic rehearsal of horror at conditions they may have experienced.[9]

Ludmilla Jordanova has suggested that only the most localised and fragmented history of children can be written, not just because they are the most temporary of social subjects – they grow up, and go away – but also because of the peculiarity of the historian's attitude towards children as a topic, an attitude that is itself a product of the developments that conventional history of childhood seeks to evade. Jordanova points out that 'childhood is a state that historians have themselves experienced [and] they are, without exception, directly personally implicated in their scholarship'. Moreover, 'historians are the products of societies that currently hold complex, deeply contradictory, and largely unarticulated views about children. Our capacity to sentimentalise, identify with, project onto, and reify children is almost infinite.'[10]

One route out of sentimentality, identification and projection is to take those attitudes and affects as the historical topic to be investigated, and this Hugh Cunningham has done, by giving an account of the tales that adults have told themselves (and children) about childhood in the past. *The Children of the Poor* (1991) confines itself to what its author calls the 'story of the history of childhood' in Britain, from the late seventeenth to the mid-twentieth century, that is, to the conventional romance in which little children carry the burden and bear the scars of industrialisation, and are finally rescued and given a 'proper' childhood – in the 1840s with the first effective factory legislation, or in 1918, when half-time labour is finally abolished, or in the 1940s, when educational legislation and the inauguration of the National Health Service bestow childhood on every child. As Cunningham says, this is a romance of nationhood as much as it is of childhood, and its 'outlines and details must rank amongst the best-known parts of the story of Britain'.[11]

Cunningham has demonstrated that the claims for a history of adult attitudes towards children, and of upsurges of interest in children and the notions of childhood they embody, are much more compelling than claims for a history of children.[12] This book too, will seek an understanding of how adults *used* the idea of childhood and the figure of the child, in various social contexts and in psychological terms. If the claim is finally that in the period under discussion childhood came to be understood as a component of selfhood – perhaps, as interiority itself – then this will have serious (and I hope helpful) implications for social histories of children that may come to be written in the future. Chapters 6, 7 and 8 of this book give some account of the dynamic and symbiotic relationship between ideas of childhood and ways of perceiving children, in the mid- and late Victorian years, in their consideration of 'street children' (street traders, hawkers, children working in trades not regulated by law) and children who worked in the entertainment industry.

Because these chapters relate the symbolisation of children to the sociology of childhood, I have found myself as puzzled as other historians by the extraordinary plasticity of the terms 'childhood' and 'child' in the period under discussion. Indeed, I have been puzzled for much longer than it has taken to work on this book, and I obviously once thought that the problem that underlay the famous encounter between Sigmund Freud and his 14-year-old patient Dora was that Freud was just rather bad at placing her on a modern developmental map, and attributed to her feelings and motives that do not, in modern terms, belong to adolescents.[13] Hugh Cunningham notes how for the purposes of early nineteenth-century campaigns against child labour, when the work of children in factories was being compared with slavery, great boys and girls in their late teens might be described as infants. The usage had a clear purpose, for 'without any precision as to the age to which it was applied, it suggested . . . helplessness'.[14] Irritated capitalists complained that '"*all* the workers in mills are spoken of as *children* . . ., or as being '*infants of tender years*"'.[15] 'Childhood' was a category of dependence, a term that defined certain relationships of powerlessness, submission and bodily inferiority or weakness, before it became descriptive of chronological age.[16] The late nineteenth century fixed childhood, not just as a category of experience, but also as a time-span. The obvious place to look for the elision of childhood with chronological age is in the development of mass schooling, and its grouping of children together by age cohort. In the same period the practices of child psychology, developmental linguistics and anthropometry also provided clearer pictures of what children were like, and how they should be expected to look at certain ages.

It is important to bear in mind these means of perceiving children, as we watch children being watched, on the stage and in the street in the mid- and late Victorian years, especially perhaps as we watch what is for us the irreducibly paedophiliac gaze turned upon the girl-child – sometimes she was five and sometimes she was 15 – who is called a 'baby' or an 'infant'. But our first mistake is not to recognise the nineteenth century's lack of interest in the actual chronological ages of its 'child' prostitutes and its 'baby' actors. In these and other circumstances the child was 'not defined or controlled by age limits, since . . . anyone between the ages of one day and 25 years or even beyond might, in different contexts, play that role'.[17]

In discussing the creation of the paedophile and the child through discourses of desire, and as 'roles necessary to our psychic and cultural life', James Kincaid could scarcely put a foot wrong, for what he describes is 'any image, body or being that we can hollow out, purify, exalt, abuse and locate sneakily in a field of desire . . . as a "child"'. This may have been a cultural development of the last two hundred years, and the interest in little girls who were stopped in the street in the 1850s, in stage fairies of the 1870s and in child acrobats of the *fin-de-siècle*, seems obviously sexual to us, from a late twentieth-century perspective. But a static and atemporal 'field of desire' cannot tell us very much about *what* was being invested in this image, body or being, nor why that investment might have been made. By dealing with the child as a unitary category in this way (which of course actually helps to some extent, in pursuing these questions) this approach also evades the implications of strenuous late nineteenth-century efforts, made across many disciplines, to create a space and a category in which it was possible to articulate sexual feelings in relationship to those who had until recently been in that vague category 'child', but who now, at a certain age became 'adolescents'.[18]

Our second mistake, in watching the child being watched, is to think that her audience always thought it important that she was a girl (thought her 'girlness' to be important in the way we now think it important). If the terms 'child' and 'childhood' present a problem of nomenclature for historical inquiry into adult investment (sexual and otherwise) in the categories themselves, then gender – the sex of the child watched, written about and wanted – is even more difficult to deal with. The least that can be done on this score is to reiterate a point that has been most elaborately and productively explored by Denise Riley, in order to say something simpler than she about gender and the category of 'woman' in history.[19] As far as the category 'child' is concerned, it is not at all clear that nineteenth-century children were distributed across the sex-gender system that modern scholarship has outlined, nor in any way that matches closely with modern conceptualisations of childhood. It is important to recognise that we currently live (and write history) at the end of a process that has both sexualised children, and very determinedly assigned to them a sex. James Kincaid suggests that because 'ungendered seeing is not quite comprehensible to our culture', it is extremely difficult for us to imagine ways in which 'a century or so ago gender was of little importance in the usual sort of thinking on children'.[20]

Though I think that this is correct, it was nevertheless the case that when the child was watched, written about and wanted, it was usually a feminised set of qualities (if not a female child) whose image was left behind for our analysis. Goethe's Mignon, after all the cultivated androgyny of her presentation, turns out to be a girl in the end. The following pages will offer some suggestions about why the images and conceptions of children that are dealt with here nearly all turn out to be girls in the end. Nevertheless, in order to present eighteenth- and nineteenth-century understandings of children and childhood in as much contemporary significance as I can retrieve, I refer to 'the child', to child-figures and to actual children – as Goethe sometimes referred to Mignon – as 'it', when that is appropriate. I use the gendered pronoun when that is what contemporaries did, and they were obviously referring to girls (or boys), though it needs emphasising that such a use did not indicate, as it now does, a set of qualities and attributes that is the symmetrical half of a larger category called 'boys-and-girls'.

Much of the claim for Mignon's importance is to do with the attention the figure draws to *littleness*, to the visceral sense of the smallness of the self that lies inside: one of the many meanings of 'mignon' is 'little one'. Sometimes, during the course of writing, I thought that what I was describing here was not 'childhood', nor 'the child', nor a development of the period 1780–1930, whereby a social and cultural understanding of a self (of the self's history, its aetiology) was most typically expressed in the shape and form of the child (by specific literary child-figures and by the complex of vocabularies, structures of explanation and typical depictions evolved by the disciplines that studied children). Sometimes, it seemed to me that what I was really describing was *littleness* itself, and the complex register of affect that has been invested in the word 'little'. One of the reasons for feeling this way is that, like others who have wanted to say something serious about childhood as a historical category, I need to eschew the emotional tawdriness that 'child' and 'childhood' bring into play, and pre-empt any tendency towards sentimentality in my readers. I can do what Hugh Cunningham has done in *Children of the Poor*, and simply say what kind of story and what kind of history we are all involved in. But the way in which 'little' and 'little one' *move* cannot be undone. 'How does she manage to move you? How?' asked one mid-nineteenth-century commentator, as she looked at the 'poor, wan, half-clothed, half-grown' Mignon depicted by Ary Scheffer in his portraits of 1839.[21] Indeed, I should acknowledge my investment as a writer in having these words – 'little', 'little one' – and that range of affect at my command, for the response they produce is the pre-eminent demonstration that this book is part of the story it is trying to tell.

The history that this book presents concerns changes and developments in uses of the idea of the child. Not so very long ago, this kind of endeavour might have been called the mapping of a change in sensibility;

and 'sensibility' is still a useful term for the way in which it draws attention to the historical development of lexes of feeling, the social structuring of ways of thinking, and the bringing of feeling and response into the realm of cognition, in particular societies, at particular points in time. One of the arguments here is that the idea of the child did allow this transmutation of feeling into thought, specifically feelings concerning the self and its history in an individual.[22] The term 'sensibility' can also serve to remind us that we have been here before, and that some of the questions posed by this book have been placed on cultural and political agendas of the past. Romantic writing in general, and in Britain the moment of thought expressed by the Wordsworthian 'Romantic Child', located individuals in time and chronology by possession of their own personal past. In this kind of account, a self was formed by the laying down and accretion of bits and pieces of a personal history, and this detritus, these little portions of the past, most readily assumed the shape of a child when reverie and memory restored them to the adult. The child within was always both immanent – ready to be drawn on in various ways – and, at the same time, always representative of a lost realm, lost in the individual past, and in the past of the culture.[23]

This apprehension and understanding of the self was written and used – used for thinking through and with – in many fields of inquiry in the nineteenth century, and in many forms of writing, not just the literary – in the fields of physiology (particularly cell theory), evolutionary biology, philology, and developmental linguistics. In particular, the dominant ideas of growth and development that were used in the investigation of all living forms (in what is now known as biology) and in the investigation of the forms of human culture (in what is now known as anthropology), implied a material progression in individual lives, which increased in symbolic importance during the course of the century, whereby that which was traversed (the course of an individual life; the growth through childhood to maturity; the development of a people or a nation) was, in the end, left behind and abandoned. In this way, childhood as scientifically described was always about that which was temporary and impermanent, always described a loss in adult life. These scientific formulations were profoundly Romantic, and in Britain were particularly shaped by the central reference point of Wordsworth's 'Ode: Intimations of Immortality'. 'It is indeed of the utmost significance,' remarked Peter Coveney, 'that the most intense emotion of the poem is one of regretful loss.'[24] We do not yet really understand how the individual's past, and larger, more historical and public pasts, came to be understood within the framework of this sadness, this apprehension of loss.

We have been here before, then, by means of inquiry mapped out by literary criticism. More recently, in *Sources of the Self* (1989) Charles Taylor surveys the whole of Western philosophy, and the grandest sweep of the

West's cultural history (Renaissance humanism, urbanisation, the rise of capitalism, Protestantism, affective individualism), in order to claim that *the thing that happened* during this period was the move from outside to inside.[25] He calls this development 'the world passed within', taking his line from Rilke's seventh *Duino Elegy*: 'Nowhere, beloved, can world exist but within.'[26] Taylor describes the development of a 'disengaged, particular self, whose identity is constituted in memory'.[27] This identity is expressed in self-narration: 'the life at any moment is the causal consequence of what has transpired earlier . . . [and] since the life to be lived has also to be *told*, its meaning is seen as something that unfolds through the events'.[28]

According to other commentators, this formulation of the self was a function of new ways of understanding the historical past that emerged in the nineteenth century. In an account like Franco Moretti's in *The Way of the World*, the modern assumptions and practices of history come into being when the meaning of events is no longer understood to be separate from the events themselves. In an earlier period of European history, what Moretti describes as an interpretative fever gave stories meaning by the hermeneutic act of interpreting and explaining them. But in the newly historicised understanding of the nineteenth century, *events in their relationship to each other* carried their own meaning with them. In this way, Moretti explains 'the centrality of *history* in nineteenth century culture . . . and . . . the centrality of *narrative* within the domain of literature'.[29] For Taylor, the important question to ask of these developments concerns the shape of the life-stories that people tell about themselves. He asks whether the narrated story of the self is simply 'the *result* of the happenings as they accumulate', or whether the shape of a life is there already, is 'already latent', simply emerging through what comes to pass. These two perspectives on the way in which 'life has to be lived as a story' are for Taylor the legacy of particular historical developments which made it quite hard for people to take over the story they were telling of themselves from 'the canonical models and archetypes'.[30] Taylor suggests that the two perspectives (the shape of a life as a result of happenings; the shape already latent, emerging through happenings) only present a problem when they are 'formalised intellectually and become a problem for philosophy'. But what follows will suggest not only that a wide variety of people living in the nineteenth century did implicitly address the problem in writing and other forms of representation, but also that their use of the child-figure and the idea of childhood actually elided the two perspectives to which Taylor draws our attention. The idea of the child was used both to recall and to express the past that each individual life contained: what was turned inside in the course of individual development was that which was also latent: the child *was* the story waiting to be told.

Taylor does not explore uses of the idea of the child in the making of modern identities; and neither did Michel Foucault, who argued in the last volume of *The History of Sexuality*, in something of the way that Taylor does, that it is not so much the sense of the self that is a development of the modern world; rather it is the *location* of the self that is new.[31] The modern self is imagined as being *inside*, and it is this spatial sense that the term 'interiority' seeks to describe: the self *within*, created by the laying down and accretion of our own childhood experiences, our own history, in a place inside. Foucault also told us, as long ago as 1970 in *The Order of Things*, that a way of explaining early nineteenth-century historical practice and history writing is to understand how people living in European societies in this period felt themselves to be 'emptied' of history, and to observe them setting about the task of discovering 'in the depths of [themselves] . . . a historicity that was linked to them, essentially'.[32]

In Foucault's account, this process was connected to a large-scale reorganisation of the way in which the natural world was perceived, from the seventeenth century onwards. Developments in scientific thinking (or, to be more precise than he was, developments in the writing of scientific accounts), especially in plant physiology, botany and comparative anatomy, provided a natural history for non-human living things. In epistemological and developmental terms, human beings were separated from a unifying narrative that had hitherto described them together with plants and animals. Now, in the last decades of the eighteenth century, and at the beginning of the new,

> things . . . received a historicity proper to them, which freed them from the continuous space that imposed the same chronology on them as upon men . . . By the fragmentation of the space over which Classical knowledge extended in its continuity, by the folding over of each separated domain upon its development, the man who appears at the beginning of the nineteenth century is 'de-historicised'.[33]

My suggestion will be that child-figures, and more generally the idea of childhood, came to be commonly used to express the depths of historicity within individuals, the historicity that was 'linked to them, essentially'. 'Childhood', 'the child', as this kind of configuring of the past, emerged at the same time as did the modern idea of history and modern conventions of historical practice. 'History' in its conventional modern meaning suggests that by a painstaking dredging through the detritus left behind – the documents and other traces – it might be possible to conjure the past before our eyes, 'in its own terms'.[34] As a practice it has certain affinities with the other discipline of the nineteenth century that concerned itself with the retrieval and representation of the past, that is with psychoanalysis, which holds out the promise that we may retrieve the lost past within us, through dreams and all sorts of error, including slips of the tongue. The proposition concerning the search for the past within individuals, and its connection with the emerging discipline of modern history, is a relatively easy one (it will be explored in Chapter 5, 'The World Turned Within', and again in the final section of the book). The real difficulty lies in discarding the account that Foucault tells out of late-eighteenth-century textbooks of morphology and plant physiology (in the *pages* of which this thing really did happen; in the *pages* of which human beings really were, in written language, removed from the great narratives that had held them in place in the natural world). The difficulty lies in moving from those pages to a social world in which men and women came to know these things about themselves, though they had no access to that science, and had not read those books. The task is not to watch this development taking place in the words on the page, but to find some means of describing how this thing might have happened in individual psychologies and in social circumstances. It involves taking the tentative first steps by which a history might be written of the way in which figures in texts become detached from their origins, become forms of thinking and feeling, used – in Mignon's case – by men and women who had never heard of Goethe, and who indeed might not have been able to read.

In Foucault's account of the *ancien régime*, thinking about the world had been ordered according to the principles of similitude and sympathy. Language itself was part of the ordering principle: in the episteme of similitude, how an entity looked, its name, its outward manifestations, were all part of its significance. In this earlier period, 'resemblance was the fundamental category of knowledge', and sign and signified were not separated.[35] Foucault did not explore the informal sets of beliefs that were attendant on this epistemological ordering of the material world, though some historians have done so, examining for example a peasant world-view of early modern Europe, by which men and women, animals and vegetables, were all understood to obey the great laws of germination and putrefaction, laws by which everything that died was born again, and no real separation was perceived between human beings and the earth from which they sprang. Knowing themselves and their bodies to be moving, changing, organic things, 'through which coursed the vital flux', men and women thought analogically, perhaps saw all the objects and entities of the natural world as being like something else, so that a plant or root shaped like a part of the human body must necessarily correspond to it and provide a cure for any ill it might suffer, and a monstrous birth could be explained by what a woman had thought, eaten or dreamed during her pregnancy.[36]

The organising principle of what Foucault called the 'Classical episteme', which emerged in the late eighteenth century (and which he dates with extraordinary – if not uncanny – precision, between 1775 and 1795), was *order*. By classifying things according to characteristics, the sign – that is, the language used in the taxonomies of natural history – was detached from that which was being named; now, the word indicated the entity, but was not part of it. In ways that are not entirely clear in Foucault's exegesis, the separation of the name from the thing was a necessary condition for the depiction of the depth and interiority of things, particularly of animal bodies. Insideness, which did not show itself and was not available to scrutiny, could be suggested, implied, and indeed figured (people could be given, or devise sets of images and analogies for thinking about interiority) in a way not possible when names and the outward signs of things had been part of their totality.

Since this archaeological shift was first described in the early 1970s, historians of science have paid much attention to the language of scientific description, to the figures of speech by which scientific imagining is effected, and, above all, to what has been called the 'metaphoric flow' between bodies of thought, not only in the bio-medical sciences of the early nineteenth century, but also between those sciences and theology, social theory, and political science.[37] In particular, the metaphoric language of Darwinian and non-Darwinian evolutionary theory has attracted much attention.[38] By proceeding in this way it was hoped to amend a history of science that had in the past merely depicted the movement of ideas towards eventual fruition in a discipline or body of thought. Attention to the language of science was also designed as a corrective to accounts that had previously placed 'science and society' in mere conjunction with each other, and read a history out of the contact between two pre-existing entities.

In undertaking this work, late twentieth-century historians of science have been much exercised by the gap between Foucault's 'wholly inferred, structuring episteme . . . and the explicitness of the historical document and debate'.[39] For many other historians as well, the procedures of their discipline are in any case likely to raise questions about differences between the large-scale, all-encompassing shifts in perception and discourse that Foucault describes, and the multiple ways in which people contemplated, argued and wrote about these matters of epistemic grand narrative. Moreover, delineation of a structuring episteme does not take into account the *problems* that shifts in ordering and perception presented to people, nor the way in which they sought solutions in conscious ways and found them – sometimes – at an unconscious level.

One method of spanning the space between the episteme and the inchoate evidence with which the historian is usually faced has been to pay even closer attention to the question of language, by the searching out of metaphor certainly, but also by looking into the depths below figurative and rhetorical usage. In pursuing the 'metaphor of organisation' in the vocabulary of physiology and natural history in the early nineteenth century, Karl Figlio, for instance, was led to the 'essential inwardness and interiority' that scientists of the period evoked to characterise living beings. He finds 'inwardness' beneath all the dichotomies that will be discussed in Chapter 3 – beneath all the conflicts and oppositions of physiological inquiry – that overtly structured the contemporary debate. According to Figlio, traces of that inwardness could be glimpsed on the surface of things by early nineteenth-century physiologists and morphologists, even though its 'nature [was] always beyond the reach of visibility or total comprehension'.[40] Then, in a strange conflation of inquiry and object, the historian's search becomes that of the nineteenth-century physiologist he is watching. Figlio recommends that the historian searching for relations between science and socio-political events must carry out the inquiry 'from a depth which sees these divisions only as surface features'. Then, extending the idea – the metaphor – of organisation to include the social theory of the period, and having discovered similar concepts there, the historian 'should compare the common ideologies carried by men and their scientific counterparts. That is what I mean by reaching the proper depth . . .'.[41]

There is no argument here with Figlio's conclusions, only an observation of the way in which the agenda and the pursuit is characterised, for it seems that in the late twentieth century we really cannot help reaching for that 'proper' depth nor – taking a step back, and before straining to apprehend it – can we help believing that it already is there to be found. That belief, and the search it engenders (the search of this book, of Figlio's article of 1976, and of many other accounts), is part of the story it is trying to tell. The quest derives from an assumption that there is *Bildung*, a wholeness in interiority, that will figure itself forth, from inside to outside. This book is about the compulsion of that belief, and its location in the child; the inquiry that follows is itself a manifestation of that compulsion. And if there is an argument with historians of science, and the methods they have evolved for linking in language archaeological shifts of perception and the commonplace and contradictory imaginings which take place under its sway, it is only argument by way of a suggestion that metaphor is not the most helpful figure of speech to employ in performing that act of historical linkage and reconstruction.

The ways in which this book attempts the move from idea to the social world, from textbooks of plant and animal physiology to the feelings, beliefs and desires of people living in societies, is first through an exploration of the practical uses of physiological inquiry. Chapters 3 and 4 deal with the images and understandings of bodies that were derived from physiology and that were conveyed as practical information about children, to parents and other educators. A further practical use of such information was in the formulation of the idea of the unconscious in psychoanalysis, a formulation partly made out of the littleness, interiority and drama of cell theory, as it had been articulated by physiologists, from the end of the eighteenth century onwards. This early part of the book, then, describes a history of physiological cell theory and its relationship to evolutionary biology from Goethe (who made some of Mignon out of it) to Freud (who used what Mignon represented to understand the unconscious). These relationships between Mignon's meanings and emergent psychoanalysis, are the subject of Chapter 5. The movement of these ideas into social worlds is then discussed in Chapters 6, 7 and 8, in which contemporary understandings of children in relationship to adults and adulthood are explored through accounts of mid-Victorian street children and children employed in the theatrical professions, particularly as acrobats. The child-acrobat – quite uncannily, for Mignon was an acrobat – was used to articulate ideas about child nurture and cruel and improper parental treatment of children in the same way as chimney sweeps and factory children were. But children working as acrobats provoked concern quite out of proportion to their actual numbers; one of the reasons for the motility and longevity of Goethe's child is that he made her an acrobat in the first place.

Many of the questions that Goethe's Mignon and her transmutations raise are questions of reading, even though they may have involved the illiterate. In his Introduction to *The Culture of Print* Roger Chartier considers 'the essential importance of plural uses and interpretations of texts used in common', and claims as a historical project an understanding of 'the process of the construction of meaning by which readers diversely appropriated the object of their reading'.[42] The studies he introduces in *The Culture of Print* make much of the fairy-tale and of the kind of material that was distributed in the *occasionels* and the *Bibliothèque bleue* (types of popular fiction and chapbooks) in the early modern period in France; and it is indeed by watching the progress of tales (and figures, plots and motifs) through chapbook fiction that we have got as far as we have in understanding the multiple appropriation of literary figures over the last four centuries in Europe.[43] Mignon's progress through nineteenth-century fiction of various kinds and through other forms of artistic representation (which will be discussed in some detail in the next chapter) is an example of a frequently observed phenomenon, whereby figures and clusters of ideas from texts (both literary and non-literary) become subject to multiple uses over time. When the journey of the literary figure is a textual one, description in historical terms is relatively easy, and it can to some extent be informed by a history of literacy in Western societies. An investigation like this might begin with an account of the creation of a particular plot, image or figure. Its coming into being in a type of text would have to be viewed as the product of a writing system, and of the constraints of that writing system. The narrative forms available to children and young adults in the society the writer operated in, the method of reading instruction experienced by him or her, and the sets of beliefs about written language that instruction may also have transmitted – all of these factors would have to be taken into consideration. Traces of other texts may appear in the one under discussion, and it might be possible to judge how far these traces helped the writer formulate ideas, make causal connections, produce linked chains of reasoning and emplotment. The author of any one individual text is then seen as belonging to a community of readers and writers whose practices are historically specifiable.

But only rarely have historians tried to describe processes of extracting meaning from text, and even less attention has been paid to the way in which meanings are altered when a specific literary figure – like Mignon – is moved across genres and forms of writing, and is altered according to new conventions. Substantial and important work on Samuel Richardson's *Pamela* shows the progress of a figure that steps out of its original literary frame to become – an organising principle, a set of political convictions, an emblem of Protestant protest: a named and characterised configuration, subject to multiple uses and many transformations.[44] But what was appropriated and used in Pamela's case was a *story*, which was both sexual and political in import. The story structure of a daughter of the people resisting the embraces of a tattered yet seductive feudalism, and triumphing over it by becoming part of it, persists in however attenuated a form, through multiple retellings. The same can be said of other case studies of this kind of figure, of J. Hillis Miller's tracking of a tale in *Versions of Pygmalion*, of Ian Donaldson's account of the transmutations of the Lucretia legend, and in Marina Warner's study of what she calls 'The Afterlife of Joan of Arc'. In these three cases, the meaning of the story that the figure embodies is transmitted with the figure.[45] Mignon, however, is not – was not – about a story, unless it is the story of her dying. Mignon is only about her oddness and incompleteness.

The finding of analytic and descriptive devices for this process has given me some difficulty. At the end of *Childhood, Culture and Class in Britain*, when I believed that I had understood why Margaret McMillan had been able to employ the idea of childhood to such political effect, and what it was that she had mobilised in her audiences when she turned Marigold the coster's child into a Mignon for her time, I had one of those moments of striking insight, which later have to be abandoned, because . . . it wasn't quite like that. I wrote then that if we wanted to understand the *use* of the idea of 'the child', then we needed to recognise that

> children are the first metaphor for all people, whether they have children or not, whether they are literate and in the business of

> constructing literary metaphors or not: a mapping of analogy and meaning for the self, always in shape and form *like us*, the visual connection plain to see.[46]

By using the term metaphor, I wanted to underline the insight of various late nineteenth-century theorists of childhood, that children gained their enormous affective power because there became available more and more ways of *seeing* their similarity with adults, and of apprehending them as part and as extension of the adult self.[47] But now, I think that what I sought to describe is not best discussed as a process of metaphor, but as one of personification.

The eighteenth century, which saw Mignon's first entrance into the world, held ambivalent, contradictory and angry opinions on the literary process of personification, of which Mignon offers an example. In reminding us of these debates in *Personification and the Sublime* Steven Knapp also alerts us to the paucity of discussion of this literary trope under the anti-humanist sway of structuralism and post-structuralism: personification has been difficult to discuss in recent years because it is so clearly the giving of a human shape to abstract ideas and notions.[48]

Eighteenth-century critics saw the same trouble in personification as they did in allegory, because the transformation of abstract ideas into animated beings was reversible, and 'once the boundaries between literal and figurative agency were erased, it seemed that nothing would prevent the imagination from metaphorizing literal agents as easily as it literalised metaphors'.[49] Knapp's account contributes to a wider literary history, in which eighteenth-century literary culture abandoned the devices of allegory, by which the personified quality was saturated with its own meaning, its own self, and moved into the modern world of symbolic forms. Under the sway of allegory, there was no space between the figure of Justice, or Charity, and what that figure meant: to a very large extent, the meaning *was* the figure. The cognitive act of personification, on the other hand, describes the bestowal of qualities upon a pre-existing entity that has other meanings besides the ones thus bestowed. There remains a space, or dislocation, between the entity and the meaning it has been given, in the way that despite all the meanings given to Mignon, something remains dislocated from them, and eludes the eye.

Marina Warner has raised the question of the teaching and learning of figurative devices like allegory and personification. She suggests that in the fifteenth century (and possibly later on as well) the cult of Joan of Arc in all its manifestations was dependent on its adherents' informal schooling in the visual and verbal conventions of Allegory, of knowing before they encountered its living emblem, the shape of Justice and Fortitude, of Chastity leading her army of virgins to the battlefield. 'Why was the girl believed and followed? . . . the answer lies in the configuration in people's minds. Joan was a familiar face, but it had hardly ever been seen in the real world before. That was the miracle.'[50]

But Mignon complicates all these pictures of prosopopoeia: she is not only the abstract that is given, or is suddenly seen, with a personal face. She was a word, and Goethe took her and made the word – not flesh, but a figure. In the gendered language of its origin, her name is a masculine adjective that also has a female form (but to say 'elle est mignon*ne*' means something quite different from 'C'est Mignon'[51]). As a figure, she was used for the purposes of personification, to give a name and a face (and a body: a deformed and damaged body) to abstract ideas and bodies of theories, particularly theories of childhood and development, and other, less articulate desires felt about childhood and children. But she stayed a word as well – an old word for new meanings. She was never really a story, nor a plot (as Pamela and Galatea and Lucretia were stories) though story-fragments and story-traces accompany her. Hillis Miller says that he deals with versions of Pygmalion and Galatea because that story is an analogue of what all storytellers must do, which is make readers fall in love with a statue. This is to say that writers must bring to life the characters they invent, by turning the marble abstraction of ideas, thoughts and propositions into living bodies. He says that because the act of personification is the responsibility of all involved (writer, reader, critic), it is an ethical act – because these various individual acts (of writing, reading that writing, writing about that writing) make something happen in the world. Mignon happened in the world, but in more than numberless individual acts of writing and reading. As Mignon was represented dramatically, visually and musically as much as she was rewritten, we cannot rely on the countless readings of countless readers (even if they were retrievable) to characterise the multiple uses that were made of her, especially as Mignon (something *like* Mignon: what she *meant*) was known to people who could not read, and who had certainly never read Goethe.

The figure of the child, released from the many texts that gave birth to it, helped shape feelings, and structure feeling into thought. Raymond Williams came close to describing this process when he wrote of the 'activation of specific relations' when poems are read, stories told, plays enacted and watched. What takes place in those moments, he claimed, are 'real processes . . . physical and material relational processes'. And he goes on to describe 'the poem first "heard" as a rhythm without words, the dramatic scene first "visualised" as a specific movement or grouping, the narrative sequence first "grasped" as a moving shape inside the body.'[52] These movements of relationship, between people and things (entities visualised, phonemic patterns given a name) are means of cognition, ways of thought. One of the problems, on the historical plane, is that the process described here is always individual, as well as often collective, not just the activation of pre-existing networks of understanding and belief and relationships, but a means of bringing them into being as well. The idea of the child was the figure that provided the largest number of people living in the recent past of Western societies with the means for thinking about and creating a self: something grasped and understood: a shape, moving in the body . . . something *inside*: an interiority.

2

Mignon's Progress

The following brief account of Mignon's extra-textual afterlife is also the beginning of an extended description of the uses to which the figure was put, in the nineteenth and early twentieth centuries. Since the beginning of this century using Mignon has involved a search for her origins, so in describing the search this chapter also records some versions of her provenance.

Although she first appeared in Goethe's draft of *Wilhelm Meister's Theatrical Mission* some time between 1777 and 1785, this particular point of Mignon's origin was not known to the nineteenth century, for the *Theatrical Mission* manuscript was not discovered until 1910.[1] What the nineteenth century knew of her was the text of *Wilhelm Meister's Apprenticeship*, published between 1795 and 1796, and known in Britain in Thomas Carlyle's translation of 1824.[2] So nineteenth-century readers did not know that in the earlier version Mignon did not die, and were not able to make comparisons between the shape and destiny of the two Mignon figures. Analysis of the final Mignon in the light of Goethe's Italian journey of 1786–8 (when he escaped from his administrative duties in the Duchy of Saxe-Weimar), his visits to the Botanical Gardens at Padua in 1786 and the understandings of physiological growth he acquired there, of growth not as replication, but as a coming into being of an essential, but not necessarily existent form, was the critical task of the period after 1910.[3]

The nineteenth century appropriated Mignon as its own, and forgot *Wilhelm Meister*. She was rewritten and re-represented across every artistic form, and became in this way a figure, a trope, an image: just a word, which is what she had been anyway when Goethe took her and used her at the eighteenth century's end. He took her and used her for a *Bildungsroman* that shows an individual's personal development in the context of a particular social order. Wilhelm Meister, a young bourgeois of the merchant class, is in love with the theatre (a passion dating from his childhood) and with a young actress, Mariane. Convinced that she has been unfaithful to him, he is plunged into a deep depression. His family think to cure him of it by getting him to carry out existing plans to travel on his father's business. Even at the outset of his journey, the theatre draws Wilhelm; he attaches himself to a company of players and makes the acquaintance of the young actress Philene (Philena in Carlyle's translation). He is lodging with the actors at an inn in a small town when he encounters the mysterious child Mignon, whom he takes into his service. At the same time as he is persuaded to provide financial support for the troupe of players, an old Harpist, whose origins are no less mysterious than the child's, also attaches himself to Wilhelm. Shortly after this, the company (with Wilhelm as their new male lead) is invited to put on a performance for the local aristocracy, and it is at the count's mansion that one of the house-guests introduces Wilhelm to the works of Shakespeare. On leaving the country seat, the actors are ambushed by robbers. The wounded Wilhelm is helped by a 'fair Amazon' on horseback who, once she has arranged for medical attention and lodgings for the injured, vanishes like a dream with her entourage. Recovering from the attack, Wilhelm continues his acting career, and makes the acquaintance of the actor–manager Serlo. He also establishes a deep friendship with Serlo's sister Auralia, who is shortly to die. Auralia has the care of a little boy called Felix, who it is assumed is her own illegitimate child. It is during this period of his life that Wilhelm learns of his own father's death.

A performance of *Hamlet* is planned (Book 5 contains an extensive discussion of the play), and Wilhelm, though extremely indecisive on this score, feels sufficiently released from the imperatives of the mercantile capitalism his father represented to take the leading role. A fire breaks out at the inn where the performance takes place and the Harpist is suspected of starting it. As the fire rages the old man is found trying to kill the three-year-old Felix. Now, in this crisis, Wilhelm comes to understand that Felix is his own son, by the now dead Mariane.

As Wilhelm broods on his recent involvement in the death of two women (Auralia and Mariane), he learns that for some time he has been watched over by a secret society, the Society of the Tower. His apprenticeship is now over, for he has grown – achieved his *Bildung* – through the interaction of inward development and outer experience. He is admitted to the Society of the Tower and becomes a Master. It is now that Mignon dies, in the care of Natalie, who turns out to be the beautiful Amazon who succoured Wilhelm when he lay wounded in the forest meadow. Wilhelm and Natalie marry, and the Society informs Wilhelm that he will have to spend some years in further travel. (This instruction is the spring of the later *Wilhelm Meisters Wanderjahre oder die Entsagenden* of 1821 and 1829, which Carlyle published as the third volume of his translation in 1839.)

My plot-summary is of the most conventional nineteenth-century type, whereby the novel of development and the account of a young man's growth through experience to some kind of maturity are subordinated to the story of the mysterious child Mignon, and Wilhelm's tale is told only to provide a setting for hers. In fact, for current purposes, we need to consider Mignon much more closely.

'From the world of the jugglers, a child springs into being'.[4] When Wilhelm first encounters Mignon she is performing as an acrobat with a troupe of Italian rope-dancers. She promotes in the young man 'intense pity', and an overwhelming sympathy and fascination (*WMA* I:87, 88–9). The bodily postures of the child-acrobats, of whom Mignon is only one, are seen – in the description that provides the title to this book – as 'strange dislocations', and Mignon herself, though very beautiful, suggests a similar deformity, for 'her limbs promised growth, or else announced a development that was retarded' (*WMA* I:87, 89). After seeing the child cruelly beaten by the acrobats' leader (the *Seiltzänger*) for refusing to perform her famous egg dance, Wilhelm buys her for the price of the clothes she stands up in. She costs him 30 *Taler*, and becomes his servant, though in her heart, the child takes the young man as her father (*WMA* I:92, 93). Particularly noted at this point are the child's attempts to rub the paint of the acrobat from her face: 'she would often stand by a vessel with water and wash her face with such great diligence and vehemence, that she almost rubbed her cheeks sore', thinking the redness thus produced to be traces of rouge (*WMA* I:95). She is in fact preternaturally clean. Wilhelm often finds her washing herself: 'Her clothes were kept clean too, although everything had been mended two or three times over' (*WMA* I:98).

Before Wilhelm watched her performing with the other children in the courtyard he had caught a glimpse of her on the stairs of the inn, when 'a young creature' leapt past him:

> A little short silk waistcoat with slit Spanish-style sleeves and long close-fitting trousers with puffs looked very well on the child . . . He looked at the figure in astonishment and could not make up his mind whether he should declare it to be a boy or a girl. (*WMA* I:83)

It *is* a girl, a gender position of which nineteenth-century re-creators of the Mignon-figure seem utterly certain, despite the child's own considerable ambiguities on this score. She holds 'fast to Wilhelm and [says] very firmly "I am a boy, I don't want to be a girl!"' (*WMA* II:10). When new clothes for her position as a member of Wilhelm's entourage are discussed, Mignon wants 'a new little waistcoat and sailors' trousers, with blue lapels and ribbons, of a style comparable to what she had seen on boys in the town' (*WMA* I:103). She puts on women's clothes for the first time after she has witnessed a sexual encounter between Wilhelm and the actress Philene, in the bedroom where she has hidden herself to wait for him (*WMA* II:110–11; III:89). Now, she is mysteriously older, taller-seeming; when she brings in the breakfast tray next morning, 'Wilhelm was surprised at the child's appearance, indeed it may be said he was startled. She seemed to have become bigger during the night; she stepped before him with a lofty noble propriety' (*WMA* II:111).

Before this moment of dignity and resolution, it is her silences, her hysteria, the complex of her *inabilities* that make her attractive to Meister. The child speaks a poor German, mixed with French and Italian, and indeed, on some days 'she was wholly mute' (*WMA* I:97–8). However, when she sings, accompanying herself on the zither, of which she is an accomplished player, 'the broken speech [is] made consistent and what was disjointed linked together' (*WMA* I:127–8). (In the century that follows, what she sings at this moment, her song of yearning in 'Kennst du das Land', *is* Mignon.) The child finds written language as difficult as spoken language, and her 'letters remained unequal and the lines crooked' (*WMA* I:118). She desperately wants to understand how maps work, what form of representation they are, but she cannot perform this cognitive task (*WMA* II:73–4). Wilhelm notes the child's 'incapacity . . . to represent anything'. He means by this her strained expression when she is asked to recite: 'in a few plays . . . her small parts had been so dryly, so stiffly done that one might say that they were not acted at all'.[5] But it is a much wider aphasia that the young man notes. There is something wrong with Mignon, 'something strange about the child, in all her comings and goings' (*WMA* I:97); 'her body seemed at variance with her mind' (*WMA* I:118). Meister means by this the way in which she finds it both extraordinarily difficult to control her body, and yet at the same time can use it with uncanny deliberation and precision. 'She did not go up and down the stairs, but leapt; she climbed up the corridor bannisters, and before you knew where you were, she was sitting high up on the wardrobe' (*WMA* I:97). But the oddness is more general than this, and permeates all aspects of his observation of her. 'Wilhelm is constantly haunted by the feeling that there is something wrong with Mignon, something that he cannot put into words and that he cannot describe'.[6]

This frantic, agitated child is always treated with great dignity by her author. The solemnity of her presentation owes much to the range of classical allusions that her most telling expression – in 'Kennst du das Land' – brings in its train.[7] Though Wilhelm cannot name the child's peculiarity, what he *is* able to describe, or to articulate in feeling, is the pity that the child produces in him. In an especially marked passage, Mignon reverses the scene with which their relationship had begun – her refusal to perform the egg dance, the consequent assault, and Wilhelm's purchase of her – and displays herself, not in the public space of an inn courtyard, but in the privacy of an upper room. The scene takes place shortly after Wilhelm has heard news of Mariane (pregnant and vanished) from a former acting companion of hers, and 'all his old wounds had been re-opened'. Fretting about the fate of his former mistress and imagining her 'straying about the world without help as a woman in childbed and as a mother, presumably with his own child', he returns home to find Mignon waiting for him. She asks to perform for him. With the embarrassment that he usually feels at being the focus of the child's intense, preoccupying attention, 'he would have preferred to refuse this, especially as he did not know what was involved. But there was nothing he could refuse this good creature.'. She places eggs at a precise distance from each other on a little rug that she has unrolled, and then, blindfolded, she dances so that not one of the eggs is broken, or even touched. As Wilhelm watches, he experiences a kind of recognition of her, articulating clearly 'all at once what he had already been sensible of on Mignon's behalf. He longed to take this forlorn being to his heart in place of a child, to feel her in his arms and with a father's love to arouse in her an enjoyment of life' (*WMA* I:102–3).

Mignon *moves*: she promotes pity and tenderness in the beholder (in the reader, as much as in Meister). Friedrich Schiller, who was Goethe's reader for the final manuscript in 1795 and 1796, was uncertain about how these feelings were promoted in him. He acknowledged Mignon's 'repellent strangeness', but wrote to her author in June 1796 that 'from the mass of impressions I have received, Mignon's image stands out most strongly . . . on opening the manuscript my eye fell first on the song, and this moved me so deeply that afterwards I could not expunge the impression'.[8] She moves the reader in the way that Franco Moretti has described in 'Kindergarten', where he discusses the power of certain child-figures, from a later period of European popular fiction, to make their audience cry.[9] But Goethe's Mignon provokes tears not so much because – to follow Moretti's argument – tears are the expression of our powerlessness to save her, but because she carries with her her own deformity and dislocation, suggests always her own unwholeness, what it is she lacks.[10] It is what eludes us in her meaning that draws the eye, as Wilhelm's was drawn: he 'could not look at her enough. His eyes and his heart were irresistibly fascinated by the mysterious condition of this being . . . he kept looking at her' (*WMA* I:89).

Goethe himself instructed his readers in Mignon's poignant qualities, claiming that

> Nothing is more moving that [*sic*] when a love which has nourished itself quietly and a loyalty that has been confirmed privately at last comes close at the right hour to the person who up to now has not been worthy of them, and are revealed to him. The bud that had for a long time been austerely closed was ready, and Wilhelm's heart could not be more receptive. (*WMA* I:124–5)

Here, Wilhelm tells the child that he is going away and leaving her. '"Sir," she called out, "if you are unhappy, what is to become of Mignon?"' The following scene shows that, in effect, the young man is *not* truly receptive, that he does not understand Mignon's feelings for him, which the child cannot name. His announcement produces in her a hysterical fit, which though it may not be the analogy of a woman in orgasm which K.R. Eissler has claimed for it, certainly is an orgasm of tears, 'a stream of tears . . . her most inward self pouring forth . . . in the confusion of the moment Wilhelm was afraid she would melt away in his arms and that he would be left with nothing of her'.[11] This moment briefly displaces the sexual desire that is later to revive, only to be thwarted in the dark of the bedroom where Mignon will see Wilhelm embrace Philene. Earlier now, as she lies convulsed in his lap, her place as a child is confirmed, and her position as child-witness to the primal scene foreshadowed:

> He held her more tightly. – 'My child!' he cried, 'my child! You are indeed mine . . . You are mine! I shall keep you, I won't leave you!' . . . 'My father!' she cried, 'you won't leave me! You will be my father! I am your child!'

Some days, some pages, later she stands watching the embrace of Wilhelm and the actress. By bearing witness in this way she begins her descent into death: she 'suffered unbearable torment, all the vigorous emotions of passionate jealousy were combined with the unrecognised demands of an obscure desire' (*WMA* III:89–90). She dies in front of Wilhelm's very eyes, welcoming the release from life with the famous line that is a response to Natalie's admonition: '"You naughty child . . . haven't you been told to avoid strenuous exercise? Look how your heart is beating" – "Let it break . . . It's been beating too long anyway"' (*WMA* III:105).

It is now revealed that Mignon was the child of an insane brother–sister relationship, that the Harpist is her father, and that she was abducted from the foster parents to whom she was sent, away from the aristocratic household where her mother wrestled madly with 'the dreadful thought that this child should not be there'. The traits that have so drawn the eye of Wilhelm (the child's suppleness and adroitness, her love of climbing and wearing of boys' clothes, her musical talents and inability to express herself verbally) are now described as showing themselves very early in life (*WMA* III:134–40). It is shortly after these revelations have been made that the Harpist kills himself (*WMA* III:152–3).

Schiller, who wrote in great detail to Goethe about the draft of the manuscript as it was sent to him in portions between the early spring of 1795 and the autumn of 1796, thought it a consummate idea to have made Mignon's death attributable to the world's failure of understanding, to have derived 'the practical enormity and terrible pathos in the fate of Mignon and the Harpist from a theoretical enormity, from monstrosities of understanding', that is, to have connected her death to the irrational fears surrounding the question of incest. He considered that in this way, 'nothing is imputed to purity and soundness. Only in the womb of superstition are those monstrous fates conceived which pursue Mignon and the

Harpist.'[12] It was after he had read of Mignon's death that Schiller told her author that he found 'everything you undertake with [her], both living and dead, quite extraordinarily beautiful'.[13]

The word 'mignon' carried its own meaning for the 1780s and 1790s: 'mignon': fondling, darling, little one, sweetheart, favourite . . . the youngest in a family. 'A pet child or simply something very charming,' says Richard Friedenthal.[14] In his *History of Childbirth* Jacques Gélis tells us that in seventeenth-century Limousin when a peasant woman was visited after her confinement the cry on seeing the baby was '"Oh! lou piti mignar [or lo pito mignardo] Que lou bonn Du li froje!" (Oh! the pretty little thing, God bless him!)'.[15] For the same period Philippe Ariès identifies 'mignotage' (best translated as 'coddling') as one of two new 'sentiments of childhood'. This, he claims, was an essentially female attitude, which developed in concert with a new kind of pedagogic attention to the development of the child's reason.[16] In his thorough study of 1927, of the etymology of 'mignon', Fritz Lachmann locates its central meaning as *littleness*: 'In French, one describes as *mignon, mignonne* someone "qui a du charme dans la petitesse" (who is charming because of their littleness), further, simply "personne qu'on chérit" (someone who you cherish).'[17] A little favourite, then; and in the courtly French used at Weimar, and in the French authors that Goethe knew (to all who knew Diderot's definition of terms in the tenth volume of *L'Encyclopédie*) a male prostitute, a *young* male prostitute; indeed, a toy boy. Diderot, and other commentators too, referred to France in the reign of Henri III, and to the *mignons* who were favourites of the king, who 'served to satisfy his pederastic desires', and were loathed by the people in this account 'pour leur accoutrements efféminés' (on account of their outrageous effeminate apparel).[18] Johann Huizinga, in *The Waning of the Middle Ages*, discusses the way in which *mignons* wore the same clothing as their lord (Lachmann reminds us of Mignon's desire to wear the colours of her master).[19] Lachmann also notes that 'there are a few instances of the use of the word "mignon" in the eighteenth century in the unambiguously pejorative sense . . . the only occurrence whose meaning can be in any doubt, and which strangely enough, refers to Goethe'. Lavater writes a postscript to a letter sent by Pfenninger to Herder in February 1776 and remarks that 'You're going to Weimar? . . . Where . . . Goethe is mignon'. From this remark, says Lachman,

> there can hardly be any doubt that in Goethe's time the meaning of the word was well known, and that it was not unknown to the poet himself. It is at least highly probable that he will have known of Henri III's mignons, whether from his reading of Fénelon's *Dialogues of the Dead* . . . or from his historical pursuits, or from material provided by dictionaries.'[20]

However, to concentrate in this way on what Goethe's contemporaries and later commentators knew about the derivation of the word he used to name his enigmatic child-figure, actually wrenches meaning away from its other connotations. *Mignon* is a word for a child, and for the delight that adults might take in a child's grace and charm – the delight that Goethe himself experienced in these years, during his care and education of little Fritz von Stein (1772–1844), the youngest son of his beloved friend, Charlotte von Stein. In 1783, in response to his mother's worries about the education Fritz was receiving and the company he was keeping, the 11-year-old was taken into Goethe's household. He stayed for three years, Goethe acting as father and tutor to the boy. It was an already well-established relationship: Goethe bought books for the younger von Stein children, read them fairy stories, encouraged their writing and drawing, and Fritz had often stayed with Goethe. The houses of the von Steins and Goethe were so close to each other that the little boy often called first thing in the morning: 'Fritz found me still in bed and so it was that the first thing I saw today was the best thing you have.'[21] Besides being the child he was – loved and educated and worried over by Goethe, helped to grow beans, keep his handwriting on a straight line, and build pretend aqueducts – Fritz was also the embodiment of Goethe's beloved: 'I love you in him, and in everything . . .'.[22] Goethe took the child with him on many trips connected with the various offices he held in the Duchy, before and after Fritz moved in with him. After one such journey in April 1779 he wrote what Nicholas Boyle has called 'the most terrifyingly erotic poem of his life'.[23] In 'The Elf King', a father rides through the night (as Goethe rode with Fritz on his saddle in front of him) with a sick child in his arms. From the desolate landscape rise spectres of lust, and the particular and perverted lust of the Elf King for the little boy's fair form.[24] 'It is the true voice of desire,' says Boyle, 'speaking to the boy with a directness scarcely paralleled elsewhere in Goethe's verse'; and he comments that 'not even Frau von Stein seems to have recognized that in it feelings she would not allow to be applied to herself were being transferred to her son, for would she then have allowed him to live three years with its author?'[25] Mignon has many origins, but one of them was surely the complex set of emotions that Goethe experienced in relationship to Fritz, the observation of a child's bodily agitation and the charm of its utter seriousness of purpose, and the erotic investment the adult makes in what is so pleasing to the eye and the imagination.

By giving a word the shape and form of a child, Goethe preserved all these meanings for the century that followed. But according to S.S Prawer there was much in Goethe's presentation of Mignon that offended as well, especially the writer's 'virtual rejection of [her], whose pathological traits seemed too much stressed in the *Apprenticeship*'. Prawer sees the Romantic novel as 'a partly conscious, partly unconscious search for an anti-*Meister*', for a narrative that will prevent the child Mignon's disintegration into death.[26] Is it this search that fuels the century's obsessive writing and re-representation of Mignon? She made an extraordinary number of appearances, across all artistic forms during the nineteenth century. For the novel in Britain, there were Sir Walter Scott's two very self-conscious writings of her, both in the pre-Carlyle translation period, in *A Legend of Montrose* (1819) and *Peveril of the Peak* (1820).[27] In the former, Annot Lyle, 'the most beautiful little fairy that ever danced upon a heath by moonlight', expresses her sorrow in song just like Mignon (though she plays the harp rather than the zither), is an orphan of mysterious provenance, and is extremely small: 'her stature, considerably less than the ordinary size of woman, gave her the appearance of extreme youth, in so much that although she was near eighteen, she might have passed for four years younger'.[28]

Goethe commented on the repetition and intensification of Mignonesque traits in Scott's figure Fenella from *Peveril of the Peak.* Not only is 'this little creature . . . of the least and slightest size of womankind', not only does she jump and slide down ropes at the least provocation, not only has she in her time been severely beaten for refusing to dance, but, as Goethe tartly observed, her author bestows total muteness on her, 'in addition to her other qualities'.[29] He thought that Scott's use of these motifs was 'repeating and detracting' – a detracting from his invention of 'something which was complete' in Mignon. It was Scott's Fenella who provided the dramatic idea of using a mute girl as a central character in opera. Eugene Scribe's libretto *Mansaniello, ou, La Muette de Portico* (1828) was adapted for British audiences as part of a series of 'Gothic melodramas, incorporating a dumb character, almost always a sympathetic figure with a terrible or mysterious past who is meant to evoke great pity'.[30]

The multifarious uses of the Mignon-figure, across all European literature, can only be sketched here. It is present in Brentano's *Godwi* (1801). She is plagiarised by August von Kotzebue as the Little Tyrolean Girl in his sketch of 1807. She is to be found as Erwine in Eichendorff's *Forebodings and the Present* (1815), as Immermann's 'Flämmchen' in *The Epigones* (1836), in Heine's *Florentinische Nächte* (Florentine Nights) (1837), and in Dostoevsky's first sketches for *The Idiot,* in the 1860s.[31] A mainstream nineteenth-century British audience did not know about these continental works, but it was well aware of Mignon's musical representations, in the settings of 'Kennst du das Land' (and Mignon's other songs) by Beethoven, Schubert, Liszt, Schumann, Duparc, Gounod and Tchaikovsky.

Schubert's arrangement was probably the best known in Britain, and acted as a main artery of cultural transmission; its melody bears a remarkable resemblance to 'Home Sweet Home'. It is important for the argument that follows (and is in line with Prawer's delineation of a nineteenth-century search for an anti-*Meister*) that the figure who so absolutely embodies the *Unheimlich* – both homelessness and the profoundly uncanny[32] – should be represented by music that epitomises, in the most naively sentimental way, the longing for home and the simple return to it.

John Howard Payne wrote 'Home Sweet Home' for his operatic melodrama *Clari, or the Maid of Milan* of 1823. This was an early domestic melodrama with a 'foreign' (actually Italian) setting, in which 'the idealisation of the village home is an important part' and from which the Maid Clari has been abducted. The melody (set by Sir Henry Bishop) is played and sung again and again during the course of the play, and each time Clari hears it, 'memories of home overpower her and she is stricken with grief'.[33] We are not to know the precise aural and figurative connections made by listeners, between Payne's and Bishop's 'Home Sweet Home' and Schubert's arrangement of Mignon's song, 'Kennst du das Land' of 1815, but the insistent repetition of nostalgia that the song itself provokes is observable in one very attenuated stage version of *Wilhelm Meister*, Herman Merivale's instant flop of 1879 'The Lord of the Manor'. The stage notes direct that every time the word 'Italy!' is uttered, 'and where an asterisk is marked, the band should play [the] old German air "Kennst du das Land", which should also be the theme of the overture'. The asterisk appears over a dozen times.[34]

Mignon and the best-known settings to her most famous song were not that distant from their origins in 1823, when Jane Welsh played – probably the Schubert, possibly the Beethoven version – on the piano during the summer when her future husband translated the first volume of *Wilhelm Meister*.[35] In July, Carlyle sent his publisher

> a *cooplet* or two from Goethe . . . The subject is Italy; the singer Mignon, a poor little girl stolen from wealth and splendour . . . while yet almost an infant, and carried by rope-dancers into Germany, where she thus expresseth her vague recollections of that magnificent region . . . tho' she cannot name it, being a child of very few words. Mignon singeth and playeth on the cithern
>
> Knowest thou the land where the fresh citrons bloom
> And the golden-orange glows in the thicket's gloom. . .?

By the time Carlyle came to write his Translator's Preface, Mignon had assumed a much more serious shape for him. He wrote now of 'this mysterious child' who is at first neglected by the reader, but who then forces herself on his attention and then 'overpowers him with an emotion . . . deep and thrilling':

> And when all the particulars of her story are at length laid together,

> and we behold in connected order the image of her hapless existence, there is, in those dim recollections, those feelings so simple, so impassioned and unspeakable, consuming the closely-shrouded, woe-struck yet ethereal spirit of the poor creature, something which searches the innermost recesses of the soul. It is not tears which her fate calls forth; but a feeling far too deep for tears . . . Her little heart, so noble and so helpless, perishes before the smallest of its beauties unfolded; and all its loves and thoughts and longings do but add another pang to death . . . It is as if the gloomy porch of Dis, and his pale kingdoms, were realised and set before us, and we heard the ineffectual wail of infants reverberating from within their prison walls forever.[36]

The structure of adult feeling that accompanies the impotent watching of children's distress and that is a feature of so much nineteenth-century observation of marginal groups of children, accompanied Mignon's entry into the English-speaking world.[37] Germaine de Staël had already provided the image of Mignon moving in the landscape of adult sensibility in her book on *Germany* of 1810, where she wrote that

> we cannot represent to ourselves without emotion the least of the feelings that agitate this young girl; there is in her I know not what of magic simplicity, that supposes a profundity of thought and feeling; we think we hear the tempest moaning at the bottom of the soul, even while we are unable to fix upon a word or a circumstance to account for the inexpressible uneasiness she makes us feel.[38]

The impulse to make Mignon un-strange, to find the homeless a home in the world, furnishes the plot of Ambroise Thomas's opera *Mignon* of 1866, in which Mignon not only marries Meister, but is found a ready-furnished *palazzo* the moment she sets foot in Italy. The English translation of the opera (by Thomas J. Williams) received its licence on 11 July 1870, though the Italian version was performed at Covent Garden earlier in the month. From 1870 until 1880 (when a new translation by A. Matthieson was performed at Her Majesty's) an English-speaking audience knew the translated libretto of Michel Carré and Jules Barbier, in which gypsies replace rope-dancers:

> The gypsy chief, Giarno, who combines the avocation of a mountebank with that of a gypsy, compels the hapless girl to dance, and go through various other performances in order to obtain money from the inhabitants of the towns through which they pass – and harshly threatens her with his stick, whenever from fatigue she refuses to do his bidding.[39]

Thomas arranged Mignon's part for a mezzo-soprano (it was initially performed by the French mezzo Celestine Galli-Marie, who sang the first Carmen nine years later). Thomas's choice of a mezzo voice, the traditional voice of the 'breeches' role' (of female characters impersonating men) when a soprano might technically have been thought more appropriate as representative of mysterious female childhood, suggests that the original Mignon's sexual ambiguity was acknowledged, at the musical level at least, in the mid-nineteenth century. Moreover, in Carré's and Barbier's libretto, *A Midsummer Night's Dream* replaces *Hamlet* as the play of Shakespeare that young Wilhelm and the company of actors are involved in, and this allowed a visual display of – and play with – the idea of cross-dressing and sexual ambiguity.

At the level of plot as well, Thomas's Mignon retains an attenuated version of her androgyny:

Filene: What ho! good sir, permit me to inquire
What hapless being is that just waking up?
Say, is't a girl or stripling lad?
Giarno: 'Tis neither one nor other, lady –
'Tis neither woman, girl, nor boy.
Filene: (laughing) What is it then, I pray?
Giarno: (raising the mantle which covers the young Gypsy) – 'Tis – Mignon.[40]

Thomas's choice of a mezzo voice anticipates an argument of 1933 concerning Mignon's androgyny. Walter Wagner said that when the girl is dressed in boy's clothing as Mignon is, the spectator or reader sees her thus clothed in the knowledge that she *is* a girl. This emphasises her essence as a girl rather than hiding it, and at the same time creates a real illusion in the psychology of the reader, which is where girl becomes boy (rather than in the text, or on the stage). For Wagner, Mignon is quite different from other literary figures because the reader (or watcher) of her is bound to become productive in relationship to her, and the *illusion* of her being a boy is what makes the reader active. 'Something happens to the reader during his reading of her . . .'.[41]

But Carré and Barbier replaced the primal scene of Goethe's story, where Mignon watches silently from the shadows as a drunken Wilhelm climbs into the bed where Philene waits, with a moment of narcissism, with Philene before her looking-glass and Mignon rouging her cheeks (and this is done to a literary child-figure who in her original version had most painfully rubbed the paints of the acrobat from her face). The turn of the plot becomes the rivalry of two young women for Wilhelm's sexual attention, which was indeed part of Mignon's story, though one she could not tell.

Thomas's Mignon travelled a very long way – as far indeed, as Barnstaple Town Hall, where Leslie F. Morton's 'Mignon. The One-Act Operatic Comi-tragique Burlesque' was performed in the summer of 1885. It retained motifs of Thomas's retelling in the heroine's cross-dressing, in her appropriation of her rival Philene's clothes, the mirror scene, and the players' preoccupation with *A Midsummer Night's Dream.* The mystery of the stolen child's provenance also endures, in the doggerel of *sério-comique*:

Mignon: I'm a travelling 'star'.
Wilhelm: You star-tle me.
Mignon: I dance at every fair
The people's idol, though not idle there.
Wilhelm: Who are your parents?
Mignon: Goodness only knows
I never had any, I suppose
Yet I remember days that once were bright
But I'm too dazed I can't recall them quite
They used to drive me in a perambulator
and once I know I went to a theatre
and saw a pantomime, I couldn't talk
But with a nursemaid
She stopped once more to speak to a marine
and that's the last of her and home I've seen
I wandered far away, until a man
carried me off to his dark caravan
There starved and ragged I had many a blow
Was taught to dance – That is all I know.[42]

Where photographs of the singers who played a more serious operatic Mignon survive, she is shown clad in a kind of universal Tyrolese or principal boy costume.[43] One photograph of Clothilde Bressler-Gianoli, the Swiss mezzo who played Mignon at the New York Metropolitan Opera House in 1907, is notable for its depiction of a bare-footed, loose-haired waif, clad in the rags of picaresque Italian peasantry.[44] This costume appears to be a close copy of one worn in Ary Scheffer's pair of portraits of Mignon produced in 1836 and 1839, the first showing the erect and foreshortened figure of a child (reputed to be that of Scheffer's daughter Cornelia, born in 1830 – though it is not clear when she posed for Mignon, nor whether she modelled more than the head of the first figure), the second the collapsed and yearning form of a fully grown woman.[45] 'One of the most unlikely candidates for a gypsy ever painted,' says Marilyn Brown of Scheffer's 'Mignon Expressing Regret for Her Native Land'. 'Critics found the insipid picture an excuse to quote

Goethe's nostalgic evocation of the oriental land of Mignon's mysterious origin,' Brown says, and she goes on to describe Théophile Gautier's regret that this pair of images had largely displaced Goethe's poetic creation, being 'too celestial . . . neither sufficiently passionate nor vivaciously Southern enough for Goethe's character'.[46]

Scheffer's pair of portraits could be seen as the artist's acknowledgement of (if not a solution to) the problem that cultural critics had long seen Mignon embodying: the inability of the reader to decide whether she was child or woman. Germaine de Staël dwelt on this conundrum in 1810, and at the same time fixed one of her meanings as a child without childhood. De Staël described 'the extraordinary creature' as 'a singular mixture of childishness and depth of understanding', whose few words are 'answerable to sentiments much stronger than those natural to her age and of which she does not possess the secret . . . it seems as if she had never known childhood . . . having been doomed to suffering in an age which nature has destined only for enjoyment'.[47] As had Schiller and de Staël, commentators of the mid-century dwelt on the problem of affect that Mignon embodied, and the inability of her many audiences to understand how the figure produced in them the feelings it did. Contemplating Scheffer's portraits in 1860, Harriet Grote mused that

> embodying this romantic creation of Goethe's fancy, the two figures . . . have always possessed peculiar interest, not only for the connoisseur, but for all educated beholders. Few have ever, I believe, gazed upon the sad, forlorn aspect of the friendless maiden without feeling profoundly touched. And why? A single figure in complete repose, – poor, wan, half-clothed, half-grown, – How does she manage to move you? How?[48]

Discussing 'countless representations of Mignon' in 1872, George Henry Lewes introduced his readers to an engraving by William Kaulbach, one that illustrated the period when Mignon is living with Natalie. The other children in Natalie's care have been discussing angels, and in order to correct their prejudices and errors, she has Mignon dress as one. The children ask '"Art thou an angel?"'

> 'Would that I were,' said Mignon.
> 'Why dost thou carry a lily?'
> 'I should be happy if my heart were as pure and open.'[49]

'And thus,' comments Lewes,

> she answered every innocent question with some suggestive words. When their curiosity began to be satisfied they wished to undress her.

> This she opposed and taking a lute sat upon the table sang with unspeakable charm [sic] . . . 'Let me retain the semblance of an angel till I become one, which will be shortly;' this is the burden of her plaintive song.

What delighted Lewes about this portrayal was not only that Kaulbach had 'seized the occasion to depict a group of children . . . [and] to express the yearning sadness of Mignon', but that he had also given Mignon's nature 'quite a novel expression'. For Lewes her 'nature' is common cultural property; quite detached from her origins, Mignon is a way of feeling, a means of expressing nostalgia, regret, loss: 'Mignon holds a mystic place in the imaginations of all Europe . . .'.

It was actually Ambroise Thomas's opera of 1866 that created a Mignon for the mid-Victorian stage in Britain. Through its many adaptations Goethe's story was rewritten. *Mignon* was first performed in Britain in 1870, when it was sung in Italian by the mezzo Christine Nilsson. Critics brooded much on the changes wrought by Carré and Barbier's libretto, but were quite united in their understanding that the part of the heroine was scored for a woman to display 'in an intensified degree all the higher and unusual characteristics of a tragic genius of the higher rank'.[50] When Emma Albani prepared herself to play the part at Covent Garden in 1874 she arranged a meeting with Thomas and the original *maître de scène* (stage manager) for the Opéra Comique production of 1866, and learned from them 'all that they could tell me of the singing and the action of "Mignon"'. Thomas made a new suggestion: that Albani should combine laughing and sobbing in one of the recitatives, and seems thereby, consciously or unconsciously, to have instructed Albani with some care in the hysteria manifested by his original.[51] But critics of her performances in 1874 and later in 1882 noted 'the tender, and essentially womanly side of the character' she presented, and her neglect of that 'touch of the untamed, passionate child of Nature', which they thought had been 'deliciously hinted at by Goethe'.[52]

The sternest criticism of Nilsson's more passionate enactment of 1870 was that Carré's and Barbier's libretto did not let Mignon die, 'but let her live, with that object entirely changing the catastrophe. Thus the most touching and pathetic incident of the romance is lost'.[53] But this did not really signify, for 'the most striking situations in which Mignon is concerned are, however modified . . . preserved. The truth is, that Mignon is Mignon . . . under any circumstances'. The same point was made eight years later, when the first English-language version was staged:

> such a character as Goethe's Mignon is immortal in whatever shape she may be brought before our eyes. Ary Scheffer's picture, is, from an artistic point of view, scarcely better than Ambroise Thomas's

> opera; both continue to live because they represent Mignon.

This critic did regret the 'unrelieved sadness and longing' the mezzo gave the part, which allowed her Mignon to gain in intensity what it lost in 'piquancy'. He conceded, however, that loss of 'piquancy' would not be felt by those who think of Goethe's original creation'.[54]

The delectable uncertainty produced by not knowing how much Mignon knew was commented on when Albani again sang the part in Italian two years later. The scene of rivalry with Philene, where Mignon rouges herself before the glass, constituted the 'delicious' hint of wildness and passion that Carré and Barbier had given Mignon, and Albani disappointed by being extremely subdued in rendering it.[55] In Britain Mrs Forrester's extraordinarily unpleasant soft-porn triple-decker *Mignon* of 1877 should probably be seen as the epitome of delicious piquancy run its course to petulancy. Her eponymous heroine certainly does not know the origins of her name, an ignorance which is marked in a novel that dwells on naming and cross-dressing, and which even has the cold-hearted teenager at its centre dress as Goethe's Marguerite (from *Faust*) for a fancy-dress ball.[56]

Mignon's uncertain age, her shifting status, between childhood and womanhood, is emphasised in derivations of Thomas's opera. Herman Merivale's 'The Lord of the Manor' is a play *about* Mignon's age and her sexual status. This play allowed its reviewers good deal of fun, with Merivale's transmogrification of Wilhelm into 'a cavalier of mature age and unusually sedate demeanour', and the absurdity of a girl of 17 falling in love with a stout man in a yellow wig.[57] Critics who knew their Goethe were able to regret the many ways in which Merivale's Sybil fell short of Mignon, and the *Daily Telegraph* reviewer delivered a touching panegyric on Mignon's soul. All of them mentioned Sybil/Mignon's age, and indeed the playtext itself made much of it. 'The Lord of the Manor' was the plagiarism of Thomas's opera without the music that all the critics said it was, but it wrestled with the question of Mignon's age and maturity in a way that Carré and Barbier had not. Sir Wilfred rescues a *child* from the mountebank Mallow when she is threatened with a beating for refusing to perform 'the famous gipsy dance', and she thanks him with a bunch of flowers. Dutifully following the Carré and Barbier libretto, he thoughtlessly gives them to Philene (called Aurora here), and the child experiences her first rejection by him. When she has painted and rouged, when she has draped herself in Philene/Aurora's jewels, and when the servants have sniggered at her appearance before Sir Wilfred, he tells her that he cannot take her to Italy as he had promised. Then, he explains, he had thought her a child; 'I do not think so now'. 'Dull and dismal' this play may have been, but it is interesting for its resolution of the piquant oscillation between girl and woman that the libretto of Thomas's opera only displayed. Resolution consists not only of giving Mignon a husband in Wilhelm – that had been done before – but by giving her an *old* husband:

Sybil. Home! I have no home where you are not!
Wil. Do you mean that? I am growing old, child.
Sybil. Old! you, Master?
Wil. Not master, husband.
Sybil. Husband!
Wil. One word. Do you love me?
Sybil. With all my heart and soul.
CURTAIN

With stunning ingenuousness, John Strange Winter (Mrs Arthur Stannard)[58] runs the gamut of pathos and paedophilia in her series of 'Mignon' novels, all published in the 1880s. In *Bootle's Baby* (1885), a baby girl of angelic prettiness and fairness is found abandoned on a bed in the officers' mess of the Scarlet Lancers, and is named first '"la figlia del wreggimento . . . petite mademoiselle"' and then 'Mignon' by the soldiers, for the snatches of French and Italian have reminded Bootles (his was the bed) of

> the girl who had been jilted by his friend and died for love. He had always called her 'Mademoiselle Mignon' . . . 'Mademoiselle Mignon', he said carelessly: 'not a bad name for her' . . . 'What a pity she ain't twenty years older . . . Pretty work she'll make of the regiment sixteen or seventeen years hence'.

Here, and in subsequent volumes, the baby's later marriage to one of the officers who stand admiring her is prefigured.[59]

The baby's mother carries a trace of Mignon's story, for she is believed to have died for love. In fact, she is not dead at all, though we must wait until the next volume to discover that. In *Mignon's Secret* (1886) – which its author declared to be 'the story of a barrack bairn . . . written in an attempt to give the world some idea of the pathos which so strongly marks some children's lives' – the repellent dark strangeness of the original Mignon is shifted to 'Private Henderson's little, ill-used, worse than motherless lass, Jack . . . whose Christian name, by-the-bye, was Geraldine'. As the child explains, '"Please, sir, father 'e calls me Jack, 'cause he'd 'ave liked a boy instead of me"'.[60] The division of characteristics and qualities between the two little girls is established long before Jack/Geraldine exists as a character: the first remark made about the abandoned baby in *Bootle's Baby* is that she '"can't be a barrack child – too dainty looking, and not slobbery enough"'.[61] One volume on it is the barrack child, whose dark hair streams wildly about her, who indulges in fits of passionate weeping, and whose body is displayed in dance for the officer she loves, in a manner reminiscent of Mignon's performance for Wilhelm.[62] This nineteenth-century dark child of slush fiction stands before Captain Lucy and 'began executing a series of wild curtseys, in which circumstances she looked . . . just like one of those wooden doll-looking things you find inside a piano, and which bob up and down as you touch the keys'.[63]

Jack/Geraldine's jealousy of the fair Mignon is immense, and passionately consuming. Her friend Polly Armstrong practically remarks that '"if he [Captain Lucy] likes that pink an' white chiney-doll sort – why, there's naught more to be said about it"'; but the barrack child feels '"just as if I could do for 'er"' which is indeed what she attempts.[64] When the two girls finally meet – 'the one . . . the embodiment of light and purity and carefully guarded and trained – the other . . . at that moment, the very picture of all the evil passions run riot'[65] – Jack/Geraldine pushes Mignon into the river. She has a rapid change of heart, and in rescuing Mignon, drowns herself.

In *Mignon's Husband* (1887) Captain Lucy changes from father-figure to lover, in 'the flash of a moment . . . In that instant, Lucy realised that his love for the child Mignon had grown and grown, until it had taken possession of all his heart and soul'.[66] However, the child has not developed into a woman to accompany the growth of his love, and at this very moment of realisation she moves towards Lucy 'with a little skip in her step and such a glad light upon her face that in an instant the *child* came back again'.[67] When the Captain proposes to her she may achieve the fulfilment of her original's desires, but only with a man who thinks himself that he may be '"too old – and too fatherly"'.[68] Hugh Moss's four-act comedy 'Bootle's Baby' of 1887, which compacted the three novels into a single plot and in its contraction stressed the sexual and social ambiguity of the Mignon-figure, will be discussed below.

Many late nineteenth-century representations of Mignon made reference to each other. Frédéric Duhomme and Piel Troisement refined Mignon's meaning to its essential in their one-act drama of 1874: there is an elegant economy in *Le Dernier jour de Mignon* (Mignon's Last Day) and its acknowledgement that her death is all that really matters. Not only does this Mignon sing Thomas's 'Connais-tu', but she is found in the opening scene 'seul . . . tournée vers une fenêtre, regardent de longues volées d'oiseaux, comme dans le tableau d'Ary Scheffer' (alone . . . looking out of the window, watching the soaring birds, as in Ary Scheffer's painting).[69]

Throughout the nineteenth century, Mignon was also what she always had been: just a word, just a name – a word for little girls on the street (in the general sense, but gesturing also towards the other sense), the word for little girls you fancy. *Trilby* (1894) is framed by this sensibility, though when Svengali croons 'Dors ma mignonne' (only doing what Limousin mothers had done three centuries before?) what might give us pause for thought is that he croons to a fully grown young woman, not a child.[70] And astonishingly, as we have seen, the same sensibility frames at least one of the Independent Labour Party's figures of reclaiming and redeeming working-class children.[71] Sometimes, on dark pavements, seen suddenly in momentarily illuminated alleyways, the wan street child of the Victorian investigative imagination becomes Mignon: a child turns and dances, utterly self-absorbed. She is then Nora on the Pavement, entrancing the grey hour; the thing you want, the little girl you fancy.[72]

Long before Margaret McMillan had used Mignon for political purposes in her child-figure Marigold, cheap fiction of the 1880s and 1890s had written her again, moving her ambiguity (of sexuality and often of provenance) to other figures in the text. Mignon's other reshapings at the century's end are do with the changing meaning of a word. Popular versions of Mignon had often been concerned with etymological questions. In the anonymous *Mignon. A Tale. Translated from the French* (1868), when a new girl arrives at a St Germaine boarding-school, and is renamed by a nun because she looks 'very mignon', it has to 'be confessed that the good nun, the parrot, and the winds of the air, in repeating the name of Mignon, truly expressed the word already idealised by poetry and art'.[73]

In February 1899, Richard Rosenbaum delivered a lecture to the Vienna Goethe Society, simply entitled 'Mignon'. This paper was representative of a new search of the 1890s, for her 'real' origins. Rosenbaum's work can be seen as exemplary of a twentieth-century and very busy search for *where Mignon came from.* This was the third version of a talk and paper, first given in Berlin in 1896, in all of which Rosenbaum sought to establish a real-life model for Mignon, in a member of an acrobatic troupe seen in Göttingen in March 1764 by one Daniel Schiebler, who was later to become a friend of Goethe's at the University of Leipzig.[74] The talks that Rosenbaum gave after 1898 also attempted to incorporate the claims of Alois Brandl that Mignon's original is to be found in the disordered maid Maria, from Sterne's *Tristram Shandy.*[75] Eugen Wolff's most thorough study of 1909 used all the biographical sources available to find the original of Mignon in Elisabeth Schmeling-Mara, a singer whom Goethe knew, and whom he mentioned in correspondence.[76]

Speculative accounts of Mignon's origins, her *Urbild,* are now to rain down on the early twentieth century, despite Rosenbaum's gentle warning (to himself as much as others) about the futility of the task. He wrote in 1898 that 'we know from our own experience that inner and outer experiences from various impressions readily combine to distil the emotional content of a particular time into a particular figure'.[77] Despite this, claims were later to be made for the origins of the real Mignon in Cervantes's *Exemplary Stories* of 1613, in the figure of 'The Little Gypsy Girl'; in Wieland's *Don Sylvio of Rosalva* (1764), in Gellert's *Swedish Countess* (1754);

the claim for Sterne has been made again and again. Commentators working within a psychoanalytic frame pursue the biographical route, and Emil Ludwig's account in 1928, *Goethe, the History of a Man*, found Mignon in little Fritz von Stein.[78]

All new quests for Mignon's origins, whether etymological, literary or biographical, returned the inquiry at some point to the eighteenth century, as does a new contribution to an obsessive twentieth-century fantasy of origins. Sarah Fielding's *The Governess* (1749) is a conduct book and reading primer, in which nine little girls learn appropriate lessons for life through the exchange of autobiographies and the telling of fairy stories. One of the fairy stories relates the 'History of the Giants Barbarico and Beneficio', in which also appears the little dwarf Mignon who with his magic fillet tames the wicked one of the pair.[79]

This feminised little miracle-worker of Fielding owes some of his own origins to the author's readings of Antoine Banier's *Mythology and Fables of the Ancients* (1739–40) (she reproduces his discourse on the meanings of dwarfism and gigantism almost word for word) and from her considerable knowledge of the writings of Salignac de Mothe Fénelon, including his *Dialogues of the Dead.*[80] *The Governess was* translated into German, and *was* published at Leipzig in 1750, the year after Goethe's birth, and it is not unlikely that he knew it. If Goethe's child-figure was born in the 1770s out of that 'theorising we cannot avoid whenever we look attentively into the world',[81] out of Goethe's own experience of child development, out of his studies in geology and botany, and out of the attention he had to pay to questions of growth (gigantism and dwarfism) as he performed the duties of recruiting soldiers for the Duchy of Saxe-Weimar,[82] then Fielding's story-within-story is a prefiguring of all these questions.

The most intense twentieth-century questioning of the Mignon-figure and her origins took place in Germany, in the inter-war years. Dorothea Flashar, in her comprehensive study of 1929, investigated biographical origins as well as literary ones.[83] Her most innovative contribution lay in a careful mapping of changes made to Mignon between the *Mission* and the *Apprenticeship*, particularly in the account she gives of Goethe's application of the law of metamorphosis to human development, and his rewriting of Mignon's life and death as an unfolding, or becoming, of what she already was. These relationships between Goethe's scientific and his literary work will be discussed in some detail in the next chapter, but it is important to note at this point that Flashar was the first commentator to notice that the Mignon of the second version of the *Bildungsroman* was historicised in a way that she had not been in the earlier one. In the *Theatrical Mission* she is described as having heart trouble, but she has no past story to explain her abnormal development, her deformities, and her possible autism. At this point of her existence (in the 1770s and 1780s) she did not have a history; and the account that made her the product of an insane brother–sister relationship was conceived after Goethe made his Italian journey. This application of the idea of metamorphosis to human development diminishes Mignon, according to Flashar. As Wilhelm changes from artistic hopeful to ordinary productive social being, Mignon's role as objective expression of his creative interiority diminishes. She gains a story, but also a death, though Flashar argues that what is taken from her in human terms is returned to her in artistic terms: 'she stands before the reader's soul with moving, pathetic vividness'.[84]

Many twentieth-century commentators have sought to establish Mignon's ethereality, and see her escape the confines of *Wilhelm Meister* 'because she is the quintessential child . . . the child as it is . . . a pure enigma'.[85] Reinhard Kuhn understands sex to be 'the secret worm that undermines her existence', and he sees Goethe anticipating 'a basic Victorian pattern which is prevalent in Dickens, the early Dostoevski, and James . . . Mignon is the incarnation of yearning, and, when fulfilment is at hand, all longing is of necessity destroyed. Thanatos follows ineluctably on the heels of Eros.' These comments certainly provide an account of what the nineteenth century *did* with Mignon, and the meaning that she came to encapsulate; she is important for the entire body of theory and structure of feeling that allowed Freud his tragic depiction, of all things returning to their former state.[86] Popular rewritings of Mignon show an obsessive desire to make Mignon a girl, to have her grow up, and to marry Meister. The strange, dreamlike sexual fluidity of the figure that Goethe wrote – in whom one psychoanalytic commentator saw the 'passionate attachment without any real capacity for love' that is the mark of the pregenital child whose sexuality is latent – is effaced by a literary history that does not take the sexualisation of childhood (which actually provides the framework for its analysis) as an object of investigation and inquiry.[87]

Possibly, Mignon is the type of 'enigmatic' child that Kuhn has discussed. Her universe is to some extent self-enclosed and non-referential. Communication between her and the adults around her is certainly difficult, and she could be said to have a speech deficiency.[88] If, however, she has a message to deliver it consists not of what she communicates (or fails to communicate) but of what those around her make of her, and how it is she is used, in the structure of the novel. The question of her being 'older than her years', which Kuhn also itemises, is difficult of application, first because her behaviour is either perceived as that of a young child by other characters in the book, or because they – of course – fail to place her upon the modern developmental map that allows Kuhn to make this point.[89] And though she is certainly doomed, she does not die because she is subject to the 'vicissitudes of time', but because she occupies such a strange relationship to temporality itself, within the structure of the novel.

In *The Way of the World: the Bildungsroman in European Culture,* Franco

Moretti tries to explain why Mignon (the first one: Goethe's Mignon; though as we already know, she has no true origin, and certainly she has no end) has to die. The argument is essentially to do with her out-of-placeness in a form of writing. The task of the *Bildungsroman*, according to Moretti, was to make time circular, to bring a linear series of events – a chronology – into a system of relationships, a kind of ring, in which the protagonists find a home to replace the original one. Mignon's nostalgia, remarks Moretti, 'is the symptom of a life in which no homeland has replaced the original one. Time here is an unchanging beat, a mechanical and exhausting effort which the organicist teleology of the classical *Bildungsroman* banishes as if it were the pounding of death.'[90] Pursuing Mignon's representations through the following two hundred years must lead us to see how very hard it is for us to accept her death – even though we may never have heard of her – and how persistent are all our attempts to rescue her, and find her a home. Since about 1890 we have given Mignon a meaning by the procedures of narrative and the procedures of history – the two forms that grew to pre-eminence in the nineteenth century and that (again, Moretti's claim) did not retreat before the onslaught of events, but instead demonstrated the possibility of giving them order and meaning: 'not only are there no "meaningless events"; there can now be meaning only through events'.[91] The story of Mignon since 1899 is a story about the permeation of these cultural needs and desires: first to find the child, and then to give the child a home; and in these ways it is not surprising if we forget that Goethe only gave his child a story once she was dead.

3

Figures and Physiology

'. . . Taking care not to forget the function of desire in relation to physiological discourse.'
(François Delaporte, *Nature's Second Kingdom*, p.8)

However it was that Mignon came into the world, she came with a great deal attached to her. To look at those attachments, as this chapter does, is to introduce other investigations that will be pursued through the course of this book, right up until its very end. First, Goethe's own scientific preoccupations of the 1780s and 1790s were important for the genesis of his child-figure and need to be introduced and discussed. But different histories of science, produced at different points throughout the nineteenth and early twentieth centuries, have much more bearing on Mignon's extra-textual afterlife. The second purpose of this chapter is to consider some of the ways in which new, nineteenth-century accounts of Goethe as scientist and poet of development shaped Mignon's new meanings. Third, and as a background to nineteenth-century interpretations of Goethe's work, this chapter also offers an account of contemporary developments in physiological thinking, particularly in the long evolution of cell theory, which have a clear bearing on the questions of childhood and interiority that are the subjects of this book. As physiological writing of the mid-nineteenth century was frequently accompanied by its own history – a history of developments in thinking that had brought the account to its current state – and as Goethe was often assigned a place in this history, one of the many connotations of his child-figure a century after her death was to do with the scientific reputation of her creator.

All of this merely adds more items to the already extensive list of Mignon's meanings. But there is a further purpose to giving an account of physiological cell theory and its figurative and imaginative force in nineteenth-century thinking, that is, to arrive at a clearer understanding of what it was that Sigmund Freud undertook when he theorised childhood in the early decades of the twentieth century; what the material for thinking the unconscious as childhood repressed actually was. Questions are raised in this chapter and the next, about little places inside, histories turned within, childhood and the unconscious, and different ways of thinking about these topics according to the protocols of nineteenth-century physiology, as opposed to the more conventionally adduced tenets of evolutionary biology.

The historical discussion of scientific work always poses questions of imagery. Edward Manier has described how in the development of a research programme (twentieth-century historians of science typically use this phrase to mean the complex of theory, work and publication built around a scientific topic) a series of tropes – figurative representations – are engaged. As the work develops, these figurative representations are replaced by 'literal, unequivocal, technical . . . expression'. Then the imaginative correlatives of the language used fade and words come to have a unitary, 'scientific' meaning. For the historian who wants to rescue the theory's full ontological significance, what is important is the dialectical relationship between the theory and its cultural contexts. This relationship can most be successfully discovered by considering the means used to represent it, that is, the language used for transmitting it as 'science'. Manier continues: 'once a theory is given a tropological representation . . . there is *no way to recover its meaning except to sort through the various possible meanings and uses associated with its central tropes or figurative expressions*'. He goes on to suggest that 'this sorting cannot be done systematically in the absence of theories of culture and cultural change'.[1] This and the next two chapters are concerned with one side of the dialectic that Manier describes – with the cultural and figurative contexts in which, throughout the nineteenth century, a physiological discourse was used to fashion a child-figure that, in its turn, explained new topographies of the human body. And in order to understand this process, we need to pay attention not only to the cultural context of Goethe's original scientific work, but also to all the meanings that it has acquired since histories first started to be written of it, and interpretations made of it. Those accreted meanings are also Mignon's meanings, personified by the histories of science by which Goethe's work has been construed, since the early years of the nineteenth century.

Since the end of the last century the most persistent questions concerning Mignon have been about where she came from, and the most determined attempts to answer them have located her in Goethe's science, in the complex set of intellectual investigations into the phenomena of form, shape and growth, which he undertook in his middle years. In the late 1770s and 1780s Goethe was directly involved in child-rearing, deeply interested in geology and botany, and his administrative position in Weimar, especially after he became involved in the War Commission in 1779, drew his attention to questions of abnormal growth.[2]

In the 1780s Goethe had also done much work in comparative anatomy, investigating the fascinating case of the supposedly missing intermaxillary bone in human beings. There is a difference between animals and human beings in the appearance of that middle part of the upper jaw which carries the incisors: in most mammals it is a separate bone, whilst in human beings the bones have grown together. Goethe was particularly concerned with the cultural meaning of this difference, studied many skulls, and found the bone which allowed him to say that

> man is most intimately allied to animals. The co-ordination of the Whole makes every creature to be that what it is, and man is as much man through the form of his upper jaw, as through the form and nature of the last joint of his little toe. And this is in every creature but a note of the great *harmony*, which must be studied in the Whole or else it is nothing but a dead letter.[3]

Goethe wrote to Johann Herder too, on the same topic, thinking of Herder's plans for a history that embraced all living things through time – his proposed *Thoughts on History* – and told him that the intermaxillary bone '"will make you . . . rejoice heartily, for it is like the keystone to humanity . . . I have thought of it in connection with your Whole, how fine it will look there".'[4] The study of botany, which Goethe began seriously in 1785, also prompted new ways of asking questions about the interconnectedness of the natural realm.[5]

He took all of these preoccupations with him to Italy, on his two-year visit in the mid-1780s. Book 6 of the *Theatrical Mission* manuscript was finished by the time he left Weimar and took the road for Rome in the autumn of 1786, and Mignon already had full figurative existence. Nevertheless, it is to the Italian journey that many recent commentators have looked for Goethe's rewriting of her. Since 1910, when it became possible to compare the Mignon of the *Theatrical Mission* manuscript with the altered – and doomed – child of the *Apprenticeship*, the work of revising and remaking Mignon has been located in the intellectual preoccupations that Goethe carried south in that sensuous form of theorising that 'we cannot avoid whenever we look attentively into the world'.[6] Nicholas Boyle has described Goethe's crossing of the Alps as the fulfilment of a desire often and long delayed, now come to emotional and intellectual fruition. Desire for Italy had already been inscribed in Mignon herself at least three years before, and in her song of longing; now, briefly, momentarily, she is acknowledged by her author as the shape of his own desire. There was a dawn start for Naples in February 1787, with oranges overhanging the road in astonishing abundance, and Goethe knows that the child-figure he had created 'was quite right to yearn for this country'.[7]

Apprehension of the interconnectedness of all the phenomena of nature (the lessons learned from bones and plants in Weimar) shaped what Goethe saw during his visits to two Italian botanical gardens in 1786.

In September, in Padua, he wrote of his 'hypothesis that it might be possible to derive all plant forms from the original plant',[8] and six months later in the Gardens at Palermo he observed that 'here where, instead of being grown in pots or under glass . . . plants are allowed to grow freely in the open air and fulfil their natural destiny, they become more intelligible'. He wondered if, among the variety before his eyes, he might not discover 'the Primal Plant'. There had to be such a thing, 'otherwise, how could I recognize that this or that form *was* a plant if all were not built upon the same model?'[9] Later, Goethe recalled that it had come to him in a flash that in

> the organ of the plant which we are accustomed to call the *leaf* lies the true Proteus who can hide or reveal himself in all vegetal forms. From first to last, the plant is nothing but leaf, which is so inseparable from the future germ that one cannot think of one without the other.[10]

Here, 'leaf' is a convenient (if a very confusing) term for the idea that a single plant is a single organ which develops (or is metamorphosed) through different shapes in the course of its existence, through a process of contraction and expansion, from inside to an external form.[11]

In order to interpret Mignon as an expression of this law of metamorphosis, twentieth-century commentators ignored a twenty-five-year gap between the letters and journal entries that recorded Goethe's contemporary botanical insights and speculations, and the publication of them in the autobiographical archive of his theories, the *Italian Journey* of 1816–17. Indeed, many of the insights and observations that he recorded between 1786 and 1788 appear to have played no part in the published text to which Mignon is most frequently referred back, the *Metamorphosis of Plants* of 1790. In particular, the idea of the primal plant, as a kind of ideal model of what the plant was to become, was quickly discarded, and it played no part in the *Metamorphosis*.[12]

In late twentieth-century accounts of the development of the theory of metamorphosis, Goethe's abandonment of the idea of the primal plant in the thesis of 1790 is not as important as the more general account that his speculations in the gardens at Padua allow historians of science to tell. Surveying the late eighteenth century, historians of science see the origins of two different, though not necessarily mutually exclusive, approaches to the study of life forms: idealistic morphology and functional morphology.[13] They describe how later in the nineteenth century (and it is largely nineteenth-century developments that these accounts of origin seek to explain), functional morphology came to focus on physiological and embryological processes, on the relationship between the structure and function of living forms, and on the present life of the organism as it actually functioned, with its structure providing the key to comprehending its function.[14] These comparative histories of scientific ideas then go on to recount how, on the other hand, idealist morphologists searched out similarity of form among different animals and plants. This could lead to the delineation of an ideal-type, or to speculation about a common ancestor or an ideal progenitor.[15] In the German university system, where so much work in morphology and physiology was advanced in the nineteenth century, the research procedure recommended by Immanuel Kant in the *Critique of Judgement* (1790) exercised a shaping force on this kind of inquiry. Kant's work stressed the need for employing the notion of a morphotype – an organisational plan – as a guiding principle in theory construction, for it was not thought possible to explain physiological organisation in terms of physical principle alone. Rather, in order to investigate the organic realm, the idea of some kind of purposive plan had to be assumed.[16] Goethe's *Metamorphosis* (as well as the notes he made for it, and the insights he had while in Italy) have been allocated to this historical account of idealist morphology; and the principle, or essence, or idea of a plant that unfolds from within has often been interpreted as his use of an *Urtyp* (ideal-type), a configuration that contained all possible morphological structures within a given scheme, and which thus permitted 'a lawlike derivation of all the variations of the original type'.[17] Accreted layers of nineteenth-century interpretation have been peeled away in order to demonstrate that Goethe did not have recourse to an explanation for development outside the plant, in some force or vital principle. Instead, as Nicholas Boyle argues, Goethe 'explained' the plant only by reference to itself, by delineating a morphological structure within a given scheme. Boyle also draws attention to the assertiveness of Goethe's use of an already established zoological concept in a treatise on botanical development, for his title of 1790 strikingly suggested that the developmental sequence observed in insect growth was also to be found in plants. The title *Versuch, die Metamorphose der Pflanzen zu erklären* (Attempt To Explain the Metamorphosis of Plants) promised to reveal a regular sequence of different forms in each individual plant, with each sequence or change showing a single principle or idea being developed from within, to the point where each plant achieved its individuality. The title undertook not only to describe each plant's formation, but also to provide an explanation for the great variety of nature's second kingdom.[18]

Earlier twentieth-century accounts of the relationship between Mignon and the idea of metamorphosis highlighted the interactive components of the theory. After the *Theatrical Mission* manuscript became available for scrutiny, the relationship between the inner nature of people (or plants), the unfolding of that nature, and the external circumstances which modify or thwart development, provided a focus for much discussion of the child-figure.[19] Indeed, Goethe himself had suggested the relationship in the

'Vorwort' to a late edition of *Dichtung und Wahrheit* (Poetry and Truth from My Own Life). In 1813 he compared the development of a child (specifically, the remembered child of his own autobiography) with that of a plant:

> before I began to write . . . I intended to form . . . [*Dichtung und Wahrheit*] according to those laws taught us by the metamorphosis of plants. In the first volume the child was intended to put out tender roots on all sides . . . in the second [part] the boy was to put forth stage by stage the brighter green of his various branches, and this burgeoning stem was in the third seed-bed to hasten into flower and show the hopeful youth.[20]

Dorothea Flashar's account of the changes perceptible in Mignon between the two versions of *Meister* suggested that metamorphosis is (and was for Goethe) a kind of quiet, organic becoming. She described a core, a shaped form (a morpheme: the smallest meaningful unit in a system) in each human being, which is made manifest through the processes of development. This was a process of rhythmic change, through which individuals might become what they already are, in essence.[21] In this exegesis Mignon was given specific status as the point of transition between the masculine and the feminine. And in something of the same way, argued Flashar, Mignon's death showed a lack of gap or rupture (between being and not being) and could thus also be seen as metamorphosis: her separation from life may be violently sudden, but her body remained, preserving the appearance of life.[22]

Explaining Goethe's theory of metamorphosis in this way, and giving it explanatory force in areas outside the botanical, had a very long history. In 1858 George Henry Lewes felt obliged to tell his British readers that what Goethe had called metamorphosis in the 1790s was not what was either generally or scientifically understood by the term. In true metamorphosis, Lewes explained, there would have to be a sequence to match the way 'a caterpillar develops into a grub, and the grub into a butterfly. This would be metamorphosis.' If readers were to understand and use Goethe's definition, Lewes said, then they must 'conceive the whole plant as a succession of repetitions of the original type variously modified; in some of these repetitions the modification has been slight, in others considerable. The two typical forms are stem and leaf.'[23]

Besides making the history of ideas clearer, Lewes's purpose was to claim Goethe as 'a thinker in science, a manipulator of scientific ideas', for a nineteenth-century British readership.[24] Lewes noted the long neglect of Goethe's theory, and then how by the mid-century across Europe it had become impossible to write a treatise of descriptive botany without reference to his *Metamorphosis*.[25] Lewes wanted to recapture the full ontological significance of Goethe's work, which he did by making strange – by historicising – conventional nineteenth-century physiological thinking. He explained how very much perception of the world had altered in the previous half-century, so as to make the conceptual changes Goethe had brought about seem unremarkable; it was Lewes's self-appointed task to make his readers understand the theoretical innovation Goethe's science embodied. The various ways in which Goethe's conceptions had been anticipated were far less important to Lewes than Goethe's innovations in scientific method. He discussed Goethe's work on the intermaxillary bone by way of example and suggested that

> the only importance of this discovery is the philosophic Method which it illustrates; the firm belief it implies that all organisms are constructed on a uniform plan. We are so accustomed to consider all the variations in organic structure as modifications of a type that we can hardly realise to ourselves any other conception.[26]

He called Goethe's Ideal Type a 'truly scientific conception', which had borne noble fruit, and emphasised that 'Goethe expressly says that we are not for a moment to believe in the *existence* of this Type as an objective reality . . . it is the generalised expression of that which really exists'.[27]

This was as selective a history of science as any other, and it did not describe the way in which, in the course of Goethe's own lifetime, what Lewes presented as an heuristic device had actually come to assume the force of 'real' existence; how the Ideal Type moved from being a regulative idea that organised research and allowed some productive thinking about evidence to take place, to being conceived as constitutive: 'as a real and identifiable historical entity', 'an actual physical force'.[28] In this way, Goethe's understandings and conceptualisations of the 1780s and 1790s were absorbed into a nineteenth-century vision of the Type.

Much nineteenth-century discussion, then, established Goethe as a thinker fundamentally concerned with the delineation of pre-existent and abstract types. This happened again when contemporary understandings of the type were read back to the late eighteenth century in order to claim him as a progenitor of the emergent social sciences. Lambert Quetelet's *Social Physics* (1835) exercised a great influence on physiological growth studies in nineteenth-century Britain and France. In particular Quetelet's belief in a perfect form or type of man, and the tendency of the race to attain that type, possessed much imaginative force and produced a good deal of anthropometric work.[29] Nineteenth- and twentieth-century accounts emphasise Quetelet's meeting with Goethe, and the influence of the older man on the younger, in his development of the idea of 'l'homme moyen'. In his *History of the Study of Human Growth* J.M. Tanner describes the meeting, and the importance of Goethe's conception for the young man's consequent theorising: 'Goethe's Type was an ideal, to which individuals by their moral and intellectual development seek to attain . . . drawn by this monistic conception of the universe, Quetelet tried to found a new science of man analogous to Goethe's Morphology of Organic Nature'.[30]

When Goethe was established as a man of science for a nineteenth-century community of professional and non-professional readers, he was depicted as a developmental theorist crucially interested in questions of growth and generation. When changes between the *Theatrical Mission* and the *Apprenticeship* became available for scrutiny in 1910, and when it became possible to make comparison between figures in the two texts (between the two Wilhelms and, above all, between the two Mignons) then an established notion of Goethe as the poet of development, with development conceived of in modern (post-Darwinian) terms, was used for analysis. Yet naturalists of the period in which Goethe worked conceived of evolution as a change *in* living things; they 'did not look at organised products as being held together by the affinity and consequently uniting the members of a great family. To them the chain of living beings was not forged by *blood and ancestry*, but by *common design and plan* revealed in their structures.'[31]

So powerful is the Darwinian myth, so numerous are the accounts of nineteenth-century evolutionary theory's cultural impact and domain, and so widely accepted are arguments about the concomitant biologising of the literary, psychological and anthropological realms (to say nothing of the scientific), that we fail to recognise that much thinking about change and development was not connected to biological thought at all, but was associated with physiology. Nineteenth-century physiological writing (especially in its popularised form) provided a series of imaginative and figurative paradigms for describing individuals, time and change. Goethe was presented as a scientific thinker within this framework. When George Henry Lewes discussed the *Metamorphosis* in 1858 and said that 'Goethe's work is very beautiful',[32] he attempted to account for the experience of reading a form of physiological writing that matched words very closely indeed to what was being apprehended. Indeed, Goethe's text of 1790 is extraordinary for the simplicity and pellucidity with which description matches not so much what is seen as what is understood in the seeing. The sentence-form, and the arrangement of the whole argument in a series of paragraphs or *aperçus* refer each moment of understanding back to the object being contemplated. The exegesis traces thought itself (these particular thoughts) as much as its subject matter. The thing-in-itself, the 'it-ness' of the thing being described, has to be represented in English by the suffixes and dashes which always imply a satire on the German language; yet it is the beauty of the essence of something-described that Lewes responded to; what he also noted were the satisfactions and the comforts of reading this form of description.[33] In calling the structure and shape of the work beautiful, he recalled what had also happened to him when he scrutinised the specimens he collected during his seaside studies of the same year, 'when the typical forms took *possession* of me'.[34]

Things-in-themselves, things as they already were in essence, the growth of those things and their turning back to what they already were in a former state: these terms provided the rhetorical and poetic structures of the physiology and morphology that was transmitted in Goethe's name in mid-nineteenth-century Britain. It is this kind of physiological thought that we need to understand in describing Mignon's progress, in the period when she lost her name and became the complex of ideas that this book seeks to describe.

In the nineteenth century, physiology took as its domain all the questions that we might now classify under the heading of biology. The term 'biology' was coined in the early years of that century, and those who promoted its use aspired to an integrated investigation into all the functional processes of organisms, in the hope that 'their aggregate effect might well be life itself'.[35] In Britain the pressure to use the term 'biology' rather than 'physiology' was social as well as theoretical, an attempt to emancipate the science from its roots in medicine and forensic anatomy.[36] However, it is important to keep the term that nineteenth-century writers and their audiences used, partly in order to understand the figurative relationships that were brought into play by the use of particular terminology, but also because in Britain physiology never did lose its associations with the medical. This association was to turn out to be important for the development of growth studies in the later nineteenth century, when biological thought came to be dominated by the idea of evolution, that is, by the imaginative force of the changes observable in living beings and populations in the context of time. Physiology, on the other hand, took the stability of phenomena as the framework for its observation, and was concerned with change and development within the time and space of an organism, rather than within the sweep of socio-historical time.[37]

But it is misleading to set up an opposition between physiology and biology in this way, for it has become clearer over the last decade or so that many historical accounts of a nineteenth-century 'Darwinian revolution' have been false, that Darwin's description of evolution (crucially, the parts of the thesis that described adaptation, and the shaping of human descent by natural events, accidents and unforeseen happenings) did not gain general acceptance until the early twentieth century, with the pioneering of Mendelian genetics. In Peter Bowler's summary of this revisionist history of biological thought and research, there was no Darwinian revolution, though there was 'a non-Darwinian revolution'.[38] This involved widespread acceptance of the idea of evolution itself from the last decades of the eighteenth century onwards. (In Goethe's letter to

Herder, when he offered him the example of the intermaxillary bone to add to his history of all living things, he used this common conception of evolution.) It was a form of evolution conceived of in terms of growth. It took as its analogy, or explanatory figure, the pattern of individual development (of a plant, an insect, an embryo, a human being). The growth model allowed those who used it to comprehend evolution as purposeful, orderly and goal directed and, perhaps, as divinely planned or ordained.

In the kind of history of science that takes a very long view, the preoccupations of early nineteenth-century physiology are presented as a manifestation of Aristotelian thought in Western culture, an obeisance to the injunction to 'describe . . . common functions, common, that is, to the whole animal kingdom, or to certain large groups, or to members of a species'.[39] In this sweep of history, the late eighteenth century is shown to display a new version of the ancient conflict in physiological explication, between mechanism and vitalism.[40] Both were structures of thought that sought an answer to the question: what is life? (though we should remember that this is itself a nineteenth-century question, and that before the changes we are here describing had taken place, there was no such thing as 'Life', only living things).[41] When eighteenth-century thinking on these questions is described, Cartesian dualism is sometimes evoked in order to define mechanism: the human body seen as an aggregate of mechanical parts, with a dynamic motor, located outside the body machine, to set it working. Much physiological work in the late eighteenth century was designed to dismantle this dualism, and by an intensive study of the human body, to demonstrate that in its entire organisation it contained all the forces necessary to its functioning.[42] At the methodological level, mechanism meant that physiologists behaved as if all the activities of the body could be explained in terms of its material composition, and the interaction of its parts at the physico-chemical level.

Vitalism, on the other hand, describes a miscellany of contemporary beliefs united in opposition to mechanism, which contended that living processes could not be entirely explained by reference to their material composition and physico-chemical activity.[43] There are many accounts of the development of the idea of an 'active principle' in matter; across Europe this idea was shaped by different research traditions and a wide variety of cultural and religious imperatives.[44] In Britain, John Hunter's late eighteenth-century exegesis is important, because of the way in which his work was received in the following century. Hunter first propounded his vital principle theory in 1786, arguing that living phenomena could not be accounted for except by the supposition that 'life resulted from the addition of a simple principle to ordinary matter'.[45] Arguments like this were structured by analogical reference to Newtonian physics. By this time scientists had given up trying to find a mechanism for gravitational action, and gravity had simply come to be considered as an intrinsic property of matter itself, something that needed no further explanation: awareness of gravity existed only because bodies gravitated. In a turn of thought like this, all phenomena could be related back to a prime cause.

Using a similar structure of explanation, life itself could be explained as a vital force. James Palmer's 1837 edition of Hunter's work transmitted the shape of an argument to the nineteenth century:

> Life then, according to this first and most simple idea, consists in a property of matter superseded to and different from all known agencies . . . It exists independently of visible organisation and spontaneous motion, it inheres more or less in every living part . . . Of its nature and immediate proximate cause we are compelled to regard it as an ultimate fact.[46]

Twenty years later, popularising cell theory in *Sea-side Studies,* George Henry Lewes described a similar 'ultimate fact', a similar end-point to physiological inquiry. He described an irreducible force of life, and told his readers that 'the fact that all organic beings are endowed with the property of Reproduction . . . must, for the present at least, be accepted as an ultimate fact, not permitting dispute, not admitting explanation'.[47] This place of no entry, the bottom line of physiological writing, was returned to again and again in the middle years of the century. The most commonly produced piece of evidence for its existence – for a vital principle that did not permit of further explanation – was the observation that the organism possessed the power to counteract the destructive effects of the atmosphere.[48]

The speculations of German *Naturphilosophen* also influenced the development of vitalist thought in British physiology. Various forms of *Naturphilosophie* were transmitted to Britain (Coleridge is well known as a transmitter of German Idealism). It had its strongest impact on British science between 1820 and 1850, providing it with a fundamental axiom: 'the idea of becoming, of the restlessness of nature, ever self-renewing and hereby life-constructing processes'.[49] We should add to this circulation of scientific ideas among scientific audiences the intermingling of vitalist notions with heterodox religion. D.M. Knight has suggested that a persistent belief in the categories of alchemy, in the unity of matter, in chemical synthesis as a unity of opposites, and the powerful impact of the idea of electrical force (especially as expressed in the international bestseller of Humphrey Davy, *Consolations*), all wedded the idea of a vital force in living matter to the categories of popular science.[50]

Formerly viewed as 'a strange and nearly impenetrable off-shoot of the Romantic movement',[51] *Naturphilosophie* has now received the respectful history that was called for thirty years ago, when L. Pearce Williams suggested that its 'deep belief in a fundamental, underlying unity of Nature' was essential for understanding all of nineteenth-century science.[52] What has also become clear through paying *Naturphilosophie* respectful attention, is the very limited historical usefulness of the traditional divisions of physiology into 'materialist' and 'vitalist'. *Naturphilosophie* provided research in physiology with a theoretical foundation, and researchers using its paradigms were often prompted to unite vitalist and mechanical theories of explanation; the complex of research and writing that was promoted between about 1790 and 1850 has been labelled 'teleomechanism'.[53]

Its theoretical foundation – the unity of all the phenomena of the living world, and the organisation of animal bodies as revelatory of the material presence of Mind (or purpose, or Spirit) in nature[54] – is now seen as a taproot of nineteenth-century recapitulation theory, for the thesis that ontogeny repeats phylogeny assumes an identity among all forces of nature.[55] This conception of the unity of all living things was the schema of Herder's vast, embracing synthesis in *Thoughts on History* (1784–91), and also dictated Goethe's response to it. Late eighteenth-century embryology also supported Herder's cultural and anthropological claims, for in 1759 Caspar Wolff had described how the organs of the chick in the egg appear one after the other in rudimentary form.[56] These scientific arguments were supported by cultural ones: Jean-Jacques Rousseau thought that the intellectual development of children retraced the steps of civilisation.[57] These broad cultural and philosophic speculations revolutionised an earlier concept of preformation, in which 'the living machine existed as a miniaturised adult in the ovum or spermatozoon, requiring only to be enlarged, scaled up, to form the full grown individual'.[58] The striking new vision meant understanding that embryos did not simply get larger; rather, they *developed.* These insights swelled 'the floodtide of Naturphilosophie', and are the theoretical and perceptual prehistory to von Baer's observation of 1828, that all young vertebrate embryos look alike.[59]

In Michel Foucault's telling of this tale, *Naturphilosophie*, and the ways of thinking and imagining that vitalist physiology made available to scientists (and to other thinkers as well) are simply manifestations of an archaeological shift in perception and understanding, which took place from the late eighteenth century onwards. He located the period 1775–95 as the one in which the idea of Life (as a force, an entity, a category of thought) became absolutely necessary to scientists attempting to categorise natural beings (formerly it was living things that were conceptualised, not 'Life'). This happened because 'the notion of Life was the only mechanism of thought that allowed a link to be made between external organs, and the organs buried deep in the body, whose existence and hidden forms perform the essential functions'.[60] From this period onwards, claimed Foucault, classifying things in the natural world would involve relating the visible to the invisible, to that which lies deep within. Characteristics of living things came to be used by natural scientists as visible signs directing the inquirer towards 'a buried depth'. Foucault does not deny that there was a difference between vitalism and mechanism, nor that vitalism triumphed over mechanism in the scientific explanation of the next half-century; his point is that in both modes of thought the attempt to 'define the specificity of life are merely the surface effects of . . . archaeological events'.[61]

These speculations among different schools of physiology proffered particular shapes and forms with which living things might be envisaged, and indeed life itself might be imagined as having contours and constitution. *Naturphilosophen* of the Romantic period described developmental sequences of organs, taking place in a geometric transformation of a basic plan or structure, and thus drew attention to the connections between organs. Other thinkers, like Goethe, speculated on changes within individual organs. For both, shape was 'the external impression in space and time of the organic formative forces'.[62]

In all European scientific communities, questions were derived from this speculative philosophy, and the animal body was scrutinised in its light. In the underlying quest for 'the type of life', or a primal element, a common research strategy was to take one of the constituent parts defined by general anatomy (mucus, for instance, or tissue) and attribute to it the function of producing the other component parts.[63] Tissue doctrine itself (connected with the researches of François Bichat) was an attempt to systematise the study of the construction of the body. Bichat defined tissues as the fundamental structural elements of the body, and grouped them in organs, which were able to form the more complex nervous, respiratory and digestive systems. Their actions were explained in terms of 'irritability', 'sensitivity', and so on – by the effect that they had on each other.[64]

The pre-existence of physiological thought like this suggests why cell theory was so easily accepted by quite divergent research traditions across Europe. Cell theory has sometimes been described as the direct result of microscopical progress, as the simple result of actually being able to *see* more of a physiological interior. But it seems clearer now that microscope technology itself should be understood as one historical manifestation of a much longer scientific attempt to describe what lies within: to give figurative shape to the body's 'minute components seen only with the mind's eye'.[65]

The history of the development of cell theory, and of the work of German, French and British scientists that anticipated its formal statement by J.M. Schleiden and Theodore Schwann in 1839, is well known. The nucleus in the cell of flowering plants had been seen by Robert Brown (1773?–1858) in 1832, using a simple microscope.[66] The fluid in the cell was being studied under its new name of 'protoplasm' by the

1830s, and cells had also been recognised in the very early stages of animal development.[67] However, compared with plant cells, animal cells were so diverse in appearance that for a very long time the idea of unity between animal and vegetable bodies was delayed.

In the 1830s Jacob Schleiden used the work of Robert Brown on the nucleus (which he renamed the 'cytoblast'). He presented it as 'a universal elementary organ of vegetables', and claimed that all plants were aggregates of fully individualised, independent, separate entities, namely cells.[68] The importance of Schleiden's work, expressed in his *Principles of Scientific Botany*, lay in his presentation of the vegetable cell as having a double existence, 'an independent one, as pertaining to its own development alone, and another incidental, in so far as it has become an integral part of a plant.' Every aspect of plant physiology was an expression of the vital activity of cells, and the cell was identified as the fundamental unit of structure and function. This perception was well established in communities wider than the scientific by the time *Principles of Scientific Botany* appeared in English translation in 1849.[69]

Schleiden communicated his unpublished findings to Theodore Schwann in the autumn of 1837, and the extension of cell theory from the plant world to the animal body was effected. In his *Microscopical Researches* of 1839, Schwann described how animal and plant physiology had hitherto developed separately, and stated that the object of his treatise was to prove 'the most intimate connection between the two kingdoms of organic nature'.[70] His study provided a description of cell formation that was 'of universal application', in his claim that

> there is, in the first instance, a *structureless* substance present, which is sometimes quite fluid, at others, more or less gelatinous. This substance possesses within itself, in a greater or lesser measure according to its chemical qualities and the degree of its vitality, the capacity to occasion the production of cells. When this takes place the nucleus usually appears to be formed first and then the cell around it . . . The cell, once formed, continues to grow by its own individual powers.[71]

'This,' he wrote, 'is the fundamental phenomenon of all animal and vegetable life.' 'There exists one general principle for the formation of all organic productions . . . the formation of cells, as well as the conclusions which may be drawn from this proposition, may be comprised under the term *cell-theory*.'[72]

When Schwann asserted that everything alive had a cellular structure, he did not mean in the modern sense that cells are only formed out of pre-existing cells; rather, he believed that the cytoblastema (this was the new name he gave to 'the structureless substance', the cell fluid) gave rise to cells, in the same way as yeast operates in fermenting liquid (he used the example of crystal formation in the extract above).[73] He also gave further figurative shape to Schleiden's original conception, when he described the double life of the cell:

> each cell is, within certain limits, an Individual, and the independent Whole . . . Individuals, however, are not ranged side by side as a mere aggregate, but so operate together, in a manner unknown to us, as to produce a harmonious Whole.[74]

Schwann himself was deeply interested in the theoretical and philosophic implications of his work, and endorsed a position that he called materialist, saying that 'the fundamental powers of organised bodies agree essentially with those of inorganic nature . . . they . . . work together blindly according to the laws of necessity and irrespective of any purpose'.[75]

His strongly anti-vitalist position – the way in which he described himself setting out 'with the supposition that an organised body is not produced by a fundamental power which is guided in its operation by a definite idea, but is developed according to the blind laws of necessity, by powers which, like those of inorganic nature are established by the very existence of matter' – serves to blur many of the clear, textbook lines between vitalism and materialism that twentieth-century history of science has drawn.[76]

The important imaginative legacy of Schwann's account lay in its detailed description of cell formation and activity. Cellular 'reality' was made in a variety of ways in the early nineteenth century,[77] that is to say, research scientists and varieties of scientific audiences were given images and analogies by which the cell could be seen and its activities watched. Indeed, the cell received one of its most visual, and, after 1847, most widely read treatments in Schwann's work. A second imaginative legacy was the movement of the idea of a force inherent in all life from the schema of vitalist theory into materialist approaches. The idea of an unreachable power at work in the human body became a generalised scientific perception, not the principle of one particular school of physiological thought. 'It will doubtless be said by many,' wrote Thomas Huxley in 1853, 'but what guides these molecular forces? Some Cause, some Force, must rule the atoms and determine their arrangements in to cells and organs; there must be something, call it what you will – Archaeus, "Bildungs-treib," "Vis Essentialis," Vital Force, Cell-force – by whose energy the vital phenomena are what they are.'[78]

L.S Jacyna has shown how British physiologists took from *Naturphilosophie* an imperative to study the totality of vegetable and animal organisms. They also took a theory of metamorphosis that made them seek out the endless derivations of the one and higher primitive type. This theory of metamorphosis and the quest it initiated promoted much work on the typical structure of lower animals, which could be taken to reveal the structure of more complex ones.[79] The search for a common structural and developmental basis underlying the heterogeneity of animal and vegetable bodies, and the easy reception of cell theory in Britain, is to be explained by these pre-existing searches and structures of explanation: 'British [scientific] workers took up the concept of the cell as a means of characterising more adequately the point of unity between the highest and lowest forms. They hoped thereby to elucidate the fundamental vital processes.'[80]

When the fourth edition of William Carpenter's *Principles of Physiology* came out in 1851, one reviewer noted that as early as 1839 (when it was originally published) Carpenter's leading idea had been to reduce

> every form of organic structure, and every functional change, to its simplest expression . . . the lowest vegetable organism, consisting of a single cell, was the continually recurred-to starting point from which to trace out the essential character of each physiological action, through its successive complications in the higher forms of vegetable life.

This reviewer thought Carpenter's work quite original on this score, but also understood that Carpenter saw himself as one of the 'numerous observers' whose work had contributed to Schleiden and Schwann's 'cell-doctrine'.[81]

Reception, use and elaboration of a scientific theory is always subject to national, cultural and sociological influences. In Britain in the 1830s and 1840s, medical science conceived of certain types of inquiry as particularly appropriate to an understanding of the human body. In the attempts to dissociate physiology from anatomy and pathology, and to meet the theoretical requirements of medical science, there was a strong tendency to abandon observation of the particular in a search for laws of very wide application. The cell 'provided the paradigm case of the degree of simplification to which physiology could attain', imitating the model of explanation provided by the physical sciences.[82] As Jacyna has put it, the cell was thus 'the "ultimate fact" that physiology needed'. And it was not only experimental physiology that needed it: a Romantic quest, for unity in diversity, for the common source of life, also reached a goal in cell theory.[83]

The third quarter of the nineteenth century witnessed the full development of cell theory. An erroneous concept of free-cell formation, according to which cells arose by a kind of precipitation around the nucleus, was replaced by a picture of their formation from the division of pre-existing cells. The search for the origin of the nucleus continued, however, and the desire to find an ultimate cause, the first place of origin, hindered the interpretation of much empirical observation of the actual behaviour of nuclei.[84] It was Ludwig Carl Virchow who, in 1855, formulated cell theory in its modern form.[85] Now there was no need to postulate the formless cytoblastema as the source of cell life: 'there is no life but through direct-succession: *omnis cellula e cellula*'. Cells are 'the last constant link in the great chain of mutually subordinated formations that form tissues, organs, systems, the individual'.[86]

Cell theory, then, was founded in the period 1840–70, and matured in the last quarter of the century. By the 1880s research physiologists understood cell division as a sequence in time which was basically the same in animals and plants; that cells in animals and plants were formed by the equal division of existing cells, and that division of the nucleus preceded division of the cells. 'Towards 1875 . . . general agreement had been reached that the cell was a recognisable entity, marked off by spatial limits . . . which possessed a nucleus itself containing further specialised structures (chromosomes) of astonishing chemical and physical complexity.' By the 1870s, physiology had entered the world of twentieth-century biology; indeed the cell had become 'the essential structural reference point for the interpretation of organic form' long before this, in the mid-century.[87]

In Britain, the empirical roots of physiology in medicine and forensic anatomy gave rise to an extraordinarily powerful functional localism. In studying animal bodies it became quite impossible to conceive of function without an organ in which to locate it. What is more, the powerful grip of natural theology in Britain (where domestic appropriation of continental vitalism had always been more theological in purpose than the original) meant that few scientists could shake off the belief of a design in nature, a plan, that had assigned each organ its proper use: 'to each structure was assigned a definite purpose working towards the maintenance of the organism as a whole'.[88] The postulation of organ and function on a unit to unit basis, with each organ being supposed to carry out a unique type of work, and the presence of the same properties in every single cell, 'eliminated the search for a unique centre directing the vital activities' among some British research physiologists of the later nineteenth century.[89]

What physiologists transmitted to more general audiences when they wrote of human organisation and cell theory was a new version of a very old debate, about continuity and discontinuity in nature. They also provided an image, of the smallest place within: the fundamental unit of life. But the cell also implied death, with its own ceaseless making and unmaking, spelling out 'the final consummation of all the functions of the material body'. That, claimed Cornelius Black in his child-care manual of

1846, was only death in the generally accepted term. Physiology, he said, recognised 'another and partial death', that is, death at the molecular level: 'thus, in strict language, we are ever dying – ever mutable – ever changing'.[90]

Surveying the century from the vantage point of 1885 and the Cambridge School of Physiology, Michael Forster saw how cell theory had provided his discipline with 'a vision of a grand simplicity of organic nature'.[91] Simple maybe, but as the *British and Foreign Medico-Chirurgical Review* noted in 1857, it had produced the most unwieldy mass of research monographs.

> The diversity of title under which the works of physiology at the present are brought before the scientific reader, appears not a little remarkable . . . if we analyse these various works, what do we find? Simply this, that each author . . . has attempted to explain the fundamental laws governing organic life.[92]

They did it everywhere. In *Sea-side Studies*, George Henry Lewes moved seamlessly from contemplating the digestive properties of sea-anemones to the 'grand impatience of the soul to free itself from the circle of individual activity, – the yearning of the creature to be united with the Creator'.[93] This popular physiology used the cell as the ideational framework for an elision of life and death, for the cell was the final place, the thing that simply could not be dispersed. Lewes wrote that

> we may consider Life itself as an ever-increasing identification with Nature. The simple cell, from which the plant or animal arises must draw light from the sun, nutrient from the surrounding world, or else it will remain quiescent . . . What we call growth, is it not a perpetual absorption of Nature, the identification of the individual with the universal?[94]

The cell was the entity and the place that was 'not capable of loss of existence'.[95]

Michael Forster thought these mid-nineteenth-century expressions of cell theory 'an absurdity'. According to the popular history of the cell that he wrote in 1885, the theory collapsed as soon as it was born in the earlier part of the century through the rapid development of protoplasmic theory when, he claimed, it had become evident that the work done by the '"cell" was the result not of its form and . . . structure but simply of the nature and properties of the apparently structureless protoplasm which formed its body'.[96]

Cells may not 'really' have existed, and cell theory may have been absurd, but it was an absurdity that was most precisely figured and that had, in fact, frequently been drawn. It is not possible to visually represent something completely structureless, and of course the line drawings accompanying Forster's *Encyclopaedia Britannica* entry on 'Physiology' gave cells a boundary in a cell membrane: the drawings made them entities, fixed on the page.

And Forster still speculated about the future of physiology at the level of the cell. His expectation was that in the twentieth century a major task would be to uncover the processes by which 'the vibrations of the nervous system originate from extrinsic and intrinsic causes', how vibrations pass through the body, acting on its various parts, and then how they break up, are disintegrated and lost. Physiology would have to show how 'these neural vibrations, often mysteriously attended with changes of consciousness . . . are wrought out of the explosive chemical decompositions of the nervous system'. The most pressing discovery to be made was how 'the energy of chemical action is transmuted into and serves as the supply of that vital energy which appears as movement, feeling, thought'. Forster told his readers that 'the physiology of the nervous system is emphatically the physiology of the future'.[97] In fact, in the year that this article was published, cell theory located itself in neurone theory and the term 'neurone' came into general use.

Most nineteenth-century histories of physiology – like Forster's brief one of 1885 – attempted to describe the same kind of archaeological shift in perception that Foucault drew attention to a century later, taking as their historical terrain a period from about 1770 to 1850. Earlier than Forster, Lewes had drawn attention to a modern, mid-nineteenth-century interest in growth, and in the history of natural forms. He thought it

> worthy of remark that the study of Development is quite a modern study. Formerly men were content with the full-statured animal – the perfected art, – the completed society. The phases of development were disregarded, or touched on in a vague, uncertain manner. A change has come over the spirit of inquiry . . . we are now all bent on tracing the phases of development. To understand the *grown* we try to follow the *growth*.[98]

It was for this reason that Goethe was so important in Lewes's account. His history of science was ahistorical – certainly in attributing this kind of historical thinking to Goethe. He is an early example of the tendency that Boyle has noted: to add structures of explanation derived from other sciences, from other periods of investigation, to Goethe's original conceptions.[99] Yet the reputation that Lewes (and other commentators) established for Goethe made it possible to see him as a scientific thinker who had embodied notions of growth and development (and thwarted development) in a literary child-figure. Lewes established him as a thinker concerned with fundamental questions of growth, and with developmental – or historical – explanation, in physiology and morphology, and who at the same time had bequeathed to the coming century apprehension of the essential *mystery* of growth and development. 'Everywhere . . .' said Lewes,

> the fundamental property of Growth – meets us as the ultimate fact, the great terminal mystery; and the simplest form under which this process is known to us is the spontaneous sub-division of a cell. Thus, to borrow Goethe's words –
>
> All the forms resemble, yet none is the same as another.
> Thus the whole of the theory points at a deep hidden law
> Points at a sacred riddle.[100]

He concluded that 'the sacred riddle awaits its Oedipus and probably will forever remain unanswered'. But Oedipus did come, and gave if not an answer at least a name to the sacred riddle. The next two chapters will suggest why the riddle had to be named as childhood.

4

Physiological Bodies

The connections between growth and death that were made by early nineteenth-century physiologists were underlined in their writing for general audiences. Two important new markets for physiological information were parents of the middle and upper classes, and medical students and practitioners. In popular child-care manuals, and in doctors' guides, childhood was added to the list of associated terms: growth and death. This chapter explores the connections between growth, death and childhood that were made in this kind of literature, as a prolegomenon to their theorisation later in the century, in the fields of child psychology and emergent psychoanalysis.

In the early and mid-nineteenth century in Britain, the fundamental laws of physiological growth were often explained to general and student audiences by the use of analogy. In his *Physiology of Common Life* (1859–60) George Henry Lewes told his readers that 'the growth and decay of an organ, is like the growth and decay of a nation or a tree: the individual cells composing the organ grow and perish . . . the life of an organism [is] the sum total of the lives of its individual cells . . . This is one of the great revelations of modern science.'[1] What needed to be elucidated was the idea of 'growth', as both a mystery and an explanatory system. In *Sea-side Studies* Lewes argued that Goethe had shown the nineteenth century the way, had believed that 'Growth and Reproduction are but different aspects of the same law'. It was growth that, for the present at least, had to be accepted as 'an ultimate fact, not permitting dispute, not admitting explanation . . . Whether new individuals or only new parts of individuals are reproduced, the fundamental process is the same'.[2] The simplest expression of 'the great terminal mystery' of Growth available to the mind's eye and common comprehension was, as we have seen, 'the spontaneous subdivision of a cell'.

Other popular physiology of the 1850s dwelt on these same terminal mysteries. W.B. Carpenter emphasised the double life that was inherent in cell theory, telling his readers that 'no fact has been more clearly ascertained by modern Physiological research than this – that each elementary part of the fabric has its own independent power of growth and development, that it has its own proper term of existence'.[3] Growth was both the bottom line – the factor beyond which explanation could not reach – and, at the same time, a mystery. Why did organic function continue, once a body or body part had attained the limits of its development? Carpenter's answer (which was not his alone) was that the process of life was destructive of itself, that every operation of the nervous or muscular system involved a necessary disintegration, which had to be repaired by continued activity. But nothing went away; or as Carpenter put it in describing the death of the material body, 'the final restoration of the components of the Human Organism to the Inorganic Universe' was but the beginning of a new 'Life of the Soul'.[4] A year later, in another textbook of physiology John Draper argued that in the growth of human beings and through all the losses and changes that such growth involved 'the immaterial principle had passed unscathed'. He suggested that just as each stage of growth was reached by abandoning the last, so the soul would endure when all material supports were finally cast away.[5] But even these material supports could not disappear, for in their essence, they were simply not capable of perishing:

> If there is a point in natural philosophy which may be regarded as finally settled, it is the imperishability of the chemical elements and the everlasting duration of force. Within the system of nature existing as it is, we cannot admit that an atom of any kind can ever be destroyed.[6]

Writing on 'Growth, Decay and Death' for the *Encyclopaedia Britannica* in 1885, Arthur Gamgee summed up a half-century's exploration of these topics, and confessed that he did not know why growth stops:

> Upon what depends this tendency to multiplication of anatomical elements, and this tendency to increase in size of individual anatomical elements of organs, until a certain approximate limit has been attained, is absolutely unknown. We know to a certain extent that the process of *growth* depends upon and is influenced by certain circumstances . . . but yet the knowledge is wanting that would tell us why, when a certain limit has been attained . . . growth ceases.[7]

For the physiologist, the end of growth marked the beginning of the material body's decline, and a century of laboratory research had not made the question that faced Arthur Gamgee substantially different from the one that had been formulated by Erasmus Darwin in 1803, in *The Temple of Nature*:

> why the same kinds of food which enlarge and invigorate the body, from infancy to the meridian of life, and then nourishe [sic] it for some years unimpaired, should at length gradually cease to do so, and the debility of age and death supervene, would be liable to surprise us, were we not in the daily habit of observing it.[8]

That the question of growth in childhood led so inexorably to the question of death when physiologists wrote for general audiences, had something to do with the tenacious hold of Aristotelian divisions of life on the depiction of childhood. Thomas Jameson, writing in 1811 on the *Changes in the Human Body at Its Different Ages*, discussed the existing methods of naming the periods of life that had been derived from classical antiquity: foetal life, infancy from 1–14 years, manhood from 28–56, old age from this point onwards. He promised to recast them upon modern physiological precepts, but in fact stayed in thrall to the 'septenary principles', for 'the septennial evolutions of the machine are remarkable . . . there does not occur seven successive years in the life of man, without some evident alteration of constitution'.[9] He thought his own innovation was to divide the 'infancy' of the ancients into two periods, calling the years 7–14 'Puerita', and describing this as the healthiest of all the terms of life, when 'the living principle is remarkably strong, and the body in perpetual action'. Jameson located the body's end in the years after 45, when 'the body begins to retrograde . . . begins to die, in the same gradual manner in which it began to live'. In 1889, senior medical students and junior doctors were still being told that 'the life of man is naturally divided into three great epochs – viz. a period of *Growth and Development*, of *Maturity* and of decline'.[10]

Jameson's uncertainty about whether growth was a property of living matter that was quite different from the vital principle was a much more general one, and one that was soon to be dramatically and publicly rehearsed in a series of debates which ran from 1814 until 1819, on the origins and nature of life, by two senior members of the Royal College of Surgeons.[11] In 1811 Jameson transmitted the terms of the debate and his full uncertainty to his audience of medical practitioners, students and parents of the polite classes of society. But the essential problem for Jameson was not the opposition of vitalism and materialism that was outlined in the last chapter, but the phenomenon of growth itself. His recourse was to tissue theory, and to the perception and structures of argument of François Bichat (1771–1802), and other continental physiologists. In 1800 and 1801 Bichat had published three works which provided a topography of the human body in terms of the deep structures into which it could be analysed. He isolated tissues as the fundamental structural and vital elements of the body, and then grouped tissues into organs which formed more complex systems. The action of tissues was to be explained by their irritability, their sensibility and their sympathy with each other.[12] Irritability might satisfactorily explain growth – indeed it might be elided with growth for some theorists, and Jameson conceded that the two must be connected, 'since simple organic bodies, especially those which are young, possess the greater share of [it], and grow faster than other older ones' – but they could not be one and the same, as growth 'ceases to exist when bodies arrive at the determined size of their species'.[13] Only an understanding of growth as *an attribute or property of young organisms* explained that 'quick circulation of nutritious fluid over the system, intended no doubt, for a speedy supply of arterial blood, containing new matter, to enlarge the size of the parts'.[14]

Jameson used the posthumous work of John Hunter in order to present his own picture of growth, telling his readers to imagine cellular tissue as the froth of soapsuds, and suggesting that in the embryo this froth might increase the growth of fibres by being spread over their surface 'like varnish'.[15] The bones of the human body were the most satisfactory analogy of growth itself: 'It occurs to us that the elongation of every fibre of the human body, proceeds in its growth after the manner of the long bones, by an accretion of assimilated fluid to its extremities, and of cellular substance to its lateral surfaces.'[16]

Jameson's was an early nineteenth-century example of the medical monograph and child-care manual that rapidly translated academic physiological debate and continental theorising for domestic audiences. The information imparted in publications such as this was subject to much revision over the next century, but the location of investigation and resolution in the phenomenon of growth would bring most of them to the end-point that Jameson reached in 1811: to the death of the body and the return of its elements whence they came. He described the way in which 'finally, the lifeless corpse, after a few days, is transmitted to the peaceful bosom of nature, that the substance may be decomposed into its original elements, and that the discharged effluvia, absorbed by the soil, may assist in the regeneration of new organic beings'.[17] Death, and a return to a previous state of things, were established as part of the scientific description of human bodies long before the cell provided a preciser image of the thing that was 'not capable of loss of existence'.[18]

The idea of death as an aspect of living bodies was not just a view for the professionals, but was routinely described for popular audiences interested in child-care. In the kind of literature that Jameson's work represents, parents and medical students (or 'the young practitioner', the 'junior medical practitioner'[19]) were closely aligned, as indeed they were in the professionalisation of child-care that took place in the early Victorian years in Britain, and in an expanding market for medical attention to children. Charles West told his audience of medical students in 1848 that 'children will form at least a third of all your patients'; and thirty years later the *Lancet* pointed out that 'the sufferings and maladies of children' were part and parcel of every general practitioner's daily round, the first means of entry and employment in most households. Each doctor who penned a treatise on physiological development claimed simplicity and accessibility in comparison with rivals in the field; some even thought their productions cheap enough to find their way into working-class homes.[20]

The *Lancet* editorial of 1879 hearkened back to a phenomenal upsurge of interest in the diseases of children in the 1840s, when 'men of mark in the profession made a show of devoting special attention to the subject. It found a place in prominent courses of lectures, and for a brief moment actually achieved what we fear must be called "popularity" among men of science.' 'The sale of this book is enormous,' exulted Pye Henry Chavasse in the Preface to the ninth edition of his *Advice to a Mother on the Management of Her Children* (1877). 'I had the good fortune, some thirty years ago, to turn up new ground – to hit upon a mine, which I have, ever since, even until now, worked with my best energy and ability.'[21] The popularity that he and other writers had enjoyed would be sniffed at by the *Lancet* thirty years on, partly because so many publications of the 1840s and 1850s had been directed at parents, particularly at mothers, but also because they kept repeating each other. 'We have been disappointed in finding how small an amount of matter . . . is drawn from the author's experience, or is an expression of his own formed opinions', said the *British and Foreign Medico-Chirurgical Review* of Fleetwood Churchill's *Diseases of Children* in 1850.[22] 'Dr Underwood's frequently re-edited and metamorphosed pages' were often noted – and 'for whom has Mr Hogg written?' asked one reviewer of *The Management of Infancy* in 1850. 'Not for his professional brethren surely, for they have already perused Adair, Sinclair, Conquest, Combe, Dick, Pereira, Mayo, Glover, and our old friend, Dr Underwood . . . from whose pages Mr Hogg has so profusely filled his book.'[23] So many of them were there that the *Lancet* referred to them familiarly and disparagingly as '"Mothers' Guides"'.

The much stricter *British and Foreign Medico-Chirurgical Review* thought their real problem was that even as early as 1850, information about the physical care and the diseases of children had advanced so much that it was no longer possible to do what so many new publications attempted, which was to deal with both the normal and the pathological in one text.[24] It was delighted to review Daniel Schreber's *Die Eigenthumlickeiten des Kindlichen Organismus* (The Peculiar Features of the Child's Organism) in 1853, because Schreber did not limit his considerations to the maladies of infancy and childhood and 'withhold from us . . . substantive work upon the general physiological and pathologic peculiarities which distinguish the youthful from the adult frame', as so many existing English-language treatments had. 'The want of such a separation . . . has been a chief cause why the subject has fallen into the hands of both *extra* and *intra* professional charlatism, and we have become overridden with so many "Mother's Guides".'[25]

Discussing the 'Necessity of Practical Instruction in the Treatment of Diseases in Children' in 1849, and the way in which 'the science of the diseases of children, from a terra incognita [had] risen up to be a flourishing colony', A. Hess pleaded for a medical education that would train students in the perception and appreciation of objective symptoms . . . in the extensive use of their perceptive faculties . . . weaning them from the abuse of, and excessive dependence on verbal examination'.[26] The same point was made again and again, whether doctors were speaking through the medium of the manual to other doctors, or to mothers: 'I speak of interrogating [children]; for though the infant cannot talk, it has yet a language of its own, and this language it must be your first language to learn . . . it is a language of signs'.[27]

The observation of children was an Enlightenment injunction, and parents of the polite classes of society had long been told to keep 'remarks made on the progress of their children in a book kept for that purpose, in order that they might attain a more distinct view of human nature'.[28] Thomas Reid's *Essays on the Intellectual Powers of Man* (1785) were the spring of Catherine Stanley's observation of her children, which she recorded between 1811 and 1820, and his work – the *Intellectual Powers* in particular – was often mentioned by Ellen Sharples, portrait painter of Bristol who started a journal of her daughter Rolinda's progress in 1803, when the child was nine.[29] Reid's discussion of the faculties guided the mother who was educating her children to the purpose that Catherine Stanley saw in her own record: to understand better the workings of human reason and intelligence. The injunction was, indeed, to observe the unfolding of the human mind, and those mothers who left records paid most attention to the development of language and of the moral sentiments in their children.

The new type of 'mothers' guide' that was published from the late 1820s onwards advised attention to the child's body, especially so that the signs and symptoms of sickness might be read (many of these books advertised themselves as home doctors); and whilst they may have built on a habit of domestic observation, they directed attention to the body's interior in a way that broke with eighteenth-century practice. Elizabeth Gaskell evidently read many of them after her first child was born in 1835 – she complained that 'books do so differ' – and certainly turned to them for advice on child-care. But her own interest was in what she considered the more important terrain of little Marianne's moral, intellectual and religious progress, and to this she devoted much the greater part of her diary. As a guide to these more significant factors of development, she turned to an older tradition of literature, represented by Mme Necker de Saussure's *Sur l'education progressive*, which allowed her to view Marianne's development in terms of faculties, and to watch her powers of intelligence, memory and will in development.[30]

However, the newer literature of child-care and observation represented by the one text Gaskell mentioned in her diary, Andrew Combe's *Principles of Physiology*, did serve her conscious needs and desires in one regard, in that it allowed her to contemplate death.[31] Modern physiology has eliminated death from its discussions, perhaps because of a tendency to believe that death may be overcome, certainly because death is nowadays considered a pathological rather than a physiological phenomenon.[32] Yet popular physiology of the mid-nineteenth century had death as a central topic, for it was the phenomenon that growth implied and that was its certain end. Gaskell, who understood that the journal of her own 'disposition and feelings was . . . intimately connected with that of [her] little baby', knew what emotional good sense it made to 'prepare her and myself for the change that may come any day', quite apart from the Christian injunction to do so. She recorded the need to dwell on death shortly after Marianne had been 'very, very ill, and I was very much afraid we should have lost her'; 'and oh! if thou shouldst call her away from "the evil to come" may I try to yield her up to him who gave her to me without a murmur'.[33] Death, its nervous anticipation, and the taming of it by evocation were the regular apostrophes of her diary. Works like Combe's promised to give meaning to death, and their exegesis could be appropriated to a Christian understanding.[34]

Because of the established practices of child observation, the reading of signs in children seems to have been taught to nineteenth-century parents long before it was recommended to doctors in training. The anonymous *Letters to a Mother on the Watchful Care of Her Infant* (1831) told the addressee that her 'little infant's countenance will offer . . . the most interesting and most intelligent page in Nature's book'. Letter IV was entirely devoted to the skill of decoding the baby's gestures: 'every change of manner, every unwonted gesture in her infant, speaks to the observant eye, of the tender mother, a language not to be misunderstood'.[35] 'The figure of a healthy infant should have no curves or angles,' wrote A.L. Pearce in 1838. 'Its form should be wavy and round, and capable of almost every position . . . It should have a bright and full eye and expanded chest . . . the flesh should be smooth and firm . . .'; and he too provided a key for decoding the child's gestures, in sickness and in health.[36] 'Children never deceive in their symptoms,' aphorised P.M. Braidwood in 1874. 'Though the cause of their malaise may be difficult of detection, it is sure to exist, and no effort should be spared which can possibly lead to its discovery.'[37] In his *Nursery Guide* of 1847, William Popham could not lay 'too much stress on the necessity of observation and attention to the smallest and most trivial symptom . . . every variation of countenance, the smile and the frown . . . every unwonted motion of the brow, or unusual roll of the eye'.[38] Writing of her nine-month-old baby girl in 1835, Elizabeth Gaskell recorded that she had been prepared for the difference that a child's 'bodily feelings' would make to its behaviour by reading Andrew Combe's *Principles of Physiology* (1834), but was still astonished to see how 'every change of temper might be deduced by some corresponding change in the body'.[39] Sara Coleridge's 'Diary of Her Children's Early Years', which she kept from 1830 to 1838, is the most obsessive reading of the signs offered by her babies' faeces, in line with the recommendations of many contemporary child-care manuals.[40]

Edward Cory, whose *Physical and Medical Management of Children, Adapted for General Perusal* went through five editions in the decade after its publication in 1834, thought that 'the study of infantine medicine' had been much neglected in Britain, and that in the early part of the century professionals and parents had been indebted to continental writers for what information they possessed on the observation of children.[41] Reviews in the British medical press in the 1850s do show an immediate reception for European works of paediatrics, and the *British and Foreign Medico-Chirurgical Review* in particular published substantial review articles in the 1850s.[42]

In urging on mothers the daily watching of children's heads, tongues, cries, gestures and faeces, Edward Cory introduced the idea of 'la sémiologie physiognomique' to British readers.[43] This technique, developed by Jules Jadelot, physician to a Parisian foundling hospital, was elaborated when M.E. Bouchut's *Practical Treatise on the Diseases of Children* was translated in 1855.[44] According to Bouchut, Jadelot had 'excelled in the difficult art of scrutinising the physiognomy of children, in order that he might discover the nature of their diseases', and he thought that an aptitude like this 'depended[ed] much upon genius'. Nevertheless, it was urged upon quite ordinary British doctors and parents, who had Bouchut's own chapters 'On the Gesture and Attitude,' and 'On the Cry' to guide them.[45]

By the end of the century this semiology of infancy had spread far beyond the home and the general practitioner's surgery. In 1890 Joanna Hill, Secretary to the Kings Norton Boarding Out Committee, was closely questioned by members of the House of Commons Committee reporting on the Infant Life Protection Bill.

> You said you had some new methods by which you could detect neglect?
>
> – Yes.
>
> You said you had been instructed in certain signs?
>
> – Yes, signs of health . . . the shape of the child and its gestures, and various things of that kind.[46]

She went on to provide the most detailed account of methods that could be used to detect ill-health or ill-treatment of children boarded out or fostered under the Poor Law. Indeed, she had written a guide called 'Instructions to Ladies for Observing Children', which described techniques she said had been copied from conventional medical practice.

'When a medical man is called in to prescribe for a baby, he notes the posture it assumes,' she explained to the Committee; 'the way it cries, whether the hands clench . . . in a like manner the boarding out visitor should watch for analogous indications of the child's condition.'[47] Miss Hill and the committee members thought all this quite new; but in fact the practice had been urged on medical students and parents for at least half a century.

Edward Cory had thought that the patient scrutiny of outward manifestations ('heads, tongues, cries, gestures') would guide watchful parents to another level of observation, of the circulatory, respiratory and digestive functions.[48] In order to observe what was not open to view, the observer had to be taught something of the organisation of the child's body; and it was to that task that these texts of popular physiology addressed themselves.

They presented parents (and medical students, where there was a dual audience) with a series of complex metaphors for envisaging and understanding the interior economy of the infant body. Sometimes a writer broke away from the idea of organisation and, as Samuel Smiles did in his immensely popular *Physical Education* (1838), used a traditional horticultural series of images to figure growth, asking, 'What success should we expect of a gardener, who was totally ignorant of the nature of plants and the relation that subsisted between them and the air around them or the soil in which they grew?' But even this appeal – delivered in traditional Lockeian terms – was only a prolegomenon to the strict lessons of organisation that he delivered.[49] Parents needed to know that 'the laws that regulate and govern human beings or organise nature, are as invariable as those which regulate the physical or material world; the changes that are perpetually occurring in the body of the human being take place only according to those certain laws of organisation'.[50] In *Popular Directions to Parents* (1829) Henry Rees told them to regard the human body as 'a complicated assemblage of vital organs, each of which is destined to perform some peculiar office or function'. All these organs, acting out their destiny, manufactured 'one general result called life'. What parents must attempt to secure in their children was health:

> when each organ is perfect in its separate action, when the secretion of every organ is prepared and poured forth in proper quantity and proper quality, then it is that animal existence shines forth in all the brightness of untroubled being; the whole countenance is lighted up with glowing beauty, and in all the system exists a pleasing sensation of happiness . . . this sensation is denominated health.[51]

The call for descriptions of the 'physiologic . . . peculiarities' of children was answered, and as physiological exegesis developed throughout the century, it isolated childhood from adulthood through its depiction of the nature of the interactions taking place within the child's body. Delivering his Lettsomian Lectures on the Surgical Diseases of Children to the Medical Society of London in 1863, Thomas Bryant conveyed what he thought to be the essential knowledge that whilst in adult life 'the vital forces, started, supported and maintained by the nervous, respitory, circulatory and glandular systems' simply operated for the maintenance of what had 'already attained its perfect growth and complete development', in young children the same vital fibres were 'mainly directed for the purposes of growth and development of their being's physical structure'. Moreover, cell life was particularly active in this period.[52]

Authors of mothers' guides frequently drew attention to the vulnerability of the growing period.[53] M.E. Bouchut's work on the influence of growth on the diseases of children was widely reported in the British medical press.[54] His own aphorisms (he called them so) on growth suggested new enigmas in the depths of the body. 'The growth of man,' he wrote, 'is the result of the same impulse as that which gives him existence. It is a phenomenon which is necessarily accomplished, and which an unknown force sustains and directs towards a determinate end.' He depicted it as being 'engendered by sexual intercourse', when a force 'suddenly takes possession of the cell which constitutes the human germ, and will only quit it on the day of its entire development in humanity'. Like all forces of nature, 'it exists before its effect . . . Matter servilely obeys it, as long as no other force happens to disturb it'. The child brought forth growth, carrying within itself that same force that had seized the cell: 'after nine months of inter-uterine operation, this force is outwardly transmitted with the infant; it continues its work in the air and light'.[55]

Karl Figlio has discussed the extreme motility of the term 'organisation' in early nineteenth-century physiological writing:

> it could suggest mere complexity, but also organic body, organised being, or the process of organising. At one extreme, it implied little that was unique to living beings and blurred the distinction between the inanimate and the animate realms; at the other extreme, it could be identified with animate processes themselves.

It engendered a metaphoric chain of associations between physiological, political and theological discourse. The opposition between materialist and vitalist physiology expressed itself in its terms; national traditions of thought and belief, which were transmitted in medical training, are observable to the historian following the path of its use. 'Organisation', then, allows the links between science and its contexts to be elucidated. Indeed, according to Figlio, 'perceiving an expression of similar ideologies by both the scientific and social concepts, concepts which are . . . carriers of covert ideological meaning' might serve to erode the boundary between ideas of 'science' and the 'social' and allow us to find a solution to the historian's problem of wedding the archaeology of Foucault's episteme to actual historical events and debates.[56]

The ideas of organisation and interiority were central topics of most motherhood manuals produced in the middle years of the century. Andrew Combe (whose bestseller Elizabeth Gaskell had found such a useful preparation for reading her child's body) described the infant in terms of organisation and function, with a sensibility finely tuned to the larger issues the terms invoked. By means of the various functions of the body, 'existence and growth' were carried on, but beyond that, those functions served no other end; involuntary in their action, they took place 'whether we are awake or asleep . . . They are common to all animals, and in a general sense, also to the vegetable world . . . to all objects possessed of *organisation*'. He was at pains to clear up any confusion caused by his use of the terms 'organic' and 'organisation', telling his readers that technically those terms simply referred to 'the support and life of the tissues of which the body is composed, without regard to the purpose for which these tissues are individually adapted'. The problem was partly one of vocabulary, because function also meant 'animal function', which referred not just to 'the *life* of man, but to the '*purpose for which life was given*'. The brain, the organs of sense and voluntary motion, the muscles, bones and nerves were 'the great organs of the *animal* functions, because it is through their instrumentality that all the operations of intelligence and emotion – acts *peculiar to animals* – are performed'. The solution to the mechanism that the vocabulary implied was not found by Combe in a process of metaphor, nor in the making of analogies between physiological theory and other social and political processes. Rather, he *embodied* these terms in the infant he was describing, and thus endowed them with meaning and purpose: 'By means of the brain and the organs of sense, the infant becomes *conscious* of his own existence, and that of beings who minister to his comfort and safety.' As the child grows, his nervous system gains in development and structure, his feelings acquire strength and permanency; he manifests kindness, and reciprocates affection'. Through ordinary interactions with those around him, the child gradually becomes 'acquainted with his own situation in the great family of mankind, [and] at length recognises the duties and obligations which it imposes upon him':

> By the nobler of these powers and capacities . . . is man distinguished from the beasts which perish; and to them he is indebted for the privilege which he alone possesses, of knowing and worshipping the one true God, and Author and Preserver of his being.[57]

In physiological discourse boundaries between inanimate and animate beings were often marked by the way in which shape was depicted. Figlio has noted how the growth of animate beings was shown as an accretion and assimilation of matter to curved and rounded surfaces, and life itself was thus depicted as 'rounded, supple and incorporating'. Inanimate structures, on the other hand, grew (often by analogy with chemical processes) by sharp, angular additions to straight surfaces; death was depicted as 'rigid, planar, impenetrable and angular'. But in the child-care manuals, where each depiction of growth was also a chronicle of death foretold, what the child embodies glides and flows, carrying what is implied in the child's beginning to its certain end.

The full articulation of cell theory in the middle years of the century not only embodied the phenomenon of growth in the child, but also more closely elided the beginning with the end, the child with death. In 1846 Cornelius Black promised readers of his *Letters on the More Evident Changes Which the Body Undergoes* 'by gradual steps . . . to lead you through the successive changes which the body undergoes from the period of birth to mature age, from which by an almost imperceptible decline it glides to the place which is destined for its last repose'.[58] In childhood, every structure attested rapid development, 'an active vital extension – the limit of which is manhood – the *ultima linea* of which is – death!'[59] Black made it clear that this perception was partly to do with the knowledge imparted by cell theory, which was of the body as a container for a daily partial death, 'in the constant change of the molecules of the material particles of the body'. Thus, said Black, 'we are ever dying – ever mutable – ever changing'.[60] Throughout the coming century this message was never delivered to parents or doctors without all the comfort that 'the religious physiologist' could supply. William Carpenter ended the massive fifth edition of his *Principles of Physiology, General and Comparative* of 1855 with the specifically Christian news that

> with the final restoration of the components of the Human Organism to the Inorganic Universe, in those very forms (or nearly so) in which they were first withdrawn from it, the Corporeal Life of Man . . . comes to a final close. But the death of the Body is but the commencement of a new Life of the Soul; in which (as the religious physiologist delights to believe) all that is pure and noble in Man's nature will be refined, elevated and progressively advanced towards perfection; whilst all that is carnal, selfish, and degrading, will be eliminated by the purifying process to which each individual must be subjected, before sin can be entirely subjugated, and Death can be completely 'swallowed up in victory'.[61]

The attention that came to be paid to normal and pathological growth in childhood in the 1850s and 1860s had another source in the 'social physics' that medical and physiological investigators learned from Lambert Quetelet, of the perfection of the average and the statistical means available for finding it.[62] In 1880 Percy Boulton, Physician to the Samaritan Hospital for Women and Children, recalled that ten years before, when he 'commenced weighing and measuring', correct averages were completely unavailable and that he had 'no idea how much a child should grow in a year, so that the scales and measures were practically useless'. He searched for some guide, came across Quetelet's work, and was taken by his conclusions, which in 1880 he summarised thus: '1. That there is a perfect form or type of man and that the tendency of the race is to attain that type. 2. That the order of growth should be *regular* towards the type. 3. The variations from the type follow a definite law, the law of accidental causes.'[63] This casting of height, weight, strength and velocity of growth upon new hierarchical tables gave rise in its turn to a physiological sociology that used the analogy of growth from childhood to death in order to write the history of 'the course of life of organs, individuals, races'.[64] John Draper told readers of the seventh edition of *Human Physiology* that the man he described in its pages as a physiological entity was 'also a member of society, and . . . History is in truth only a branch of Physiology'.[65] Things would be very different, he said, 'when dynamical physiology begins to be cultivated'. Draper delivered his own first thoughts on dynamical physiology to the 1860 Oxford meeting of the British Association for the Advancement of Science, when he discussed 'the mental progress of Europe', and made a full statement of his belief that 'social advancement is as completely under the control of natural law as is bodily growth'.[66]

> The procession of nations does not move forward like a dream, without reason or order, but there is a predetermined, a solemn march, in which all must join, ever moving, ever restlessly advancing . . . individual life and its advancement through successive stages is the model of social life and its secular variations.[67]

The work of anthropometry (the measurement of the human body), was also engendered by a wider system of reckoning and counting populations. The eleventh edition of Combe's *Principles of Physiology* (1842) found a new rhetoric in statistics of infant mortality published in the First Annual Report of the Registrar-General.[68] Compelled by such findings, local doctors, especially those appointed under local arrangements to schools and under the Poor Law, began the work of anthropometric investigation as early as the 1860s.[69] The school in particular offered a large field for the observation of child pathology as well as a slowly emerging account of normal growth and development.[70] The attention focused on the physical development of children by the 1863 Select Committee on

Children's Employment (and the very wide attention paid its finding by the medical press) should also be noted.[71]

In 1879 the editor of the *Lancet* discussed the development of anthropometry as part of the upsurge in growth studies in the 1850s and 1860s, and adduced new attention to children as citizens as the medical motive for weighing and measuring them.[72] Charles Roberts's appeal to *Lancet* readers for help in completing a series of observations on the height, weight and chest girth of English children was made within an international framework, but also with the framework of class difference. Roberts already had 15,000 observations on boys and men from different strata of society, but his standard series was incomplete, from birth to eight years, and his labouring children's series needed making up for the years 1–5:

> As my observations vary considerably with the social position, occupation, etc., of the persons on whom the measurements were made, I have divided them into two series: one for the wealthier classes, whose physique has not been influenced by the manual labour either of the children or their parents, and who have been well fed and nurtured; the other consists of the labouring classes and their children.[73]

Joanna Hill's 'Instructions to Ladies' had also been framed by this comparative vision, quite as much as they had been influenced by the 'physiognomie sémiotique' available in child-care literature from the 1840s onwards.

Physiological exegesis in these popular forms explored its own terminal mysteries by considering the puzzle of the child, who embodied growth yet whose growth stopped. What these ordinary everyday uses of physiology in the mid-Victorian years in Britain suggest is that for some medical practitioners, and for some parents of the polite classes of society, the child the manuals showed them was a means of aligning and amalgamating a phenomenon and a name for the phenomenon, of eliding growth and childhood and childhood and death. Another way of understanding these movements of thought that were articulated in the texts that have just been discussed, is to say that by embodying the problem of growth and disintegration in children, children became the problem they represented: they became the question of interiority. The problems that physiology's vision of childhood posed were not answered by physiology. As the next chapter suggests, the child study that it inaugurated in fact adopted evolutionary theory in order to reverse the link between childhood and death, and to give a new transcendence to the figure of the child.

5

The World Turned Within

Long established associations between littleness and interiority and between history and childhood were theorised in emergent psychoanalysis between about 1895 and 1920. In establishing psychoanalysis as a body of theory and as a cognitive form, Sigmund Freud worked with the imaginative legacy of cell theory, that is to say with notions of littleness, of entities composed of smaller parts, and with the idea of the smallest possible entity as the birthplace, or progenitor, of memory and consciousness of time. He used a different set of connections and formulations in his delineation of childhood itself as something which, though lost and gone, has left behind memories and traces. This chapter will discuss both formulations and uses of the idea of childhood.

The quest for the origins of psychoanalysis has had a long run and is not exhausted yet.[1] Many searchers discover how inadequate the 'background' – in neuro-anatomy, or physiology, or whatever – is to explain the extraordinary innovation of the idea of the unconscious revealed through dreams and the phenomenon of transference.[2] Rather than searching for origins, this chapter describes the material used for thinking and theorising at a particular point in time, material available to Freud from many heterogeneous late eighteenth- and early nineteenth-century cultural, literary and scientific sources. I take Freud to be a typical user of this material, however innovative and extraordinary in impact his theory construction turned out to be. The connections sought here are between ideas, figures and bodies of thought, connections that lie in their own history, and in the history of their later effect. Their claim to importance is the meaning of childhood that Freudian psychoanalysis bequeathed to Western thought. I make some suggestions about *how* that might have happened: in what manner childhood (the idea of the child) came to encapsulate and articulate what it did about an adult sense of interiority, in both formal and informal expression. This fragment of history about to be told is connected to the development of 'history' itself.

We know a good deal about the self-conscious embrace of history by different European cultural traditions from the late eighteenth century onwards. In Britain it has been described in reference to the popularity of historical fiction, the founding of antiquarian and archaeological societies and historical reviews and journals, and the establishment of history as a university discipline.[3] More generally, the nineteenth-century emergence of the modern discipline of history has been aligned with historical explanation in the life sciences. In their purposiveness, natural history and history both offered the comforts of narrative exegesis: the comforts of a story.[4]

Evidence of a desire for reconciliation to the social order by means of history and historical explanation has also been found in literary forms and devices. Franco Moretti calls the *Bildungsroman* a 'comfort of civilisation', because of the way in which it uses historical explanation to make the world a homeland – a place to be at home in – for its characters and its readers. According to Moretti, the novel of growth, development and formation produced this effect by denying any place outside the circle of story and history that the text itself created.[5] In the circle of time of the *Bildungsroman* there can be no meaningless events. Moretti aligns this narrative form with the development of historical explanation in the life sciences and, indeed, with nineteenth-century historical studies themselves: 'narrative and history . . . do not retreat before the onslaught of events, but demonstrate the possibility of giving them order and meaning'.[6]

In this discussion of history's centrality to nineteenth-century thought, a prominent place has recently been given to melodrama. Christina Crosby has described mid-nineteenth-century English stage melodrama as both a literary form and a force that domesticated history by identifying the social with the familial and making the past a subject for nostalgia. She argues that in the many plots that melodrama employed, the past was presented as something that was lost, but that was also there to be found: a place to find a home in.[7] Crosby's argument depends much on the idea of what it is that is found; depends on the idea of women, or 'Woman'. Defining 'history' as the truth of 'man' entailed creating various categories like 'savages' or 'primitive man' and 'women', which related to history in quite a different way. They are history's Others, outside it (or in the case of the last category, both outside history proper and inside, indoors, in the domestic realm). The imaginative and intellectual move that Crosby describes is summed up thus: 'Men are constituted as historical subjects and find "man" in history by virtue of locating woman elsewhere.'[8]

What is sought in the melodramatic mode, and in the fictions and stage presentations that Crosby discusses, is the maternal woman, she who was once present but is now absent: 'it is she who is an originary site of total love and complete satisfaction that must be found again'.[9] In the melodrama that Crosby discusses in most detail, Wilkie Collins's *The Frozen Deep*, though the actual setting for Acts II and III is the icy and arid wastes of Greenland and the Arctic, and though what is literally found is the supine and frozen body of Frank, it is actually Clara, the woman in question, who is 'Found!'[10] Wardour, who loves her as deeply as Frank, saves the life of his rival because of Clara's saving image. This image allows him to struggle 'towards the light of home, towards the perfect union with the perfect woman' – though he actually dies in striving towards the ideal. The point is that 'home and woman-in-the-home together constitute an absent present that may be recovered'.[11] However, it really is not clear that what is found in this plot structure is Woman (or indeed, a woman) because it is not certain that that is what had been lost. What was actually lost and found, in the many plot structures that articulated the quest, this and the following chapters will attempt to relate.

Long before Christina Crosby discussed the importance of history to nineteenth-century thinking by locating Victorian Woman as that which is lost, Peter Brooks told us that melodrama is 'a mode of excess', and the exemplary genre of the post-Romantic age. Because the world is desacralised, the conflict between good and evil must be brought into people's very existence and being, and ethical conflicts must be spoken aloud, by figures utterly opposed to each other, in exaggerated conflict and in hyperbolic exchange. Brooks accounts for the social origins of this mode in French post-Revolutionary theatre, but his thesis is more centrally concerned with melodrama as 'a mode of conception and expression . . . a certain fictional system for making sense of experience, [and] as a semantic field of force'.[12] He is particularly interested in charting the movement of melodramatic modes and gesture into the novel, and into a collective imagination. Nevertheless, stage melodrama is crucial to later and more general uses, particularly in 'the desire to express all', and the range of gesture, stance and movement by which the absent could be made present, the unfathomable discovered.

> Nothing is spared [in melodrama] because nothing is left unsaid; the characters stand on the stage and utter the unspeakable, give voice to their deepest feelings, dramatise through their heightened and polarised words and gestures the whole lesson of their relationship. They assume primary psychic roles, father, mother, child and express basic psychic conditions.[13]

The many points of analogy between melodrama and psychoanalysis (between the melodramatic imagination and the imagination stocked by psychoanalytic models and paradigms) leads Brooks to the conclusion that psychoanalysis is 'the modern fulfilment and codification of melodrama', and that it has become 'a necessary mode within modern consciousness'.[14] Christina Crosby describes Freud as 'an historian of subjectivity . . . of an Oedipal past which makes its indelible, obscure mark on the present'.[15] We shall be in a better position to understand the shape and form of this history of subjectivity, the place where it was lost and where it was found, if we map out the kind of past that was described in the physiological and biological thought that shaped it.

Evolution conceived of on a growth and development model was assimilated and used because it did not necessarily demand the abandonment of belief in an orderly and purposeful creation developing towards a goal.[16] As a structure of thought and inquiry it also provided the satisfactions – and the comforts – of historical explanation: if a pattern of progressive development is built into the very nature of things – if things contain, or encapsulate in some way, what they are to become – then following the course of their history will allow predictions about the future.[17] Rather than post-Darwinian questions of descent and modification through time being adapted for the historicisation of other fields of inquiry (cultural anthropology, emergent sociology, and history itself are the fields commonly mentioned) it seems more likely that evolutionary biology shared with these other disciplines a general cultivation of developmental, or historical explanation.[18]

If 'historical . . . explanation was satisfactory explanation', we need to understand why was this so.[19] Stephen Bann discusses the development of historical thought in the nineteenth century, paying particular attention to the contemporary means of representing history (historical ideas, theories, information) in the novel, in the visual arts, and in the organisation of museums and archives.[20] He discusses the 'historian as taxidermist', desperate to give what is in fact dead and gone – the past – the appearance of life. His work raises an important series of questions about the development of historical thinking in the nineteenth century, and the emergence of the modern belief that it is the historian's task to produce an account of the past that parallels or resembles it. 'At what stage, and in what domains,' asks Bann, 'does the idea of *life-like representation* achieve expression both in theoretical and in practical terms?'[21]

This question has often been answered by making reference to the historical writing of Leopold von Ranke and the historical procedures and assertions connected with his name: that accuracy of data must be the foundation of historical writing, that the historian's task is to consider the past from its own perspective rather than from a 'present-centred' one, and that events viewed in this way must be narrated – in a much-repeated phrase 'as they actually happened'. Indeed, Ranke's subordinate clause – *wie es eigentlich gewesen* (as it actually was) – has achieved a kind of iconic status among historiographers of the late twentieth century. Bann understands the anxious repetition of the phrase 'actually happened', and indeed Ranke's original formulation, to be part of a much wider search by nineteenth- and twentieth-century historians (and their various audiences) for lifelike representation, or *vérité*.[22]

The principle of *vérité* was that historical writing must be faithful to the events it sought to describe, so that it might render them lifelike, 'as they really were', or 'as they really happened'. The distance between *vérité* and eighteenth-century theories of representation was immense. An earlier tenet of *vraisemblance* acknowledged a distance between the entity and its representation; by a process of mimesis it imitated it, stood in for it: represented it. When Bann asks about this change, and attempts to answer the question 'what, on the anthropological level, necessitates the abandonment of the rule of mimesis, or mediated representation?' he has recourse to an argument that has already appeared in these pages, that is to the argument embodied in Michel Foucault's Man, who at the beginning of the nineteenth century feels himself to be emptied of history as he contemplates a world in which there is no longer a unified narrative to hold him in place at its centre, only many competing histories, natural histories and philologies, none of which is anthropocentric.[23] But it is Bann's insight, not Foucault's, that 'the restoration of the life-like is . . . a response to a sense of loss'; it is he who notices that 'the Utopia of life-like reproduction depends upon, and reacts to, the fact of death'.[24]

The post-Romantic historical search for the past 'as it really was' was made possible by a new, 'scientific' attention to the texts and documents and other traces in which the past might be found. Modern historiographers have noted how attention to fragments and traces of past cultures in nineteenth-century historical writing actually slowed time down, as the disparate and fragmented elements of social life were put together under the heading of cultural coherence. Carl Schorske argues that in Johann Jacob Burkhardt's *Civilisation of the Renaissance in Italy* (1860), for example, time as it was represented 'did not stop . . . but it was . . . slowed down. Not transformation but cultural coherence became the focus of attention.'[25] Historiographers of the late nineteenth century were often quite clear about these changes that had been wrought by a new attention to time and narrative, and dated their development with some precision. Charles Langlois's and Charles Seignobos's *Introduction to the Study of History* (1898) surveyed a century of history writing from the vantage point of the century's end, and noted the great change that took place in the 1850s and 1860s, locating narrative changes in the first period of 'scientific research, in the mid-century:

> up to about 1850, history continued to be, both for historians and the public, a branch of literature. An excellent proof of this lies in the fact that up till then, historians were accustomed to publish new editions of their works . . . without making any change in them, and that the public tolerated this practice. Now every scientific work needs to be continually recast, revised, brought up to date . . . transformed by subsequent researches . . . it is enough for [historians] that their labours should have contributed to the production of works by which their own have been superseded, and which will be, sooner or later, superseded in their turn. It is only works of art that enjoy perpetual youth.[26]

Attempts like this, to make change, alteration and all of history's terrors part of the epistemological and procedural basis of a discipline, were a strategy forced by the historical tale that Darwinian thought implied.

In *Darwin's Plots*, Gillian Beer has described the metaphors, narrative structures and ordinary everyday acts of the imagination that were used in nineteenth-century society in order to absorb and assimilate evolutionary theory. What was it that people needed to understand and assimilate? The great order of consanguinity and relationship in nature's first kingdom is sometimes described as the first lesson to be learned from Darwin, but Beer (and other commentators) draw our attention to the much greater impact of the idea that 'everything was subject to irreversible change', that 'whole species had vanished and that even the evidence of their existence had crumbled away'. The evolutionary theory that Darwin's *Origin of Species* crystallised and made overt reinforced other evidence from geology and natural history and 'suggested irretrievable loss'.[27] What is more, the theory implied that any individual creature was both – or just – 'a vehicle and dead end'. Individual organisms did not evolve during the course of their own life; they 'merely took part in a generational process'.[28] Added to this, Darwin's theory seemed to require extinction, and 'death was extended from the individual organism to the whole species'.[29] John Draper's dynamical, or historical, physiology, 'which speaks of the course of life, of organs, individuals, races . . .', was an earlier example of the way in which physiological understanding of human bodies and their course through growth to death was applied to the external world, in order to depict vast tracts of social and cultural time. Non-Darwinian evolutionary thought was adapted to explain large-scale social and cultural developments: the rise and fall of peoples, races and nations.[30] A physiologist like Draper believed that the analogy he was using to describe cultural and historical developments through time was that of individual human growth. In giving an account of the intellectual development of Europe he suggested that 'the life of a nation may be said to be no longer than the life of a person . . .':

> The origin, existence, and death of nations depend . . . on physical influences, which are themselves the result of immutable laws. Nations . . . must undergo transitional forms offered by the animal series. There is no more immortality for them than there is an immortality for an embryo in any one of the manifold forms passed through in its progress of development.[31]

Yet social and cultural appropriation of this bleak message of extinction could transform it into one of comfort. In evolutionary anthropology, for example, the idea of the potential for growth was moved from the individual to the collective. Entire peoples and races might then be seen as part of the childhood of the human race, in need of guidance and protection certainly, but with the potential (however distant in prospect) for achieving the adult state. Growth in children was observable, natural and undeniable, and 'evolution of the race could be confirmed in the same way'.[32] Observers of 'childlike' peoples also had the great satisfaction of presuming themselves to be at a peak of development.[33] Hugh Cunningham has shown how, by use of a complex set of analogies, children of the urban poor in nineteenth-century Britain were connected with the 'savages' of the anthropological imagination. Yet even the act of discovering 'savagery' among prosaic little street traders and crossing-sweepers carried its own compensation, for if savages represented the childhood of the human race, or were themselves children, then they were necessarily capable of development and change, for these were the essential potentialities of childhood. By a complicated doubling back of an analogy, the dirty, wild children of the very poor could be assigned to 'childhood' by virtue of their savagery. Evolutionary theory used in this way implied loss and disintegration, but it also proffered powerful images of progress and ascent. In its Darwinian and non-Darwinian forms, evolutionary theory described hope, by depicting children as the embodiments of the history that ostensibly implied death and extinction.

Darwin himself was interested in the evidence that children presented, and made connections between evolutionary progress and the development of the faculties in young children.[34] George Romanes, Darwin's younger collaborator and pupil, published a good deal of the older man's manuscript material in *Mental Evolution in Animals* (1883), and *Mental Evolution in Man* (1888). By 1888, having used notes left by Darwin, Romanes was in a position to suggest that 'the emotional life of animals is so strikingly similar to the emotional life of man – and especially young children – that I think the similarity ought to be taken as direct evidence of a genetic continuity between them'.[35] In describing mental development, Romanes showed that the higher order of ideation – the human ability to conceptualise the abstract – involved self-consciousness, that is, a mind that not only knew, but knew that it knew. The question to be answered in *Mental Evolution in Man* was whether the self-consciousness manifested by human beings was different in degree or kind from mental processes in animals. The organism that posed this question was conceived of in physiological terms; it was 'one connected whole; all parts . . . mutually related in the unity of individual sensibility'. Indeed, physiological cell theory shaped the language in which Romanes wrote about self-consciousness; he claimed that 'self-consciousness arises out of an admixture of the protoplasm of judgement with the protoplasm of sign-making'.[36] But answers to questions posed by self-consciousness were framed by reference not to physiology but to evolutionary biology. Romanes claimed that the only way to discover whether human self-consciousness differed in kind from the range of emotions displayed by animals was to consider its rise 'in the only place where [it] . . . can be observed, namely, in the psycho-genesis of a child'.[37] In this exegesis, the child was a piece of living evidence for certain psychogenetic processes. Conceived of in this way, the child was the most perfect encapsulation of the idea that had animated both materialist and vitalist life sciences throughout the century: the insight that in the course of development a living organism repeats the evolutionary stages of its genus; that ontogeny repeats phylogeny.

Romanes also used the striking findings of contemporary philology in order to define language itself as an 'unconscious record of the growth and decay of ideas . . . as the stratified deposit of thoughts'.[38] He suggested that in 'the growing intelligence of a child we have . . . as complete a history of "ontogeny", in its relation to "phylogeny" as that upon which the embryologist is accustomed to rely when he reads the morphological history in the epitome which is furnished by the development of an individual'.[39] No one, said Romanes, who opposed the idea of the evolution of mind could ever have paid any attention at all to the actual process of psychogenesis 'as this occurs in the growing child'.[40]

Mental Evolution in Man was read and annotated by Freud in the early 1890s.[41] Indeed, Freud could be taken as a typical user of the new branch of child study exemplified by Romanes's work, and his own theory development as an example of what was done with the idea of recapitulation in fields of inquiry other than the biological. Freud was to claim some years later that the child entered the world with a sum of instinctual knowledge, and in 1909, when he published his only case study actually involving a young child, he attributed many of Little Hans's problems to a phylogenetic endowment of fear and other instinctual primitive emotions.[42] Later, Freud made direct theoretical claims on Darwin (a reading of Darwin filtered through Romanes) to argue that many childhood fears, especially neurotic phobias, were the result of the history of the race that the child encapsulated, that is, were phylogenetically caused.[43]

None of this was unusual. Frank Sulloway has described 'Darwin's pervasive influence on child psychology', and the way in which in the second half of the nineteenth century it became increasingly common for psychologists like William Preyer in Germany, James Sully in Britain, and Mark Baldwin in the United States to compare the emergence of instincts in childhood with those in the lower animals.[44] Freud received Mark Baldwin's 'rampantly biogenetic' *Mental Development in the Child and the Race* in 1897, three years after it was published, and commented to Wilhelm Fliess that it was interesting to see how 'writers are now turning so much to child psychology . . . one still remains a child of one's age, even with something one had thought was one's very own'.[45] Freud was very familiar with recapitulatory child psychology and made explicit reference to the works of Sully, Preyer, Baldwin and Groos in his 'Three Essays on the Theory of Sexuality'.[46]

Language and the child, seen both as evidence and epitome of the processes of evolution, were used figuratively to outline the project of a scientific child psychology. Introducing the first volume of *The Mind of the Child*, William Preyer opposed the psychology of the *tabula rasa*, arguing that the tablet had already been written upon 'before birth, with many illegible, nay, unrecognisable and invisible marks, the traces of long-gone generations'. The more closely and attentively a child was observed, the more easily legible became the traces, even though 'it is hard to discern and decipher the mysterious writing on the mind of the child'.[47]

The psychology that framed Freud's development of psychoanalysis was certainly evolutionary, though perhaps not Darwinian. The motor of evolution in Darwin's argument was accidental: natural selection was not part of an unfolding plan, but the result of random, incidental events. The older, pre- or non-Darwinian biology that is now understood to have shaped much late nineteenth-century evolutionary thinking was also used in the construction of childhood in the new child-study movement, from which Freud learned so much.[48] Non-Darwinian evolutionary theory used by psychologists of the child-study movement expressed an inherent teleology, with the idea of progress being embedded in the idea of development. In this way, the child's developing body and mind could be understood as an epitome of a more general historical progress. When W.B. Drummond published his popular and summative *Introduction to Child Study* in 1907, he suggested in his epigraph that 'child-study marks the introduction of evolutionary thought into the human soul'. The anthropologist, 'unable to discover a living specimen of primitive man, turns to the child as his nearest representative'. This course of human development, revelatory of so much more than itself, began in pre-natal life, in the first place in 'a division and subdivision of the original cell into a little mass of cells'.[49]

Growth, conceived of in biological terms, demanded historical explanation. A progression through the stages of development, observable in all embryos and young creatures, carried evidence of a human cultural past and of a biological past; and the young child, possessed of language (or the capacity for language), carried linguistic evidence as well of the distant and lost processes of acculturation. 'Growth', understood in this way, was a biological and therefore a historical phenomenon, and the child of the species was used as working material for its investigation. A child psychology was partly constructed in the expectation that cultural and historical evidence enclosed within the child's body and mind could be retrieved and used.

In some late nineteenth-century psychological accounts, the child's understanding of its own body and its own interiority was used as a form of historical evidence. James Sully thought that the child's ideas of 'origin, growth and final shrinkage' mirrored 'the development of the idea of the soul by the race', for among the ancient peoples 'its seat was placed in the trunk . . . long before it was localised in the head'.[50] When the child is able to grasp the idea of 'a conscious thinking "I", the head will become a principal portion of the bodily self'. This conscious self, the self that 'thinks, suffers and wills', comes to be 'dimly discerned' by the end of the third year.[51] As it came into being, this self historicised itself, by constructing 'the unreachable past'. Sully observed how 'very curious are the directions of the first thought about the past self'. The child had to encounter the 'terrible mystery, time'. Sully described how children seem at first 'quite unable to think of it as we think of it, in an abstract way. "Today," "tomorrow," and "yesterday" are spoken of as things that move.' When he pointed to the child's inability to grasp 'great lengths of time', he gave expression to the great sadness that evolution and history had bequeathed. He made a curious elision of adult and child when he suggested that 'possibly [a] sense of immeasurable lengths of certain experiences of childhood gives the child's sense of past time something of an aching sadness which older people can hardly understand'. In Sully's description the subject feeling loss is at once adult and child (or neither; both are ageless subjects of time and history): 'Do not the words "long, long ago," when we use them in telling a child a story carry with them for our ears a strangely far-off sound?'[52]

For William Preyer, consciousness of time came into being in the same way, when

> to the original consciousness belonging to sensation is added the experience of succession, and with that the consciousness of time; then the simultaneousness of the sensations of contact, and with this the consciousness of space; finally, the consciousness of the causal connection of two or more contacts that have come to consciousness in time and space, and with this the idea of the body touched.[53]

He made similar points about time and loss when he discussed the infant sucking, how it 'awakens the recollection of the sweet taste; the sweet taste of itself causes sucking. This succession is already a separation *in time* of two sensations (the sweet and the motor sensation in sucking).' The separation in space requires the child to recall two sensations and, with this, 'the first act of intellect is performed, the first perception made, i.e., a sensation first localised in time and space'.[54]

When Sigmund Freud turned his attention to childhood (to adult memories and uses of childhood rather than to actual children) in the 1890s, he certainly worked within a framework of understanding that was derived from evolutionary child study. His belief in the existence of an instinctual, or phylogenetic, endowment is well documented. Perhaps of more significance for the mature development of his theory was his growing understanding that a particular form of time came into being in the child's body. This understanding was first arrived at when he paid attention to the processes of pathological defence observable in the adult's memory (and repression of memory) of bodily trauma in childhood.

What Freud believed at this stage was that sexual abuse (precocious sexual stimulation, or 'seduction', in contemporary terms) could have no immediate psychopathological repercussions on the nervous system at the time of its occurrence, because the sexual instinct was not developed in infancy and the child could not comprehend what was being done to it. Nevertheless, the memory would remain; indeed, according to Freud sexual abuse exerted 'a uniquely delayed psychophysical effect upon the human nervous system'.[55] At the arrival of puberty 'this mnemic psychical trace', long since forgotten and relegated to the unconscious portion of the mind, would suddenly be reawakened. Then, due to the physiological changes wrought by puberty, this memory would now 'display a power which was completely lacking from the event itself. The memory [would] operate as though it were a contemporary event'.[56] The hysterical symptoms displayed by many of Freud's patients in the 1890s were often taken as evidence of earlier sexual trauma.

Gradually between 1897 and 1905, Freud came to an understanding – or at least to a public understanding – that what many of his patients were describing was not actual sexual abuse in childhood, but a fantasised seduction.[57] It was in November 1899 that he described clearly for the first time how fantasies might operate at the unconscious level in order to produce an alternative form of reality. In *The Interpretation of Dreams* he wrote that 'if we look at unconscious wishes reduced to their most fundamental and truest shape, we shall have to conclude . . . that *psychical* reality is a particular form of existence not to be confused with *material* reality'.[58] The abandonment of belief that adult neuroses and psychotic amnesia were caused by childhood sexual abuse and the move towards a conviction that fantasised events operated in the psyche *as if* they were real events, was an early stage in a very long process of theory construction, which is often traced through Freud's uncovering and formulation of the Oedipal crisis in a child's life.

Though the crisis, or complex, was not named until 1910 (in the *Five Lectures on Psycho-analysis*) it was discussed in a roundabout way in *Interpretation of Dreams* of 1900; the idea was at work in the 'Dora' case study of 1905, and in the *Three Essays on Sexuality* of the same year, but again, was not directly discussed. The theory is outlined more clearly in 'Family Romances' (1908) and in 'The Sexual Theories of Children' (1909).[59] The perceived threat of castration by the father, who prohibits the child's incestuous desire for the mother, forces a resolution of the child's Oedipal crisis. The child accepts the societal proscription on incest, introjects the universal, patriarchal law, and thus begins to form the voice of conscience and prohibition within itself. It is through the Oedipal crisis that the child develops an individual identity, and a place in social, family and sexual organisation; but the child can only do this by splitting off its guilty desires, and repressing them into the unconscious. So the human being who emerges from this crisis is a split subject, torn between consciousness and the unconscious. Childhood, as a cluster of desires, happenings, experiences, assaults and traumas, is relocated, put into another place – a place that for the moment we only need to label as not the conscious mind, under the sway of a radically different form of time.

The prehistory of how Freud came to theorise this other form of time (time that is not the same as social time, nor narrated time) is not to be found in *The Interpretation of Dreams.* Something else was written by him on this question in the early months of the last year of the century, in which childhood was clearly formulated as its basis. In 'Screen Memories', published in September, childhood was pivotal to the argument.[60] 'Screen Memories' is an account of his discovery that the earliest of childhood memories – Freud's own and those of his patients – had been found never to have taken place, never to have 'really happened'. It is an argument claiming that the importance of childhood memories actually lies in what they reveal of the adult's unresolved conflicts about current circumstances. Of this realisation, this moment, this paper (written in the early months of 1899) Jacqueline Rose says that we have been reading the wrong Freud on the subject of children, and that 'we do not realise that Freud was first brought up against the unconscious when asking how we remember ourselves as a child'.[61] This, then, is the place where Freud discovered a particular meaning of childhood (began to evolve his theory of childhood), its status as a form of history, and its import for the narration of time.[62] What Freud used in this formulation was not the grand sweep of external, evolutionary time (though evolutionary inheritance, embodied in the child, certainly did have a place in his depiction of *childhood,* and of the few children he wrote about). But when he described an interiorised time coming into being in a child's body, his new formulations were made within the paradigms of the neurological physiology in which he had been educated, in the 1870s and 1880s.

Freud had experienced intellectual formation through debates waged between materialism and vitalism in the Viennese Physiological Institute, of which he was a member between 1876 and 1882. In 1873 he had become a student in a medical school in which materialist physiology had been given enormous theoretical force and *élan* by Ernst Brücke.[63] In 1874 Brücke had published his *Lectures in Physiology,* which offered a powerful vision of organic bodies as systems of smaller parts moved by forces. The smaller parts interact with each other, combine, are transformative through their action within an enclosed system.[64] Siegfried Bernfeld reminds us that as late as 1929 it was with this vision and this vocabulary that Freud described 'Psycho-analysis', for the *Encyclopaedia Britannica*, as an investigation into the forces in the human organism 'which assist or inhibit one another, combine with one another, enter into compromises with one another'.[65] He was quoting here from Brücke's *Lectures on Physiology*. So as a young man, Freud was taught by men who had been extraordinarily vocal anti-vitalists in their own youth, in the 1840s and 1850s, pledged to proving that 'no other forces than the common physical-chemical ones are active within the organism'.[66]

Tracing Freud's development of psychoanalysis, Frank Sulloway has described the way in which, by the mid-1890s, Freud was content to formulate psychological explanations for ordinary everyday repressions, that is, repression following on childhood seduction. But the highly pathological repression that resulted in complete amnesia forced a physiological explanation. In Freud's schema, neuroses were the *toxological* consequence of wrongly utilised libido, and so whatever inhibited them 'must be something quantitative and thus physiological'.[67] Freud's search for the precise chemical and neurological details of the process of pathological repression prompted his *Project for a Scientific Psychology* of 1895. This was written out of his understanding of recent cell theory, a conceptualisation of the nervous system as consisting of distinct yet similarly constructed neurones. He understood neurones to have contact with each other through the substance surrounding them. Through this substance, contact lines were laid down, along the tracks made when the neurones received stimulus and gave it off. He described this stimulus as deriving from the ordinary cellular processes going on in the body. They, too, had to be discharged, and the organism could not withdraw from them as it could from external stimuli.[68] Freud thought it likely that neurone structure meant that resistances would take place in the contacts between one neurone and the other: 'in this way they receive the value of barriers'.[69] He thought there might be two types of neurone: those with no contact barriers, through which stuff passes, and which remain as they were before stimulus; and those whose contact barriers operate, and which are changed by each excitation, thus affording '*a possibility of representing memory*'.[70] The distinction between two types of neurone, the perceptual and the mnemonic, was important for Freud's outline of the processes of repression, which had been observed in victims of childhood abuse, and which he here described as taking place at the cellular level.

Freud returned to these questions in his 'Beyond the Pleasure Principle', written twenty years later, in which he still pursued an answer at the level of the cell. This is to say that the arguments that he felt obliged to consider in 1920, about the compulsion to repeat unpleasurable experiences, were structured by reference to the picture of 'a living organism in its most simplified form . . . an undifferentiated vesicle of a substance that is susceptible to stimulation'. This 'little fragment of a living substance' acquires a kind of shield, as a result of 'the ceaseless impact of external stimuli'; in this way, a kind of crust was formed around it, 'which at last would have been so thoroughly "baked through" by stimulation that it would present the most favourable possible conditions for the reception of stimuli and become incapable of any further modification'. This was the way in which the shield became capable of giving rise to consciousness; also, having become inorganic, the energies of the external world could pass through it, into the underlying layers, though its main function remained protection against those outside stimuli.

Freud described the way in which there was no such protection from the excitations coming from within the little fragment of living substance; those feelings and excitations were of much greater intensity. In an attempt to deal with them and provide a barrier against them, the vesicle treated them as if they came from outside, so that it might be possible 'to bring the shield . . . into operation as a means of defence against them'. This, said Freud, was one of the origins of projection.[71]

Freud believed that the compulsion to repeat those unpleasurable sensations that came from within was caused by 'a universal attribute of instincts and perhaps of organic life in general which has not hitherto been clearly recognised', that is, the 'urge inherent in organic life to restore an earlier state of things . . . an *old* state of things, an initial state from which the living entity has at one time or other departed'.[72] He described a course of desire, for the quietude of inorganic being, and used the vicissitude of the cell to provide the image of psychological processes.

Pondering his own use of language in 'Beyond the Pleasure Principle', Freud suggested that the difficulty with his exegesis of 1920 was the way in which he chose to use the figurative language of metapsychology ('death instinct', 'pleasure and unpleasure'); its deficiencies might vanish if he were 'in a position to replace the psychological [terms] by physiological or chemical ones', for whilst it was true that 'they too are only part of figurative language', it was at least a language with which he and his readers had 'been long familiar and which is perhaps a simpler one as well'. But in 'Beyond the Pleasure Principle' he had used physiological terms and images, in the way he had in 'Project', when he first described the progress of time, memory and consciousness. The resources of the nineteenth-century physiological imagination were used to depict psychological processes embodied in a tiny fragment of living matter, that is, in a cell. Discovery of the processes of repression through the uncovered traumas of childhood sexual abuse lay at the basis of Freud's formulation of the unconscious. That an account of its aetiology was given at the level of the cell (in the neurone and its relationships) does not merely delineate some kind of false start on Freud's part, nor a misdirection in the development of psychoanalytic theory (though many accounts like this have been written, of physiological explanation replaced by a more mature psychological vision). What concerns us here is the process of envisaging: the little place within was the child at the heart of the theory, as well as at the heart of the psychoanalytic body.

We need to return briefly to a fantasy. Freud's theory of phantasy involves the imagined scene, or event, or happening, which is the fulfilment of a wish (this phantasy can be conscious or unconscious). Freud's evolution of the idea of phantasy is inextricably bound up with the question of whether or not *it really happened.* We know the accusatory account of how Freud abandoned the seduction theory between 1897 and – when? 1900? 1905? possibly not at all – from Jeffrey Masson's book of 1984, and his version of the events which led Freud to claim that his hysterical patients were not describing actual sexual abuse in childhood, but rather, a fantasised seduction.[73] Then 1988 gave us Larry Wolff's *Postcards from the End of the World,* and a similar charge against Freud, not of betraying women, but of forsaking the battered children of *fin-de-siècle* Vienna (and of the twentieth century in general). Wolff depicts Freud anxiously combing his morning newspaper all through November and December 1899, for reviews of *The Interpretation of Dreams.* The charge is this: that the one man in Europe who could have explained contemporary cases of child battering, did not even comment on the column inches devoted to them.[74]

The year 1899 matters very much in the account we have of Freud's recantation of his earlier theories, for it was in *The Interpretation of Dreams,* published in November, that he can be seen to have made the first and enduring distinction between psychical reality and material reality.[75] Here he postulated a different kind of time from social time and narrated time, though the fact that it was indeed time and narrative with which he dealt here would not become clear until he had written up the case of 'Dora' (in 1901; not published until 1905) and that of the Wolf-man (in 1918).[76] In this last case history, Freud made it abundantly clear, for the first time, that narrative truth, order and sequence do not much signify in the eliciting of a life-story, for we get the same story in the end, whichever way we tell it or construct it: the individual's account of how she or he got to be the way she or he is.[77]

In the long twentieth-century process of claiming Freud by rewriting the history of his ideas, the abandonment of the seduction theory – a first step in the formulation of the Oedipal theory – has been a matter for celebration as much as it has been condemned as a betrayal of abused women and children, for here Freud can be seen to make a move from physiological to psychical explanation. Moreover, with the abandonment of the seduction theory, Freud can be seen to leave behind a notion (or naïve belief) that the events of the past can be retrieved, the past itself reconstructed as it really was; and he can be watched moving towards 'the mature psycho-analytic theory of history as making meaning out of memory in the service of the present'.[78] By the procedures of this teleological history of ideas, a theory of the unconscious can be seen being formulated very early on indeed, and recognised in all its radical and desirable otherness. Indeed in the modern desire to see Freud forsake physiology and the belief that psychic processes are based in the functioning of the body, it has been argued that even in the 'Project' of 1892 Freud adopted a structure of explanation that was metaphoric rather than material and physiological. Using a spatial metaphor in the reading of Freud's early work, and ascribing the same metaphorical use to his writing, it has been argued that the 'Project for a Scientific Psychology' can be read so as to see the mind possessing both place and hierarchy, with the unbearable and unthinkable pushed below – or at least, somewhere – into repression.[79] In this line of argument it is considered important that 'the concept of repression presupposes a topographical *division* of the mind – that is, a division of the mind based on a figurative representation of the psyche by means of a spatial metaphor'.[80]

In fact, this argument might equally serve to remind us of the material with which the spatial metaphor did its work, that is, with the cell. The metaphorical structures utilised by Freud involved the irreducible unit of physical organisation, the entity that was both a place, and a place where things happened: the topos of the cell. The cell, the smallest place within, promoted another set of analogies, for what the cell carried was the child turned within, an individual's childhood history laid down inside its body, a place inside that was indeed very small, but that carried with it the utter enormity of a *history*.

So powerful is the image of evolution's sway in the nineteenth century, so frequently are we reminded of the way in which evolutionary thought made its mark on every field of human thought and endeavour, that it is possible to forget the means that were available for resisting the plot – of growth, development, history, death – that was brought in its train. In physiology and physiological cell theory a different kind of time was configured and employed, one that bore some relationship to older concepts of metamorphosis. 'Transformation and metamorphosis may take place almost without time,' Gillian Beer reminds us. 'Growth cannot. It is therefore in some measure equivalent to history.'[81] As she points out, the idea of metamorphosis expressed 'continuance, survival, the essential self transposed but not obliterated by transformation'.[82] Cell theorists had most firmly confronted death, in all their writings, and stared it down, because what they learned from that long nineteenth-century encounter was that there simply could not be final extinction. 'If there is a point in natural philosophy which may be regarded as finally settled,' said Draper in 1856, 'it is the imperishability of the chemical elements and the everlasting duration of force. With the system of nature existing as it is, we cannot admit that an atom of any kind can ever be destroyed'.[83] 'Perhaps in some age hereafter,' he mused, 'physiology will find herself sufficiently advanced to offer her opinion on this profound topic, for I cannot think that GOD has left us without a witness in this matter, even in the structure and development of the body itself'.[84] With this vision, it was possible to dehistoricise history, and remove it from time. This was not done by denying change or death, and certainly physiologists like Draper used the grand analogy between national types and the individual, both with their 'Infancy, Childhood, Youth, Old Age and Death, respectively'.[85] But death was not extinction, as long as the structure of thought allowed 'the death of particles in the individual [to answer] the death of persons in the nation'. The point was, as Draper explained, that 'through all these losses and changes, the immaterial principle has passed unscathed . . . In the broadest manner that a fact can be set forth, we see herein the complete subordination of structure and the enduring character of spirit.'[86]

Gillian Beer has described how metamorphosis and growth offered the nineteenth century 'two radical orders for narrative', and she shows the tension between them at work in several examples of Victorian fiction. Metamorphosis and growth also constituted orders for narrative outside the fictional realm, for physiology and psychoanalysis – to point to current examples. But writing like Draper's shows that though they offered radical orders, they were not radically opposed to each other, and a notable feature of mid-nineteenth cell theory was its formulation to encompass the problems presented by evolutionary theories of growth, development and history. Cell theory, like many other bodies of thought in the period, was indelibly marked by evolutionary theory; but it used the individual as working material rather than the species; it operated by procedures that excluded the chance that provided the motor of Darwinian thinking; and it worked within the framework of a determinism that explained the action of body parts in terms of their function. In this way, the radical alternative vision offered by cell theory lay in its denial of extinction: nothing goes away. It was this understanding that Freud used to delineate the unconscious: the place where childhood (an individual history) is put, and thus released from time. George Henry Lewes wanted an Oedipus to come, to unlock the gates to the terminal mystery of growth. The theory that Freud constructed in the name of the King of Thebes was a slowly formulated strategy, by which the mystery (which *was* only a mystery because of time) could be removed from the temporal order, and childhood turned within, to the timeless interiority of the unconscious.

In the version of *Wilhelm Meister* that the nineteenth century knew,

Mignon dies with a shriek and a melodramatically explicit gesture. In the same moment she indicates both the cause of her death ('"Let it break . . . It's been beating too long anyway"') and a fleeting repulsion of what she says she welcomes: 'Mignon suddenly felt for her heart with her left hand, and stretching out her right arm with a violent movement, she collapsed' (*WMA* III:105).[87] A doctor and a surgeon are called, and pronounce her dead. The doctor asks for permission to 'give some permanence to the remains of this strange being . . . I wish to apply immediately to this dear creature the beautiful art of not only embalming a body, but also of preserving in it an appearance of life' (*WMA* III:106, 107). Wilhelm is intensely interested in the young surgeon's bag of instruments, for he is sure that he has seen it before, when his wounds were tended after the ambush in the forest.[88] But Schiller thought that this response, which seems to exclude mourning for Mignon, would jar with the 'sentimental' demands of Goethe's audience. He was not the first reader to find it odd that Wilhelm, 'who is after all the cause of her death and knows it, has at this moment eyes for the instrument case and can lose himself in memories of past scenes when the present should possess him utterly'.[89]

It is now as Mignon lies in her angel garments – 'as if asleep in a very pleasing manner' – and is lowered into the depths of a marble sarcophagus, that her story is told for the first time and we learn of the insanity of her inheritance. Nineteenth-century retellings of *Wilhelm Meister* repeated the story that is given to Mignon's corpse, for the plots of restoration and refusal of death in which she found herself had to reveal the endowment that made her a bride worthy of Meister. Almost without exception, the plot of restoration removed incest and insanity and left Mignon's abduction by rope-dancers or gypsies, finding its conclusion in the alternative end-stop of the *Bildungsroman*, that is, in marriage rather than death.[90]

Forgotten – or repressed – by nineteenth-century operatic and melodramatic versions of *Wilhelm Meister*, this scene can serve as an epitome of the topics of childhood, death and history, their centrality and their connection, in nineteenth-century Western culture. The ideas of growth and development came to be more and more articulated around observation of the young of the species, and particularly in terms of human children. What emerged in this way was a collection of concepts and understandings of children's bodies that became one of the components of 'childhood'. The puzzle of growth, its cessation, and its prewritten end in death, all of which caused so much physiological deliberation in the mid-century, was also subject to exploration in other fields of inquiry. Evolutionary thought and exegesis (in its non-Darwinian and Darwinian modes) provided some solution to the problem of growth, for it was able to find meaning in the child's early and rapid development. The meaning it found was historical, that is to say, it made the stages of a child's development analogous to a more general human history.

The embalming of the child Mignon, her horribly rouged, dead-yet-alive appearance as she is lowered to her marble bed, the vulgarity of it all so remarked upon across the centuries, can only act as the allegory of the preceding discussion. Only in the structure of this book can the scene in which death is resisted by restoring the appearance of life be taken as gesture towards the changes in epistemology and historiography to which Stephen Bann draws our attention in *The Clothing of Clio.*[91] Goethe foreshadowed nothing; but in the trajectory of this argument, which draws its evidence from a two-hundred-year time–span, the scene he wrote points to the missing term of Bann's argument, which is that loss and death, and the ways in which they were thought and imagined, were connected with the idea of growth and its necessary cessation. Growth, most apparent in the young of the species, was observed, written about and theorised most consistently in connection with childhood. History and childhood, as ways of thinking and ways of knowing, both strenuously attempted to delimit and resist the implications of growth, and both ways of thought pushed these questions to the interior. The vast, historicised world was turned inside, so that history itself might be de-historicised, removed from the time that allowed growth and decay, so that they might be overcome, in the lost and – crucially – timeless place within. Bann shows nineteenth-century history-writing attempting to triumph over the terrible implications of history itself; and childhood, as a personification of vast tracts of evolutionary and cultural history, was a similar kind of strategy. Moreover, the agenda of emergent psychoanalysis was set by conceptualisations of childhood made familiar by evolutionary thought, and by the questions of growth, time and death that had been raised by physiological cell theory over the preceding half-century. Part of the purpose of this chapter has been to understand the idea of the unconscious as a meta-theory of childhood which drew on the two currents of scientific thought that have been outlined, those of evolutionary theory and physiology. To understand the ways in which these ideas were employed in nineteenth-century society we need a clearer conception of childhood's – and indeed Mignon's – meaning in nineteenth-century culture, for we have not yet exhausted use of her.

6

Strange Dislocations: Child as Acrobat

> Wilhelm could not look at her enough. His eyes and his heart were irresistibly fascinated by the mysterious condition of this being . . . he kept on looking at her . . .
> (Goethe, *Wilhelm Meister*, Volume I, Book 2, Chapter 4)

From the end of the eighteenth century onwards, there came into being complex ways of understanding childhood as a component of the adult self, and of envisaging the depths of the self to which childhood – the adult's personal history – was relegated. The discussion so far has focused on the ways of imagining the body and its interiority that made this act of cognition possible. At the end of the period under discussion, it has been suggested, Freud drew on two orders of thought, the physiological and the evolutionary, in order to establish childhood in its relationship to the unconscious, so that the unconscious mind was conceptualised as the timeless repository for what was formerly the matter of time and history, that is, an actual childhood, an actual period of growth and its vicissitudes. In this way, through the images that Freud used, and by the networks of understanding that he activated when he described these processes in neuro-physiological terms, his account of the unconscious repeated the imperative of nineteenth-century physiology, which was to confront death with the idea of endlessness.

Children, and the complex of beliefs, attitudes and projections that constitute childhood, have been subject to much speculation and theorisation over the last two centuries, though conclusions regarding the changes discussed above have been reached by different routes and using different kinds of evidence from that which is adduced here. Connections between childhood and adult self have been discussed in relation to the Romantic movement in literature, as have nineteenth-century developments in autobiographical writing that produced the genre of 'the childhood'. Literary child-figures also helped shape political policy on childhood at the end of the nineteenth century – at least in Britain, and in the Independent Labour Party and Labour Party.[1]

Literary analysis allows the child to be understood as an intricate matter of adult projection and desire, and once this is done James Kincaid's conclusion in *Child-loving. The Erotic Child and Victorian Culture* (1992), that the child 'is not, in itself, anything', is very easy to reach (and quite irresponsible proposals may follow on it).[2] It is particularly easy to write about childhood in the past from this perspective, for the commentator is released from the obligation to find evidence for happenings and events, and is only obliged to pursue the desires, opinions and observations of those who 'wrote' childhood (or, to use an older language, only obliged to uncover the 'attitudes' of adults towards children). Yet the historical dilemma – what makes the topic worthy of historical inquiry – is that children were *both* the repositories of adults' desires (or a text, to be 'written' and 'rewritten', to use a newer language), *and* social beings, who lived in social worlds and networks of social and economic relationships, as well as in the adult imagination. If it is this dual existence that makes childhood a problem worthy of historical attention, then the historiographical difficulties attendant on recovering evidence about childhood needs to be indicated, if not adumbrated, once again.[3]

However, it is possible to proceed more positively, and to use these complexities – the muddied relationship between desire and social being – as a means of historical inquiry. This and the next two chapters consider the locations in which Victorian childhood was enacted for various audiences: on the stage and in the street. These were places where the meanings attached to childhood were not so much *performed* – for that suggests children's intention and complicity in enacting something – as *recognised* by adults watching them. Outside the setting of the home and before the development of compulsory mass schooling, these were the two situations in which more than any other in Britain, children were observed, written about and, indeed, had desires projected on to them. It is sometimes possible to dimly perceive children conscious of – and puzzled about – the exhibition that was required of them. Though it is not the purpose of this book to reconstruct that experience, the knowledge that types of childhood were among the many things that adults wanted – and still want – from children should probably be a component of any social history of them that might come to be written. Indeed, the adults' beliefs and desires out of which children were described should probably be regarded as an unfortunate factor of their social existence, now and in the recent past, and one which the historian discussing them must take into account.

Focusing on street children and stage children in this way also has the advantage of bringing a thesis to the testing place of social class and social division, for on the face of it there was not much to be found that was less *like* the gentleman stopping the child in the street than the dirty, verminous and illiterate little crossing-sweeper he questioned about hours of work and habits of life. But then Mignon was not much like Wilhelm, though she turned out to be his very self, as we shall see. Once more, Mignon will set the terms of the ensuing argument, not only because she embodies it, but because she appears again and again – on the street and on the stage – in many guises, and in the most unsettling ways.

In the pages of *Wilhelm Meister*, it is Mignon's gestures and motions as an acrobat that carry the burden of her oddness. It is the strange dislocations of Mignon's body that Goethe marked in his text of 1795–6, and it was the strange dislocations of her performances and dance that appeared again and again in the course of the nineteenth century. In Britain – and in a quite uncanny way – these questions were pursued through a campaign of the 1870s and 1880s, to rescue actual child acrobats from all the exploitation and distress with which Goethe marked his eighteenth-century fictional child.

Mignon is made conspicuous by the clothes, appearance and demeanour of an acrobat, from the very first moment that Meister (and the reader) encounters her. Her apparel, and the way in which she leaps towards him make it obvious that she is 'a member of the troupe of acrobats and dancers' that has just arrived in the town (*WMA* I:83)[4]. In performance, she and the other children put themselves in 'strange postures', and their bodies portray the efforts with which these are achieved (*WMA* I:87); but off duty as well, Mignon is often found in the peculiar attitude of the acrobat. 'There was something strange about the child in all her comings and goings. She did not go up and down the stairs, but leapt; she climbed up the corridor bannisters, and before you knew where you were, she was sitting high up on the wardrobe where she would stay quiet for a while' (*WMA* I:97–8).

Mignon chooses these postures for her singing and music-making as well:

> At one time she would sit on the topmost rung of a ladder, with her legs crossed under her, like a Turk on his carpet; at others she promenaded on the eaves of the courtyard buildings, where the plaintive tone of her strings, which she sometimes accompanied with an agreeable but somewhat rough voice, made everyone listen, surprised and startled. Some compared her to an ape, others to some strange animal; but all concurred in saying that there was something insular, foreign and romantic in the child.[5]

When Wilhelm notes her 'good physique', and 'the limbs [that] promised stronger growth, or else announced a development that was retarded', Goethe may well have been working with an understanding of *Bildung*, and using Mignon as some kind of symbol of thwarted growth; but he was also quite prosaically referring to the habits and practices of an acrobatic training, in which the maintenance of a low body weight was of paramount importance, and which were well known at the end of the eighteenth century.[6] When Hughes Le Roux and Jules Garnier produced their account of training for the acrobatic profession in 1890, they summed up a century of detailed observation of preparation for slack- and tight-wire dancing, for trapeze work, and for gymnastic and contortionist performance.[7] Le Roux and Garnier wrote in the age of the connoisseur, when appreciation of all the lessons that the acrobat taught was heightened by the possession of handbooks and guides, and when the instruction in aesthetics that the acrobat had long offered – 'the inspirational power of perfect equilibrium' – was elaborated by technical analysis.[8] The extensive commentary on the acrobat produced out of this 'true obsession of the European fin-de-siècle' was part of a quest for the satisfactions of *knowing*, of understanding how effects and appearances were produced, how sexual ambiguity and mystique were acquired in training.[9] But the detailed attention to the acrobat's use of his or her body – and the development of a vocabulary, a kind of aestheticised physiology, for describing it – that started to be paid to the adult stars of the acrobatic firmament in the 1880s and 1890s, had been a feature of British writing on acrobat children since the middle years of the century.

Descriptions of training programmes for acrobatic performance by children were fantastically detailed. In talking to street performers in 1851, Henry Mayhew found a most elaborate analysis of training procedures, whether in an interview with a rope-dancer father describing the tender pedagogical methods he used with his two little girls, or in the remembered agony of the street-posturer who across thirty-five years recalled 'being "cricked"' by his father: 'he used to take my legs and stretch them, and work them round in their sockets, and put them up straight by my side . . .'.[10] No process of child labour save chimney-sweeping had so much attention paid to it in nineteenth-century Britain. Acrobat children had a good deal more to learn, and over a much longer period than most other child workers, and the minutiae of observation had something to do with that fact. But this precise and itemised description was also an elaborate questioning of the relationship between parents (or adults in general) and children. Details of acrobatic training showed the literal making of children's bodies, under the hands of their parents. Ellen Barlee's *Pantomime Waifs* of 1884 (written as part of a campaign against the acrobatic training of children) devoted several pages to the adult's manipulation of the child's body, describing a literal moulding of its limbs until the required flexibility was achieved.[11] Barlee did not describe the training process for trapeze work, nor preparation for general stage performance, in the same detail, though both were more central topics of her book. It was the handling of the child's body in acrobat training that drew attention. Barlee described training for touching heels with the hands thrown backwards over the head, and how the trainer always supported the child's body and constantly and gently rubbed the spine: 'presumably but for this aid the bone would suddenly snap in two'. 'It is well known,' she reported

> that to be a successful Acrobat or Contortionist the training must really commence at a very tender age, for then, and then alone, before their bones and muscles have attained firmness and strength, before . . . the frame is knit, can the bones be rendered sufficiently supple to perform the duties required of them.[12]

In the very earliest observations of children trained for acrobatic performance, the pity and sympathy of the reader is invoked by itemising the feelings of the narrator or fictional character involved in the observation, in the same way as are Wilhelm's, when he watches the children in the inn-yard, and notes the effort with which they attain their strange postures. The withholding of food from children was common knowledge (which is not to say that it was common practice) and it is likely that Goethe alluded to it in his description of Mignon's retarded growth. Sir Walter Scott's Fenella, whose *Seiltänzer* (tightrope walker) Adrian Brackel 'beat her when she would not dance the rope, and starved her when she did to prevent her growth', may well have familiarised the novel's audience with the idea that acrobat children were starved children.[13]

Barlee's book was one of the many campaigning texts inspired by Lord Shaftesbury's last – and little known – campaign to rescue child workers. As an appendix to *Pantomime Waifs* Barlee reproduced a speech on the topic of juvenile acrobats that had been made by Shaftesbury in the House of Lords in August 1883. He was concerned here with the Children's Dangerous Performances Act of 1879, and the clauses it contained which made anyone putting a child under fourteen through a performance that was likely to endanger life or limb liable to summary jurisdiction. The provisions of that act had been altogether ignored, said Shaftesbury, and 'the evil prevailed to a greater extent than before'. By way of illustration, he told of 'the human serpent'. 'This is a little girl,' he explained, who

> . . . is made to throw her head backwards and to bend her spine so that her head not only touches the ground, but is bent completely under her, so that her face looks out from between her legs. In this painful position she is compelled to remain and to perform tricks until the blood rushes into her face and she is forced to unbend upon which she pants fearfully.[14]

Legislation had singularly failed to prevent a scene 'disgusting to humanity'. During the earlier campaign for the Children's Dangerous Performances Bill he had pointed out that acrobatic performance was to be treated as an aspect of child labour rather than as a question of children's moral welfare. All debates over children's work moved between two principles, that of the parents' right to the labour of their children, and the developing autonomy of the child, first as an educational and moral and then as a legal subject existing in its own right. The striking feature of Shaftesbury's campaign, which it had in common with the revived campaign of the mid-century against the use of climbing boys, was the lines it drew between parental rights and parental cruelty. Though an Act of 1840 forbade climbing by anyone under the age of 21, the legislation was widely flouted, and campaigners worked until the mid-1870s to achieve final abolition. The revived campaign of the 1860s and 1870s drew new attention to the adult cruelty involved in training, to the manipulation and alteration of the child's body, in the same way as did the campaign against child-acrobats.[15]

During the nineteenth century the labour of children had been very slowly brought within the regulatory framework of factory legislation. Legislation of the 1860s extended the Factory Acts to many trades employing children, and a consolidating Act of 1870 closed many loopholes.[16] Children who worked in the entertainment business escaped this legislation for the main part. The Acrobats Bill, brought before the House of Commons in 1872, had been an attempt to subject children like this to the framework of protection by prohibiting the employment of young persons (those under 16 at first, then after amendment, those under 12), in any gymnastic performance by way of trade or for the purpose of gain. Shaftesbury's misgivings about this piece of proposed legislation were to do with its focus on performance rather than on training. When the Bill was introduced, the debate concentrated on the nature of children's bodies, and what constituted ill-treatment of them. Some might continue to think that 'the physical conformation which enabled people to twist and turn themselves . . . ran through families, and was handed down through successive generations';[17] but at committee stage Shaftesbury insistently directed attention to the role of parents in the making of the child performer's body. He read out a letter from a 17-year-old boy who movingly described a training that had started – for him at least – at the age of two. 'No other chap in the world is so supple and can tumble and twist himself like me,' he wrote.

> My father trained me into it. He began by twisting my limbs and backbone when I was a little baby. I used to suffer dreadful, and I remember when I was from four to nine years of age, he used to make me twist myself, and remain twisted up, till my bones seemed to come away from each other, and I was often ill from the pain.

He went on to explain that training had to begin at a very young age 'when there was no bone, but when all that subsequently became bone was mere gristle'.[18] As far as Shaftesbury was concerned, legislation that outlawed performance would leave untouched the cruelty of this system of private family training.

The Bill proposed in 1872 did not become law; but the Children's Dangerous Performances Bill of 1879 did. In Committee again, Shaftesbury made the point he had made seven years before, that 'in preventing only such performances as were, in the opinion of a Court of Summary Jurisdiction, dangerous to life and limb', it failed to touch the cruelties of the training process. The trick he mentioned this time was '"the back slide trick"'. Whilst this was not dangerous to life or limb, 'training commenced for it when the children were very young, and taught them to completely hoop their bodies . . . it inflicted an enormous amount of torture upon the unfortunate victims for the amusement of the people, and was a fearful detriment to their health and strength in after years'.[19]

To some extent the focus on adult cruelty within the family was to do with the powerful 'story' that Hugh Cunningham sees told in the history of childhood, with the way in which the drama of intervention, rescue and amelioration was less likely to be subverted if the child labour that continued after the great triumph of factory legislation in the mid-century were ignored. This is certainly a strategy of much twentieth-century history of childhood, but the 'story' was written contemporaneously as well, when the ambiguities of labour in the entertainment industry were evaded by condemnation of cruel and unfeeling parents, who were depicted in obverse relationship to that approval they gained when exactly the same system of training in a family craft was portrayed in all the symbiosis, trust and responsibility that is so charmingly presumed and evoked in Frederick Barnard's 'A Dress Rehearsal'. This painting of 1868 shows an affectionate (though tense) father putting his little boy through acrobatic rehearsal in a shabby but respectable working-class interior.[20]

The medical press played an important part in developing a perception of adult power and cruelty in relation to the child acrobat. In particular, it contributed a technical language for discussing the abnormality of the little acrobat's experience and of the body that training had given it. 'We have no great sympathy with many of the more sentimental sorts of philanthropy which take the form of "grandmotherly government",' announced the *Lancet* in 1883,

> but it is impossible not to feel that something – and something decisive – needs to be done to put a stop to certain of the practices carried on by the trainers of young children for acrobatic performances. The cruelties inflicted on those who are being prepared for

> exhibition as contortionists are terrible to think of, and must be horrible to endure.[21]

Fifty years' exploration of growth in the child-care manuals had anyway drawn attention to the evils attendant on flouting 'a natural law of the constitution', and 'the evils arising from ignorance of the structure and functions of the human body, and . . . the aid which might be derived from a general acquaintance with physiology'.[22] These complex understandings of children's bodies made the pain and suffering involved in acrobatic training easy enough to see; the vision of cruelty was sharpened by the knowledge that the anatomical and physiological depths of the little acrobat's body were also scarred. It was finally the Prevention of Cruelty Acts of 1889 and 1894 that forbade the training of any child under 16 as an acrobat or contortionist outside the family, though domestic training was still specifically excluded from this protective legislation.[23]

The idea of parental cruelty structured the campaigning literature that accompanied the progress (and demise) of the aborted legislation of the early 1870s. In *The Little Acrobat and His Mother* (1872) a parent of baroque awfulness is responsible for her child's unhappy state. Though it promises the narrative of 'a little German boy, who is in the service of travelling gymnasts, his adventures, hardships and subsequent deliverance from an evil course of life', the final message of the book concerns the psychology of family love and offers a dreadful picture of what ensues when the love of a mother fails.[24] The linguistically handicapped child hero ('"What is your name?" . . . "Acrobat." "I know your profession is that of an acrobat, but what is your Christian name?" "Acrobat."') is textually produced by his mother's failures as much as by the bodily distortion to which he is forced to submit.[25] 'Acrobat' is

> obliged to fast when ordered, to twist his body and limbs into all sorts of strange shapes, and sometimes to remain for a long time in the same position, mostly a fatiguing one. If he showed the slightest carelessness or inattention in performing his feats of agility, it was sure to draw upon him a storm of hard words and even severe punishment.[26]

The kindly philanthropists who finally come to Acrobat's rescue discuss his age, thinking that he is probably older than the 10 his *Seiltänzer* says he is, for 'children who lead that sort of life seldom grow'.[27]

Mignon's appearances in the nineteenth-century representational realm are so many, and so frequent, that it is no surprise to find her transmogrified into a wooden little German boy in a piece of Religious Tract Society pulp fiction. But the processes of social and political history that brought her from the pages of *Wilhelm Meister* to tumble and to perform her dance on British streets in the 1870s and 1880s make that appearance seem uncanny indeed. Sigmund Freud would presumably have placed reactions to the following item of social history under the heading of uncanny effects produced out of an 'old, animistic conception of the universe', an example of the way in which 'people experience the feeling in the highest degree in relation to death and dead bodies, and to spirits and ghosts'.[28] He remarked that few things had 'changed so little since the very earliest times . . . as our relation to death'. Moreover, he pointed out that nineteenth-century science had done little to dispel an original emotional reaction to death, and 'biology [had] not yet been able to decide whether death is the inevitable fate of every living being or whether it is only a regular but perhaps unavoidable event in life'.[29] Freud's discussion is useful, perhaps, for reconstructing the perception of those contemporary passers-by who threw the little Italian street performer a penny, though we have to retain the strong suspicion that most of them did not know what it was that had been brought back from Dis's kingdom by the sound of the barrel organ. It is more helpful for the twentieth-century observer of that nineteenth-century audience. Mignon twirling on the Holborn pavement is not uncanny because our primitive fear of the dead is still strong within us, so we believe that she can do us harm, but rather because she is there at all, brought from the fictional realm into the realm of social history. Because she is thus animated and brought to life we understand, perhaps for the first time, that she (the child she represents) has always been, and still is dead.

Mignon arrived in Holborn by the following route: in 1873 the Italian Parliament enacted legislation that forbade the employment of children in the vagrant professions.[30] By the time Charles Bradlaugh asked whether the clauses of the proposed Cruelty to Children Bill (1889) prohibiting the employment of different categories of children 'would touch the case of the Italian *padrones* in this country', the organisation of the import and employment of children into Britain was extremely well known.[31] In 1877 the Charity Organisation Society produced a report explaining 'the ordinary circumstances under which this system is carried on':

> Persons known as padroni, acting generally two together and working alternate six months in Italy and England, obtain the children from their parents in the Neapolitan districts, which are the least advanced of the Italian kingdom. They enter into a verbal contract with the parents to pay a fixed sum for the service of the children at the end of two years, and undertake to clothe and feed them during that period, and teach them a 'virtu', that is, to sing and play a musical instrument, 'so that they might become as rich as the padroni themselves'. They are not brought by railroad, but are made to walk the whole way through France, singing, playing, and dancing in the

> villages through which they pass . . . they are then placed in depots in London, whence they are distributed throughout the country . . . They are sent into the streets by day to play, or pretend to play, a musical instrument, singing and dancing in time to it, and at night they perform in a like manner in public houses.[32]

The *padrone* system had developed rapidly after European borders were opened up at the end of the Napoleonic Wars. It was a way for migrants, especially young men who sought employment as street musicians, to be provided with lodgings and employment in return for a proportion – or all – of their wages.[33] In Britain, the distribution centres of Brighton, Worthing, Bristol, Manchester, Birmingham and Sheffield were noted in the Charity Organisation report. Liverpool and Bradford were particularly important and flourishing centres for the dispersal of children.[34] In London, the Saffron Hill and Leather Lane areas of Holborn had long been known as centres of Italian settlement, and the trade located itself there. Many journalists besides Henry Mayhew were eager to report on the exotic corner of London that was home to the *padroni* and their charges. Charles Manby Smith surveyed these 'curiosities of the Metropolis' with a most detailed eye in 1853, telling his readers of nine classes of music grinders, and specifying their regions of birth.[35] His last category, the hurdy-gurdy players, could be further subdivided if the observer took note of 'little hopping, skipping, jumping, reeling Savoyard or Swiss urchins . . . whom you expect every moment to see rolling on the pavement, but who contrive, like so many kittens to pitch on their feet at last'. His attention then turned to the 'men with sallow complexions, large dark eyes and silver ear-rings, who stand erect and tranquil, and confer a dignity, not to say grace, upon the performance'.[36] James Greenwood's series of pieces for the *Daily Telegraph* provide a sociology of the trade.[36] Published in book form in 1873 as *In Strange Company*, these articles feature a Holborn organ grinder who 'for the goodness knows how many years, had been the companion of various members of that fiendish Italian horde who, by means of a barrel organ, grind us mad to make their bread', and 'whose colony, as everybody knows, is within a stone's throw of Leather Lane'. Before the Italian legislation of 1873 increased the import of children (as opposed to young men) into Britain, Greenwood's informant thought the boys had used the sympathies of local magistrates to gain ascendancy over their *padroni*: a 'naturally . . . laying-about, lazy lot of little beggards in their own country', they took immediate advantage of a legal system that obliged 'the man that hired 'em . . . to feed 'em' and not to 'wallop 'em'.[38]

In his account of the several thousand Italian street performers who were active around the world during the 1860s and 1870s, John Zucchi records the range of reactions to their presence in northern European and North American cities, the juxtaposition of the threat to social order they represented with 'sentimental depictions of those same children as helpless victims'.[39] The same mixture of vilification and appreciation extended to their *padroni* who, in the portraits of journalists and social investigators who visited Britain's Italian quarters, either cringed before the children who had discovered that 'the magistrate was on their side' or as 'gentlemen of the pavement' surveyed the children and the white mice under their care with benevolent and soulful eye. However, it was the motivelessly cruel *padrone* who was to become the stock-type of socio-fiction and campaigning melodrama.

Most reports of the system paid a good deal of attention to the appearance and visual appeal of Italian children, to their pretty, puppyish ways. Dark, good-looking children made a striking contrast with the native inhabitants of the city street who, at least in representational terms, were always stunted, dirty, unkempt and deeply unattractive; in Lord Shaftesbury's enduring perception 'pale, feeble . . . their appearance wild', with 'matted hair [and] . . . disgusting filth that renders necessary a closer inspection before the flesh can be discerned between the rags which hang about it'.[40] Moreover, the weight of contemporary evidence was that after 1873 the import of girls increased. Their extreme attractiveness, the reputed earlier sexual maturity of Italian girls compared with English ones, and the consistent charge that they were imported for the purposes of prostitution, made them infinitely watchable.[41] The *padrone* system was frequently referred to as a 'white slave' system, and although the term did not assume its full sexual connotations until the 'Maiden Tribute of Modern Babylon' scandal broke in 1885 (when the campaigning editor of the *Pall Mall Gazette*, W.T. Stead bought a child from her mother in order to demonstrate the existence of a system of child prostitution), the Charity Organisation Society was quite certain that 'mere children may be found in the street almost within a stone's throw of the Home Office, acting as prostitutes under the guise of street selling'.[42]

When clauses of the Prevention of Cruelty to Children Bill that dealt with theatrical performance were being debated in 1889, Charles Bradlaugh evoked the dangers of prostitution among Italian girls, in order to discuss a more disturbing type of psychological ruin or corruption of such children. He claimed that 'the evidence is that these unfortunates, if they do not get ruined entirely . . . never settle down to any industrial occupation; but when they become sufficiently well off, those who were themselves stolen set themselves to steal other children'.[43] One of the enduring effects of the 'Maiden Tribute of Modern Babylon' scandal had been its linking of the questions of child sale, child stealing and child prostitution, and it is probable that Bradlaugh framed his questions under its effect. However, a system of apprenticeship in the acrobat profession had been understood as a system of buying and selling children for much longer than five years, and campaigners against the *padrone* system often condemned it by telling stories of cruel foreigners (usually Italians) who purchased children for the purposes of exploitation.[44]

When Wilhelm buys Mignon from the leader of the rope-dancing troupe, he pays 30 crowns for her, though the child is told that she cost a great deal more than that.[45] Cavalier Buzzegoli, Secretary of the Italian consulate in London in the 1870s, told the Charity Organisation Society that the sum paid to parents for children amounted to about 50 ducats (about £8), usually paid in three instalments. The children were expected to pull in about £220 during the course of their career in northern Europe.[46]

These children were, in the evocative phrase of their historian John Zucchi, 'little slaves of the harp', not acrobats. Little Italian street musicians did dance, and some did handstands and simple tumbling tricks between showing white mice and shaking tambourines; but it was a musical instrument – a harp, violin, pipe or hurdy-gurdy – that the usual contract between the *padrone* and the parents specified, along with the obligation of the *padrone* to teach the child to play.[47] The Italian street musician became elided with the child acrobat in campaigning literature, and in two campaigning melodramas of the 1880s, written by G.R. Sims and Clement Scott. 'Jack in the Box', their joint venture of 1885, shows a pathetic, passive and suffering little boy acrobat from the Savoy, who is contrasted with a new type of melodramatic child, the ebullient embodiment of juvenile Englishness, Jack Merryweather, 'a prodigy of vitality'.[48] Four years later, in 'Master and Man', written by Sims in collaboration with Henry Petitt, the target for reform is the training and exploitation of acrobat children in general, not just fictive Italian ones, though in both dramas the cruel and exploitative adult involved in their training has Italian connections.

The second act of 'Jack in the Box' opens 'at Toroni's . . . an Italian padrone's den in Saffron Hill'. 'Italian Organ girls and men, Hurdy gurdy boys &c' throng the stage, and against this background the little Savoyard (like the Religious Tract Society's 'Acrobat' he has no name) speaks for the first time, in a paradigmatic longing for home and the south: 'I shall die & never see dear Italy again. I was so warm there. It is so cold here.'[49] Mignon speaks here, as we should expect, though the voice echoes the libretto of Ambroise Thomas's opera as much as it does the words Goethe gave his child. The framework imposed by Carré and Barbier's libretto is particularly apparent when Toroni's physical abuse of the children in his care is exposed before a fairground crowd. Here, like Giarno the gypsy, he compels a hapless child to perform.[50]

Marilyn Brown discusses similar uses of the figure of the gypsy in France in this period, in *Gypsies and Other Bohemians.* Operating under an extremely stringent system of registration and policing after the mid-century, a host of ambulant entertainers with a wide range of occupations were obliged to register with local authorities. The *saltimbanque* (mountebank, juggler, travelling clown), became more visible and became noticeable not just because of regulatory attention but also because new waves of musicians and other entertainers pouring into France inspired 'hatred bordering on racial prejudice'. In her discussion of the various ways in which all categories of vagabondage were mythologised in France, Brown shows how the gypsy was able to represent at one and the same time the soul of the artist struggling to be free, and all sorts of fakery, hucksterism and criminality. Child theft was only one of the calumnies that attached to the *saltimbanque.*[51]

In 'Master and Man', a Lancashire child is stolen so that his mother (who has in her possession her imprisoned husband's blueprints for innovative agricultural machinery) will follow him. The villain has hired the gypsy Lee (who calls himself 'Signor Lee-Vane' in his profession as acrobat) to steal the child Little Johnny (or Jackie: the script wavers on this point), who immediately loses his name (whatever it might be) and becomes 'Boy'.[52] Lee-Vane discourses on parenthood to his companion, suggesting how easily children may mistake the bad father for the good:

> Talk about the voice o' nature, eh, Jim? Mother tells the boy to love his father and be a good boy to him – voice o' nature – Boy finds out that his father is a convict what is wanted by the police. Voice o' nature tells him – Boy never see his father, mistook me – I took the boy – told him I was his father and that his mother wished him to come along wi' me, and the boy believes it – 'Cos it's the Voice of Nature.[53]

The questions of the child's hunger and being forced to tumble on an empty stomach are frequently raised in the script. The Boy says that often he does not get enough to eat 'because I'm a bad boy – and I can't stand on my head long enough. And then I only get stick pie.'[54] When the child's real father arrives on the scene, well-established techniques for depicting innocence are brought into play, especially in the child's incomprehension of adult language, and the aching gap between the adult's meaning and the child's. In the moment of misrecognition, Little Jack shows the pathetic endurance of the good child:

> Jack: Why, you ought to be playing instead of crying.
> Boy: But I don't like playing, at least I don't like the kind of playing I have. But it's no good crying about it if I have to do it, is it?
> Jack: Why you are quite a philosopher.

Boy: No, sir; I'm not; I'm an acrobat.[55]

Lee is finally exposed before a crowd gathered to watch his little troupe perform. Pointedly, this scene is set outside a boys' school, a backdrop which evokes not only other ways of dealing with children, but also all the connections that Dickens had established between Dotheboys Hall and the Infant Phenomenon in *Nicholas Nickleby* (1839).

Lee: This here is my boy Johnny, and he's going to do a spring and jump onto my shoulder, and then turn a double somerset on the ground
Crowd: And what are you going to do with yourself?
Lee: Why, take the money!

According to the *Era*'s reviewer, 'a thrill of horror' moved the Birmingham first-night audience watching Lee-Vane beating the boy 'with a brutal ferocity as a preliminary to its difficult performance'.[56] The trick fails, and the child falls exhausted to the ground. At this moment his true father Jack enters, and rescues the boy from violence. Lee asks what right he has to interfere between father and son, and Jack responds that his right is that of every man 'to protect a helpless child from a coward and a brute'.[57]

The *Era* reviewer watched the Birmingham audience at this moment quite as carefully as he watched the performance. The whole thing was a bit derivative, he thought; the material had been used before, in Sims's own 'Jack in the Box' and in that most famous of nineteenth-century melodramas, 'Harbour Lights'.[58] But the use of stale material and worn-out convention did not signify; this audience (who numbered 'Aeschylus not among them') loved it. The thrill of horror that moved it in the beating scene, the palpable release of tension when the child's true father came to the rescue were where the true interest of the performance lay, though there was no speculation as to why this was so. We can speculate, however, on an aesthetic that had been shaped by the spectacle of cruelty to children, a cruelty in which bodily exploitation and distortion were closely tied to questions about the parental role.

These questions had certainly been dramatically enacted in the 'Maiden Tribute' scandal of four years before; it is important to remember that Sims's 'Jack in the Box' made its provincial tour during the months when the campaign orchestrated by the *Pall Mall Gazette* against an 'Old Corruption' that bought and abused the daughters of the poor was at its height. 'Jack in the Box' continued to play to audiences who had the opportunity not only of reading an account of the child bought by W.T. Stead and whose story was sensationally told throughout July in the columns of the *Pall Mall Gazette* (the Eliza Armstrong case came to trial in

October 1885), but perhaps too of making connections between the pathetic and exploited child acrobat longing for his mother and his home, and the London 'Mother Seeking a Lost Child'.[59] Judith Walkowitz has described how in the aftermath of the 'Maiden Tribute' scandal the reporting of sex crimes by the *Pall Mall Gazette* increased dramatically.[60] There was a concomitant decrease in the stories of child exploitation that had been the prolegomenon to the Eliza Armstrong case. Between the end of March and the publication of the 'Maiden Tribute' series in July, the *Gazette* published eight pieces on the training of children for acrobatic and contortionist performance in the circus. Prompted by a reader's letter of 28 March, journalists were dispatched around the country to investigate alleged cruelty to 'the young gentleman in pink tights and spangles . . . his sallow cheeks smeared with rouge'. These children could most conveniently be evoked as 'Master Alfonso . . . [and] Miss Ella'.[61]

The aesthetic response that looked for the pallor beneath the rouge, the traces of violence on the child's body, and that wondered 'what becomes of the elves and fairies . . . when the performance is over', was not a new development of the 1880s.[62] Conceptualisation of cruelty to children was a development of these years, but the means of seeing and writing about the physical abuse and distortion of children's bodies had been available from investigations into children's work undertaken from the 1830s onwards. The chimney sweep and the acrobat bore the marks of adult intervention in a strikingly visual manner. The little acrobat had the aesthetic advantage over the sweep of being pleasing in appearance, and bearing witness to the most elaborate system of adult intervention. The child acrobat thus raised questions about the nature of child development and of childhood itself; it was those questions that provoked the thrill of horror in the audience for 'Master and Man'. As an aesthetic it was disconnected from the *fin-de-siècle* appreciation of the adult *funambule*. Le Roux and Garnier celebrated the sight of the acrobat's 'youthful form flying through the friezes' as 'a delight to those pagans who appreciate pure curved lines', but it was a young woman who offered 'a subject for meditation to . . . philosophers'. What they saw in that moment was the impossible, lustrous movement or configuration that made no reference at all to the preparation, training, tears and pain involved in its beautiful impossibility. 'The little acrobat unconsciously gives a symbolic lesson', for when

> she has exhausted in an ascending scale of difficulties all the most unexpected combinations of equilibrist art, upright upon her globe, supported by the trapeze only, she pauses, and upon this vantage point of unsurpassable perfection, feeling sure that *nothing more is possible*, she smiles, sends a kiss from the tip of her fingers to her admirers, then abruptly, as though struck by lightning, she falls into the net.[63]

The child could not inscribe the course of Thanatos like this, for the child brought with it the story of its progress to that point; what its audience noted were its 'fearful panting', its painful concentration of effort, the strangeness of its postures, the heart-wrenching seriousness of its efforts to please, and all the slips it made. The child as acrobat could not conceal its art, and was a highly resonant figure for the idea of childhood shaped and forced by adult hand. The strange dislocations were not simply those of the child's body but of the adult imagination too, in the uneasy understanding that what was being watched was not quite separate from the watcher.

All of Pierre Loti's *Le Roman d'un enfant* (1890) is the expression for 'la bonne histoire' of childhood's 'vanished years and long dead summers', and has been treated as such in discussions of the literature of childhood in the century since it was written.[64] But the piercing recognition comes – comes only – when a circus manager makes Loti see how his 'muscles . . . acted like steel springs'; see what could have been, if only . . . and then utters the truest words the author has 'ever heard spoken': '"What a pity, Monsieur that your training began so late"!'[65] The acrobat is always an expression of regret for one's lost native land.

7

Children of the Street

The trade of acrobat existed for a small number of children in mid-Victorian Britain, one minor category of work among the myriad available to them.[1] As a trade, contemporaries categorised it in three ways. First there were the children of the profession, in all its subdivisions of status, who were trained in a family craft. Second (and this category of child will be dealt with in more detail in the next chapter) were those trained to perform on a seasonal basis, mainly for the pantomime market that developed from the 1870s onwards. Third were children attached to street performers and entertainers, whose natural propensity to tumble and play were marshalled into something that could be called performance – somersaults and dances – and who carried round a cap for payment afterwards. Italian children, whose presence on British streets was much commented upon in the 1870s, belonged to this last category. Though their main reputation on both sides of the Atlantic was as street musicians – as 'little slaves of the harp'[2] – in Britain at least they were also seen as belonging to the category of acrobat, contortionist, and tight- and slack-rope walker. The last chapter described how the campaign designed to expose and eradicate the cruelty involved in an acrobatic training became elided with various attempts to eradicate the *padrone* system, in the 1870s and 1880s. Campaigning literature and melodrama used the composite figure of the exploited and abused *Italian* child acrobat; in a most striking way Scott's 'Master and Man' gave the guise of an Italian to a gypsy, before he practised cruelty on the body of the little boy he had stolen.

Observing the elision of the gypsy and the Italian in the *padrone*, of the abused child and the acrobat in the little street entertainers he had charge of, and the story told in campaigning work like that of Sims and Scott, it is very difficult not to see Mignon born again, in a specifically British context. It was Thomas's opera *Mignon* (1866) that turned the original Mignon's *Seiltänzer* into a gypsy and provided campaigning melodrama and literature with its specific story content. However, that was not a primary contemporary understanding. Italian street entertainers, like all children taken or sent on to the streets to earn a living, were first of all a police problem. The little Italian 'slaves of the harp' were a nuisance, in the specific meaning of the term established under English by-law and local Act. There were several attempts to reduce the noise pollution they produced: in 1864 when the powers of the Metropolitan police to 'move on' street performers were extended, and after 1882, under the Police and Sanitary Regulations of that year.[3] In England, the Vagrancy Act of 1824 had conferred a statutory and universal power on all policemen in their surveillance of the streets and highways. As one of the most consistently used pieces of legislation of the nineteenth century, it made the connection between homelessness (or the appearance of homelessness) and criminality particularly easy to make.[4]

These children posed a severe problem of vagrancy and mendicity. As John Zucchi has pointed out, street performers, including children who danced and sang and then asked for money, proved a difficult case for legislators, police, charity workers and child rescuers, for whilst they were not technically beggars, their occupation was useless; they asked for money from onlookers in exchange for their performance, but they did not have a scale of charges, as they would if selling in the street or hawking. What they did resembled begging, but blurred the line between mendicity and labour.[5]

The 'street child', a new category of child, who emerged to be written about and legislated for from the 1830s onwards, was a third way of classifying and understanding the problem that little Italian musicians represented – though as Hugh Cunningham has pointed out, it was an understanding largely confined to the metropolis. The street child, as he or she was contemporaneously described, was not attached to an adult but ran wildly and independently through the thoroughfare that has 'always had a connotation of freedom, even licence'.[6] Hugh Cunningham has isolated three 'overlapping discourses' concerning street children in the period from 1840 to 1870. There were first of all religious attempts to rescue such children and restore them to order through voluntary efforts like the Ragged Schools. Second were far more 'professional' attempts to deal with the problem of juvenile delinquency; and finally Cunningham discusses those who watched, wrote about and represented such children to various audiences. Whilst earlier accounts of 'street children' and 'street arabs' had been apocalyptic in tone, with the wild child of the urban poor representing a serious threat of civil disorder, Cunningham notes an increasing tendency to treat them as humorous, quaint pieces of street furniture or street theatre – 'an accepted part of the social scene, and a part not without a picturesque appeal'. Cunningham also suggests that the street child who attracted attention was almost always a boy, and that a tolerant appreciation of the working-class 'card' of a child celebrated qualities of brashness and cheekiness deemed inappropriate in girls.[7] This differentiation is partly to do with terminology; with a definition of the street child as the street arab, who was certainly written and depicted as a boy. But when the whole contemporary category of street children is taken into account, and children who traded on the streets and earned money there in other ways are considered along with those who appeared to run wild, then girls appear much more frequently. Even so, it was probably the case that girls were depicted out of proportion to their numbers, in something of the way that Cunningham's own evidence belies his assertion of the preponderance of boys over girls. His most sustained contemplation of a street child is of a little girl – the much watched (and about to be watched again) street trader in watercresses interviewed by Henry Mayhew in the winter of 1850. It is arguable that in representational terms – in the massive transmission of information about the lives and sentiments of poor children that melodrama and various forms of slush fiction effected in the mid-century – girls were more often depicted than boys.

Indeed, Cunningham pays very close attention to the type of reclaiming child of fiction for children typified in Hesba Stretton's *Jessica's Last Prayer*, and the importance Stretton gave to her child-heroine's physical appearance, the state of her dress and hair, as well as to her state of mind.[8] In her analysis of this genre of fiction Claudia Nelson has made it very clear that, textually at least, the child redeemer was feminine, whether he or she appeared as a boy or girl in the text.[9] Moreover, the bestowal of qualities through the act of watching is an activity that cuts both ways. The pathos that frames the quite considerable literature on the little girl of the mid-Victorian street also came to be attached to boy children. Describing the processes by which a society comes to represent and envisage groups within it (in this case the criminal, in all his or her manifestations), Martin Wiener has noted how 'whereas Mayhew's street children had appeared to overflow with vigor, however misdirected, late-Victorian street children . . . seemed more pathetic than dangerous, but just as problematic'.[10] The Italian street entertainer is an acute example of this transference of qualities, for he was nearly always presented as feminised by the cruelty done him, as well as by his littleness, grace and physical beauty. If James Kincaid is right, and the sustained child-watching that Western culture has indulged in over the last two hundred years has rendered the sex of the child irrelevant in the watcher's pursuit of remoteness, beauty and androgyny, then the fictional and dramatic depiction of the poor children of British urban conurbations is certainly a case in point.[11] Goethe's portrayal of Mignon was concerned with aloofness and androgyny; and what we are about to examine – which is the bestowal of Mignon's graces on one dirty and disturbingly unattractive street child of the 1850s – can only testify to the power that lies in the looking.

To some extent, the children that Mayhew (and other commentators) watched and reported on were seen through the conventions of melodrama, specifically in the meaning urban melodrama gave to children before the 1880s, as heightened embodiments of the suffering of the adults connected with them.[12] In order to explore these relationships between melodrama, the means of representing working-class childhood, their history and the history of legislation concerning them, we need also to explore the relationship between the street and the stage, as the places where the child was most consistently watched. This chapter, then, begins an exploration that will be continued in the next.

'Street children', in all their contemporary divisions and subdivisions, were deeply unattractive, very poor children, who were consistently represented as such. The greater burden of distaste fell on the girls, to be sure, probably because they wore the length of 'foul matted hair, which looks as if it would defy sponge, comb or brush to purify it' – though 'the broken and filthy boots and stockings which they seem never to button or to garter' belonged to both sexes.[13] William Locke, Honorary Secretary of the Ragged School Union, said in 1861 that candidates for his kind of school could always be told 'from seeing them in the streets, from their peculiar habits, their filthy appearance, their uncombed hair and their manners which are peculiar';[14] and in one of the many fictional rewritings of Mayhew's street children that will be discussed below, a girl-child is described as looking 'elfish and wild,/With nought but the size, that bespoke it a child'.[15]

In 1851 Henry Mayhew reckoned that there were about 10,000 children earning a living on the streets of the metropolis, most of them selling things:

> money-bags, lucifer match-boxes, leather straps, belts, firewood . . . fly-papers, a variety of fruits, especially nuts, oranges and apples; onions, radishes, water-cresses, cut flowers and lavender (mostly sold by girls), sweet-briar, India rubber, garters and other little articles of the same material, including elastic rings to encircle rolls of paper-music, toys of the smaller kinds, cakes, steel pens and penholders with glass handles, exhibition medals and cards, gelatine cards, glass and other cheap seals, brass watch-guards, chains and rings; small tin ware, nutmeg-graters and other articles of a similar description such as are easily portable; iron skewers, fuzees, shirt buttons, boot and stay-laces, pins (and more rarely, needles), cotton bobbins, Christmassing (holly and other evergreens at Christmas-tide), May-flowers, coat-studs, toy-pottery, blackberries, groundsel and chick-weed, and clothes pegs.[16]

Here, the press of child activity is made an analogue of the highly visible swarms of children that appear in written and pictorial representation from the mid-century. Dickens's observation of scavenging children, hopping about 'like wild birds, pilfering the crumbs which fell from the table of the country's wealth', is repeated again and again by modern historians, in a manner reminiscent of the Victorian reiteration of Lord Shaftesbury's perception of 1850, of street folk as 'bold, and pert, and dirty as London sparrows, but pale, feeble and sadly inferior to them in plumpness of outline'.[17] These were children whose activities lay outside the structure of regulatory legislation that by the 1850s had restricted juvenile employment in the textile trades and mining.[18] The great parliamentary surveys of the 1860s that investigated the labour of children not already protected by law prompted later legislation covering the work of all children employed in factories and workshops. In urban places, street trading could be regulated under local Act of Parliament, and by bylaw; the Municipal Corporations Act of 1882 offered easy provision for this kind of regulation of children working in the streets. Many of the street traders that Mayhew talked to were also very well aware of the Vagrancy Act and its provisions against mendicity.

Definitions of juvenile delinquency widened in the mid-century. The Industrial School system developed, and an enactment of 1866 extended eligibility for commitment to industrial schooling to include the state of being orphaned, to children of a surviving parent who was undergoing penal servitude or imprisonment, and to refractory children in general. In fact, since 1857 magistrates and Boards of Guardians had been able to send vagrant, but non-criminal, children aged 7 to 14 to industrial schools, for the purposes of moral and vocational training. This legislation 'multiplied committals to industrial schools, dramatically expanding state control over children of the criminal classes'.[19]

These tightenings of the legal net around children working as street traders are important. But we should acknowledge, along with contemporary observers, that educational legislation from the late 1870s onwards had a more profound effect on the regulation of child labour. One witness before the Royal Commission on the Working of the Elementary Education Acts (1886) suggested that they had as their fundamental intention an extension of the provisions of the Factory Acts to all children.[20] G.R. Sims, whose theatrical writing of the 1880s featured varieties of melodramatic children, observed the great changes in childhood that had been brought about by the Education Acts. His *How the Poor Live* (1883) and *How the Poor Live and Horrible London* (1889) bear striking witness to the effect of educational legislation in changing the appearance of working-class children: the foul and matted hair combed neat, clothing become tidy – the motley abandoned, pinafores on, boots buttoned and hands and faces clean – under the new requirements of the school.[21] What should capture our attention here is not so much an actual change in demeanour, deportment and dress (these were real enough, though after 1877 rather than 1870) but a change in the aesthetic of childhood that Sims bears witness to, and newly evolved ways of looking at children and responding to them, as the street disappeared as the common background to their performance.

Surveying a century of child labour from the vantage point of 1914,

Frederic Keeling understood the Prevention of Cruelty to Children Acts of 1889 and 1894 as the apogee of a half-century of attempts to deal with street trading.[22] Certainly the London Society for the Prevention of Cruelty to Children promulgated the view that 'street trading by children was one of the most fruitful sources of suffering and demoralisation';[23] and in his socio-fiction its founder Benjamin Waugh consistently located scenes of cruelty to children in the families of street traders and beggars.[24] The House of Commons, debating the Cruelty to Children Prevention Bill in Committee in June 1889, heard that 'Nothing is more common in vagrancy that [*sic*] the taking of children into the streets for the purposes of singing, taking part in performance, or selling some small article, but this being merely a cover for begging . . . [the children being] cruelly beaten if they do not bring home a certain amount of money.'[25] In fact, the effect of the large-scale reorganisation of the law regarding children that took place in the late 1880s and early 1890s was to make a much closer connection between children on the street and vagrancy in general. At the end of the century children became part of the perishing and dangerous classes.

In December 1850 Henry Mayhew had visited the green markets of London as part of his *Morning Chronicle* series on 'Labour and the Poor'. 'Farringdon,' he reported, 'is the great watercress mart'; and he particularly noticed the 'poor shivering, half-clad boys and girls surrounding the dealers' stands'.[26] It was here and during this month that we may assume he met the Little Watercress Girl (though it is possible that the interview took place a month or so later, in January 1851).[27] This eight-year-old told Mayhew of her life at home with her mother (a former worker in the fur trade, though now a charwoman), her brother and two sisters, and her mother's common-law husband, a scissor-grinder by trade. This is the man whom the child insists is a 'father-in-law' rather than a stepfather: '"No; mother ain't married again – he's a father-in-law."' In Mayhew's transcription of her words, she starts by denying her status as a child: '"I ain't a child, and I shan't be a woman till I'm twenty, but I'm past eight, I am"', and her apparent self-definition is entirely as a worker. Mayhew recorded what she told him of her street trading in cresses (the system of trading is described in great detail; this after all was Mayhew's purpose in interviewing workers in the green marts), and her Saturday job as helper to a Jewish couple on their Sabbath, as baby-minder and cleaner, but the later part of the transcript tells in some detail of toys and games; the child also had much to say about family relationships and affections.

Of all Mayhew's street children, the Little Watercress Girl captured the imagination in a way that no other did. She captured Mayhew's first of course, partly because of her inexplicableness, and the transcript of her narrative is much longer than that of any other child he interviewed. In May 1851, when he came to some conclusions about the children he had talked to, he made clear distinctions between boy and girl street traders. 'The female child,' he said, 'can do little but *sell* (when a livelihood is to be gained without resource to immorality); a boy can not only sell, but *work*.'[28] This child, however, *did* work, and had told Mayhew not only about her labour at the watercress mart preparatory to street selling, and about her Saturday job, but also about long periods as a child-minder and helper to her mother, when she still worked as a skin-dresser. Perhaps it was the narrative of labour, so precisely delineated, that made her particularly noticeable to Mayhew.

In all of Mayhew's discussions with female children there hovers the idea of a more common reason for gentlemen stopping little girls on crowded pavements than investigation into their work and home circumstances. Mayhew sometimes asked the little girl street traders he interviewed about the problem of being stopped and importuned by strange men, though more often reported that he himself had been followed by them, 'most perseveringly'.[29] He was well aware of a common prejudice against 'girls selling watercress and so on; we know that in many cases that is an excuse for begging'[30] – and for other sorts of selling.

By the end of January 1851, Mayhew was issuing his newspaper articles in pamphlet form, bound with his 'Answers to Correspondents', and in the middle of February a lady sent a sovereign to him, writing that 'should a Young Flower Girl, or the little Cress girl mentioned . . . be still in distress her own sympathies go first with the *young* in sorrow'. The seller of watercress was the only child to whom Mayhew's correspondents responded in this way, although many of his adult interviewees received considerable doles.

It has been suggested that Mayhew dramatised his own work for the London stage under the title 'How We Live in the World of London', though if such a play was ever performed, it has proved impossible to trace.[31] A melodrama entitled 'How We Live or London Labour and London Poor' was certainly staged at the Surrey Theatre in March 1856, but is ascribed to J.B. Johnstone.[32] There was an even earlier version than this, produced at the Royal Pavilion in March 1854, and entitled 'London Labour & London Poor, or Want and Vice'. This two-act melodrama written by James Elphinstone concerns a son of the gentry, disinherited for marrying a milliner and fallen on hard times. Once his good-hearted brother comes into the inheritance, he searches for him and his little family through the streets, dens and lodging-houses of Farringdon, failing to find either the father or the destitute and abandoned mother and children, or to prevent the parish officers removing the dead baby in its coffin from a 'Pauper Lodging House' in Clerkenwell. The drama includes a full cast of London street folk, beggars, thieves, down-and-outs and ambulant musicians, but there are no street children among them, and the only children in the cast, the lost brother's little son and daughter

(Boy and Mary), exist solely to highlight the awful misery of the adults around them.[33]

Two years later, those playgoers who had 'grown tired of the ordinary quiet phases of amusement' and who really wanted to know what a sensation was, could go over to the Surrey, and see 'How We Live in the World of London', which, to be sure, offered 'nothing very striking from the literary point of view, for the best of the language is a mere transcript from the "Labour and the Poor" of Henry Mayhew'. What would promote tears, however, was its verisimilitude and its 'vivid pictures of those familiar episodes of street life, truthfully rendered'.[34]

> The gentleman who does the adaptations and general hack literature for the Surrey, has . . . succeeded in weaving into a tolerably connected tale many of the facts with which Mr Mayhew makes us familiar . . . the chief merit of the play consists in the dioramic truthfulness of the scenes . . . a faithful daguerreotype of low life in London . . . it is the *vraisemblance* of the portraiture which constitutes its excellence.[35]

This version of 1856 does number child street traders among the cast, though the watercress seller of 'How We Live' bears little resemblance to Mayhew's complicated child, and makes her entrance with an utterly familiar and bucolic 'street cry of old London', and in order to punctuate a conventional debate of urban melodrama, on the virtues and disadvantages of town and country life.[36] She is called 'Betty Clearbrook', and a gentleman called Arthur stops her – as gentlemen must – saying

> There – there's a cry without tears – a London melody, a tune that ever dwells on the ears when the Bell has rung – a strong reminder of white tablecloths and wet doorsteps here my beauty of the running brook, here's 2d for six bundles.[37]

(The child Mayhew talked to had told him prosaically that 'I go about the streets with watercresses, crying "Four bunches a penny, watercresses".') The point of the stage exchange is that Arthur has overpaid Betty Clearbrook, indeed does not want the cresses at all, and is making a dole in a way designed to acknowledge that its recipient was not begging.[38] The social realism in the discourse on Betty Clearbrook sits uneasily with the pastoral figure she actually presents to the audience. 'Ah poor little thing,' cries Arthur

> hers is a hard lot, she might walk a long distance before she'd clear as much as the trifle I have given her. Cold – heat – wet or dry, her little feet must walk her weary round, day break sees her up & on her

> way to market & then from street to street until her little stock is sold & then wet & weary to her unhealthy cellar dwelling to eat her humble crust in dirt and darkness.[39]

In fact, the Little Lucifer Girl and 'Fanny George' the Wallflower Seller are much closer readings of Mayhew's interviews in *London Labour and the London Poor*, showing the 'generalised suffering enacted by children in [early] urban melodramas'.[40] In this second stage version of Mayhew's investigations the visual and other figurative associations of the watercress seller brought social realism to a border with the pastoral that it could not breach. But 'Betty Clearbrook' is sexualised in a way that the match, wallflower and beggar girls who throng the stage are not, and she sells something that Mayhew himself alluded to in his general observation 'Of the Children Street Sellers of London', that is, her response. When she is given twopence for six bundles Arthur's companion Charles remarks that money has been well spent on such a smile of gratitude. Mayhew sometimes made reference to the pleasures of making a little girl smile.[41]

William Travers's two-act melodrama *The Watercress Girl* stunned audiences at the City of London Theatre in October 1865, with its astonishing depiction of Covent Garden Market on the stage. Here the watercress seller is called Alice Green, and she performs an act of rescue for another child, her friend Dick, who is softened and civilised by the reading lessons Alice gives him, and her recounting of what she has learned in Sunday School.[42] The child Alice is victim both of a social evil and of melodramatic convention. Her father believes her to be dead, having paid Mrs Blane, a notorious baby-farmer, to do away with her at birth so that he might incarcerate her mother and lay hands on her fortune. The secret of Alice's past is revealed as early as Act I, scene 2, for here we learn that as 'this little watercress Girl is John Leicester's child and not dead after all' her father will need to make another attempt on her life. Mrs Blane the baby-farmer elaborates, debating familiar points about good and bad parenting.

> Well, yer see. I knowed as how Mr Leicester wanted the child out of the way and I thought he'd give an ansome sum if he knowed she was dead, so I goes to him a month arter I'd took the child, so I puts it to him straightforward – he says to me Miss Blane, let me that child in her coffin and there's a 100 for yer. all right says I. you shall see her, an away I goes. well I'd got a poor sickly brat a nussing as I know'd us die in a day or two which it did and I brings Mr Leicester to my lodins [lodgings] and shows him the young un, he thinks it vos own says I'm a trump and down's with his 100 and away he goes. O' course I'd got a valiable secret in my hands . . .[43]

'The plot, though garnished with the usual number of exciting incidents demanded by the public hereabouts, is clear and simple enough to satisfy the most homely playgoer,' thought one reviewer, for 'the abduction of an infant child, and her subsequent persecutions, are good themes for sensational stories in cheap periodicals or sensational dramas in minor Theatres'.[44] John Leicester finally confesses his crimes in a dramatic scene at Swallow Falls in Wales where, under attack by gypsies, he names himself 'the husband of this lady and the father of this child – a guilty lost wretch – none have more deeply wronged wife and child than I'. He perishes in the Falls, as a great storm arises. As the gypsies chorus 'Ah, the waters', all fall to their death except Alice the putative watercress girl and her mother; the waters cover the entire stage. With this tableau – 'the visual summary of the emotional situation' of melodrama – the play ends.[45] The water that obliterates the past and removes the wicked (though finally repentant) father is the only attenuated connection with the icy water of the Farringdon Market pump where actual watercress sellers washed their wares. Indeed, watercress selling is chosen as this child's fate only in order to show the extraordinary and unspeakable dangers of the street to which her father's cruelty has abandoned her.

The mid-century saw efforts to establish missions and rescue systems for girls selling flowers and watercress on London streets. Two such rescue operations were the Emily Loan Fund, which Lord Shaftesbury supported, and John Groom's Watercress and Flower Girls' Mission.[46] The connection between flower and cress selling and prostitution was very easily made – a case in Travers's 'Watercress Girl' not of melodrama uttering the unspeakable, but of melodrama gesturing towards quite ordinary horrors of the streets using quite conventionalised figures.[47]

The Little Watercress Girl – the original one: Mayhew's child – had in fact made a much earlier fictional appearance than this one effected by Travers in 1865; earlier even than Johnstone's depiction of 1856. In Sarah Maria Fry's *The Little Watercress Sellers* (1854), a fictionalised version of Mayhew's interview, the child is named Hetty, and is given a brother called Jack. There is a mother, but no father (and certainly no 'father-in-law'); not a dead father, not a father 'gone away', but simply, none. The complicated esteem and affection in which Mayhew's child had held her mother – 'I always gives mother my money, she's so very good to me. She doesn't often beat me; but when she does, she don't play with me' – is translated into an account of horrifyingly bad mothering. Hetty tells the kind lady who befriends her and her brother that '"we have a mother sometimes, but not very often . . . she often goes away for a long, long time, and then comes back just for a little while; but we're always sorry then, for she beats us, and takes our money away, and spends it on herself; we don't like her at all."'[48]

Like Mayhew's child, these two live in a 'narrow court'[49] and the details Fry presents, of Jack and Hetty's day, follow quite closely those that Mayhew learned from the child he spoke to (though this information could easily have been elicited from any child selling cress in the streets, or one hailed from the basement steps just 'when the Bell has rung' for tea and the white tablecloth laid). 'Every morning,' reported Fry

> they had to rise very early indeed, and go to market to buy their watercresses to sell again . . . They used to buy a large bundle, and then sit down in some place where they would not be disturbed, and divide it into a great many little bunches, some to sell for a half-penny, and some for a penny.[50]

Mayhew's observation of a 'little face, pale and wrinkled with privation . . . wrinkled where the dimples ought to have been', is echoed in Fry's description of Harriet's 'thin, old look, which ill suited her childish age and figure'.[51]

The charitable endeavours that ease the lot of these two fictional children have their most dramatic effect on Hetty's appearance; her author notes at the end of her tale, and after Jesus has spoken successfully to the children's better nature, that

> their little watercress trade was much better than it used to be, for many persons who had not fancied water-cresses from the basket of a ragged, slovenly little girl, or disliked the bold, harsh tones of a dirty-looking boy, gladly purchased a bright green bunch from the tidy maid that Hetty had now become.[52]

Mary Sewell's ballad *Our Father's Care*, issued as a Household Tract for the People in 1861, is a much more interesting recasting of Mayhew's child. In the 1880s it was claimed that over a quarter of a century's popularity it had 'familiarised most persons with the early toil and hard education for the . . . calling'.[53] It can be seen, then, as part of that massive transmission of information about child destitution that even by the mid-century made the details of childhood in poverty well known.[54] The reader of Sewell's ballad was assured that 'the age, occupation, and early maturity of Little Nelly, are sketched from life', though many details match those that Mayhew's child imparted. Not only is this fictional child named 'Nelly', but in one moment of heart-wrenching determination she acquires a type-name as well, and becomes 'Nelly Hardy'.

This child has a mother brought to bed, a father in hospital, and is the stay and prop of her little family:

> Says I, 'Father, cheer up, and don't be afraid
> For you may depend on your own little maid';
> So now, I'll be going to Farringdon Street,
> That we may have fire, and something to eat.[55]

It is five o'clock on a wintry morn when Nelly lets herself out and slips into 'the shuddering, wrestling, struggle of life/The pitiless crush, and the perilous strife' of London, clad in the same kind of ragged motley worn by all the poor girl-children to whom Mayhew spoke. Mayhew had recorded that the eight-year-old he spoke to 'had entirely lost all childish ways, and was indeed, in thoughts and manner, a woman'; and Mary Sewell noted that in Nelly's case 'nought but the size . . . bespoke it a child;/And quaint were her speeches and womanly wise'. Mayhew's child spoke of her own precocious maturity at some length, and in Sewell's ballad this becomes a refrain, as Nelly Hardy says again and again 'with a shake of her little rough head, – /"But I am the woman that works for their bread".'[56] The 'calm earnestness' with which Mayhew's child talked of 'the bitterest struggles of life' is called courage by Sewell, and she has a most piercing description of the cold and exposure that Mayhew noted in Farringdon watercress mart, and that his eight-year-old told him about ('I never see any children crying – it's no use'):

> But see – pushing through the confusion and din,
> That mite of a child is now hurrying in:
> She elbows her way on to look at the cress,
> And chooses her lot, be it many or less.
> She stops not to question what others may do
> If they purchase many, or only a few.
> She carefully reckons her number of pence,
> And that is the measure for Nelly's expense.
> There's none to advise her, there's no one to feel,
> 'Tis each for himself, and 'tis all for a meal.
> She pays for her bundle and hurries along,
> And pushes her way through the jostling throng;
> Then squats on her heels in the slippery street,
> To pick the cress over, and tie it up neat.
> Then off to the pump she courageously goes –
> Ah me! for those poor little half-frozen toes;
> And splashes below, on the stones of the street –
> A sob and a shudder, that nobody heard,
> A quiver of anguish, but never a word.
> She dashes away a poor trickling tear,
> ''Tis childish to cry, although nobody's near'.[57]

It misses the serious purpose of this ballad not to understand Nelly Hardy as the type of child-rescuer, or child-redeemer, who is able to comfort her father on his deathbed by telling the story of Elijah fed by the ravens and about the clothing of righteousness that will be given to 'poor humble people . . . glad of this dress,/I think mother called it "Christ's righteousness".'[58]

The man may die content because through her considerably long and (almost) perfectly recalled biblical narratives, his daughter can assure him that

> I dare say we'll do, as we have done before,
> Mother says there's no end of the heavenly store.
> She bid me tell you some words that God said,
> I don't think I've got them exact in my head . . .
> 'Thy fatherless children' – yes, that is the word –
> 'I will certainly keep them alive,' saith the Lord;
> And then, says the promise as plain as can be
> 'And let the poor widow depend upon me –
> And so you may leave us contentedly here,
> If God will preserve us, we've nothing to fear'.

It is the child's solemn illustration of the text '"Therefore take no thought, saying, What shall we eat? or what shall we drink? or wherewithal shall we be clothed? – for your Heavenly father knoweth that ye have need of all these things"' that allows her earthly father to die 'with light on his brow', as the verse slips from its firm, hurrying dactyls to a calm knell:

> And the soul had fled
> From the silent dead,
> And free as the lark,
> And above the dark,
> And above the cloud
> And the toiling crowd,
> Had entered the rest
> Of the good and blest;
> But the hand that was grasped,
> And so firmly clasped,
> Now helpless and cold,
> Had relaxed its hold
> And the orphan child
> Was left in the wild.[59]

(Who is able to avoid the Little Girl Lost, the child left 'among tigers wild', when writing of childhood destitution?)[60]

The child's heavenly Father is represented on earth by the charity of a working man – she tells this to her earthly father on his hospital bed – who accidentally pushes against her in the pouring rain and then takes her home with him:

> '. . . if you come with me

My missis will give you a cup of hot tea,
And maybe, she'll find you a bit of dry clothes,
Or old pair of shoes just to cover your toes;
I've three little girls not much bigger than you,
Amongst them they'll find up a trifle or two.'[61]

In a quite determined break from a source in Mayhew's transcript, which shows his child utterly clear that she is not an object of care or compassion – '"No; people never pities me in the street"' – this fictional child becomes an object of pity and philanthropy. When she has battled her way to Farringdon through a winter storm, 'the saleswomen fell pitying me',[62] and, in by far the most interesting encounter she has with charitable men, she is used to achieve a transfiguration of the social relations noted by the real child out of whom she was created.

The child Mayhew interviewed was quite certain that no one had ever cast her a pitying glance, '"excepting one gentleman, and he says, says he 'What do you do out so soon in the morning?' but he give me nothink – he only walked away".' Fry's child by way of contrast, does not know that a gentleman sitting in his window seat, his Evangelical conscience racked by the luxury he lives in, has determined to succour and uplift the widowed and the orphaned by way of thanking God for the material mercies bestowed upon him. Suddenly, there falls upon his ear the cry of the watercress girl, and he finds in her appearance on the other side of the glass '"A lamb of the fold, who is looking for thee".' He taps on the window pane, attracts Nelly's attention, and then goes to the door himself, carrying a handful of bread from his breakfast table. She tells him of the troubles at home; he tells her to call the next day, 'And gave her a sixpence on going away'.[63]

On his meagre charity, the little fatherless family comes finally to depend; the gentleman is the true agent of 'Our Father's Care', for he seeks out Nelly's lodging house, 'And he became their comforter,/He wiped away their tears/He softened all their poverty,/Through many coming years.'[64] Hugh Cunningham elides Evangelical efforts to succour abandoned children with later understandings of the street child as savage, in need of civilising.[65] However, the belief of many of those who took part in early efforts to reclaim lost childhood, was that they were making such children aware of their existence and worth in the eyes of God, and Mary Sewell's charitable gentleman is a very powerful writing of this belief. His actions stand in marked contrast to those of the gentleman the actual Farringdon child remembered, though what apotheosis of Mignon's desire his giving the child something actually represents must await later discussion.

Mid-Victorian society was a society of the young: between 1800 and 1900 children under 15 consistently represented between 30 and 40 per cent of the population.[66] In societies like this, children are usually highly visible on the streets. Children, moving at a different pace from adults, drawing the eye down from the line of sight established by the adults moving there, children – running, playing, crouched in the gutter, dancing, begging, importuning – are noticeable. The street makes them objects for the eye, in a way that other settings outside the theatre do not.[67] When the street is empty, it becomes a backdrop for the child's lonely necessity; Nelly Hardy, like the policeman who does *not* stop her, and who does *not* speak to her, is there as a stark representative of much larger dramas of law, and labour, and necessity, being enacted in a great city:

> None speak to Nelly, and she speaks to none,
> Through all the great City, she's passing alone.
> The morning patrol, on his earliest beat,
> Sees fluttering garments and hurrying feet;
> And lets her pass by, with a half-dreamy eye,
> Nor asks her a question, nor seeks a reply.

This loneliness and isolation is not the anonymity that prompts the twittering and twitching of Dickens's cockney sparrows (and less pretty vermin, in other perceptions); loneliness and isolation are the aperture of the child's meaning, of what it is she represents. The contemporary commentators we have been observing made great efforts to know these children, to give them names, to follow them, by some means or other (even if the means are only fictional) into the fetid courts and alleys that spawned them – where they find, not malodorous horror, but a floor scrubbed 'three or four times a week' by Mayhew's child, and a 'poor upper room' – Nelly's lodging – where 'A small fire is burning, the water is hot,/The tea is put into the little teapot,/And all things are carefully set in their place'.[68] Both Fry's and Sewell's accounts open in the children's home: they are not arrested in the street as are the real and stage watercress girls. They seek, too, to know these children on the inside, and to depict a psychology. Sewell's detailed depiction of Nelly's state of mind and cognitive development is both a reading of Mayhew's interview with the Little Watercress Girl, and the repetition of a sequence of his observations, gleaned from his interviews with many children:

> Thinks she of a dolly, a book, or a ball? –
> She never had played with a dolly at all.
> Thinks she of a game, when the school hours are done –
> Of school-fellows romping, and laughing, and fun?
> She never had been in a schoolroom to learn:
> Poor Nelly has long had a living to earn –

She's thinking perhaps 'tis a hardship for her
To get up so early, and travel so far;
Whilst other girls always have plenty of food,
And she has not anything, pretty or good? –
No – trifles like these are not filling her mind,
As street after street she is leaving behind –
She's thinking about the poor baby's that come,
And mother so weak and helpless at home;
And says, with a shake of her rough little head, –
'But I am the woman that works for their bread'.

When Mayhew took down his own child's narrative, he framed it with anonymity and with her own ignorance – 'all her knowledge seemed to begin and end with watercresses and what they fetched' – but in fact took from her a detailed account of family organisation, at the economic and domestic level; an organisation that was revealed by nearly all the children he spoke to. Investigators like Mayhew could not help doing this: their very attempts to present the children as utterly strange, remote, filthy beyond belief and products of unspeakable home circumstances produced quite different evidence. The 1861 Select Committee on the Education of Destitute Children certainly heard how it was always possible to tell such children 'from seeing them in the streets'. But it also heard from an agent of the Ragged School Union who sometimes watched the children in the schools he visited eating their dinner, and who had seen some of them 'with some nice yellow slices, which have turned out to be boiled mangold wurzle, and they have said it was quite a treat', and who was thus forced to present evidence about a system of domestic organisation and planning that could keep a pot on a fire going at a rolling boil for the twenty minutes it takes to cook a slice of swede.[69]

It is when a child like this dances that the observer is able to lay bare the aetiology of pathos and to come as close as possible to consciousness of what he or she wants from watching it. Mayhew noted that many child street traders made a living as entertainers, as 'tumblers . . . ballad singers, bagpiper boys . . . street musicians (especially Italian boys with organs . . .)'. It would be neat indeed to have the Little Watercress Girl dance in her court to the music of the 'Italian boys with organs', but in fact she only mentions playing at two singing and dancing games during which she and her friend carried the little ones whilst they sang (though she was too tired to dance, she informed Mayhew).

When the poet and aesthete Arthur Symons strolled the London pavements in the 1890s, he was taking part in what John Lucás has called a kind of domestic orientalism, so that the panoply of street life – prostitutes, street musicians, vagrants, entertainers, children importuning – could thus be safely distanced into the exotic.[70] Symons compared the English city crowd most unfavourably with those of the Continent, finding it sadly wanting in visual appeal, as a mass of human beings 'to whom nature has given no grace or charm, whom life has made vulgar'.[71] As he walked the Edgware Road, he wondered 'why these people exist, why they take the trouble to go on existing'. Then as the barrel organ starts up violently, and 'one or two children hold out their skirts in their hands and begin to dance in tune', he notices the grey narrow face of the child whose thin legs are too tired to dance . . .'.[72] Some years later he has a child of these people, 'Nora;/Child, and most blithe, and wild as any elf', leap free from the crowd and from herself, and dance wildly on the pavement.

As Nora on the pavement
Dances, and she entrances the grey hour
Into the laughing circle of her power,
The magic circle of her glances,
As Nora dances on the midnight pavement;

Petulant and bewildered,
Thronging glances and longing looks recur,
And memorably re-incarnate her,
As I remember that old longing,
A footlight fancy, petulant and bewildered;

There where the ballet circles,
See her, but ah! not free her from the race
Of glittering lines that link and interlace;
This colour now, now that, may be her,
In the bright web of those harmonious circles.

But what are these dance-measures,
Leaping and joyous, keeping time alone
With life's capricious rhythm, and all her own,
Life's rhythm and hers, long sleeping,
That wakes, and knows not why, in these dance measures?

It is the very Nora . . .

Lucás is surely correct to see the tiredness still present, in the poem's enervated rhythm and the way in which, belying its subject matter, it never lets go of itself, the first and last line of each stanza mirroring and repeating each other. Its self-containment and self-referentiality express an adult desire much more than they do a child's abandonment, a desire embodied in many visions of the child dancing: *that the child be itself*, in all its 'earnestness of purpose' in order to be watched.

In Laurence Binyon's *London Visions* (1896) 'Two children, all alone and no one by' hear the organ start and 'Holding out their tattered frocks . . . dance sedately: face to face they gaze,/Their eyes shining with perfect pleasure'.[73] A good deal of knowledge was brought to bear on these observed moments of childish self-absorption and concentration; the least that the child-study movement had done was to delineate the pleasures of watching the child's wonderful self-referentiality. After the Froebelian movement taught the dances of the people to the children of the people in a variety of summer play schools towards the end of the 1890s, it is hard not to see that deliberate turning up of the child's skirt in a preliminary to dance as a taught gesture, at least in London, where play schemes were most consistently run.[74]

Lucás suggests that 'Nora' briefly allows a glimpse – against the grain of the poet's earlier perceptions of 'the people' – of altered social and aesthetic circumstances, allows the briefest vision of a possibility, 'of a life whose heritability is not entirely determined by circumstances'. The moment of Mignon dancing for Wilhelm could not possibly be repeated, across a century, and across many other historical boundaries – even if any commentator on the street child dancing, from the 1850s or the 1890s, had known that Mignon's dance once took place, in some now lost fictional realm. But the desire that Goethe wrote in that scene was reiterated, and most insistently, when the child was watched in movement, and sometimes stopped and spoken to. This happened in British conurbations from the 1830s onwards, so that a whole register of aesthetic and emotional response developed, and of course also changed, in accordance with the material circumstances from which the child emerges, and the ways available for seeing it. The desire is that the child become itself, and that by becoming itself its connection to the watching adult become plain. That desire was there, even in Mayhew's confused and disgusted attempts to see the street-seller standing before him, and in the many rewritings of her. And yet Symons's desire that the child be who she is – 'the very Nora' – involves imagining her not only in a transfigured social setting, but quite specifically on the stage, in the ballet chorus, watched and fancied from the other side of the footlights.[75] It is to the continuum between children whose existence on the street merged with entertainment, theatrical children and children represented on the stage, that our attention must now turn.

8

Children of the Stage

The deregulation of the British theatre in the mid-1840s increased employment opportunities on the stage for women and children of the working and lower-middle classes.[1] Until the Theatre Regulation Act of 1843, only licensed theatres were allowed to present entirely 'spoken theatrical activity'. In order to stay within the letter of the law, all other places of entertainment had used the strategy of interspersing music, dance, acrobat, gymnastic and other novelty turns with drama and melodrama. In the same period, music hall developed out of the entertainments provided for drinkers in pubs, taverns and halls. Here, performing dogs, families of acrobats, and little female impersonators found an audience, along with short dramas and vignettes.[2] The Theatre Act freed the theatre from monopoly, but also helped bring about the stratification of the entertainment industry, distinguishing clearly between the theatre and other premises where the sale and consumption of drink was allowed in the auditorium. There followed a rapid expansion of theatrical outlets at all levels of the market, particularly as working-class entertainment.[3]

Theatrical agents, managers and actors who gave evidence before parliamentary inquiries in the 1860s and the 1890s bore witness to the popularity of ballet, the turns and choruses of music hall, and above all, the processional and transformation scenes of pantomime, all of which called for the employment of large numbers of children, as stage props, stage furnishings, and costumed as fairies, imps and other creatures.[4] The following account, of the ways in which representations of childhood on the stage and children's presence there (not necessarily playing child parts) were seen and understood, has a context in a much commented upon increase in their theatrical employment in the mid-Victorian years. Earlier in the century, children had certainly been a stage presence, in the traditional drama and in early domestic melodrama, with parts often taken by players' own children, or children of other theatrical workers.[5] The development of the mid-Victorian years that concerns us here was an increase in seasonal work for much larger numbers of children, many of whom had no family connection with the theatre. Moreover, an increase in the number of places licensed for public entertainment and the working-up of turns (dances, displays of contortion, acrobatic and gymnastic displays) for such premises often involved children, and created a new kind of child performer, present on the stage because of an interest in its own capacities.[6] Sometimes these performances were integrated into the more 'legitimate' theatre. In the 1870s and 1880s, in the music halls and during the pantomime season, a career trajectory was mapped out for the child supernumerary, who, according to Eileen Barlee might start its life running between a Giant's legs, next get a chance as a Page in a processional chorus, then as a Lion Couchant or sent up in a balloon, graduating to the costumed parts of Frog, Black Beetle and Big Spider. At the end of this progress, there might be a one-line part for the able and bright child.[7]

When she gave evidence to the Royal Commission on the Education Acts in 1887, Millicent Fawcett estimated that there were about 1,000 London children employed as supernumeraries during the London pantomime season; and in her recent account of the employment of children in the Victorian theatre, Tracy Davis suggests that perhaps five times that number were employed across the country.[8] Many contemporary statistics were collected for the purposes of propaganda – Millicent Fawcett was speaking on behalf of the National Vigilance Association – but having taken motives for gathering and imparting them into account, what is striking is the testimony to a huge increase of children on the stage, during the 1870s and 1880s. In 1884 Eileen Barlee reckoned that the licensing of travelling theatres, circuses, and the 'low' kind of music hall that she called 'gaffs' for dancing and gymnastic exhibitions, had increased the number of girls who adopted chorus life as a permanent means of livelihood from 4,000 to 12,000 across the country.[9] Though these figures are impossible to verify from contemporary sources, a belief in the trend they indicated helped promote the campaign for regulation of the theatre and the 'rescue' of theatrical children in the late 1870s and 1880s.

The pantomime season lasted from Boxing Day until the end of April (it was shorter in the cheaper venues), and children employed during these months either worked at some other trade during the rest of the year, or (after 1876, and if they were under 13) had to gain exemption from schooling, on a full- or part-time basis. The Education Act of 1876 prohibited the employment of children between the ages of 5 and 10, and children of 10 to 13 had to demonstrate a certain level of educational attainment before they were granted exemption.[10] The get-out clause that concerned theatrical reformers was a section of the 1876 Act which permitted the employment of school-age children during school holidays and out of school hours, as long as this did not materially interfere with their education.[11] Advocates of theatrical regulation saw use of this clause as wholesale flouting of the law, and also drew attention to the complete lack of legislative attention to children under five who, ignored by the Education Acts, could be employed without any reference to this system of certification.

The employment of large numbers of children in this way, usually on a seasonal basis, reinforced an already rigid hierarchy of employment in the profession: a new marker of the classical theatre became the relatively small number of children that it employed. Eileen Barlee's sociology of theatrical employment distributed children from high to low, from those tiny numbers who appeared in 'the Drama', the Oratorio and the Opera, whose lineage was respectable and who belonged for the main part, to well-established theatrical families. Descent down the scale of probity and respectability began with the Opéra Comique, which often featured a ballet performance by a troupe of children. It was the increased use of ballet, and special effect and transformation scenes at all levels below the classical stage – in melodrama, in the music halls, travelling booths and circuses – that was thought to constitute the main danger to children.[12]

The legislative protection of 'novelty' performers – acrobats, stilt-walkers, rope-dancers, children shot from cannons, contortionists – had been effected by the Children's Dangerous Performances Act of 1879, which prohibited the employment of any child under 14 in a performance that was dangerous to life or limb, in the opinion of magistrates sitting in petty sessions.[13] Shaftesbury's exposure of the alleged cruelty of training practices and continued evasion of the law received wide publicity, but the target of protectionist campaigners shifted away from acrobat children, towards the question of theatrical children in general. But even though children employed in dangerous performances represented a tiny proportion of all children who worked in the entertainment industry, and whilst protectionists and the theatrical lobby alike agreed that their case was distinct and their protection necessary, the figure of the little acrobat bequeathed important perceptions, of naturalness and unnaturalness, forced and unforced childhood, to those watching quite a different spectacle of childhood upon the stage. The legacy of the little acrobat was much to do with a deep and pleasurable uncertainty about what was natural in its contortions, and what was the product of cruel parenting.

After the mid-1870s more mundane suspicions than those of physical cruelty and abuse were involved in watching the troupes of elves, fairies, frogs and flowers that thronged the pantomime stage: that the child inside the costume was – or ought to be – a schoolchild. Supporters of regulation worked hard to sharpen an audience's suspicions – they were among the first campaigners to condemn part-time labour for children on the grounds that it unfitted them for school work – but they also tried hard to make amateur and professional observers of children aware of children's theatrical work as labour, as an aspect of what Hugh Cunningham has called the 'story' of child labour under capitalism.[14] This was done by drawing constant attention to the relationship between the Factory Acts and more recent educational legislation in Britain, by mastering the extraordinarily complex relationship of these two bodies of legislation over the past half-century, and by aligning the employment of children in the theatre to a shameful history of child exploitation. In 1889 the House of Commons was reminded that half a century before, when Lord Shaftesbury had promoted protectionist legislation in the textile trades, he had been met with exactly similar arguments to those of the contemporary theatre lobby: 'instances were given of great factories in Lancashire conducted in the most admirable manner . . . It was also said that if not trained early they would not be fit for labour in factories. The same was said even of mines, and it was argued that if the employment of children was stopped the race of miners would come to an end.'[15] Whilst the parliamentary theatre lobby spoke movingly of the little stage-fairy and the virtues and necessity of training up Peasecod and Mustard-seed as early as possible, its opponents pointed out that it operated by the principles that had 'governed . . . legislation over the last 40 or 50 years', that is by way of the tortuous arguments, which had to be rehearsed again and again, about parents' rights in their children's labour.[16]

It was the Factory Acts (under which a system of half-time labour in the textile trades had developed from 1833 onwards) that had provided the first compulsory system of education for children in Britain, and it was to these origins that members of the Preventative and Rescue Sub-Committee of the National Vigilance Association referred when they made their most substantial campaigning point, that educational legislation from 1870 onwards seemed to have as its intention 'the extension of the provisions of the Factory Acts to all children'.[17] By making this point, the Association meant to promote the idea that the stage was an industry, not just in its liability to regulation and inspection because of its employment of children, but as part of a recent industrial history in which 'children under ten [had been] debarred, with admittedly good results from all other employments: why should they not also be debarred from theatrical employment?'[18]

The protectionist strategy was to make their audiences understand children's labour and children's schooling as inextricably bound up with each other and, indeed, both were aspects of a larger question, of what kind of social and legal subject a working-class child was. This question became particularly pressing in the last decades of the nineteenth century, in the period in which Viviana Zelizer has seen the emergence of childhood 'sacralisation'. From the sixteenth century at least, a primary function of the children of the poor had been to work, to prevent the habit of idleness and its consequences in social disorder, and to contribute to the family economy. When large-scale shifts in labour requirement and in sentiment transformed children (or the ideal of what children should be) from workers into scholars, then the phenomenon that Zelizer observes took place: having become economically useless to their family, children became emotionally priceless.[19]

The campaign against the theatrical employment of children – like the movement against the half-time system in the textile trades that gained momentum in the 1890s – can be used to make qualifications to the thesis, to point out, for instance, how very long it took for children in Britain to become absolutely useless in economic terms, and to discuss an emotional investment in children that actually derived from their economic worth.[20] What the question of theatrical children can do is to offer some further insight into the process of sacralisation, of the way in which the child on the stage, or in performance in general, brought about affective involvement and attachment quite beyond the immediate family, which is the locus of Zelizer's thesis. The artful display of childhood's artless little ways on the stage started to be called 'priceless' towards the end of the century. The word described that access of tenderness and amusement felt at the absurdity of it all – the child up there, on display and in performance and dressed as a pantomime fairy, or in its tiny little suit of adult clothes; the child up there and just being – a child.[21]

For working families in this period all their children's earnings, however small, were useful, and it is for this reason that the spirit if not the letter of educational and industrial legislation was flouted so consistently. Children worked at baby-minding, errand running, 'helping', fetching and carrying, in all the nooks and crannies of time that the Education Acts did not specify, in the hours before school and in the dinner break.[22] But the interest of the child working in the entertainment industry is that its wages were far from small: no matter what level of the theatrical hierarchy it worked at, it was a very valuable child indeed, to both its parents and to theatrical managements. Regulationists had some success in effecting an imaginative connection between stage labour and factory labour when they presented evidence about children's health, the extremes of temperatures they experienced, the effects of ill-ventilated and insanitary dressing-rooms.[23] But the most effective way to counter arguments about the romance of play-acting for slum children, and to connect stage work with industrial labour, was to discuss the wages children received. All commentators agreed that children could earn much more by pantomime employment than they could in any other way, and the theatrical lobby produced many accounts of children making significant contributions to family income.[24] On the other side of the argument, when for instance Eileen Barlee described the efforts of the Theatrical Missions to woo children from the stage, she furnished one vignette of a rescued child so evangelically powerful that its ostensible plot, of a seven-year-old stage fairy come to Jesus, was quite effaced by the starker economic story it told. Barlee recounted how the little girl

> of her own accord under her new light, not wishing to continue on the stage, both herself and her sister quitted it, and took

> employment at a blacklead factory where they each received in payment two pence half penny a gross for making the lead into paper packets, a tithe of what her stage earnings would have been, and a sum on which life could scarcely be sustained.[25]

Arguments about the benefits of the stage fairy's wage to working-class families were often accompanied by praise for the elevating and educational effects of the theatrical experience.[26] It was said that the theatre got children out of the crowded rooms that were their home and kept them off the streets, that the stage experience disciplined them, and taught them the virtues of cleanliness and good manners. Even Millicent Fawcett conceded that the stage child had to be a tended child, that 'half-starved children would not do; they must be children who are fairly well-nourished and able to stand the work' – a point that belied her claim that most pantomime children came from 'homes that are hardly worth the name'.[27] What struck other observers of theatrical children was 'the extremely gentle manners of the girls . . . their laugh and their way of talking being so much more refined than girls of that age and class usually are'.[28]

Connoisseurs of the pantomime fairy, who saw before them a bright-faced intelligent child, a child who had been taught to breathe properly and who was even now, as they watched, taking disciplined and healthy exercise, were eager to discuss children's own investment in their work, and their enjoyment of it. 'In the Drury Lane pantomime last year there was a very pretty scene in which a number of girls were dressed up to represent dolls', reminisced the Member for Stockport in 1889. 'They took a great interest in the performance. I spoke to one of them, and she told me she was seven years old, and was receiving 15s. a week'.[29] In 1914 when he surveyed a century of child labour in the United Kingdom, Frederic Keeling noted drily how often 'bright pictures' had been drawn by the theatrical lobby 'of the romance of life as a stage fairy for the slum child'.[30] Certainly theatre critics and reviewers of all productions featuring children were sensitive to any forced appearance on the part of the child, to any shadow of suspicion that a child might have been 'pinched or slapped' into performance.[31] The child's manifestation of spontaneity and enjoyment was part of what was purchased with the ticket. 'There is no prettier baby in London than La Petite Mignonne,' declared *Pearson's Magazine* in 1897. The men of Whitechapel had lost their hearts to this little girl because she could dance and perform acrobatic tricks 'without any physical effort, and without special training'.[32]

Though the appearance of effortlessness was much sought after, the debate over theatrical children actually highlighted stage training and its rigours. The argument for children's enjoyment of their work, evocation of the touching 'earnestness of purpose [they] seemed to put into their efforts', was on a continuum with the cruelty that was supposed to be involved in their training, at least as far as the reformist lobby was concerned, though detailed, graphic description of 'child torture' was reserved for the acrobat profession, and for the preparation of children for costumed animal parts in the pantomime. John Weylland's account of 1872, of the supply of children to represent 'the huge frogs, cats and other animals' needed by the theatres, and his harrowing description of getting children '"into shape"', in tight, claustrophobic skins, was rehearsed again during the campaign of the 1880s.[33]

Allegations of cruelty were part of a serious effort – on both sides of the campaign – to map out psychological changes undergone by theatrical children that were understood to be analogous to the bodily distortions of the acrobat, or the babe inside the imp's costume. One witness before the Royal Commission on the Education Acts thought that stage work unfitted children for scholarship because it made them 'much less childlike, and demand more excitement'.[34] There were also concerns about stage children's terrible knowingness. When the reformer Eileen Barlee invited the Crystal Palace Ballet Troupe to tea, she noted 'a precocious undercurrent, not of a too refined nature'.[35] This was to be expected, perhaps, of the not too refined boys and girls who, once the pantomime season was over, were snapped up by managements promoting the novelty of children's ballet.[36] But Barlee saw the same effect in children playing the high-class drama, who were taught 'to accompany every word by studied gesture and look', and who were 'made to practise the various expressions of passions – pride, contempt, love, hatred, pleasure, etc – until each can be assumed at command'.[37] What marked all stage children, of whatever class, was their 'insatiable thirst for admiration'.[38] They were children who were very used to being watched, and to seeing themselves as objects of someone else's contemplation. What was crucial to Barlee's analysis was her perception that stage children were not only knowing, but had knowledge of their own knowingness. She questioned one young actress, who had spent her 'whole life' in the theatre on this point, asking her what drew her to it. '"It's the power of moving others by my pathos,"' she replied, '"of seeing hundreds of faces change and soften as I speak. I would not give up the stage . . . for anything on Earth . . . no, not to save myself from Hell."'[39] Barlee observed a young woman conscious of herself, and of her power to produce an effect in others.

Pressure for legislation by the Society for the Prevention of Cruelty to Children and the National Vigilance Association framed the discussion of theatrical children that took place when the Cruelty to Children Prevention Bill was debated in the summer of 1889. The theatrical clauses of this portmanteau piece of legislation were the most hotly debated, and more than one MP remarked on the self-interest embodied in an amendment to exempt the theatre from the restrictions proposed for music halls and other 'low' places of entertainment. It was 'an effort to make an exemption in favour of theatres, on behalf of the theatre-going public'. 'If you want to employ . . . children to minister to the amusement of the upper and middle classes, you will have to make out a very much stronger case than has been yet made.'[40]

At first the House of Commons supported prohibiting the employment of all children under 10, but in the event and in the face of an extremely strong theatrical lobby, a House of Lords amendment fixed 7 as the minimum age for theatrical employment. Would-be employers of children over 7 and under 10 were required to obtain a magistrates' licence.[41] The Act also contained provisions for the inspection of places of entertainment, and the appearance of children was prohibited between 10p.m. and 5a.m.

An amending Act of 1894 raised the age below which a licence was required to 11 (in line with the raising of the school-leaving age in 1892), and provisions for acrobat, contortionist and circus children were aligned with those affecting stage children.[42] Tracy Davis has described the effect of this legislation on theatrical practice, particularly in the retiming of the standard transformation scene of the pantomime, so that children could vacate the theatre by 10p.m. (9p.m. after 1894).[43] The theatre lobby of the late 1880s, which promoted so tenaciously the need for little Peasecod and Mustard-seed to be played by children, and which painted absurd pictures of what would happen if legislation replaced them with adult performers – of Norma 'staggering across the stage with two overgrown tomboys instead of children' – was largely middle-class, representative of 'the slow but sure upper-middle-class takeover of the theatre and the drama from the middle years of the century'.[44] Some contemporary analyses allocated responsibility for the 'modern innovation' of putting children on the stage to this audience, as an exploitation of the children of the masses for the pleasure of the classes.[45] Legislative weakness and evasion of the theatrical clauses of the Cruelty Prevention Acts have usually been attributed to an extremely powerful theatrical lobby, itself a manifestation of a deep public attachment to the pleasures of watching children on the stage. If children were in such demand, if theatrical management and investors responded to the demand, and if in Davis's words 'audiences simply liked to see children on stage',[46] what was it they liked watching?

If watching children has been made a 'self-contained leisure-time industry' over the last two hundred years, then it is instructive to consider some of the social locations where the pleasures of watching were made manifest, were overtly and commercially catered for, and about which contemporary audiences articulated a range of feelings, responses and theories. James Kincaid describes a domestic practice of child-observation, established towards the end of the eighteenth century and professionalised in the following century by the huge weight of medical and pedagogical advice that then became available to the watcher. A sub-genre of this advice literature, the physiological advice manual, was discussed in Chapter 4.[47]

In the light of Kincaid's observations, there are advantages to considering children in performance on the stage, in one particular social context. If what pleased the eye did not have to be specified by age, needed only to fill a space 'that could be thought of as a child',[48] then nineteenth-century British audiences' attitudes towards the stage-fairy are illuminating. At the least, they will allow us to see audience desire met by the market and, in a British context at least, specify a late-nineteenth century development in the long history of child-watching that Kincaid describes.

For most Victorian audiences the chronological age of children on the stage was of far less importance than their presence. Strapping 12-year-olds could be called babies, and long before the chubby and pubescent Petite Mignonne was given her name, Charles Dickens had much cruel fun in *Nicholas Nickleby* (1839) with audiences' willingness to be bamboozled by infant phenomena. However, a pantomime was a sentient and plastic event, and a physiological development and a child's appearance offered some constraints to the imagination in the way that other fictional depictions of children did not. After the post-1843 expansion of child employment in the theatre and before protective and educational legislation of the late 1860s and 1870s, children of all ages were likely to be found in performance. In the late 1870s and 1880s, it was easier for very young children and children over 10 to find employment, and after 1889 it was very rare indeed to find children under 7 employed on the stage. It then became more common to dissemble about chronological age, in order to fit apparent age to audience preference, though it is an audience's interest in the question of age itself that should probably draw our attention.

Walter Sickert's painting of 'Little Dot Hetherington at the Old Bedford' (1888–9) has been much commented on, in an attempt to explore a general question of the watcher's relationship to the child in performance. It shows a little white figure enclosed not only by the concentrated gaze of her audience (Sickert showed one woman among them), but also by the large mirror in which we see both Little Dot and the sinister, watching men. The figure of Little Dot draws the sympathy of the twentieth-century observer, who sees a fragile child menaced by the bull-necked, faceless men.[49] Indeed, we do not need Sickert's composition to feel empathy with a child who, like the four-year-old Vesta Tilley (1864–1952) was carried on to the stage of the Theatre Royal in Gloucester by her father (employed there as music hall chairman) set down 'amid the all-male and probably drunken audience', with the instruction not to be frightened, to '"sing as if you mean it. Do not cough.

Speak up."'[50] We have learned a response from the child's own embarrassment and fear, the edgy sense that something unnameable emanated from the audience, which is recorded again and again in memoirs of former child performers.[51]

Twentieth-century commentators agree that the female child performer gave an audience something of what it wanted, and that when she sang 'the same love songs and comic songs, filled with innuendo, as adult stars', it was her youth that gave the act 'an added frisson'.[52] The argument here that what the audience wanted was sexual in nature is not weakened by replacing Sickert's middle-aged men and the all-male drunken crowd of the historian's imagination with a more recent sociology of music-hall attendance in this period, which estimates that about one-third of any audience for little girls like Dot Hetherington would actually have been female.[53] It has also been suggested that Little Dot's appeal can be explained by 'the popularity of child prostitutes and to the incipient market in young virgins', which had been exposed in the *Pall Mall Gazette* four years before.[54] This suggestion comes quite close to asking us to forget that the fact that none of the cases W.T. Stead wrote about in 'The Maiden Tribute of Modern Babylon' involved girls under 13, that the number of children known to the Metropolitan police as prostitutes was tiny in number, and that the most certain thing we can know about the material that Stead used was that it constituted 'a narrative of sexual danger' (or, in the words of Ann Gruetzner Robins whose argument this is, it 'appealed to the popular imagination')[55] rather than being descriptive of an actual system of child prostitution. Sickert's painting uses some of the conventions of this popular narrative, of innocence menaced by the satyr whose face we never see. The intent, bulky concentration of Little Dot's audience repeats the configuration that Stead used for describing the crisis of the narrative he published in the *Pall Mall Gazette* in 1885. Judith Walkowitz describes how in 'The Maiden Tribute' we witness the defilement of the child Eliza Armstrong 'through the eyes of the omniscient narrator' Stead himself, whose face we never actually see. The child is undressed, put to bed in the brothel to which she has been taken, and chloroformed. She wakes to find a man in the room: 'And then there rose a wild piteous cry . . . like the bleat of a frightened lamb. And the child's voice was heard crying in accents of terror, "There's a man in the room. Take me home; oh, take me home!" . . . And then all once more was still. *****************'[56]

Stead's 'Maiden Tribute' may well draw on melodramatic convention at the level of plot: it is a retelling of the ancient story of a daughter of the people used and exploited for the pleasure of the upper classes.[57] But that row of asterisks did not draw on the conventions of melodrama in performance, for the point and purpose of stage melodrama was that it showed not only the face but the shape and bodily form of villainy: it not only spoke the unspeakable, but demonstrated it too, through its entire repertoire of gesture and stance. The row of asterisks is the visual analogue of Sickert's composition, allowing the reader and the viewer a complicated access to the figure on the stage and the figure in the bed, over the shoulder of the faceless and actual audience. The anxiety of our own contemplation of 'Little Dot Hetherington', of the child all alone in her little white smock, is partly produced by the extreme visual uncertainty that the painting provokes. Even when it is understood that what seems like a decorated ledge, running horizontally across the forefront, is actually the frame of a mirror, and that reflection constitutes the whole reality of the image, it is still extremely difficult to work out *where* Little Dot is in relationship to all her different audiences, and indeed where you are, as viewer. As a watcher of Sickert's child, there is simply no place to be.[58]

The modern observer can make tentative suggestions about the relationship between Stead's narrative of sexual danger and a visual composition like that of Sickert; but some commentators of the 1880s were utterly certain of the correlation between sexual desire for the child and its public display. One correspondent to the *Pall Mall Gazette* in July 1885 mused on these questions, describing himself as an 'Altered Man' (though Stead, determined to work with the mythological references of the 'Maiden Tribute', labelled him a 'Saunterer in the Labyrinth'). He thought that 'immorality [had] descended into a positive depravity' in his time, claiming that 'the peculiar evil against which the *Pall Mall Gazette* has been warring was unknown at the West end of London when I began life. It came in with the roller skating at Prince's', he asserted, when

> for the first time, the great body of men about town were brought into daily contact with beautiful children, not members of their own family. The little things, in their nescience, were only too prodigal of smiles and glances. A passion sprang up for little children. The ruin of the children themselves was out of the question, but the procuresses found little east-enders to bear the curse vicariously.[59]

Eileen Barlee thought that nothing so specific as roller-skating displays but rather that the pantomime in general had developed a new and erotic attention to children. Pantomime drew 'the world's dilettanti, who seemingly have no better purpose in life than an hour's amusement, and the gratification of the senses'. She described how

> when the London season is over, and the theatres closed, certain money-making agents have instituted companies of small children, selected for their good looks, girls mostly, who dressed in boys' costumes, are taken down to the various racecourses to sell

> programmes, ices, and other light refreshment. While thus engaged they are called upon to perform feats of agility, dancing, tumbling, etc. . . . Petted and spoilt, these children are introduced to the worst phases of fast life.[60]

Sometimes, she said, these children were also hired out to photographers, 'to pose for the nude in classical groups and subjects'.[61]

If Sickert's complex use of the mirrored space surrounding Little Dot Hetherington raises the question of our own ambiguity and anxiety about where and what the child is, and what we want from it, and if it simultaneously allows us to understand the seriousness with which contemporary commentators explored questions of childhood and eroticism, then we also have to allow that these matters were pursued with more levity at the time Little Dot actually pointed her finger up at the gallery. The child performer raised with a delicious acuteness the question that provoked so much late nineteenth-century theorising of childhood – by emergent psychoanalysis as much as by the novel: what was it that Maisie *really* knew?[62]

Much of the historical interest of the late nineteenth-century debate over the regulation of theatre children lies in the adult consciousness it reveals: both sides were clear about the kind of campaign they were participating in, and what images and theories of childhood they were promulgating. Children on the stage embodied the question of how childhood was to be seen, both literally and figuratively. The visual connection of the stage child to the actress was very plain. Tracy Davis has raised a series of striking questions about the very appearance and demeanour of the actress, and the references her appearance made to the 'bodily coverings, gestures and spatial relationships lodged in [the] separate but symbiotically dependent source' of pornography.[63] Pressure groups like the National Vigilance Association and other parties interested in stage censorship often experienced extreme difficulty in bringing charges of obscenity against certain stage performances, because they were unable either to read or to articulate the pornographic code that made some acts so disturbing: 'those who wanted to suppress or reform the theatre, were least equipped to deal with it'.[64]

The costumes, gesture and movements of children on the stage often made reference to the same range of pornographic sources, and the related questions of tights and nudity are informative on this point. There was intense concentration on the appearance of 'the little ballet girl', above all on her legs and their covering. Davis has described how tights effaced the divisions of the leg that training for the classical dance had established (foot, ankle, knee and thigh), and how, by a single sweep of flesh-pink worsted, they drew the eye smoothly upwards, towards the place where they ended.[65] Tights were understood as a deliberate evocation of the nakedness they covered. Victorian actresses were not divested of their clothes; rather, costumes that simulated nudity 'kept the referential body to the fore'.[66]

Albert Smith's stunningly coy *Natural History of the Ballet Girl* of 1847 anticipated the leers of those 'Gents' who imagined from the title that they '"were going to be put up to a thing or two," or that there [was] anything in it which might, with propriety, exclude it from the dining-room table'. His promise 'to touch but lightly upon pink-tights and gauze petticoats' suggests that tights and tarlatan constituted the visual code through which any account of the little ballet girl had to be read.[67]

Literature produced by campaigns for the regulation of children's theatrical employment made much of young girls' awareness of the sexual meaning of this clothing, and the kind of attention it attracted. One of the most disturbing scenes of Eileen Barlee's *Pantomime Waifs* depicts a young girl in a state of terrified embarrassment and shame at being required to put on tights in the rehearsal room.[68] This felt outrage to a young girl's modesty can be read in many actresses' accounts of their childhood. Claire Tomalin draws on these for her account of stage childhood in early nineteenth-century professional families, remarking that there was only one reason for dressing a young girl in this way, and that the young performer's visible embarrassment at appearing in flesh-coloured tights was part of what her audience wanted, quite as much as the glimpse of the female form they provided.[69] Perhaps, as Tomalin says, nobody talked or wrote about 'the messages sent by tights' in the period of Ellen Ternan's childhood that she describes, but a child's acute awareness of the assault on her modesty that wearing them constituted was an important aspect of the psychology of performance that anti-theatrical campaigners of the 1880s triedto highlight. For Barlee, the immodesty imparted by tights was a certain contributor to the disturbing self-consciousness of theatrical children. Tights made children conscious of their bodies, in the same way that nakedness did.[70] But though the female child was sexualised by the wearing of tights, the chronological age of the pantomime fairy was a very uncertain thing. Young women of 15 to 24 who represented 'Mashers' ('a term applied in "fast life" to effeminate young men of the age; much as "dandy" was formerly') on the stage were 'children' in Barlee's account, their performance disturbing not so much for any display of androgyny, but because their stage costume of tight trousers and the swagger they affected drew attention to their body.[71]

If the stage costume of little girls acquired erotic connotations because it was usually inhabited by an adult woman, much of the erotic appeal of the young actress lay in her connection with childishness and the childlike.[72] After about 1850 the 'little ballet girl' became symbolic of the actress herself. The short dress, its skirt composed of many muslin layers (its length shifted, but settled at the knee by the mid-century), *décolletage*, ribbon round the throat, a bow in the hair, and . . . pink tights, was the costume universally adopted by the *corps de ballet* of music halls, pantomime and circus.[73] As a costume it signalled youth, if not infantilisation. Albert Smith's ballet girl of 1847 was charted through a course of natural development. In a Preface of hyperbolic whimsy he referred to the grand, classificatory and 'unceasing labours of Cuvier, Linneaus, Buffon . . . and other animal fanciers', and hoped that his own efforts in the ensuing pages might be read more like 'the Natural History of Selbourne [sic]; and its sparrows, grubs, and tortoises'.[74] He botanised his member of the *corps de ballet* through a life-cycle, from her first appearance in the green room, where is found 'a small pale child undergoing a lesson from the Ballet-mistress before the others arrive', through all her stages of development from flying fairy – 'the stages being Fairy, Extra, Corps de Ballet, and Coryphee' – to young womanhood and marriage.[75]

In fact, Smith's voyeuristic investment was far more in the erotics of the little girl's labour than it was in her tights, and he lovingly detailed her arduous day of rehearsal, the long walk home at night, her exhaustion, and the way in which 'the effects of this artificial existence are painfully visible' in all the members of the troupe: 'their lips are parched and fevered, their cheeks hollowed and pale . . . their limbs nipped and wasted'.[76] Later, as his ballet girl grows, he reveals in fascinated detail her behaviour in her domestic habitat, her housework and washing, and the 'little iron, which she regards as the head of her household gods'.[77] Smith's erotics of female labour did not achieve the heights of classificatory investment that Arthur Munby's did, when he pursued working women in order to photograph them in working dress and have them describe a process of labour, or repeat work endlessly in writing, as Hannah Cullwick was required to do.[78] Smith's work is much shorter, and much more fey in tone, but it takes part in the same pornography of work as Munby's did.

Smith's ballet girl is tiny – 'she is small, trim, *une petite taille bien prise*' (with a nice little figure) – but she does grow up to marry and wield her little iron. This is not allowed to the little ballet girl featured by the Theatrical Mission, who was recommended as an object of affectionate charity to the seven hundred ladies registered to write letters to the young of the profession, from 1870 onwards.[79] The figure that the lady correspondent was asked to imagine, in order to put pen to paper, was a little girl who covers her tutu with a threadbare cloak after the show is over and makes her swift way to her attic dwelling. As she falls asleep clutching the letter she has found waiting for her but that she is too tired to read, it is, in all but chronological terms, a child who lies there. The little ballet girl's appeal was in her very littleness, and her status as a kind of child.

The majority of children employed on the Victorian stage did not play child parts. Most of them were animated stage props who, costumed as elves, sprites and woodland animals, swelled processional scenes or decorated landscapes. Some were asked to speak a line or two, and their voices were added to the chorus; but for the main part they were mute. The child with a child-part to play was a much rarer phenomenon (though the theatre lobby made a great deal of the roles Shakespeare and the classical drama provided for children), and needs to be distinguished from the child on the stage playing itself, by showing its skills in acrobatics, dance or impersonation, to music-hall audiences. There was always some cross-over between these types of performance, particularly via the pantomime, which came to employ music-hall stars on a regular basis in the 1870s. G.R. Sims and Clement Scott's 'Jack in the Box', which was discussed in Chapter 6, was an unusual attempt to combine music hall and melodrama, when the *sério-comique* and burlesque music-hall star Fanny Leslie (1857–1935) played the juvenile lead Jack Merryweather.[80] A series of acrobatic tricks was performed by the 18-year-old star before the play started, though the enforced play and tumbling extracted by the cruel *padrone* that the script called for was left to Little Ada Reeves.[81]

In his discussion of childhood on the London stage between 1880 and 1905, Brian Crozier has drawn on the evidence of child-parts, played by children, in the legitimate theatre. A middle-class appreciation of the child on the stage was of a miniature participant in adult life, with much delight taken in the contrast of size and perception between adults and children. This perception – of the relative size and shape of children's understanding as well as of their bodies – was an important component of the kind of sentimentality that stimulated early twentieth-century attempts to write an entirely new 'world of childhood' for the stage, and to create plots which were constructed around children's 'unique imagination' and integrity.[82] What is 'priceless' in the child's performance is its attempt to be part of the adult world, and the very uselessness of that attempt. Audiences for earlier melodramatic children – like seven-year-old Mary in Elphinstone's version of *London Labour and the London Poor* – saw no rupture, or dislocation between the adult's and the child's understanding of events. The feature of children's parts written later, and with new repertoires of reading and understanding childhood provided by child-study, mass schooling and child psychology, was the adult's understanding that the children could not possibly understand.

The changing notions of childhood that were expressed on the stage during this period, that were read – and perhaps learned – by various audiences, cannot be confined to parts written for children (or for the slight, trim young women who played figures like Jack Merryweather), nor to the meanings encoded in those parts. The child had a meaning that existed quite apart from the child-part it played, which connected with all the crowds of anonymous little fairies who thronged the stage whether 'high' or 'low', with the little acrobat who performed its routine before or afterwards, and who suddenly, surprisingly might bring into the plot itself an aetiolated version of another story, of the child in forced performance, in the dance insisted upon.

Goethe's Mignon never was a child upon the British stage, though much of her story was used to develop new notions and conventions of childhood that were displayed in dramatic performance throughout the century. Sir Walter Scott's rewriting of Mignon in *A Legend of Montrose* and *Peveril of the Peak* was so consciously done, and by making reference to his original he instructed his audience so clearly how to read Fenella and Anott Lyle, that Goethe's child was hard to lose sight of, even for those who had never encountered her in pristine form (both books were written in the pre-Carlyle translation period). This was done despite Scott's depiction of them both as young women rather than children. Scott's sensationalism, pageantry and romanticism, and his unconfused confrontations of virtue and vice, made his plots excellent sources for melodrama, and nearly all his novels were adapted for the stage.[83] 'Montrose; or the Children of the Mist. A Musical Drama in Three Acts' was performed at the Theatre Royal, Covent Garden in 1822. The scriptwriter Isaac Pocock moved Anott Lyle a great distance from the Mignon that Scott had mawkishly modelled his character on: the stage Anott is of quite ordinary stature (indeed, is 'beautiful and elegant'), a 'cheerfulness ever fills her mind', and she sings upbeat Scottish airs whenever the opportunity arises.[84] However, in the childhood that does not appear on the stage and that is outside its time frame, she was a little girl of the mist, found in the forest – a child without provenance. Fenella was made the central character of both melodramatic versions of *Peveril of the Peak*, the first staged at Covent Garden in 1826 as a 'comic opera', again written by Isaac Pocock and scored by Charles Horn.[85] Music accompanies the dumb girl everywhere she goes, and several times 'Fenella intimates her organic deficiency by pointing to her mouth and uttering a soft and plaintive but imperfect sound'.[86] She is certainly a lost child found, and, as in Scott's novel and in Goethe's original, her social status turns out to be very high indeed. Pocock actually altered her lineage from the one Scott gave her, but it remains resolutely aristocratic. But this Fenella is a woman – small, elastic, perfectly formed – but a woman, nevertheless. Scott's next adaptor, Edward Fitzball, who wrote his melodramatic version in 1829, recalled its first run many years later. He remembered clearly the precocious appearance of 'Little Miss Vincent' when she walked on the stage out of a fiddle case, in role as the diminutive Sir Jeffery Hudson, but his Fenella was also a grown woman.[87]

Stage Mignons of the mid- and late Victorian years in Britain made their central reference to Ambroise Thomas's opera of 1866, though Hugh Moss's four-act comedy 'Bootle's Baby' of 1887 brought John Strange Winter's Mignon directly from modern fiction to the stage. Moss contracted Mrs Stannard's three volumes into a single plot, and in its contraction emphasised the sexual and social ambiguity of the Mignon-figure that most rereadings of Goethe through Carré and Barbier had evaded. There is a regimental dance, and one of the guests asks what tune the band is playing. She is told that it is '"La Fille de Madame Angot . . . It's an opera – a girl who was adopted by a lot of – like you Mignon."'[88] Here, Moss made reference to C.H. Lecoq's opera of 1873 (set in the period of the Directory), in which the heroine Clairette is left on the death of her mother to be brought up by market folk. Madame Angot had died 'poor as a Madeleine, she, who had been so rich'; everyone believes that Clairette had been born 'in the seraglio at Constantinople . . . she is perhaps, the daughter of the Grand Turk'. She is certainly her mother's daughter – which is the plot's point – and shakes off 'the innocence/And candour' that the market people have been so keen to inculcate in her. As she tells them, modesty 'was not in my nature/You know from whence I came:/Of mother Angot I am the daughter,/And the daughter of Angot/Resembles her family.' Being her mother's daughter does not mean going to the bad; it means, rather, being recognised for what she really is. Indeed, the formerly demure 'flower of sin' ends up rejecting the glamorous and fickle Ange Pitou, songwriter, Bohemian and revolutionary Royalist poet, on passion for whom much of the plot has hinged. In the end, she accepts the sedate and middle-aged Pomponnet, whom she rejected at the beginning of the story, because he is old and responsible. This may have been an important reference for Mrs Stannard, for her trilogy ends with Mignon finding a husband in an equally fatherly figure. But in the stage version of 1888 it is the abandoned mother of Mignon who achieves marriage and who brought down the curtain upon 'a shower of rice and old slippers'.[89] It is this stage version of Winter's trilogy that makes very clear indeed that in her use of Mignon's name she discusses illegitimacy: 'Mignon' is the word for a child without provenance, an illegitimate child, legitimised in this version by her mother's marriage to the kindly officer on whose bed she was placed as a tiny baby. In the last of the series, Winter's Mignon reflects that 'She had never been called by her own name of Mary Gilchrist, but always by that which she had borne in the days when she was a child of uncertainty.'[90]

Moss's stage Mignon denies the analogy with Clairette when she hears the band play (though she does not know what it is she denies in her babyish lisp):

Mignon: No, I'm La figlia del wregimento, am I not Lal?
Lucy: Yes, my sweetheart.
Miles: So you are la fille de madame Angot, and we've adopted you . . .

There was no end to operatic girls lost and found. Gaetano Donizetti's *opéra-comique* 'La Fille du régiment' had the little Italian/Tyrolese Marie found as an infant on one of the battlefields of the Napoleonic Wars and raised as the regiment's daughter. An aristocratic inheritance finally revealed does not stop her marrying her common love, helped by Sergeant Sulpice, a figure much like Lal of 'Bootle's Baby'. The idea of collective fatherhood informed 'La Fille de Madame Angot' and 'La Figlia del Regimento'.[91]

Reviewers found Moss's scene of collective fatherhood very striking. 'Little Mignon, having been surreptitiously laid in Bootle's bed, is discovered by the large-hearted officer and held up for the astonished admiration of the whole scarlet-coated mess.' It was the contrast between 'the tiny, helpless, dumb, staring infant, and the huge moustached, spurred and gold-braided cavalrymen' that was reckoned to make up so 'fresh, ingenious and diverting' a stage picture. This moment was compared with the discovery of Eppie in *Silas Marner*, and Mr Allworthy's finding of the foundling Tom Jones.

The little angel discovered on the bed was played by an anonymous baby, but the child Mignon was impersonated by Little Minnie Terry. There was much discussion in the theatrical press about Minnie Terry's real age, but universal agreement that this 'charmingly artless little maiden' was conspicuously free from 'the precocious airs and graces that usually mar the pleasure to be derived from juvenile performers'.[92] It is a cheap charge to bring against an entire cultural form and many decades of theatrical effort and audience response: that the movements, gestures, demeanour and voice of childhood were taught to generations of child performers, who became liable to rejection and dismissal if their repertoire appeared too studied or forced. Charming artlessness could be learned too, and child stars of the second half of the nineteenth century were the ones who had studied the 'quaint and pretty ways of childhood' most assiduously.[93] The artlessness, the unknowingness of the female child could best be maintained if her presence was able to signal the process of growth and physiological maturity in which she was implicated, but without overt recognition of it.

In all the strange transformations of *Wilhelm Meister* that the nineteenth-century British stage presented, there was one scene that was never represented. In all the versions of Goethe's novel that have been discussed, however distant from the original, however truncated or attenuated, a cruel master (who is either an Italian or a gypsy) tries to force a child or a young girl to dance or to perform a series of acrobatic turns. 'Saute, Mignon!' (Jump, Mignon!) cries the gypsy chief Jarno in Carré and Barbier's libretto; then 'Danse Mignon,/Méchant démon' (Dance, Mignon, you wicked devil), leaving quite unclear what she actually would have done, had she not refused. An old gypsy woman has unrolled the carpet, a child has placed the eggs at regular intervals, but we never do find out what Mignon would have done on that carpet. In later versions of the story, in which we have seen Mignon become a pathetic little Savoyard, or a Boy without a name, the abused child may take a few faltering steps before collapsing, but, true to the original, the dance is promulgated, but not performed. The child's refusal – or inability – to perform brings a beating, and at that point it is rescued, by some version of Wilhelm, and given a home. In the original published version of the *Bildungsroman* however, Mignon does finally dance privately for Wilhelm. In that performance, Wilhelm finally *sees* the child, and takes her as his own.

The scene is never repeated, partly and practically, it must be remarked, because an *opéra-comique* could scarcely demand that its mezzo also be a novelty performer, and it was from Thomas's characterisation of Mignon that all late nineteenth-century versions of Mignon derived, in some form or other. But the absence of the dance continued when there were no practical constraints on its performance; and its absence, which the next chapter considers, was as much Mignon's meaning as were her manifold presences.

9

Childhood and the Uncanny

In Freud's essay on 'The Uncanny' of 1919, much of the argument is to do with the way in which the strange and the inexplicable, the most unhomely and weird of things or places, will turn out in the end to be not strange at all, but that which is familiar and well known, though subjected to suppression, usually in early childhood.[1] Part of the essay is devoted to testing a proposition of the psychologist Ernst Jentsch, who suggested in a paper of 1906 that one of the most effective means available to writers wishing to create an uncanny effect is to leave the reader in doubt about whether a particular figure is human, or some lifeless thing that is made to move.[2] Freud concluded his own exploration of the same literature that Jentsch had used in evidence, by pointing out that the effect is produced not by any intellectual uncertainty like this about whether figures are alive or dead, but because certain stories awaken long-repressed fears and anxieties in the reader. In the course of his discussion, Freud urged readers to make a distinction between the experience of the uncanny in real life, and the uncanny as it is depicted in fiction. He also asked the reader to note that many strange and peculiar things in literature, particularly in the world of the fairy-tale, are not uncanny at all; indeed, that in the fairy-tale, the severed limbs and the hands and feet and noses that move all by themselves usually produce a comic effect rather than one of fear and apprehension. He also drew attention to the position the reader is invited to take in relationship to the peculiar event or happening in the story. He did not explore in any detail the question of reader identification with the character feeling the sensation of uncanniness in the story; but he did point out that as soon as a writer allows a distance between the character and the reader – allows objectivity or irony to enter the text – then the uncanny cannot take place, as a literary effect.[3]

It is also the case, claimed Freud, that as long as strange figures and happenings remain within the setting of poetic reality, they do not produce an uncanny effect. Nevertheless, literature is 'a much more fertile province' for the uncanny than real life, 'for it contains the whole of the latter and something more beside', and it is open to the writer to move his or her magical effects into 'the world of common reality'. Then the uncanny comes into operation, for by this move the writer has available everything that would have an uncanny effect in reality: 'we react to his inventions as we would have reacted to real experiences; by the time we have seen through his trick it is too late and the author has achieved his object'.[4]

These distinctions, between the fictional realm and the realm of reality, between intellectual uncertainty and the deepest sources of the body as the foundation of the uncanny, have been useful in an exploration of nineteenth-century uses of Mignon. We have seen Goethe's child-figure constantly referred to as strange and inexplicable, as she was by her first author, and for those who know her story her afterlife shows her achieving an uncanny effect that was not the same as the one she evoked when she was confined within the pages of *Wilhelm Meister*. At the same time, Mignon's progress, the dances she performs in the consciousness of generations who never read a word of Goethe's original text, should at the least make us uneasy about the formal division Freud made between the operation of the uncanny in literature and life. The elision that Mignon effects, of the uncanny in literature and life, is to do with the role she plays in the depiction of Wilhelm's very self. This interiorised self is presented by Goethe as the story of his childhood.

In the published version of *Wilhelm Meister*, the volumes of the mid-1790s, Wilhelm's childhood is placed at a distance from the reader. It is conjured as the after-dinner recollection of a young man telling his mistress Mariane about the puppet show he was presented with as a Christmas treat when he was 10 years old. Wilhelm describes how after the festivities were over, he found the box of lifeless dolls and tangled wires in the spice-laden air of the larder, and how he stole the playtext – the drama of David and Goliath – lying on top of the heap. He goes on to recount his ensuing obsession with the theatre up in the attic, which his austere but kindly parents turned into a miniature playhouse for him. Mariane (Mariane the actress, still wearing the scarlet soldier's coat from her evening performance, 'the little female officer') is tired, and falls asleep in the middle of Wilhelm's recital.

What had delighted the child-in-memory, the young Wilhelm, was the *littleness* of the puppet figures, 'the strange caperings' he could effect among 'the Moors and the Mooresses . . . shepherds and shepherdesses . . . dwarfs and dwarfesses'; the way in which, though but a child himself, he could 'hover aloft over all that little world'.[5] The puppets thus performed the function of dolls for Wilhelm, and indeed it was his sisters' 'dressing and undressing' of their own that gave him the idea of doing the same. He 'slit the scraps of cloth from their bodies; tacked the fragments together as well as possible; saved a particle of money to buy new ribbons and lace; begged many a rag of taffeta; and so formed by degrees, a full theatrical wardrobe'.

This delight in littleness, in the manipulability of these figures (they are dolls that can be made to move), and of the world the child invents for them, all describe the little boy's own situation, and his understanding of his own childishness. Goethe wrote that

> in well adjusted and regulated houses, children have a feeling not unlike that what I conceive rats and mice to have; they keep a sharp eye on all crevices and holes, where they may come at any forbidden dainty; they enjoy it also with a fearful, stolen satisfaction . . .[6]

In the earlier version – the *Theatrical Mission* manuscript of the 1770s and 1780s – we enter directly into the narrative of Wilhelm's childhood, close to Christmas, some time in the 1750s. In the *Theatrical Mission* not only does the child actually scamper and creep, mouse-like, about the house, but his littleness is turned inward, into a visceral sense of himself. This visceral sense is related to the way in which he has become 'estranged from his mother, and was most unfortunately situated, because his father was also a hard man; so that nothing seemed left for him but to creep into himself, a fate which with children and old folks is of serious consequence'.[7] And in this early version, the obsessive curiosity that the little boy experiences after the first puppet show is aligned to the child's quest for sexual enlightenment: his was 'the rapture of observation and inquiry. How the business was managed was what he sought to know.'

The puppet theatre has been erected for a second time when some neighbours' children come to visit, and after the performance the company takes to the dance floor. The show is being dismantled, and little Wilhelm slips towards the table that has been placed across a doorway to serve as a stage. He lifts the green carpet that covers it; 'a maid servant spied him from behind and drew him back'; but

> in that momentary glimpse, he had seen them packing friends and foes, Saul and Goliath, Moors and dwarfs into a drawer, and this sight was fresh food for his half-sated curiosity. As children at a certain period, when first made conscious of sex-differences, feel the stirrings of wonderful emotions throughout their nature, excited by a glimpse beyond the veil which hides these secrets, so it was with Wilhelm after his discovery; he was quieter yet more restless than before, fancied he had learned something, only to find thereby that he knew nothing.[8]

The boy pursues his inquiries with the puppets and the playscript that he keeps in 'the little chamber in the roof'. 'In passing,' observed Goethe,

> I cannot leave unnoticed the magical effect which garrets, stables and secret chambers often have upon children, in which . . . they revel in the fact of being alone, a sensation which in later years

> slowly passes away, yet sometimes returns again, when places of unclean necessity must provide the secret chancellory for unhappy lovers.[9]

It has often been observed that when Mignon springs into existence, a rewriting of Wilhelm's childhood takes place; an objectification of the moments of psychological and sexual development that Goethe describes in both versions of *Wilhelm Meister* has frequently been noted. Early twentieth-century psychoanalytic commentary used the textual relationship between Wilhelm and Mignon to explore the function that Mignon served Goethe in reworking his own childhood experiences. This was done in a period when much critical attention was paid to Goethe's sister Cornelia, to her brief life (reluctantly married, she died in childbirth at the age of 27), to her neuroses, and to her character which was 'peculiar and difficult to discuss'.[10]

In 1929, encouraged by Freud's interest in Mignon, Philipp Sarasin elaborated the insights of 'A Childhood Recollection from *Dichtung und Wahrheit*' (1917) in order to give an account of Mignon and the Harpist as a mysterious, ambiguous reworking of Goethe's own family situation as a child, his curious absence of concern at the death of four younger siblings, his relationship with Cornelia, and with his parents and grandfather.[11] There was much speculation in the early twentieth century about Goethe's childhood, about the possibility that the Frankfurt household in which he grew up harboured tuberculosis, and that Goethe himself suffered from the disease. It was suggested that it caused the early death of four younger brothers and sisters.[12] According to Sarasin, Freud supported his own conjecture that Cornelia finally died from consumption. Both of them saw in Mignon's hysterical crying fit the traces of Cornelia's childish tubercular convulsions, which they assumed had been witnessed by her brother:

> Freud has encouraged me several times to express an assumption which I will here add . . . Wolfgang will hardly have been spared the sight of his seriously ill siblings, nor that of convulsive attacks if we assume a vesicular tuberculosis with meningitic irritation . . . Mignon's crying fit hereby acquires a unique and organic interpretation. Doubtless not only Cornelia . . . but the whole sequence of siblings are mirrored in Mignon.[13]

Much later K.R. Eissler was to claim that the strangeness of Mignon on which Wilhelm dwells so much, and her androgynous appearance, are the result of the way in which the boy Goethe experienced his sister's body at a certain point of his psychosexual development – as 'a boy in whom something was missing'. According to Eissler, when the child Mignon sings 'What have they done to you?' in the third verse of 'Kennst du das Land?', reference is made to her castration, and the egg dance is an expression of her invincibility, for the girl-child has been castrated and nothing more can happen to her.[14] For Eissler the crying fit is no memory of tubercular convulsions at all, but admitted of 'only one interpretation, realistic down to the smallest detail, of a girl having an orgasm'. Making this claim involved arguing for the existence of orgasms in little girls in the pre-genital stage of sexual development, for Cornelia having experienced orgasm, and her brother having watched her.[15] Though the mature Goethe left many lines to read between in his descriptions of Cornelia, and though he certainly implied that her later unhappiness in marriage was due to her being unable to love the one man in the world she wanted to love, namely her brother, it has to be pointed out that Eissler's argument for incestuous fantasies of Cornelia being embodied in Mignon rests entirely on the evidence of the text of *Wilhelm Meister*.[16] However, his assessment of Wilhelm's experience of Mignon's 'orgasm' as kinaesthetic rather than visual is important, not so much because he locates a reality behind the hysterical fit, but because the child's sexual experience and search for sexual knowledge that Goethe wrote about in the *Theatrical Mission* is something that takes place in the dark holes and corners of a household, in which mice and children scamper and creep. And of course for our purposes the true interest of Eissler's claims lie in his making Mignon the product of recollections, fantasies and experiences of Goethe's own childhood. Sarasin's was the same move, though his embodiment and reactivation of Goethe's childhood in Mignon is refracted through what she means to Wilhelm, in the context of the *Bildungsroman*.

Sarasin described the child Goethe's actual possession of a puppet theatre, and the tightrope walkers and child-actors he encountered in Frankfurt after the city was occupied by French troops in 1759. The soldiery brought the French theatre in its train, and the child Goethe was encouraged by his grandfather to spend time at the playhouse, much against the wishes of his own father (the outbreak of the Seven Years' War in 1756 had politically split the Goethe family). Sarasin acknowledged the differences between the Mignon-figure of the *Theatrical Mission* and the *Apprenticeship*, whilst arguing at the same time that the whole complex of meaning and affect embodied in it 'was taken over unaltered from the first version into the new; it was a creation of the first Weimar period and arose during his love affair with Frau von Stein'.[17] He used Freud's account in 'Creative Writers and Day-dreaming' (1908) to suggest that before he made the Italian journey, the writer's psychological situation in Weimar pressed him to rework recent experiences with unconscious material from his earliest childhood.[18]

The changes that Sarasin did find between the two versions were to do with the writer's relationship to his own past, which he understood to be articulated in the two Wilhelms and the differences between them. Sarasin discussed a dream sequence of the *Apprenticeship* (which does not appear in the *Theatrical Mission*) in which Wilhelm watches calmly from a window all the people and figures and entities from his own past that the mad, frantic child Mignon had represented. In this dream of the *Apprenticeship* 'they appear in peaceful coexistence, without friction, without the strange madness of secret misunderstandings'. If Wilhelm's dream, in which Mignon appears quietly lying on the grass next to Felix, is the 'true image of the mature Goethe, who in Italy had discovered his inner equilibrium', then in the actual time frame of the novel, Mignon is still utterly strange and quite mad.[19] But it is certainly the case that the only points in the text at which she is ever still, and not in some frantic, bodily agitation, are in Wilhelm's dream, and in her death.

In his paper of 1949, 'The Symbolic Equation: Girl = Phallus', Otto Fenichel relied much on Mignon and on 'Mignon-figures'. Here, Fenichel summarised his own clinical inquiries and a whole corpus of work on the equation of the penis with a child (with a baby, or with 'a little one') in order to describe what he thought was an already well established cycle within psychoanalytic thinking, that is the way that what is introjected by the very small child is projected later in fantasy. For Fenichel, the phallus-girl was simply the end of a line, of faeces, milk, babies – all the contents of the mother's body introjected by the very young child. What he sought to understand was why 'the little one', or the penis, was so frequently fantasised as a *girl*.[20]

Fenichel suggested that the fantasy revealed in analysis connected with

> recurrent motives of legend and fairy-tale . . . [in which] little girl rescuers who protect great men in all their adventures occur not infrequently. Miracle-performing little companions (who do not necessarily have to be female), such as dwarfs, mandrakes, talisman figures of all kinds, have often been analysed, and the 'little double' has been recognised as a phallic figure . . . in her smallness, her outward weakness which stands in such contrast to her magic strength.[21]

Fenichel dealt with the symbolic equation first from a female perspective, in an account that goes: 'the fantasy "I am a penis" represents a way out of two conflicting tendencies, "I want to have a penis" and "I want to love a man as a woman"'. The fantasy of being a man's penis is then a fantasy of being united with him in inseparable harmony. It is also a quite ordinary way out for a little girl whose infantile omnipotence has been threatened by discovery of the penis (and the discovery that she does not have one); omnipotence is restored to the child by identification with the phallus.[22] From the male perspective, Fenichel noted that 'men fall in love with little girls in whom they see themselves embodied, and to whom they give what their mothers denied them'. He thought this structure – a man seeing in a little girl his own self, his desire to give her what his own mother did not give him – was very probably 'the decisive mechanism in paedophilia'.[23] Always, he said, male fantasies like this were combined with the idea of mutual protection: 'the little woman is rescued by the great man in actuality, the latter by the former in magical fashion'. The fantasy is circular, for girl-phalluses (or Mignon-figures; all the small, magically powerful little tokens of legend and fiction) represent the man who fantasises himself as a girl, and at the same time they allow him to be the great man who – he himself – rescues the little one. Fenichel also speculated on the persistence with which the little girl rescuer is garbed as a page in folk and fairy-tale, as 'a primarily helpless little fellow inseparably devoted to a great person, in order in magical fashion to help or save him'. He concluded that such 'half-girl figures' are no different from other phallic symbols, 'which despised at first on account of their smallness, turn out later to be powerful'.[24]

Given the deep satisfactions of the explanatory structure presented in 'The Symbolic Equation', and the mutuality of the fantasy as it is outlined (its satisfactions for the little girl and the man – who is also the little girl) Fenichel was bound to find Sarasin's reading of Mignon inadequate, and his account of Mignon as a condensation of Goethe's memories of Cornelia and his other dead brothers and sisters as correct, but not sufficient. Fenichel's contribution to the intensified biographical search for Mignon's origins of the inter-war years was his understanding that 'Mignon's male characteristics stem from the fact that she represents the poet himself'. It is by paying attention to the whole context of the early part of *Wilhelm Meister*, to the writer's childhood, and the circumstances in which the novel was written that they can be discerned.[25]

The symbolism of Mignon dancing was crucial to Fenichel's discovery of Mignon as a phallus-girl and thus as representative of the poet's own self. The egg dance performed by Mignon was also central to Hellmut Ammerlahn's study of 1968, which drew close connections between Wilhelm, Mariane and Mignon but which, restricting itself to the function of Mignon in the text of *Wilhelm Meister*, did not need to describe the sequences of the symbolic equation in order to disinter Mignon as the embodiment of Wilhelm's refracted feelings and impulses. Taking Mignon's egg dance as a starting point, Ammerlahn showed how the little carpet that the child places on the bedroom floor represents a stage, on which Mignon dances like a marionette. Both of these images (stage and puppet) draw the young man to early memories of his own theatre in the attic, and this memory in turn connects with his telling Mariane its story. As he watches Mignon dance, Wilhelm is in a state of some emotional turmoil, for he believes that Mariane has been unfaithful to him.

Nevertheless, Ammerlahn claims that the two happiest periods of Wilhelm's life (his little theatre; the affair with Mariane) and the saddest (the loss of both) are tied to the image of Mignon-as-marionette, dancing.

What is more, Mignon's age – the span of her fictional existence – links these two events in Meister's life. Meister reckons that the strange child-acrobat is 12 or so (*WMA* I:88–9) and twelve is the number of years between the loss of his theatre at the age of 10, and the loss of Mariane at the age of 22: 'Mignon's development and existence prove to be constituted by those two events and the time-span between them'. Ammerlahn pursues many of his arguments in etymological terms: Mignon comes from Italy, and *marionette* (*marionetta* in Italian) is a little-Maria figure that also originates in Italy. 'And is it just chance that Wilhelm's beloved, of whom Mignon, the "little Maria" constantly reminds him, is called "Mariane"?'[26]

In this interpretation, then, Mignon – an embodiment of Wilhelm's desires and fantasies – is refracted through his sexual feelings as an adult. More recent analysis of the function of Mignon in the text has understood her as both a window on to Meister's soul and a symbolic representation of his developmental predicament: Mignon is 'a dark, awkward figure whose physical growth has obviously been retarded, but at the same time, her yearnings and actions reflect Wilhelm's will to grow, to overcome his self-denial'. She is, in this way, quite precisely 'the child of his troubled spirit', his troubles being to do with the way in which he is arrested by circumstance and personality from pursuing his own course of development.[27]

These are all important claims about Mignon's function as a figure in the structure of the text, about the way in which, at the level of time-sequence and imagery, she literally holds the book together. But the claims of Mignon's physical littleness (she *is* 'little one'), her associations with Wilhelm's boyhood, the way in which he uses her as a means of interpreting his own dilemmas, suggest something more: that Mignon (among all the other things she is) is Wilhelm's own past, there, dancing on the carpet, and his own childhood, turned within himself, and now projected; that the child on the stage – dancing, twisting, tumbling – is the self in performance.

In 1810 Heinreich von Kleist published his much-reproduced and referred to article on puppets, and the paradoxes that the dancing puppet presents to the beholder, in the *Berlin Abendblätter*.[28] 'Über das Marionettentheater' was one of a series of short works by Kleist demonstrating a difficult or paradoxical phenomenon, explored in this case through a dialogue between a professional dancer and a narrator. The paradox of the puppet theatre is that wooden dolls, controlled by strings – inanimate wooden things, their limbs 'mere pendula' – exhibit more 'symmetry, mobility and lightness' than living dancers. The explanation for this phenomenon that is adduced by the living dancer who has just watched a marionette performance, is that the centre of gravity in the puppet is fixed in one point, which the operator controls through the wires. All the wooden limbs simply follow the line etched by their movement around this centre, in perfect co-ordination. The professional dancer who makes these comments is certain that it is absolutely impossible for a human being even to equal a puppet in this regard. He believes that the feelings of the puppetmaster are of some importance to the performance, that the line inscribed by movement around the centre of gravity is 'something very mysterious', that it probably could not be done 'unless the operator imagines himself as the puppet's centre of gravity', and that the line followed by the dead pendulous limbs is 'the path of the dancer's soul'. Nevertheless, he also believes that 'even the last fragment of spirit . . . could be removed from the marionette' and that its dance could take place entirely in 'the realm of mechanical forces'. Not only is there a contradiction within the argument about the puppetmaster's role, but the contradiction fuels the larger paradox, that 'in the organic world, to the extent that reflection grows dimmer and weaker, the grace therein becomes more brilliant and powerful . . . it appears purest simultaneously in the human body that has either none at all or else infinite consciousness – that is, in the puppet or the god'. The human dancer has knowledge, and also consciousness of that knowledge: reflection – self-reflection – is very strong indeed. It does not matter how well the human dancer may understand the laws that bind him or her to the earth; all conscious attempts to defy gravity cannot produce the grace of the unreasoning, unknowing wooden doll.

The dancer who thus propounds his philosophy of puppets describes our fallen state: the loss that is attendant upon knowledge and consciousness. He also expresses the hope that divine grace might be restored to human beings, by consciousness passing 'through the infinite' and becoming at one with the divine. For the time being, locked out of paradise and with the gates barred against us, we can only watch divinity at play in the dance of an inanimate object, suffused with the appearance of life: in the marionette.

In Goethe's description of Mignon's egg dance the marionette is certainly evoked. The child blindfolds herself, so that she dances unseeing. Her movements begin like 'wound-up clockwork'; 'she took her course without stopping, like a piece of clockwork'; 'the strange music gave a new impulse to the dance as it continually started again at the beginning and whirled on its ways at each repetition' (*WMA* I:102). But although the perfection of the mechanical and the lifeless is evoked, Mignon does not become whole in her dance, nor does she inscribe the divinity of one who has no self-consciousness. Indeed, Mignon's dance is not only the place in the text where Mignon is her own self, but also the place where Wilhelm sees her plainly for the first time, marvelling at 'how excellently her character developed in this dance'. The child shows herself as 'severe, dry, forcible and, in gentle postures, solemn rather than agreeable'. It is while watching the performance of Mignon's own self that Wilhelm feels for the first time 'what he had already been sensible of on Mignon's behalf. He longed to take this forlorn being to his heart in place of a child, to feel her in his arms and with a father's love to arouse in her an enjoyment of life' (*WMA* I:103).

Indeed, in depicting the dance and Wilhelm's reaction to it, Goethe wrote about the finding of a child in two senses: it is the point at which all that Mignon represents and personifies of Wilhelm and his past is brought together and recognised; and the point where Wilhelm sees a real child and recognises her, in the social world of the novel. The dignity of this moment, its inscription of Mignon's self-possession, was not attractive to a post-Romantic aesthetic that sought the effacement of the dancer in the dance, an image of the moving body and the vacuous face.[29]

Towards the end of a book there is a desire to discuss endings themselves, and to assign to all that has been discussed its full meaning. Now that Mignon's shape, form and significance is clearer, and now that it can be pointed out that all she represented was theorised in the period from 1890 to 1930, it would be satisfying to make the end of a century's use of her the ending to this book, and to have her embody the sense of an ending. From the very beginning, the search for Mignon has offered the complex comfort of all the quests that Frank Kermode discussed in *The Sense of an Ending*, when something is not so much found as seen to have happened, to be over and done, in however arbitrary a way.[30] But another of Mignon's meanings was about resisting the end. That resistance was largely to do with the discoveries about past time that were attendant on the theorisation of childhood as the unconscious in the period 1895–1920, in particular the discovery that preoccupations with the past are revelatory of an unresolved conflict about the present. A new kind of time came into being at the end of the nineteenth century, which was born both of recastings and rewritings of the historical past, and also of a long development, of an interior space or place within human beings, expressed most clearly in the shape of a child. This second origin of a new kind of time – the idea of human interiority shaped in the form of a child – throughout the century and across many discourses, is the one that Freud inherited, and that he theorised between 1899 and 1920.

The new, historicised attention to Mignon at the century's end that has been noted was connected to the form of historical reconstruction forced by the new status of historical evidence, its effects on historical narrative, and its promulgation of the belief that the past – that Mignon – could be found, as she really was. The search for the child – it does not matter who the child is, for it is the search itself that concerns us here – is the expression of a desire to give the child a home: to find her a home in the world: to give her a history, a psychology, and a meaning. Angela Carter's rewriting of Mignon, in the setting of 1899 but actually for the 1980s, is especially interesting on this score. This Mignon, the Mignon of *Nights at the Circus*, is not written out of Goethe's child-figure at all, but out of the fall to prostitution described to Henry Mayhew in 1850 by interviewees quite different from the Watercress Girl, taking in Trilby along the way, via Philip Larkin's drugged and raped child of 'Deception' (in *The Less Deceived*, 1955) and with an acute late twentieth-century sensibility.[31] In one heart-wrenching moment, however, she does evoke the child after whom she is named, when she sings the *Lied* composed by Schubert out of the original Mignon's 'Kennst du das Land' (words taught to her by an English stable-boy, repeated in a language she does not understand). She learns Byron's 'We'll go no more a-roving' in this way too, unknowingly reminding her audience of the way her original died:

> We'll go no more a-roving . . .
> For the sword outwears the sheath
> And the heart outwears the breast
> And love itself must cease
> And the heart itself take rest. (p.134)[32]

It is with an aetiology of the victim (the many mid-twentieth-century writings of the abused, and battered and raped woman and girl-child) that Carter sets about normalising her fictional figure, by writing a pathological case study that 'explains' her Mignon. This 'broken blossom of the present tense' (pp.139–40), with 'the scarcely to be imagined tragedy of her life, the sea of misery and disaster in which she swam' (p.132), her 'febrile gaiety of being without a past . . . without memory or history' (pp.139–40) is actually given both by the narrator: a father who murders her mother; an orphanage; abuse in her place as a servant; a street child for a time, she sells bunches of discarded flowers – 'begging with paint on its face' – casual prostitution, posing for the dead, a con-man's mistress . . . The casework notes are very full; the life-story told in immense detail. She is found a home as well, in the idea of childhood, both in her author's insistence that in spite of it all she is *still a child*; and, more interestingly, in the childlike syntactic structure with which portions of her story are told. For instance, Mignon meets the medium, Herr M. and 'for the first time in her life . . . got enough to eat; but she did not put on any weight, it was as though something inside her ate it all up before she could get at it but she didn't have worms' (p.133).

Carter's Mignon is finally found that most proper of late twentieth-century homes, in the love and the arms of another woman, the Abyssinian Princess, the Keeper of the Tigers. We should be reminded here, for Carter certainly must have been, of Freud's argument in 'The Uncanny', that that which seems most *unheimlich*, most strange, most uncanny, is in fact the most familiar of places, a woman's body: 'the home of all human beings' – in Freud's extraordinary use of the language of the fairy-tales – 'the place where each one of us lived once upon a time and in the beginning'. He went on to remark that 'the *unheimlich* is what was once *heimisch*, familiar; the prefix "un" is the token of repression'.[33] The narrator of *Nights at the Circus* remarks of the relationship between Mignon and the Princess that 'perhaps it was that homeless look of Mignon's that made up the Princess's mind for her' (pp.153–4).

Carter's Mignon, then, is found a home in an exemplary late twentieth-century way. But the desire to do this for the child-figure is nothing new. '"Do you know that land where the lemon trees grow?", asked, implored [Carter's] Mignon' (ibid.). The Princess's tigers rustle and stir. Carter writes: 'For might not this land be the Eden of our first beginnings, where innocent beasts and wise children play together under the lovely lemon trees, the tiger abnegates its ferocity, the child her cunning.' We cannot, it seems, stop wanting this child, nor performing all our acts of rescue. For as Carter's Mignon sings her *Lied* in the tiger's cage, Blake's 'Little Girl Found' is evoked. 'Follow me,' says Blake's kindly beast to the child's parents:

> 'Weep not for the maid;
> In my palace deep
> Lyca lies asleep.'
>
> Then they followed
> Where the vision led,
> And found their sleeping child
> Among tygers wild.[34]

10

The Child-figure and the Melodramatic Imagination

Then there comes the insistent pressure of a new story – a new account of Mignon's story – a new meaning for it. Having witnessed the preoccupations, anxieties and fantasies that this child-figure has condensed and represented during her extra-textual afterlife, we are in a better position now to discern the weight of a modern preoccupation that ineluctably draws the reader's attention to the silences in the life-story that Goethe wrote for her, and the impossibility, in the late twentieth century, of locating her meaning anywhere else.

Philipp Sarasin claimed that when he came to revise the *Theatrical Mission* manuscript in the 1790s, Goethe – seeing himself, perhaps, as no more than editor of a collection of papers he had himself produced earlier in life – adopted the 'Mignon-complex' in its entirety from the earlier work.[1] If Mignon represented a family history and pathology and the writer's conflicts concerning his own childhood, and if, as Sarasin argues, these difficulties were dispelled by the mature man who had found an inner equilibrium in Italy, then there was little for the writer to do but to kill off the dark, ambiguous figure taken over from an earlier period to serve her function in a new version of *Wilhelm Meister.*

The depiction of a deeply disturbed child is, indeed, virtually unaltered between the two versions of the *Bildungsroman.* Mignon's pathological traits – her neurotic ordering of her physical environment, her obsessive washing, her frequent muteness, her extreme difficulties with speech and writing, and her frantic bodily agitation – were continually brought before the reader, in both versions of the text. These traits appear emphasised in the second version because there Mignon dies, in a kind of apotheosis of oddness, but also because in the second version she is given a history that explains her strangeness and her death, when the reader learns of the incestuous relationship that produced her, and the circumstances of her very early childhood and of her abduction.

The story told as Mignon lies in her marble tomb is of a mother – Sperata – protected from the knowledge that her priestly lover was also her brother. She was recommended to the spiritual care of another priest who 'believed himself obliged to practise deception on the nursing mother'. He brought her false news of the man now locked away in a monastery and with whom he has never actually communicated. But as soon as the child was weaned, Sperata's confessor began to emphasise the horror of having yielded to a priest, an act which he named 'a sin against nature . . . a form of incest' in itself. The tactic was to produce in her a remorse equal to that which she would have felt had she known that the priest was also her brother. Meanwhile the child grew, showing 'a singular nature', walking very early and displaying adroitness and dexterity in movement; it was 'only in words that she could not express herself, and the impediment seemed to be in her ability to think, rather than in her vocal organs' (*WMA* III:134–45).

The priest's ploy – to have the mother feel a guilt equal to the nature of a crime of which she remained ignorant – was successful and Sperata rejected the little girl, who was sent to live with foster parents on the shores of Lake Maggiore. 'With the increased freedom which the child now had, her particular pleasure in climbing soon emerged. It was a natural urge on her part to climb the highest peaks . . . and to imitate the strangest tricks of the tight-rope walkers who appeared in the locality from time to time.' She enjoyed swapping clothes with the local boys so that she could do all these things more easily. She wandered off and frequently got lost, but always returned home. Often, when she came back, she would sit down beneath 'the columns of the portals of a country house in the neighbourhood . . . then she would run into the great hall and look at the statues'. (These were the marble statues of her 'Kennst du das Land?' which held her in their view and asked 'Oh you poor child, what have they done to you?') One day the child went missing for good; her hat was found 'floating on the water, not far from the spot where the mountain torrent ran down to the lake'. The body was never recovered, and the poor mad mother haunted the lake-shore, collecting animal bones washed up there, which she thought were her daughter's.

The text is silent about the abducted child and the time she spends with the rope-dancers; uncertainty about these years is very marked. When Mignon is first brought before Wilhelm and asked how old she is, she replies that '"Nobody has counted the years."' When she is asked about her father, she answers that '"The big devil is dead"' (*WMA* I:88). It is assumed that she is a stolen child: when Wilhelm sees the *Seiltänzer* laying about her with a whip he shouts that the man is not to '"see or touch this creature again until you have given an account, in a court of justice of where you stole her"' (*WMA* I:92). When negotiations are over and the child has been purchased by Wilhelm, 'the black-bearded ferocious Italian' completely cedes his claim in her, but is unwilling to say any more about her origins 'than that he had been looking after her since the death of his brother, who had been called "the big devil" because of his extraordinary skill' (*WMA* I:93). Much later, on the night when Mignon's wildest behaviour and hysterical merriment preceded her slipping away to await a drunken Wilhelm in his bedroom, she is shown to be still preoccupied with 'her supposed father the "big devil"', though on this occasion she denies her fear of him (*WMA* II:109–10).

The modern eye is drawn irresistibly to those spaces in the text where Mignon – for how long? five years? seven years? – is on the road with the acrobats, first on the passage across the Alps, and then from small south German town to town. The eye is drawn to the dead 'devil', and the range of symptoms that the child presents which, against the grain of the explanation that Goethe wrote in the summer of 1796, make absolutely intelligible for us Mignon's pathology, provide the aetiology of her story and, indeed, of her very existence.

We are accustomed to children arriving from nowhere, out of the silences of a piece of fiction, or out of actual Aveyron forests, bearing the bodily and psychic marks of terrible harm done them. The child later called Victor was sighted several times between 1797 and 1800 by farmers living in the Lacaune region of France, and was finally captured in 1800, when he was given into the care of the doctor and psychologist Jean-Marc Itard. He was assumed to be about 11 or 12 years old.[2] Harlan Lane has described the encounter between the Wild Boy and the doctor as forming the stuff of modern legend, particularly in a kind of pedagogic epic, in which a heroic teacher attempts to make human a child who is completely ignorant not only of language, but of the intellectual and cultural traditions of a society which abandoned him to the wild.[3] This conception – the meaning extracted from Itard's care, education and study of Victor – has so much appeal, remarks Lane, that we must surely ask what need it fulfils in parents and other adults.[4]

Besides embodying a set of educational fantasies, and providing a large number of people with the means for thinking through ideas of noble savagery in relationship to post-Romantic conceptions of childhood, Victor's story has also always been the tale of an abandoned and abused child. J.E. Esquirol was not the first to postulate a family nightmare that explained Victor, to imagine 'a reprehensible mother, a poverty-stricken family abandon[ing] their idiot or imbecile child'.[5] The mark on Victor's throat left by the adult who had – presumably – attempted to kill him before leaving has always been noted by the many educators, psychologists and anthropologists who have debated the causes of his disabilities over the last two hundred years.

What must interest us here is the shifting focus of attention to Victor's pathological traits, which Lane has described in some detail. In the 1950s and 1960s, after a century and a half of psychological discussion and in the context of an intense popular and professional interest in the topic, many child psychiatrists and psychologists suggested that the Wild Boy was in fact an autistic child. Case studies of Victor from the 1800s were used to adumbrate the symptoms of a personality disorder, characterised by withdrawal from human contact, by abilities in motor skills and co-ordination that are not matched by abilities in speech and intelligence, by obsessive and repetitive patterns of behaviour and by the child's use of a language that does not serve the purposes of human communication.[6] The claim for the fictional Mignon as an autistic child was prompted by this literature, but it was made at one remove, showing the Romantic child belonging to a self-enclosed, non-referential universe, and finding communication (and sometimes speech itself) extraordinarily difficult.[7]

Tracing the movement of melodramatic modes and conventions from the early nineteenth-century stage to the fiction of Honoré de Balzac and Henry James, Peter Brooks has conceptualised a melodramatic imagination. This practice of modern consciousness is a 'mode of conception and expression . . . a certain fictional system for making sense of experience, a semantic field of force', that operates in regions very distant from the theatre where it was first expressed.[8] Brooks pays attention to the mute gesture of stage drama and the way in which its function alters once it is used in the novel. The dramaturgy of 'gesture and inarticulate cry' on the early nineteenth-century melodramatic stage can be seen to make reference to an eighteenth-century debate on the origins of language, as an attempt to recover 'something like the mythical primal language, a language of presence, purity, immediacy', which could evoke 'the extremism and hyperbole of ethical conflict and manichaeistic struggle'.[9] It was also this debate that very largely dictated how Victor was taught language by Jean Itard.

In a de-sacralised world, within what Brooks calls 'the broad context of Romanticism', where language was held in suspicion because it could so easily be used to disguise or misrepresent thought, mute physical signs offered what mere words cannot offer, which is the hope of recovering and revealing a true, deep meaning and of bringing into the present the ineffable and the absent. Later in the century, the other site for the elaboration of the melodramatic imagination outside the drama was in psychoanalysis. Brooks maintains that 'the full logic of the text of muteness is in fact realised in Freud's discovery of the dream rhetoric, which treats words and concepts as plastic representations'.[10]

The cases of the historical child Victor and the child-figure Mignon, and the evidence of late twentieth-century interpretations of them show that we are all readers after melodrama now (indeed, all readers after Freud). Not only (in company with Sir Walter Scott and Eugene Scribe) do we insist on a muteness and failure of communication in Mignon that Goethe never wrote, but we also *know* that her muteness is a sign of the unspeakable now spoken. We know by the sign of her silence that damage has been done to her.

All of Lane's objections to the labelling of the Wild Boy of Aveyron as autistic also apply to Mignon. Goethe's child-figure was not dumb. Victor was mute, but like Mignon was highly communicative within his own limitations, wanted to make contact with and to please many of the adults around him, and knew a full range of human affect and response. Moreover, Goethe's fictional child is shown knowing these things about herself: she tells Wilhelm that she is 'sufficiently educated to love and to mourn' (*WMA* III:60).

Twentieth-century attempts to find in Victor the symptoms of childhood autism and psychosis belong to a period in which the existence of extensive physical abuse of children was revealed for the first time. The aetiology of autism was extensively written as the child's reaction to its own history and experience, usually one of inadequate and cold, if not cruel, parenting. The precise configuration belongs to the mid-twentieth century, but reinterpretation of Victor's 150-year-old symptoms and patterns of behaviour to serve a modern contemplation of these questions was nothing new.

Now, in the 1990s, the compelling spaces in Mignon's story suggest not so much physical abuse, for that has always been easy of interpretation: Mignon is an acrobat and *thus* the embodiment of cruel adult attention to her body; in the text a child is beaten before our very eyes. Rather, the gaps in Mignon's story, the behaviour she presents, and her elliptical references to her own silence, lead the modern reader unswervingly to the charge of child sexual abuse, probably against the 'big devil': 'Bid me not speak; be nothing spoken/ . . . Fate forbids that aught be told'.[11] In late twentieth-century melodramatic language, 'My poor child, what have they done to you?' *can* only be a question about sexual abuse. To point all of this out is not to claim a final explanation of Mignon; such a move is not only ahistorical, but clearly wrong. The focus of attention is rather the latest in a long series of uses of the Mignon-figure, uses which for nearly two hundred years have given convoluted expression to formal and informal theories of childhood; to all the ways of understanding its meaning that have been outlined in these pages.

Modern fascination with the sexual abuse of children is quite new. Reviewing Otto Rank's *The Incest Theme in Literature and Legend*, which has been translated into English for the first time since its publication in 1912, Liam Hudson suggested that it was 'scarcely five years since incest erupted in our midst as a vehicle for journalists in search of copy, and for all those paediatricians, psychologists and social workers who know in their bones that parents do their children irreparable harm'.[12] Jeffrey Masson's *Assault on Truth* (1985) was a sign that the upheaval was under way, and the belated translation of Rank's text far less to do with its intrinsic interest than with the way in which the topic is, in Kincaid's words, 'pursued with gusto into every nook and cranny of our collective experience'.

The child molested and abused is one of the most commonly told stories of the late twentieth century in Europe and the US, though it is important to note that what is related is usually a story of 'sexual abuse' rather than 'incest'. The British stories that Hudson evokes in mentioning 'the Cleveland fiasco; the rush of dawn raids and care orders,' rarely employ the term 'incest', which as Hudson notes is reserved for more literary manifestations of the obsession and the searching out of the incest theme in Jane Austen (and, indeed, in *Wilhelm Meister*).

In the marginalising of the paedophile that most of these stories involve and their making of him a monster (and also always a man) James R. Kincaid finds inscribed a universal involvement in 'child-loving':

> Admiring children, responding to children as erotic forms, investing one's primary emotions in children, desiring children, engaging in sex with children, helping children, molesting children, worshipping children, devoting one's life to children, living for children: all these forms (and more) are available to us under the general rubric of 'child–love'.[13]

Child-loving makes paedophiles of us all, historical legatees of the sexualisation and eroticisation of the child, our common desire repressed, overlaid and disavowed in the clamour of defamation: 'in the very strength of our denial, the need we have to tell the story so strenuously and so often, always in the same terms exactly, lies a . . . clue to our involvement'.[14] Kincaid describes the rapid development of popular entertainment – made-for-television film in particular – that focuses insistently on abducted, molested and raped children, in documentary and fictional narratives.[15]

The purpose of *Child-loving* is to discover why we all talk about this subject so much: 'why this hypnotic interest? And what is it we are in need of hearing? Exactly the same thing, said or represented over and over again . . .'.[16] Kincaid finds answers by bringing paedophilia in from the margins and making it central to the cultural history of the West, an inevitable response to developments (some of which have been discussed in these pages) which have reified and sexualised 'the child'. This placing of paedophilia on a continuum with the massive psychical and affective investment that is made in children is illuminating; and in so far as it helps us come to some understanding of how that investment has been eroticised, Kincaid's account is unexceptionable and useful. However his conclusions – which are not altogether to the point here, though his means of reaching them are – seem irresponsible as well as illogical. Part of the difficulty lies in his use of and dissatisfaction with Foucauldian definitions of 'power' when used to understand social relationships in the past, and his avowed intention to replace a discourse of 'power' with one of 'play'. (The other problem is the belief that 'power' as a historical concept, explains anything at all.) Kincaid reaches the end of his arguments with a suggestion that the legal prohibition on adult–child sexual relations should be waived. Ending proscription would bring about 'a refiguring of the fields of being and desire, so that bodies and pleasures, released from power, would also be released from abuse and molestation'. He does not think that 'in play there would be an open season on children'.[17]

This solution is a response to the wrong question. Kincaid asks 'why do our children so often engage in sexual relations with adults?' He puts much effort into obliterating the stereotype of the paedophile as monstrous stranger, and replacing him with a quiet, gentle man, whose attentions children often seek out and whose friendship brings them benefits. But the image of paedophile as beneficial friend quite occludes the probability that a sexual relationship like this is one between family members, as indeed does the absence of the term 'incest' from his account. He fails to remind his readers often enough that the adult is much more likely to be a father (or someone occupying the father's place) than a friend, though he is very interested in the narrative aspect of this absence. He indeed points out that children are continuously told to beware of strangers in the face of evidence that most acts of abuse are performed by people the child knows, and then asks why, knowing this,

> we do not have deep explanations of this sort of family romance that animates the tight circle of child and parent [and] family friend . . . Where are the extensive studies of 'pedophilia' as a form of incest? . . . why not investigate the possibility that the substantive term, the motivating activity, is incest, not pedophilia?[18]

His answer to these questions is that the narrative told 'demands the abducting stranger'. Resort to narrative in this way as the motor of explanation involves an evasion of other tales that are told about precisely the same events. It involves ignoring, for instance, the weight of evidence that we possess taken from those who experienced such relationships as children, which suggests that *it hurts*, either physically or psychically. It is strange not to be reminded of this point. Moreover, replacing one image with another, one 'story' with another potential story, resolutely maintains the adult as male, and gives no space at all to consideration of the incestuous or paedophiliac impulses of women (though Kincaid does briefly discuss the way in which the 'story' of paedophilia has effaced the woman's role).[19]

Kincaid notes the 'positive response' of many children engaging in such relationships, and their naming of the paedophile as their '"best friend"'. It is odd indeed to produce as evidence the feelings and desires of those who have quite rigorously been depicted as 'nothing' throughout *Child-loving*, as those who are not in themselves anything, but rather images, bodies, beings located in a field of adult desire. In the terms Kincaid establishes, being 'nothing', children surely cannot *want* anything.

Children's desires (or presumed desires) have been appealed to by many commentators (particularly educators) since the early years of the nineteenth century, as some kind of bottom line of argument for all kinds of behaviour on the part of adults. The appeal was (and still is) connected to the same post-Romantic exaltation of the child that shaped the erotic imagination that it is Kincaid's self-imposed task to deconstruct. His recourse to it, to the 'natural' child, who knows what it wants (in this case, the attentions of a paedophile) is interesting, if completely inconsistent. The much larger part of the problem with Kincaid's proposed solution is that he puts the question the way he does, asking why children want sexual relations with adults, rather than asking the more obvious one, which is forced by his own evidence, of why adults seek all kinds of attachment to children, including sexual attachment. The severer predicament in which the argument finds itself is due to thinking that history proffers any kind of solution at all to the weird problems it allows us to see taking shape and form during the recent past.

The violent and sinister strangers whom Kincaid has revealed as our own desires in paedophiliac guise and their multiple appearances in modern fictions, are often called melodramatic – by Kincaid and many others. In generic terms, they might more accurately be called Gothic, particularly – in the British context – in their resemblance to that central narrative of child abduction and abuse, paedophilia and prostitution, the 'Maiden Tribute of Modern Babylon' of 1885.[20] In her recent discussion of this piece of campaigning journalism and its aftermath, Judith Walkowitz has shown W.T. Stead drawing on English melodrama, particularly in its dramatisation of class exploitation as sexual exploitation, in order to write his sensational story, but also grafting on to it newer elements of pornography and the Gothic fairy-tale.[21] Late nineteenth-century Gothic adds layers of reference to the small dark rooms in which the – possible – defilement of the child Lily takes place, but only if the reader is aware of its conventions. We may need to be schooled in these conventions, but can presume along with Walkowitz that a contemporary audience for the 'Maiden Tribute' did not. In fact, Walkowitz provides the late twentieth-century reader with a careful education in genre and motif and this education allows extremely interesting readings of Stead, as both voyeur and villain. But it is popular Gothic rather than stage melodrama that allows the elaboration of our uncertainty about him, makes us ponder on what he was *really* up to (the paedophile in the guise of rescuer?), and on what *really* happened in the space of that row of asterisks. Stead's rapid movement between different styles and genres in the 'Maiden Tribute' also reinforces the device of uncertainty that is crucial to the Gothic. For very long stretches of the narrative it is simply impossible to decide whether he is hero or villain, sinister or not, because the kind of story one is in changes so often. (It is the *reader* of Stead's text who is uncertain here; there are different questions to ask about the story-content and how it worked when it was released from the printed page and *told*, in many different social contexts, in the summer and autumn of 1885.) This uncertainty of affect was as much a legacy of the 'Maiden Tribute' as was its content, but it was not melodramatic in form, only in motif, for melodrama does not disguise its villains, and everyone involved in its plots is absolutely insistent on speaking the unspeakable.

We have seen the melodramatic in operation with a particular clarity, in the many rewritings and re-representations of Mignon that have been discussed in the preceding pages. Her case may lead us to some conclusions about ways in which the melodramatic imagination was brought into being during the nineteenth and early part of the twentieth centuries. Discussion of the form of stage melodrama and its use of child-figures is helpful here, but ultimately restrictive unless its use and meaning are followed into the modern imagination, in the path Brooks has laid out. In his account of classic nineteenth-century French melodrama, the child accompanies the heroine as a kind of handmaiden of virtue, and is sometimes introduced in its own right, as a sign of innocence. Because children on the melodramatic stage are themselves tropes and gestures, living emblems of innocence and purity, they serve as catalysts for virtuous or vicious actions; their very existence speaks the providential, for 'they suggest the workings of a higher and more enlightened design'.[22] We have seen this structure endure, even in the aetiolated versions of Mignon that were shown on the English melodramatic stage in the 1870s and 1880s. But we have watched the audience too, behind the bull-necked men and the woman in the large hat gazing at Little Dot and at all the little stage fairies who are Mignon's shades, and what we have seen is the knowledge that was brought to bear on that moment of watching, the reformulations and refiguring of childhood, that made the child an aspect of the self, and all that the self had experienced and endured. Among all the other things members of that audience wanted, looking at the child, was their own self.

Having taken a long hard look at Mignon and Mignon-figures, Otto Fenichel concluded that the desire of adult men was precisely this desire, for they saw themselves embodied in the child. They sought to rescue, save, *have* that child, he thought, so they might give to her 'what their own mothers denied them', specifically a baby, in more general terms what they had lost, what all of us have lost, which is the baby or child one formerly was.[23] This was not the only component of the equation Girl = Phallus that Fenichel discussed, but it was the one he thought decisive in paedophilia.

What is important here, and open to investigation, is how that self that the adult embodies in the child is understood by the adult performing that act of the imagination (and sometimes of the flesh). This book has attempted a partial description of some of the knowledge (things read, heard, known, believed, figured and felt), by which strange acts of personification took place, that is, the giving of abstract information about children and children's bodies, shape and form in actual children, not by bringing statues to life through the force of prosopopeia, but by using living bodies as expressions of the deepest springs of the self.

The advantage of seeing developments in the history of the idea of selfhood in this light – quite apart from its intrinsic claim (which is not, of course, exhaustive) that something like this happened in the recent past – is that it removes historical events and developments from the linguistic model of meaning that has prevented many recent commentators from saying that anything much ever did happen in the past, in one way rather than another. In *How Societies Remember*, Paul Connerton discusses the role of bodily practices and habitual actions in preserving and re-enacting the past. There are the commemorative and ritual ceremonies that are the pre-eminent instances of this, but also the whole range of ordinary, everyday taught skills and procedures that effectively re-enact the past.[24]

If one believes that societies are analogous to linguistic systems, or are structured in the way that languages are structured, then there is no place for human bodies except as signs, endowed with meanings by the larger structure. The bodies are only important as vehicles for the expression of something that actually exists elsewhere, in the larger edifice of meaning, or language, or discourse.[25] But Connerton shows ways in which meaning, and knowledge, remembering and affect, actually *come into existence* in human bodies. I have chosen a literary figure or trope, that of personification, to describe that kind of active making of something out of ideas, information heard about or read, stories, realisations, because that whole range was best summed up in the living child, whoever he or she was, there before your very eyes. I think that this act of embodiment was the same kind of material activity as the ones that Connerton describes, that it was something people actively performed in particular societies in a particular historical epoch (which is not finished yet), and that those countless individual acts of recognition and embodiment were not shaped or forced by pre-existing languages, or discourses outside the places and the times where people performed the act of making children's bodies the living emblems of their self and its history.

The knowledge later revealed by psychoanalysis, that the lost thing is not to be found, was not arcane knowledge in the nineteenth century. The elegiac sadness with which the attempt to find the child was usually expressed shows a keen awareness that the child grows up and goes away, that the lost object is not to be found, for the very search alters it, as it goes along, so that the lost thing is not the same now, as it was before.[26] (It is true, however, that this knowledge was not taught by history, the discipline and structure of thought that carried the society's preoccupations with the past; it was much more likely to be learned from the loss described by dynamical physiology.)

This book has not told the whole story. It has said nothing about contemporary commentators who saw these things happening and who saw a denial of the self in the act of embodiment; who suggested that the cry 'I want children' really meant 'I do not want myself'. Friedrich Nietzsche thought that only suffering wanted heirs and wanted to reproduce itself, whilst 'joy . . . does not want heirs, or children – joy wants itself, wants eternity, wants recurrence, wants everything eternally the same'.[27] But the bull-necked men watching the little stage fairy were the children of suffering too. The cry for them was for the self, long lost and gone: possibly a bid for recurrence, eternity, sameness. The end of this particular story that has just been told is the beginning of another, which must be to do with the social effects of embodying these desires in other people, or rather, in human beings just about to become legal subjects and people: that is, in children.

All of this – what has just been read – masks the historian's compulsive search for a child who did once actually exist, that is the eight-year-old street trader in watercresses interviewed by Henry Mayhew some time in the winter of 1850–51. Chapter 7 effaces a very long and tedious search for this child, through every household in Farringdon enumerated in the Census for 1851.

Historical obsessions are about knowing that there is something to be found, though one does not yet quite understand what that thing is. The anonymous street child of the 1850s mattered because, as I have attempted to show, she became caught up in the same set of reworkings that mark the history of the child who never actually existed. The extra-textual afterlife of Goethe's abducted Italian child coincided with the history that Mayhew's child represented. That after 1873 the British investigative imagination was forced to contemplate the spectacle of *Italian* child-acrobats and entertainers on the streets of London and other major cities, has made the disentanglement of the real and the figurative, of the Little Watercress Girl and Mignon, of sociology and personification, especially difficult to effect.

To disentangle the child selling, begging, importuning on the pavement (or weeping, or stoically going about her business, but always, always, *watched*) from the ways available for seeing her is difficult indeed, because Mignon and the Little Watercress Girl were not one and the same; one was more than a name, more than a word. However the

Farringdon child was used and in whatever figurative forms she appeared in the mid-Victorian years, she carried with her the irreducible traces of actual social relations. But in a book which asserts that figurative existence is a form of historical existence, there has been a particular problem in asserting that the child interviewed by Mayhew actually lived, that her existence was recorded, that she could have been found, in one of the entries off Brook Hill, behind Brown's Court and Foy's Court, in one of Clerkenwell's enumerated dwelling places, if only the family had not moved, gone away . . . some time between December 1850 and the day the enumerator called, three months later.

It is the figurative forms of grace and beauty and dignity bestowed by perception and personification upon prosaic little street traders that can lead to those much larger questions of the relationship between the public and the private, which Richard Sennett gives an account of in *The Fall of Public Man*. Here, in discussing the way in which the meaning of life has shifted from the public to the private realm over the last two hundred years, he shows us the eighteenth-century street as a place for performance, for bodies dressed and displayed as if upon a stage, with meaning discernible in that display. By the end of the nineteenth century, he argues, the meaning of life – what a man or woman was, what they *meant* – lay in the articulation of the deepest resources of an interiorised self.[28] Do we see in the eight-year-old street trader, or in the child dancing to the hurdy-gurdy, the attenuated rendition of these large questions, of performance in everyday life, with the child carrying the great burden of the historical distinction between public and private? Certainly, the idea of the street as theatre (in the real and the figurative sense) had not been erased by the time Henry Mayhew stopped the Little Watercress Girl and talked with her; and twenty years later than this, parliamentary debates on the employment and protection of children made their unswerving course of connection between child labour, street hawking, children begging in the streets or singing in public houses, to theatre children, children of the stage. These were public children, children in which the idea of a public life, a life lived in public, a life *performed*, is concomitant with the meaning of the child that this book has sought to explore: the child as interiority, privacy, the deepest place inside: not to be found.

It is important as well to acknowledge that nineteenth-century observers and commentators had rather less difficulty than the twentieth-century historian in both seeing and understanding a relationship between the figurative and the real. A sensibility shaped by a thousand renditions of Mignon's most famous song, her infinitely sad song of yearning for Italy, 'Kennst du das Land', permitted observers of and campaigners on behalf of outcast childhood to know that the child performing its tricks in the street was *cold*. In Goethe's text of 1795–6, Mignon finishes her song and looks meaningfully at young Wilhelm. '"Do you know the land?" "It must be Italy that is meant," answered Wilhelm; "Where did you learn the little song?" "Italy!" Mignon said in a significant manner; "if you go to Italy, take me with you, I'm freezing here"' (*WMA* I:126). She repeats her desire to be warm more than once. In G.R. Sims and Clement Scott's melodrama of 1885 'Jack in the Box', one of the Italian children trapped 'at Toroni's . . . an Italian padrone's den in Saffron Hill', laments thus: '"I want to go back to Italy – To my mother. My father sold me to the padrone & my mother kissed me & cried, & said I should never see her again – and I shan't. I shall die & never see dear Italy again. I was so warm there. I'm so cold here."'[29] Henry Mayhew had made particular note of the cold appearance of the children clustering around the watercress dealers' stands in Farringdon Market, noted how the snow sometimes fell on their 'numbed fingers' as they sat on neighbouring doorsteps, stringing their bundles.[30] But when he asked the child he interviewed about this aspect of her work, she said '"I bears the cold – you must . . . No; I never see any children crying – it's no use".'[31]

Out of the several thousand households in the Farringdon district visited by the Census enumerator in the spring of 1851, there were two recorded to which the street trader in watercresses might have belonged. I was looking for a single-parent household, headed by a woman, who may have given her trade as 'furrier' or as 'fur-skin dresser' – though the child told Mayhew that her mother 'goes out cleaning rooms sometimes, now she don't work at the fur'. There were four children in the family, a boy and a girl, both older than the Little Watercress Girl, and a younger sister who, according to what the child said, must have been two or three years old at the time of the enumeration. The man who lived with her mother was a scissor-grinder, but he would not necessarily appear in the enumeration as part of the household. Ideally, the family sought should have lived in a 'court' rather than a street, lane, alley, place or buildings, and 'Carry H.', another child of the same age as the street trader, might live there.

In March 1851, in enumeration district 219, St-James's 9, 29-year-old Mary-Ann Flodden, an Islington-born furrier, was recorded as living at 9 Bishop Court. Her nine-year-old daughter Ann had been born in Clerkenwell, and there were two other little girls in the family, six-year-old Jane, and a baby of three months: Harriet. The older brother and sister mentioned by the watercress seller could have been absent from home; but there was no mention of a two- or three-year-old, and the absence of any child in the court matching the description of Carry H. makes this an unlikely household.

In enumeration district 20, St-James's 1, at 3 Pigeon Court lived Hannah Hardwick, 44 years old, a fur-skin dresser, and native of County Cork. Her daughter of 20, Mary Ann, and her 16-year old son Henry had been born in the Middlesex parish of St-Andrews. Hannah, 10 years old, was described as a scholar, as was seven-year-old Margaret. No three-year-old was mentioned. Hannah could be the watercress girl, older than she told Mayhew (or perhaps 'past eight' meant that some mid nineteenth-century coming of age had been reached), in which case we must ask where the seven-year-old Margaret came from. Or Margaret could be the watercress girl, younger than she told Mayhew, with two older sisters. Despite these discrepancies, this is the more likely household of the two: Pigeon Court and the whole district was alive with skin dressers, and for the employment of the unnamed 'father-in-law' there was a master cutler's in Key Street. There were, as well, many Jewish households in Turnwell Street ('On Friday night . . . I goes to a Jew's house till eleven o'clock on Saturday night. All I have to do is snuff the candles and poke the fire. You see they keep their Sabbath then, and they won't touch anything . . .').

Sometimes Mayhew amalgamated two (or even three) 'characters' for his journalism; in both households a two-year-old may have died, and an older brother and sister may have left the first. In the first quarter of 1851, the Little Watercress Girl's family may have left the district – '"moved"', as Margaret McMillan was to write sixty years later of a Deptford coster family, her inverted commas suggesting an unwritable horror of family disintegration and dislocation.[32] Anyway, as a witness before the Royal Commission on the Housing of the Working Classes said of Clerkenwell in 1884, 'out of the 35,000 poor people, 3,000 are always on the move'.[33] Given all of this, Hannah Hardwick's 10-year-old is the most likely candidate. But of course it is not her; she is not to be found . . . The search is not the historian's alone. The search is for the self, and the past that is lost and gone; and some of the ways in which, since the end of the eighteenth century, the lost object has come to assume the shape and form of a child.

Notes

(The place of publication is London, unless otherwise indicated.)

Preface

1 Mary Shelley, *Frankenstein* (1818), Penguin, Harmondsworth, 1985. See Ann Mellor, *Mary Shelley. Her Life, Her Fiction, Her Monsters*, Routledge, 1988, for a reading of the Monster as a child. By describing *Frankenstein* as a myth of parturition and motherhood, it was Ellen Moers who first understood Frankenstein's Creature as a child-figure. Ellen Moers, *Literary Women*, Women's Press, 1978, pp.92–110.

2 William H. Sewell, 'Review of Joan Wallach Scott, *Gender and the Politics of History*', *History and Theory*, 29:1 (1990), pp.71–82.

1 *Introduction: Lost and Found*

1 Margaret McMillan, 'In a Garden', *Highway*, June 1911, pp.132–3; 'In Our Garden – Chapterette II', *Highway*, July 1911, pp.148–9; 'Marigold – An English Mignon', *Highway*, September 1911, pp.185–7. The series continued in the issues for May to September, 1912. See Carolyn Steedman, *Childhood, Culture and Class in Britain. Margaret McMillan, 1860–1931*, Virago, 1990, pp.76–80.

2 McMillan's involvement in the land question and contemporary movements that employed the economic theories of Henry George were probably also indicated by her use of this quotation. See Steedman, *Childhood*, pp.85–7. Richard Lesuer of Ann Arbor, Michigan has traced 82 nineteenth-century settings of 'Kennst du das Land'. The well-known ones are by Beethoven (1809), Schubert (1815), Liszt (1842), Schumann (two versions of 1849), Tchaikovsky (1874), and Wolf (1888).

3 Christina Crosby, *The Ends of History. Victorians and 'The Woman Question'*, Routledge, 1991, p.75. British Library, Lord Chamberlain's Collection, Add. Ms 53054N, 'The Frozen Deep. A Drama in Three Acts. By Wilkie Collins, 1866'. Its first public performance was at the Olympia Theatre, in October 1866. It was performed privately in 1857. See Claire Tomalin, *The Invisible Woman. The Story of Nelly Ternan and Charles Dickens*, Viking, 1990, pp.71–3, 96–100.

4 'A clever and pleasing *voltige* on horseback was performed by Miss Mignon, a young rider who made her first appearance in this country.' 'Wulff's Circus', *The Times*, 28 November 1893, p.3.

5 Robert Miles, 'Radcliffe and Interiority: Towards the Making of the

Mysteries of Udolpho', in *Gothic Writing, 1750–1820. A Genealogy*, Routledge, 1993, pp.124–42; p.124.

6 See Robert Pattison, *The Child-figure in English Literature*, Georgia University Press, Athens, 1978.

7 Ibid., p.44. William Wordsworth, 'Ode: Intimations of Immortality from Recollections of Early Childhood' (1807), IV, l.49.

8 Reinhard Kuhn, *Corruption in Paradise. The Child in Western Literature*, University Press of New England for Brown University Press, Hanover, Pennsylvania and London, 1982, p.65. Here Kuhn actually describes this determination as 'an effort'.

9 Lionel Rose, *The Erosion of Childhood. Child Oppression in Britain, 1860–1918*, Routledge, 1991, offers a recent example of this type of history of childhood. But see also E.P. Thompson, *The Making of the English Working Class* (1963), Penguin, Harmondsworth, 1968, pp.366–84.

10 Ludmilla Jordanova, 'New Worlds for Children in the Eighteenth Century: Problems of Historical Explanation', *History of the Human Sciences*, 3:1 (1990), pp.69–83; p.79. See also Anthony Easthope, 'Romancing the Stone: History-writing and Rhetoric', *Social History*, 18:2 (May 1993), pp.235–49.

11 Hugh Cunningham, *The Children of the Poor. Representations of Childhood since the Seventeenth Century*, Blackwell, Oxford, 1991, pp.8–17; pp.9, 218–33.

12 For an earlier and thoughtful discussion of this point see Brian Crozier, 'Notions of Childhood in the London Theatre, 1880–1905', PhD, Cambridge University, 1981, p.12.

13 Carolyn Steedman, *Landscape for a Good Woman*, Virago, 1986, pp.125–6.

14 Cunningham, *Children*, p.88. Catherine Gallagher, *The Industrial Reformation of English Fiction*, University of Chicago Press, Chicago, 1985, pp.3–35.

15 Quoted in Cunningham, *Children*, pp.80–1.

16 For a discussion of the common-law doctrine of *potestas*, and those categories of people who were not to rule but to be ruled, or to be held under the protection and control of a master, see Leonore Davidoff, 'Mastered for Life: Servant and Wife in Victorian and Edwardian England', *Journal of Social History*, 7:4 (1974), pp.406–28; pp.406–7.

17 James R. Kincaid, *Child-loving. The Erotic Child and Victorian Culture*, Routledge, 1992, pp.5, 76–7.

18 John Neubauer, *The Fin-de-Siècle Culture of Adolescence*, Yale University Press, New Haven, 1992.

19 Denise Riley, *'Am I That Name?' Feminism and the Category of 'Woman' in History*, Macmillan, 1988.

20 Kincaid, *Child-loving*, p.15.

21 Mrs Grote (Harriet Grote, née Lewin), *Memoir of the Life of Ary Scheffer*, John Murray, 1860, p.58. See below, pp.33–4 for further discussion of these paintings.
22 For feelings, or affects as 'thoughts embodied', see Michelle Z. Rosaldo, 'Towards an Anthropology of Self and Feeling', in Richard A. Shweder and Robert A. LeVine (eds), *Culture Theory. Essays on Mind, Self and Emotion*, Cambridge University Press, Cambridge, 1984, pp.137–57.
23 Pattison, *The Child-figure*, pp.47–74. Robert Rosenblum, *The Romantic Child. From Runge to Sendak*, Thames & Hudson, 1988.
24 Peter Coveney, *The Image of Childhood. The Individual and Society: A Study of the Theme in English Literature* (originally *Poor Monkey*, 1957), Penguin, Harmondsworth, 1967, p.80. See also John R. Morss, *The Biologising of Childhood. Developmental Psychology and the Darwinian Myth*, Lawrence Erlbaum, Hove, 1990, p.83, p.112, n.1 for an interesting note on Wordsworth, and his legacy of the infant trailing phylogenetic clouds.
25 Charles Taylor, *Sources of the Self. The Making of Modern Identity*, Cambridge University Press, Cambridge, 1989.
26 Ibid., p.501. Rainer Maria Rilke, *Duino Elegies*, trans. J.B. Leishman and Stephen Spender, Hogarth Press, 1963, p.71.
27 Taylor, *Sources of the Self*, p.288.
28 Ibid., p.289. For an extended reading of this point see Mark Freeman, *Rewriting the Self. History, Memory, Narrative*, Routledge, 1993.
29 Franco Moretti, *The Way of the World. The Bildungsroman in European Culture*, Verso, 1987, pp.6–7.
30 Taylor, *Sources of the Self*, p.289. However, historical research on autobiographical writing of the seventeenth and eighteenth centuries, and on the print culture of early modern Europe, has shown us that however hard it may have been for people to find a story for the self, they nevertheless managed to do so. See Roger Chartier (ed.), *The Culture of Print, Power and the Uses of Print in Early Modern Europe*, Polity Press, Cambridge, 1989, pp.1–10. See also David Vincent, *Literacy and Popular Culture*, Cambridge University Press, Cambridge, 1989, pp.54–66.
31 Michel Foucault, *The Care of the Self. Volume 3. The History of Sexuality* (1984), trans. Robert Hurley, Allen Lane, Harmondsworth, 1988.
32 Michel Foucault, *The Order of Things. An Archaeology of the Human Sciences*, Tavistock, 1970, p.369. See also *The Archaeology of Human Knowledge*, Harper & Row, New York, 1972, p.12.
33 Foucault, *The Order of Things*, pp.368–9.
34 Timothy Ashplant and Adrian Wilson, 'Present-Centred History and the Problem of Historical Knowledge', *The Historical Journal*, 31:2 (1988), pp.253–74.

35 Foucault, *The Order of Things*, pp.54–5.

36 Jacques Gélis, *History of Childbirth: Fertility, Pregnancy and Birth in Early Modern Europe*, trans. Rosemary Morris, Polity Press, Cambridge, 1991, p.9.

37 Karl Figlio's account of the concept of 'organisation' in physiology is a striking example of attention paid to the naturalisation of ideology in the language of science. Karl M. Figlio, 'The Metaphor of Organisation. An Historical Perspective on the Bio-medical Sciences of the Early Nineteenth Century', *History of Science*, 14 (1976), pp.17–53; p.26.

38 Robert M. Young, 'Darwin's Metaphor: Does Nature Select?', *Monist*, 55 (1971), pp.442–503; Robert M. Young, *Darwin's Metaphor. Nature's Place in Victorian Culture*, Cambridge University Press, Cambridge, 1985. Gillian Beer, *Darwin's Plots. Evolutionary Narrative in Darwin, George Eliot and Nineteenth Century Fiction*, Routledge & Kegan Paul, 1983, pp.43–69. Evelleen Richards, '"Metaphorical Mystifications": the Romantic Gestation of Nature in British Biology', in Andrew Cunningham and Nicholas Jardine (eds), *Romanticism and the Sciences*, Cambridge University Press, Cambridge, 1990, pp.130–43.

39 Figlio, 'Metaphor of Organisation', p.29.

40 Ibid., p.38.

41 Ibid., pp.42–3.

42 Chartier, *Culture of Print*, p.4.

43 Margaret Spufford, *Small Books and Pleasant Histories. Popular Fiction and Its Readership in Seventeenth Century England*, Cambridge University Press, Cambridge, 1981.

44 Austin Dobson, *Samuel Richardson*, Macmillan, 1902, p.31. *The Rape of Clarissa*, Blackwell, Oxford, 1982, p.5, p.17. Jocelyn Harris, *Samuel Richardson*, Cambridge University Press, Cambridge, 1987, p.9. A.D. Harvey, *Literature into History*, Macmillan, 1978, pp.32–3. Morris Golden, 'Public Context and Imagining Self in *Pamela* and *Shamela*', *English Literary History*, 53:2 (1986), pp.311–29. *Richardsonia XII. Pamela: Four Versions, 1741–1746, by Dance, Clifford, Edge and Goldoni*, Garland, New York, 1976. D.C. Mueke, 'Beauty and Mr. B.', *Studies in English Literature*, 7 (1967), pp.467–74. Margaret Ann Doody, *A Natural Passion. A Study of the Novels of Samuel Richardson*, Clarendon, Oxford, 1974, pp.35–70.

45 J. Hillis Miller, *Versions of Pygmalion*, Harvard University Press, Cambridge, Mass., 1990. Ian Donaldson, *The Rapes of Lucretia: A Myth and its Transformations*, Clarendon, Oxford, 1982. Marina Warner, *Joan of Arc: The Image of Female Heroism*, Weidenfeld & Nicolson, 1981, pp.185–275.

46 Steedman, *Childhood*, p.259.

47 I was particularly concerned to evaluate the influential and

revisionary evolutionism of Henry Drummond, and his belief that with the development of human children, altruism entered the world, and altered existing evolutionary accounts of human history. Henry Drummond, *Lowell Lectures on the Ascent of Man*, Hodder & Stoughton, 1894. See Steedman, *Childhood*, pp.73–4.

48 Steven Knapp, *Personification and the Sublime. Milton to Coleridge*, Harvard University Press, Cambridge, Mass., 1985.

49 Ibid., pp.2–3.

50 Warner, *Joan of Arc*, p.236.

51 'C'est Mignon!' was the phrase with which the many stage versions of Mignon were constantly greeted, after the first performance of Ambroise Thomas's opera *Mignon*, in 1868. See below, pp.31–3, 35–6.

52 Raymond Williams, *Marxism and Literature*, Oxford University Press, 1977, p.190.

2 *Mignon's Progress*

1 *Wilhelm Meisters Theatricalische Sendung, Von Goethe*, Rascher, Zurich, 1910. *Wilhelm Meisters Theatricalische Sendung*, Stuttgart, 1911. *Wilhelm Meister's Theatrical Mission*, trans. Gregory A. Page, Heinemann, 1913. For the discovery of the *Mission* manuscript, see *The Times*, 22 and 28 February, 22 April 1910; *The Times Literary Supplement*, 14 April 1910. The first references to the *Mission* manuscript in Goethe's diary occur in the early part of 1777, though he clearly started work on it in 1776. Nicholas Boyle, *Goethe. The Poet and His Age. Volume I. The Poetry of Desire (1749–1790)*, Clarendon, Oxford, 1991, pp.162, 289.

2 In 1839 Carlyle also translated *Wilhelm Meister's Travels* (originally published in the German in 1821 and 1829). From this date, *Wilhelm Meister's Apprenticeship and Travels, Three Volumes in Two*, became the standard texts for British readers. However, references here are to the most recent, six-volume, English translation of 1977, that of H.M. Waidson. Volumes 1–4 of this contain the text of the *Apprenticeship*, and 5 and 6, the *Years of Travel*. References are made to the volume and page of Waidson's translation, thus: (*WMA* III:105). When reference is made to the final Carlyle translation of 1839, references in the notes are to the volume, book and chapter of his text, e.g. 1,I,iv. The Chapman and Hall edition of 1894 has been used for reference to Carlyle's translation.

3 One that Goethe himself had suggested in his 'Vorwort' to a late edition of *Dichtung und Wahrheit* (Poetry and Truth), and which now became more salient in the early twentieth century. See below, p.47–8.

4 Richard Friedenthal, *Goethe. His Life and Times*, Weidenfeld & Nicolson, 1965, pp.360–1.

5 Johann Wolfgang von Goethe, *Wilhelm Meister's Theatrical Mission*, trans. Gregory H. Page, Heinemann, 1913, p.154.

6 K.R. Eissler, *Goethe. A Psycho-analytic Study, 1775–1786*, 2 volumes, Wayne State University Press, Detroit, 1963, vol. 2, p.757.

7 See Arnd Bohm, '"O Vater, lass uns ziehn!": A Mythological Background to "Mignon's Italian Song"', *Modern Language Notes*, 100:3 (April 1985), pp.651–9, in which the song is discussed in relationship to the myth of Demeter and Persephone. Textual allusions in 'Kennst du das Land' also seem to make specific reference to the *Aeneid* of Virgil, Book 6 – allusions which bestow enormous remoteness and dignity on the mysterious child – though myths of stolen and abducted childhood were clearly of much greater importance for nineteenth- and twentieth-century tellings of Mignon's story. I owe my understanding of Virgilian references in 'Kennst du das Land' to Sabrina Peck.

8 *Briefwechsel zwischen Schiller und Goethe*, ed. Heinz Amerlung, 3 volumes, Deutsche Bibliothek, Berlin, n.d. vol. 1, pp.164–6. Letter 177, Schiller to Goethe, 28 June 1796, trans. Richard Parker. Hereafter *Schiller–Goethe Correspondence.*

9 Franco Moretti, 'Kindergarten', in *Signs Taken for Wonders*, Verso, 1983, pp.157–81.

10 Steven Knapp, *Personification and the Sublime. Milton to Coleridge*, Harvard University Press, Cambridge, Mass., 1985, p.3.

11 Eissler, *Goethe*, pp.758–63. See below, pp.152–3.

12 *Schiller–Goethe Correspondence*, Letter 180, Schiller to Goethe, 2 July 1796, trans. Richard Parker. See Georg Lukács, *Goethe and His Age*, Merlin, 1968, pp.58–9. See also Friedenthal, *Goethe*, p. 366, and Emil Ludwig, *Goethe. The History of a Man. Two Volumes*, Putnam, 1928, vol. 2, p.33 on this correspondence.

13 *Schiller–Goethe Correspondence*, Letter 180. Schiller to Goethe, 2 July 1796, trans. Richard Parker.

14 Friedenthal, *Goethe*, pp.360–1.

15 Jacques Gélis, *History of Childbirth. Fertility, Pregnancy and Birth in Early Modern Europe*, trans. Rosemary Morris, Polity Press, Cambridge, 1991, p.189.

16 Philippe Ariès, *Centuries of Childhood* (1960), Penguin, Harmondsworth, 1973, pp.127–30. Adrian Wilson, 'The Infancy of the History of Childhood: An Appraisal of Philippe Ariès', *History and Theory*, 19 (1980), pp.132–53; p.134.

17 Fritz R. Lachmann, 'Goethes Mignon', *Germanisch-Romanische Monatsschrift*, 15 (1927), pp.103–5, trans. Richard Parker.

18 *Encyclopédie, ou Dictionnaire raisonné des sciences, des arts et des métiers* (The Encyclopedia, or Systematic Dictionary of the sciences, arts and crafts), Tome Dixième [vol.10], Neufchastel, 1765.

19 Johann Huizinga, *The Waning of the Middle Ages* (1924), Arnold, 1970, pp.43–4.

20 Salignac de la Mothe Fénelon, *Dialogues of the Dead*, D. Browne, 1735, pp.393–6. See below, p.40.
21 Robert M. Browning, *Selections from Goethe's Letters to Frau von Stein, 1776–1789*, Camden House, Columbia, 1990, p.162. Letter dated 22 April 1781.
22 Johann Wolfgang von Goethe, *Gedenkausgabe der Werke. Briefe und Gespräche* (Memorial Edition of Goethe's Works. Letters and Conversations), ed. Ernst Beutler, Artemis, Zurich, 1949. vol. 18, p.669, Letter 618, 25 May 1782, trans. Richard Parker. For Goethe's educational care of Fritz von Stein see Ludwig Fertig, *Johann Wolfgang von Goethe, der Mentor*, Wissenschaftliche Buchgesellschaft, Darmstadt, 1991, pp.88–97.
23 Boyle, *Goethe: The Poet and His Age*, p.339.
24 'Erlkonig' ('Elf King'), in Christopher Middleton (ed.), *Johann Wolfgang von Goethe. Selected Poems*, Suhrkamp/Insel, Boston, 1983, pp.86–7.
25 Boyle, *Goethe: The Poet and His Age*, p.340.
26 S.S Prawer, Mignon's Revenge: a Study of Mörike's *Maler Nolten*', *English Goethe Society, Publications*, New Series, 25 (1955–6), pp.63–85.
27 Sir Walter Scott, *A Legend of Montrose* (1819), Adam & Charles Black, Edinburgh, 1883. *Peveril of the Peak* (1828), Adam & Charles Black, Edinburgh, 1883. The 1831 Preface to *Peveril* makes reference to Mignon.
28 Scott, *Legend of Montrose*, pp.60, 66.
29 Scott, *Peveril of the Peak*, pp.189, 236–7. James Boyd, *Goethe's Knowledge of English Literature*, Clarendon, Oxford, 1932, pp.214–16.
30 Michael R. Booth, *English Melodrama*, Herbert Jenkins, 1965, p.71, for the theme of muteness in English melodrama. See Jerome Mitchell, *The Walter Scott Operas. An Analysis of Operas Based on the Work of Sir Walter Scott*, University of Alabama Press, Alabama, 1977, pp.260–70, for operatic reworkings of Fenella. Jane F. Fulcher, *The Nation's Image. French Grand Opera as Politics and Politicised Art*, Cambridge University Press, Cambridge, 1987, pp.23–45 for Eugene Scribe's use of the Fenella figure.
31 Erika Tunner, '"L'Esprit de Mignon": Bilder von der Klassk bis zur Gegenwart' (Mignon – Images from Classicism to the Present), *Goethe-Jahrbuch*, 106 (1989), pp.11–21, trans. Richard Parker. See also Julia König, 'Das Leben im Kunstwerk: Studien zu Goethes Mignon und ihre Rezeption', Lang, Berlin, 1991. Gerhart Hoffmeister (ed.), *Goethe's Mignon und ihre Schwestern in Literatur, Psychologie und Kunst* (Goethe's Mignon and her sisters in Literature, Philosophy and Art), Lang, Frankfurt, forthcoming.
32 Sigmund Freud, 'The Uncanny' (1919), in *Standard Edition of the Collected Works*, vol. 17, Hogarth Press, 1955, pp.217–56. See below, pp.149–50, and chapter 9, passim.

33 John Howard Payne, *Clari; or, The Maid of Milan. An Opera in Two Acts* (1923), Cumberland's British Theatre, 1829; *Home, Sweet Home,* Walker, 1888. Michael R. Booth, *English Melodrama,* Herbert Jenkins, 1965, pp.120–1; 'The Metropolis on the Stage', in H.J Dyos and Michael Wolff, *The Victorian City. Volume I, Images and Reality,* Routledge & Kegan Paul, 1973, pp.211–24.

34 Herman Merivale, 'The Lord of the Manor. A Drama in Three Acts. Founded Upon Goethe's *Wilhelm Meister*', 1879. British Museum, Lord Chamberlain's Collection. Add. Ms 532230. 'A stage work weak, bald, tame and somewhat dreary . . . the first failure of the New Year', *The Era,* 11 January 1880, p.5.

35 C.R. Sanders and K.J. Fielding (eds), *The Collected Letters of Thomas and Jane Welsh Carlyle,* 7 volumes (1970–7), Duke University Press, Durham, North Carolina, vol. 2 (1822–3), 1970, pp.395–6.

36 Thomas Carlyle, *William Meister's Apprenticeship and Travels,* trans. from the German of Goethe, three vols in two, Chapman and Hall, 1894. Translator's Preface to the first edition of *Meister's Apprenticeship,* Edinburgh, 1824.

37 See Robert Pattison, *The Child Figure in English Literature,* University of Georgia Press, Athens, 1978, pp.47–75.

38 Anne-Louise-Germaine de Staël-Holstein, *Germany. Translated from the French. In Three Volumes* (1810), John Murray, 1813, vol. 2, pp.326–8.

39 *Mignon. Opéra Comique. Paroles de Michel Carré et Jules Barbier. Musique de Ambroise Thomas* (Mignon. A Comic Opera. Words by Michel Cavié and Jules Barbier. Music by Ambrose Thomas.) (1866), Calmann-Levy, Paris, 1870. 'Mignon. Opera in Three Acts. English Translation by Thomas J. Williams', 1870, British Library, Lord Chamberlain's Collection, Add. Ms 53086.

40 'Mignon. Opera in Three Acts. English Translation by Thomas J. Williams', Act I, p.9.

41 Walter Wagner, 'Goethes Mignon', *Germanisch-Romanische Monatsschrift,* 21 (1933), pp.401–15; p.411.

42 F. Leslie Morton, 'Mignon. The One-Act Operatic Comi-tragique Burlesque, or, The Egg-dancer's Pet and the Artful Coquette', 1886. British Library, Lord Chamberlain's Collection, Add. Ms 53357K, p.14.

43 Tracy C. Davis, 'The Spectacle of Absent Costume. Nudity on the Victorian Stage', *New Theatre Quarterly,* 5:20 (1989), pp.321–47 for the variety of costume and bodily display experienced by Victorian women performers. Marilyn R. Brown, *Gypsies and Other Bohemians. The Myth of the Artist in Nineteenth Century France,* UMI Research Press, Ann Arbor, Michigan, 1985 for the fantasies embodied in this kind of costume.

44 This photograph appears in Robert R. Tuggle, *The Golden Age of Opera,* Holt, Reinhart & Winston, New York, 1983, p.41.

45 *Catalogue*, Museum Ary Scheffer, Dordrecht, 1934. Leo Ewals, Ary Scheffer, Sa Vie et son oeuvre (Ary Scheffer. His Life and Work.), s.l, s.n, Nijmegen, 1987, pp.276–7; p.287. See also p.298 for the 'Mignon et le vieux jouer de harpe' (Mignon and the Old Harpist) of 1844.
46 Brown, *Gypsies*, p.43. It is not clear which passage of Goethe Brown refers to here. His Mignon is never vivacious, let alone vivaciously 'Southern'. Théophile Gautier, 'Ary Scheffer', *L'Artiste*, 20 June 1858, p.99.
47 De Staël-Holstein, *Germany*, vol. 2, pp.326–8.
48 Mrs Grote, *Memoir of the Life of Ary Scheffer*, John Murray, 1860, p.58.
49 This appears to be Lewes's own translation – not Carlyle's (*WM*, 1, VIII, i). George Henry Lewes, *Female Characters of Goethe, from the Original Drawings of William Kaulbach. With Explanatory Text by G.H. Lewes*, Frederick Buckmann, 1872, Plates 18 and 19.
50 *The Era*, 10 July 1870, p.10.
51 Emma Albani, *Forty Years of Song*, Mills & Boon, 1911, pp.53–62.
52 *The Times*, 6 July 1874, p.14; 18 May 1882, p.14.
53 Ibid., 11 July 1870, p.5.
54 Ibid., 14 January 1880, p.10.
55 *The Times*, 18 May 1882.
56 Mrs Forrester, *Mignon*, 3 vols, Hurst & Blackett, 1877, vol. 1, pp.67–9; vol. 2, pp.4–5; 264–5; vol. 3, pp.42–3. As far as Mrs Forrester is concerned, 'connue comme Mrs Bridges', says the Bibliothèque Nationale catalogue, unhelpfully.
57 Merivale, 'Lord of the Manor'. *The Era*, 11 January 1880, p.5. *Daily Telegraph*, 5 January 1880, p.6. Clement Scott and Cecil Howard, *The Life and Reminiscences of E.L Blanchard, with Notes from the Diary of Wm. Blanchard, in Two Volumes*, Hutchinson, 1891, vol. 2, pp.495–6.
58 Or Henrietta Eliza Vaughan – considered by Ruskin to be the author 'to whom we owe the most finished and faithful rendering yet given of the character of the British soldier'! *Who Was Who*, vol. 1, 1856–1911.
59 J.S Winter, *Bootle's Baby. A Story of the Scarlet Lancers*, Frederic Warne, 1885, pp.16–19; p.47. See below, pp.145–6 for 'La Figlia del Regimento'.
60 John Strange Winter, *Mignon's Secret*, F.V. White, 1886, Preface; pp.10–15, 23, 46. This portrait of barrack life is presumably the reason for Ruskin's judgement of Mrs Stannard. See n.58.
61 Winter, *Bootle's Baby*, p.19.
62 Winter, *Mignon's Secret*, pp.42, 44, 58–9.
63 Ibid., pp.63–4.
64 Ibid., pp.83, 89.
65 Ibid., p.98.
66 John Strange Winter, *Mignon's Husband*, F.V. White, 1887, p.58.
67 Ibid., p.63.

68 Ibid., p.111.
69 Frédéric Duhomme et Piel de Troisements, *Le Dernier jour de Mignon. Drame en un acte, en vers. Répresenté pour la première fois, à Paris, sur le théâtre de la Porte-St-Martin, le 19 avril 1874* (Mignon's Last Day. A Verse Drama in one Act. Staged for the first time at the Porte-St-Martin Theatre, 19 April 1874), Barbré, Paris, 1874.
70 George du Maurier, *Trilby. A Novel*, Osgood McIlvaine, 1895, pp.379, 441.
71 See above, pp.1–2.
72 Arthur Symons, 'Nora on the Pavement' (1909), in *Poems by Arthur Symons*, vol. 1, John Lane, New York, 1911, pp.83–4. See below, pp.127–8.
73 *Mignon. A Tale. Translated from the French*, P. O'Shea, New York, 1868, pp.22, 32. Like Winter's versions, this text is interesting for its displacement of Mignon's silences and her androgyny on to another female character.
74 Richard Rosenbaum, 'Mignons Urbild' (Mignon's Original). This talk given to the Berlin Society for German Literature on 21 October 1896 was reported in the *Deutsche Literatur-Zeitung* (7 November 1896) as Richard Rosenbaum, 'Mignons Urbild', *Chronik der Wiener Goethe-Vereins*, vol. 11 (10 March 1897), pp.5–6, trans. Richard Parker. Richard Rosenbaum, 'Mignons Herkunft' (Mignon's Origin), *Archiv für das Studium der neueren Sprachen und Literaturen*, 100 (1898), pp.1–22.
75 Rosenbaum discussed Alois Brandl's lecture to the Society for German Literature, Berlin, given in November 1896 and reported in *Vossische Zeitung*, 577 (9 December 1896), and in *Euphorion*, 4 (1896), p.437.
76 Eugen Wolff, *Mignon. Ein Beitrag zur Geschichte des Wilhelm Meister* (A Contribution to the History of Wilhelm Meister), C.H. Becksche, Munich, 1909.
77 Rosenbaum 'Mignons Herkunft', p.22.
78 Emil Ludwig, *Goethe: The History of a Man*, 2 volumes, Putnam, 1928, vol. 1, pp.217, 268–9.
79 Sarah Fielding, *The Governess, or, the Little Female Academy* (1749), Women's Press, 1987, pp.20–34.
80 Abbé Antoine Banier, *Mythology and Fables of the Ancients. Translated from the French*, 4 vols, Andrew Millar, Edinburgh, 1739–40. Fénelon, *Dialogues of the Dead.*
81 W.H. Bruford, *Culture and Society in Classical Weimar, 1775–1806*, Cambridge University Press, Cambridge, 1962, p.145.
82 Ibid., pp.110–11. J.M Tanner, *A History of the Study of Human Growth*, Cambridge University Press, Cambridge, p.99.
83 Dorothea Flashar, *Bedeutung, Entwicklung und literarische Nachwirkung von Goethes Mignongestalt* (Significance, Development and Literary

After-effects of Goethe's Mignon figure), E. Ebering, Berlin, 1929. See also Walter Wagner, 'Goethes Mignon', *Germanisch-Romanische Monatsschrift*, 21 (1933), pp.401–15.

84 Flashar *Bedeutung*, p.100.

85 Reinhard Kuhn, *Corruption in Paradise. The Child in Western Literature*, Brown University Press/University Press of New England, Hanover, Pennsylvania, 1982, pp.186, 187.

86 Sigmund Freud, 'Beyond the Pleasure Principle' (1920), in *Standard Edition of the Complete Psychological Works of Sigmund Freud*, vol. 18, Hogarth Press, 1950. See below, pp.90 and n. 72.

87 Philipp Sarasin, 'Goethes Mignon. Eine psychoanalytische Studie' (Goethe's Mignon. A psychoanalytic study), *Imago*, 15 (1929), pp.349–99; 388–9, trans. Richard Parker.

88 Kuhn, *Corruption*, pp.60–5.

89 See Sarasin, 'Goethes Mignon', p.388, on uncertainty of age in Mignon. See Wolff, *Mignon*.

90 Franco Moretti, *The Way of the World: the Bildungsroman in European Culture*, Verso, 1987, p.19.

91 Ibid., pp.6–7.

3 *Figures and Physiology*

1 Edward Manier, 'History, Philosophy and Sociology of Biology. A Family Romance', *Studies in the History and Philosophy of Science*, 11:1 (1980), pp.1–24; p.17 (Manier's emphasis).

2 J.M. Tanner, *A History of the Study of Human Growth*, Cambridge University Press, Cambridge, 1981, p.99. W.H. Bruford, *Culture and Society in Classical Weimar, 1775–1806*, Cambridge University Press, 1962, pp.110–11. T.J. Reed, *Goethe*, Oxford University Press, Oxford, 1984, pp.43–53. Nicholas Boyle, *Goethe. The Poet and the Age. Volume 1. The Poetry of Desire*, Clarendon, Oxford, 1991, pp.252–6, 277–9, 335–7, 346–50. This fascination with questions of gigantism and dwarfism was general in the eighteenth century, according to Geoffroy Saint-Hilaire, *Histoire générale et particulière des anomalies de l'organisation chez l'homme et les animaux* (A General and Specific Account of Organisational Irregularities in Man and Animals), 3 vols, Ballière, Paris, 1832–7, vol. 1, pp.140–2; p.142. Antoine Banier, *Mythology and Fables of the Ancients. Translated from the French*, 4 vols, Andrew Millar, Edinburgh, 1739–1840, vol. 2, pp.192–207.

3 Bruford, *Culture and Society*, pp.145–7. George Henry Lewes, *The Life and Works of Goethe* (1858), Dent, 1908, p.295, quoting a letter from Goethe to Knebel. Johann Wolfgang von Goethe, *Gedenkausgabe der Werke. Briefe und Gespräche*, ed. Ernst Beutler, Artemis, Zurich, 1949, vol. 18, p.813. Letter 778, 17 November 1784.

4 Quoted by Emery Neff, *The Poetry of History. The Contribution of*

Literature and Literary Scholarship to the Writing of History since Voltaire, Columbia University Press, New York, 1947, p.68.

5 Boyle, *Goethe: The Poet and His Age*, pp.385–6.

6 Bruford, *Culture and Society*, p.145.

7 Boyle, *Goethe: The Poet and His Age*, pp.355, 368–9, 446, 477. Johann Wolfgang von Goethe, *Italian Journey*, 1786–1788, trans. W.H. Auden and Elizabeth Mayer (1962), North Point Press, San Francisco, 1982, p.172.

8 Goethe, *Italian Journey*, p.55.

9 Ibid., p.251.

10 Ibid., p.363.

11 Agnes Arber, 'Goethe's Botany. The Metamorphosis of Plants (1790) and Tobler's Ode to Nature (1782)', *Chronica Botanica*, 10:2 (1946), pp.63–126; p.75 discusses nineteenth-century attempts to provide a term that was not hampered by everyday associations as 'leaf' is. Goethe sought to describe a part of the plant that undergoes successive changes, appearing as one lateral appendage after the other. The foliage leaf is no more his 'Leaf' than is the cotyledon or the stamen.

12 Boyle, *Goethe: The Poet and His Age*, p.594. Arber 'Goethe's Botany', pp.89–115. The first English translation appeared in 1863 (ibid., p.87).

13 Garland E. Allen, *Life Sciences in the Twentieth Century*, Cambridge University Press, Cambridge, 1978, pp.161–2.

14 William Coleman, *Biology in the Nineteenth Century. Problems of Form, Function and Transformation*, Cambridge University Press, Cambridge, 1977, p.14. J. Schiller, 'Physiology's Struggle for Independence in the First Half of the Nineteenth Century', *History of Science*, 7 (1968), pp.64–89; p.73. Timothy Lenoir, 'Teleology without Regrets. The Transformation of Physiology in Germany, 1790–1847', *Studies in the History and Philosophy of Science*, 12:4 (1981), pp.293–354.

15 Allen, *Life Sciences*, pp.162–3.

16 Timothy Lenoir, *The Strategy of Life. Teleology and Mechanism in Nineteenth Century German Biology*, Reidel, Dordrecht, 1982, p.305. See p.298 for the way in which a 'research programme' was generated when this principle was applied to science: a negative heuristic came into being through the generation of a succession of refutable variants, each of which reflected some aspect of its predecessor and thus 'ultimately extend[ed] its explanatory domain'.

17 Ibid., pp.69–70.

18 Boyle, *Goethe: The Poet and His Age*, pp.594–5. Lenoir, *Strategy*, p.28. François Delaporte, *Nature's Second Kingdom. Explorations of Vegetality in the Eighteenth Century*, trans. Arthur Goldhammer, MIT Press, Cambridge, Mass., 1982.

19 Bruford, *Culture and Society*, p.257. Dorothea Flashar, *Bedeutung, Entwicklung und literarische Nachwirkung von Goethes Mignongestalt*

(Significance, Development and Literary After-effects of Goethe's Mignon figure), Ebering, Berlin, 1929, Chapter 6. William Gilby, 'The Structural Significance of Mignon in *Wilhelm Meister*, *Seminar*, 16:3 (1980), pp.136–50; p.137.

20 *Dichtung und Wahrheit*, Part Three, in vol. 28 of the *Sophienausgabe*, edn, 133 vols in 143, 1887–1919, Boehlau, Weimar. This passage is given in the apparatus to vol. 28 as 'Goethe's corrected drafts of a Preface to the Third Part of *Dichtung and Wahrheit*'. This was originally published in 1813, trans. Richard Parker. See Mary Gies Hatch, 'Mignon: Goethe's Study of Affectional Frustration in Childhood', in Alexej Ugrinsky (ed.), *Goethe in the Twentieth Century*, Greenwood Press, New York, pp.133–8; p.137, n.9; and also Bruford, *Culture and Society*, pp.142–51, 236–54, 256–7; also Boyle, *Goethe: The Poet And His Age*, pp.415–530.

21 Flashar, *Bedeutung*, p.56.

22 Ibid., p.60.

23 Lewes, *Life and Works*, p.359.

24 Ibid., p.353.

25 Ibid., p.338.

26 Ibid., pp.338–9, 358–9.

27 Ibid., p.369. Walther Riese, 'Goethe's Conception of Evolution and Its Survival in Medical Thought', *Bulletin of the History of Medicine*, 23 (1949), pp.546–53; p.553.

28 Timothy Lenoir, 'Generational Factors in the Origin of Romantische Naturphilosophie', *Journal of the History of Biology*, 11:1 (1978), pp.57–110; pp.70–1, p.83.

29 Lambert J. Quetelet, *Physique social. Essai sur le developpement des facultés de l'homme*, 2 vols, Muquardt, Brussels, 1835. *A Treatise on Man and the Development of His Faculties* (1842), Scholars Facsimiles and Reprints, Gainsville, Florida, 1962. Percy Boulton, 'On the Physical Development of Children or the Bearing of Anthropometry to Hygiene', *Lancet*, (1880 Part 2), pp.610–11.

30 Tanner, *A History*, pp.123–4. V. John, *Quetelet bei Goethe* (Quetelet in Goethe), Fischer, Jena, 1898, p.328.

31 Riese, 'Goethe's Conception', p.546. Emphasis in original. See also Lenoir, *Strategy*, p.76.

32 Lewes, *Life and Works*, p.363.

33 See T.J. Reed, *Goethe*, Oxford University Press, Oxford, 1984, pp.45–50.

34 George Henry Lewes, *Sea-side Studies at Ilfracombe, Tenby, the Scilly Isles and Jersey*, Blackwood, Edinburgh, 1858, p.34. Lewes underlined 'possession' three times.

35 Coleman, *Biology*, pp.2–3.

36 Ibid., p.3. Schiller, 'Physiology's Struggle'.

37 'Physiology's Struggle', p.64.
38 Peter J. Bowler, *The Non-Darwinian Revolution. Reinterpreting a Historical Myth*, Johns Hopkins University Press, Baltimore, Maryland, 1988.
39 Coleman, *Biology*, p.18.
40 Lois N. Magner, *A History of the Life Sciences*, Dekker, New York, 1979, pp.288–340.
41 Michel Foucault, *The Order of Things. An Archaeology of the Human Sciences*, Tavistock, 1970, p.228.
42 Sergio Moravia, 'The Enlightenment and the Sciences of Man', *History of Science*, 18 (1980), pp.247–68; p.253. Schiller, 'Physiology's Struggle', p.80.
43 E. Benton, 'Vitalism in Nineteenth Century Scientific Thought. A Typology and Reassessment', *Studies in the History and Philosophy of Science*, 5:1 (1974–5), pp.17–48; pp.18, 20.
44 Magner, *Life Sciences*, pp.302–15.
45 June Goodfield-Toulmin, 'Some Aspects of English Physiology, 1780–1940', *Journal of the History of Biology*, 2 (1969), pp.283–320; pp.291–2. Stephen J. Cross, 'John Hunter, the Animal Oeconomy and Late Eighteenth Century Physiological Discourse', *Studies in the History of Biology*, 5 (1981), pp.1–110. John Hunter, *The Works of John Hunter*, ed. J.F. Palmer, 4 vols, Longman, 1835–7, vol. 1, pp.221–8.
46 Goodfield-Toulmin, 'English Physiology', pp.291–2, quoting Hunter, ibid.
47 Lewes, *Life and Works*, p.322.
48 Goodfield-Toulmin, 'English Physiology', p.290.
49 L.S Jacyna, 'The Romantic Programme and the Reception of Cell Theory in Britain', *Journal of the History of Biology*, 17:1 (1984), pp.13–48, quoting G. Valentin, *Handbuch der Entwickelungsgeschichte des Menschen* (Guide to the History of the Development of Human Beings), Rucker, Berlin, 1835. Anon., 'Coleridge and Freke on Life, Review of *Hints Towards the Formation of a More Comprehensive Theory of Life*. By S.T. Coleridge. Edited by Seth Watson, London, 1848', *British and Foreign Medico-Chirurgical Review*, 3 (January 1849), pp.194–8. Walter F. Cannon, 'History in Depth: The Early Victorian Period', *History and Science*, 3 (1964), pp.20–38; p.23.
50 D.M. Knight, 'The Physical Sciences and the Romantic Movement', *History of Science*, 9 (1970), pp.54–75; pp.57–9. Edward Royle, *Radicals, Secularists and Republicans. Popular Freethought in Britain, 1866–1915*, Manchester University Press, Manchester, 1980, pp.88–177, and *Victorian Infidels. The Origins of the British Secularist Movement, 1791–1866*, Manchester University Press, Manchester, 1974, for some discussion of the place of science in popular freethought. Humphrey Davy, *Consolations in Travel, or, The Last Days of a Philosopher*, John Murray, 1830, especially 'Dialogue the Fourth. The Proteus, or Immortality'.

51 Lenoir, 'Generational Factors', p.57.
52 L. Pearce Williams, 'The Physical Sciences in the First Half of the Nineteenth Century. Problems and Sources', *History of Science*, 1 (1962), pp.1–15; p.1.
53 Lenoir, *Teleology*, p.298.
54 Ibid., p.215.
55 Coleman, *Biology*, p.48. John R. Morss, *The Biologising of Childhood. Developmental Psychology and the Darwinian Myth*, Lawrence Erlbaum, Hove, 1990, pp.11–29.
56 See above, n.4.
57 Neff, *Poetry of History*, p.68. See also Morss, *Biologising*, pp.33–4.
58 C.U.M. Smith, 'Evolution and the Problem of Mind. Part I. Herbert Spencer', *Journal of the History of Biology*, 51:1 (1982), pp.56–88; p.56.
59 Ibid., p.56. Karl Ernst von Baer, *Über Entwickelungsgeschichte der Thiere* (On the History of the Development of Animals), Borntrager, Königsberg, 1828.
60 Foucault, *The Order of Things* (1970), p.228.
61 Ibid., pp.229–32.
62 Lenoir, *Strategy*, p.76.
63 Jacyna, 'Romantic Programme', p.20.
64 Magner, *Life Sciences*, p.215. François Bichat, *Anatomie générale, appliqué à la physiologie et à la médicine* (1801), trans. as *General Anatomy applied to Physiology and the Practice of Medicine*, trans. Constant Coffin, and privately printed, 2 vols, 1824. W.R. Albury, 'Experiment and Explanation in the Physiology of Bichat and Magendie', *Studies in the History of Biology*, 1 (1977), pp.47–131.
65 Magner, *Life Sciences*, p.215.
66 Ibid., p.217.
67 For earlier conceptualisations of protoplasm, see L.S. Jacyna 'Romantic Thought and the Origins of Cell Theory', in Andrew Cunningham and Nicholas Jardine (eds), *Romanticism and the Sciences*, Cambridge University Press, Cambridge, 1991, pp.161–8.
68 J.M. Schleiden, *Principles of Scientific Botany, or, Botany as an Inductive Science*, trans. Edwin Lankester, Longman, 1849, pp.31–80.
69 'Review of J.M. Schleiden, *The Plant: a Biography. In a Series of Popular Lectures*, Translated by Arthur Henfrey, London, 1848', *British and Foreign Medico-Chirurgical Review*, 2 (October 1848), pp.368–82.
70 Theodore Schwann, *Microscopical Researches into the Accordance of the Structure and Growth of Animals and Plants* (1839), trans. Henry Smith, Sydenham Society, 1847, p.ix.
71 Schwann, *Microscopical*, p.39.
72 Ibid., pp.39, 161, 165–6.
73 Everett Mendelsohn, 'The Biological Sciences in the Nineteenth

Century. Some Problems and Sources', *History of Science*, 3 (1964), pp.39–59; p.42.

74 Schwann, *Microscopical*, p.2.

75 Ibid., pp.186–8.

76 Oswei Temkin, Materialism in French and German Physiology of the Early Nineteenth Century', in *The Double Face of Janus and Other Essays in the History of Medicine*, Johns Hopkins University Press, Baltimore, Maryland, 1977, pp.340–4; p.342.

77 L.S. Jacyna, 'John Goodsir and the Making of Cellular Reality', *Journal of the History of Biology*, 16:1 (1983), pp.75–99.

78 T.H. Huxley, 'The Cell-Theory', *British and Foreign Medico-Chirurgical Review*, 12 (October 1853), pp.15–243. Erling Eng, 'Thomas Henry Huxley's Understanding of Evolution', *History of Science*, 16 (1978), pp.291–303.

79 Jacyna, 'Romantic Programme', pp.14, 16, 20.

80 Ibid., p.22.

81 Anon., 'Dr Carpenter's Principles of Human Physiology', *British and Foreign Medico-Chirurgical Review*, 8 (October 1851), pp.509–25.

82 Jacyna, 'Romantic Programme', pp.41–2.

83 Jacyna, 'Romantic Thought', p.167.

84 Magner, *Life Sciences*, pp.228–36.

85 Rudolph Ludwig Carl Virchow, *Cellular Pathology as based upon Physiological and Pathological Histology* (1859), trans. F. Chance, John Churchill, 1860. Oswei Temkin, 'Metaphors of Human Biology', in *The Double Face of Janus*, pp.271–83, on the political importance of the cell.

86 Magner, *Life Sciences*, pp.231–2.

87 Coleman, *Biology*, pp.17, 30.

88 Gerald L. Geison, *Michael Foster and the Cambridge School of Physiology*, Princeton University Press, Princeton, 1978, p.21.

89 Schiller, 'Physiology's Struggle', p.73.

90 Cornelius Black, *Letters on the More Evident Changes Which the Body Undergoes, and, The Management of Health in Infancy and Adult Age*, Whittaker, 1846, pp.47–9. Schleiden, *Principles*, p.80.

91 *Encyclopaedia Britannica*, 9th edn, vol. 19, Adam & Charles Black, Edinburgh, 1885, p.12.

92 Anon., 'Physical Physiology', *British and Foreign Medico-Chirurgical Review*, 19 (April 1857), pp.261–74.

93 Lewes, *Life and Works*, p.218.

94 Ibid., p.218.

95 John William Draper, *Human Physiology, Statistical and Dynamical; or the Conditions and Course of the Life of Man* (1856), Harper, New York, 1868, p.549.

96 *Encyclopaedia Britannica*, 9th edn, vol. 19, p.12. Magner, 'Cell Theory', *Life Sciences*, p.228. Huxley, p.314.

97 *Encyclopaedia Britannica*, 9th edn, vol. 19, pp.9, 17. See J. Hughlings Jackson, 'Croonian Lectures on the Evolution and Dissolution of the Nervous System', *British Medical Journal*, (1884 Part 1), pp.591, 660, 703. Also reported in the *Lancet*, (1884 Part 1), pp.555, 660, 739. See also Jackson's 'On Some Implications of the Dissolution of the Nervous System', *Medical Press and Circular*, (1883 Part 2), pp.64, 84; (1884 Part 2), pp.411, 433. See C.U.M. Smith, 'Evolution and the Problem of Mind. Part II, John Hughlings Jackson', *Journal of the History of Biology*, 15:2 (1982), pp.241–62. E.A Stengal, 'Hughlings Jackson's Influence on Psychiatry', *British Journal of Psychiatry*, 109 (1963), pp.348–55.

98 Lewes, *Life and Works*, pp.366–7. Emphasis in original.

99 Boyle, *Goethe: The Poet and His Age*, p.596.

100 Lewes, *Life and Works*, p.322. Here Lewes provided his own translation of the second apostrophe of Tobler's *Die Natur* (Nature) 1782, which was attributed to the young Goethe by the old, and by many other commentators. See Arber 'Goethe's Botany', pp.121–4 for the *Ode* itself, and p.120 for an account of Thomas Huxley's translation for the first volume of *Nature* in 1869, and of other nineteenth-century English-language versions.

4 *Physiological Bodies*

1 George Henry Lewes, *The Physiology of Common Life*, 2 vols, Blackwood, Edinburgh, 1859–60, vol. 2, p.428.

2 George Henry Lewes, *Sea-side Studies at Ilfracombe, Tenby, the Scilly Isles and Jersey*, Blackwood, Edinburgh, 1858, p.322.

3 William B. Carpenter, *Principles of Human Physiology, General and Comparative*, 5th edition, John Churchill, 1855, p.14. (Originally published as *Principles of General and Comparative Physiology*, 1839). *British and Foreign Medico-Chirurgical Review*, 11 (January 1853), pp.155–6.

4 Carpenter, *Principles*, p.928.

5 John William Draper, *Human Physiology, Statistical and Dynamical; or, the Conditions and the Course of the Life of Man* (1856), Harper, New York, 1868, p.550.

6 Ibid., p.548.

7 *Encyclopaedia Britannica*, 9th edition, vol. 17, Adam & Charles Black, Edinburgh, 1884, pp.686–7. J.M. Tanner, *A History of the Study of Human Growth*, Cambridge University Press, Cambridge, 1981, p.372 makes a similar point about the puzzle that growth presents to modern physiology.

8 Erasmus Darwin, *The Temple of Nature, or The Origin of Society* (1803), in *The Golden Age. The Temple of Nature*, ed. Donald A. Reiman, Garland, New York, 1978, p.43.

9 Thomas Jameson, *Essays on the Changes of the Human Body, at Its*

Different Ages; the Diseases to Which It is Predisposed in each Period of Life: and the Physiological Principles of Its Longevity, Longman, 1811, p.24, pp.25–31.

10 Henry Ashby and G.A. Wright, *The Diseases of Children, Medical and Surgical*, Longman, Green, 1889, pp.1–13.

11 Karl M. Figlio, 'The Metaphor of Organisation. An Historical Perspective on the Bio-medical Sciences of the Early Nineteenth Century', *History of Science*, 14 (1976), pp.17–53; pp.32–7. Oswei Temkin, 'Basic Science, Medicine and the Romantic Era', *Bulletin of the History of Medicine*, 37 (1963), pp.97–129. Marilyn Butler, 'Introduction' to Mary Shelley, *Frankenstein*, Pickering and Chatto, 1993.

12 See above, p.55.

13 Jameson, *Essays*, p.11.

14 Ibid., pp.12–13.

15 Ibid., p.16.

16 Ibid., p.16.

17 Ibid., pp.103–4, 138.

18 Draper, *Human Physiology*, p.549.

19 J.B. Harrison, *Familiar Letters on the Diseases of Children, Addressed to a Young Practitioner*, John Churchill, 1862. Ashby and Wright, *Diseases*, p.1.

20 Charles West, *Lectures on the Diseases of Infancy and Childhood* (1848), Longman, 1859, pp.1–13. 'Editorial', *Lancet*, (1879 Part 2), pp.472–3. P.M. Braidwood, *The Domestic Management of Children*, Smith Elder, 1874, was typical in naming rivals in his Preface. He considered them to be Henry Pye Chavasse in his many manifestations and editions; as Combe's *Principles of Physiology*, which according to its author achieved sales of 45,000 in the UK and the US between 1834 and 1842; and interestingly, as Jean Baptiste Fonssagrives's *De la Régeneration physique de l'espèce humaine par l'hygiène de la famille, et en particulier du rôle de la mère dans les maladies des enfants* (A Treatise on the Physical Regeneration of the Human Race, by means of family hygiene, and in particular the role of mothers in the care of sick children), Coulet, Montpelier, 1867. Braidwood claimed his own book to be both simpler and cheaper – 'so cheap that it can find its way into *every* home'.

21 Henry Pye Chavasse, *Advice to a Mother on the Management of Her Children, to which is added Counsel to a Mother*, Lippincott, Philadelphia, 1877, p.v. This includes his often revised *Advice to Mothers on the Management of Their Offspring*, which was originally published in Britain in 1839. The 1877 edition includes two volumes, paginated separately, the full title being *Advice to a Mother on the Management of Her Children, and on the Treatment on the Moment of Their More Pressing Illnesses and Accidents. Sixteenth Edition, and, Counsel to a Mother: Being a Continuation and Completion of 'Advice to a Mother.'* This included several of Chavasse's prefaces to earlier editions.

22 *British and Foreign Medico-Chirurgical Review*, 6 (July 1850), pp.131–68. Fleetwood Churchill, *Diseases of Children*, Hodges & Smith, Dublin, 1850.

23 *Lancet*, (1855 Part 1), pp.218–19. Dr Underwood's manual was very old indeed, and its author actually dead. He had published his *Treatise on the Disorders of Childhood, and Management of Infants from Birth, Adapted to Domestic Use*, in 1797. It was in its tenth edition by 1846. Henry Davies, *Dr Underwood's Treatise on the Diseases of Children; with Directions for the Management of Infants*, John Churchill, 1846. John Tricker Conquest, *Letters to a Mother on the Management of Herself and Her Children in Health and Disease*, Longman, 1848. Andrew Combe, *A Treatise on the Physiological and Moral Management of Infancy*, McLachlan, Stewart, Edinburgh, 1840. Robert Dick, *Diet and Regimen, Physical, Intellectual, Moral, as Means in the Cure and Prevention of Disease*, Symington, Glasgow, 1838. Jonathan Pereira, *A Treatise on Food and Diet*, Longman, 1843. *British and Foreign Medico-Chirurgical Review*, 8 (July 1851), pp.56–77. Charles Hogg, *On the Management of Infancy. With Remarks on the Influence of Diet and Regimen*, John Churchill, 1849.

24 *British and Foreign Medico-Chirurgical Review*, 6 (July 1850), pp.131–68. *Lancet*, 1 (1855), pp.218–19.

25 *British and Foreign Medico-Chirurgical Review*, 11 (January 1853), pp.93–104. This was a review of four German-language texts.

26 A. Hess, 'On the Necessity of Practical Instruction in the Treatment of Diseases in Children', *Lancet*, (1849 Part 1), pp.341–2.

27 West, *Lectures*, p.1.

28 Christian Augustus Struve, *A Familiar View of the Domestic Education of Children. Translated from the German. To Which Are Prefaced Three Introductory Lectures on the Same Subject by A.F.M. Willich* (1800), Murray & Highley, 1812, p.144. Thomas Reid, *Essays on the Intellectual Powers of Man* (1785), in Sir William Hamilton (ed.), *The Works of Thomas Reid*, 2 vols, Maclachlan & Stewart, Edinburgh, 1846–63, vol. 1, pp.215–598. Gwen Raverat, *Period Piece. A Cambridge Childhood* (1941), Faber & Faber, 1962, pp.154–5 for Josiah Wedgwood II's diary of child observation, kept between 1797 and 1799. His nephew Charles Darwin continued this common domestic practice, publishing his observations of the 1840s in *Mind*, 2:7 (July 1877), pp.285–94. See Ben S. Bradley, *Visions of Infancy. A Critical Introduction to Child Psychology*, Polity Press, Cambridge, 1989, pp.11–27. See Carolyn Steedman, *The Tidy House*, Virago, 1982, pp.85–7; p.230, n.5.

29 Catherine Stanley of Alderley, 'Journal of Her Four Children', Cheshire Record Office, DSA 75. Ellen Sharples, 'Diaries, 1803–1832', City of Bristol Museum and Art Gallery.

30 Elizabeth Cleghorn Gaskell, *My Diary*, ed. Clement Shorter, privately

printed, San Francisco, 1923. Bradley, *Visions*, pp.25–6 for the importance of faculty psychology (what he calls 'common sense philosophy') to parents of this period. Mme. Necker de Saussure, *Progressive Education; or, Considerations on the Course of Life* (1828–32), Longmans, 1839.

31 Andrew Combe, *Principles of Physiology Applied to the Preservation of Health and to the Improvement of Physical and Medical Education* (1834), MacLachlan, Edinburgh, 1842.

32 Oswei Temkin, 'German Concepts of Ontogeny and History Around 1800', in *The Double Face of Janus and Other Essays in the History of Medicine*, Johns Hopkins University Press, Baltimore, Maryland, 1977, pp.373–89; p.373. See also Sigmund Freud, 'The Uncanny' (1919), in *Standard Edition of the Collected Works*, vol. 17, Hogarth Press, 1955, pp.217–56; p.242. Freud wrote at the turning point of physiological conceptions of death.

33 Gaskell, *My Diary*, pp.9, 11, 17.

34 On Elizabeth Gaskell's baby-journal, see Jenny Uglow, *Elizabeth Gaskell. A Habit of Stories*, Faber & Faber, 1993, pp.93–8.

35 Anon., *Letters to a Mother on the Watchful Care of Her Infant*, Seeley & Burnside, 1831, p.32.

36 A.L. Pearce, *An Essay on Children, and the Disease Designated Mesenteric Obstruction, Atrophy or Marasmus. Adapted Partly for Parents*, privately printed, 1838, pp.15, 24. See also Braidwood, *Domestic Management*, p.1.

37 Braidwood, *Domestic Management*, p.82.

38 William Home Popham, *Nursery Guide, or, Practical Hints on the Diseases and Management of Children*, Simkin, Marshall, 1847, pp.22–3.

39 Gaskell, *My Diary*, p.14.

40 Sara Coleridge, 'Diary of Her Children's Early Years, 1830–1838', Humanities Research Centre, University of Texas at Austin. See the section on 'Of the Condition of the Bowels', in Anon., *Letters to a Mother*, pp.72–7. See Henry Rees, *Popular Directions to Parents on the Management of Children in Health and Disease*, Sherwood, Gilbert & Piper, 1829, p.20.

41 Edward Augustus Cory, *The Physical and Medical Management of Children, Adapted for General Perusal* (1834), Draper, 1844, pp.77–8.

42 *Lancet* (1855 Part 1), 218–19, for a useful survey of current literature. For continental works reviewed by the *British and Foreign Medico-Chirurgical Review*, see 3 (April 1849), pp.406–32; 10 (July 1852), pp.1–19; 11 (January 1853), pp.93–104.

43 Cory, *Physical and Medical*, p.78.

44 J. Jules Jadelot presented his thesis on *Quelques considérations sur la physiologie et la pathologie de l'enfance* (Some thoughts on the Physiology and Pathology of Infancy) in 1835. *Collections des Thèses soutenues à la*

*Faculté de Médicine de Paris (*Theses defended at the Faculty of Medicine, Paris), Tome Huitième [vol. 8] thèse 240, Didot, Paris, 1835. His work on infant semiology was known through journal articles, and through M.E Bouchut, *Treatise on the Diseases of Children and Infants at the Breast, including the Hygiene and Physical Education of Young Children. Translated from the French of . . . With Notes and Additions by Peter Hinkes Bird*, John Churchill, 1855.

45 Bouchut, *Treatise*, pp.98–102, 102–6.
46 British Parliamentary Papers, *Report from the Select Committee on the Infant Life Protection Bill*, 1890, vol. 13, p.694.
47 Ibid., p.730 and Appendix 10.
48 Cory, *Physical and Medical*, pp.77–8.
49 Samuel Smiles, *Physical Education; or, the Nurture and Management of Children, Founded on the Study of their Nature and Constitution*, Oliver & Boyd, Edinburgh, 1838, p.3. John Locke, *Some Thoughts Concerning Education* (1693), ed. J.W. and Jean S. Yolton, Clarendon, Oxford, 1989, p.90 and *passim* for the analogies and metaphors of land husbandry that recommended generations of parents to 'Let Nature have Scope to Fashion the Body as she thinks best.'
50 Samuel Smiles, *Physical Education*, pp.9–10.
51 Rees, *Popular Directions*, pp.10–11.
52 Thomas Bryant, 'Lettsomian Lectures on the Surgical Diseases of Children', *British Medical Journal*, (1863 Part 1), pp.287–8, 415–17, 669–71; pp.287–8.
53 Combe, *Principles*, p.291.
54 Bouchut, *Treatise*, pp.710–25. *Lancet*, (1855 Part 1), pp.218–19. *British Medical Journal*, (1862 Part 1), p.69.
55 Bouchut, *Treatise*, p.710.
56 Figlio, *Metaphor*, pp.42–3, 45. See above, pp.14–15.
57 Combe, *Principles*, pp.104–5.
58 Cornelius Black, *Letters on the More Evident Changes Which the Body Undergoes and the Management of Health from Infancy and Adult Age*, Whittaker, 1846, p.63.
59 Ibid., p.47.
60 Ibid., p.48.
61 Carpenter, *Principles*, p.928.
62 Lambert A.J. Quetelet, *Physique social. Essai sur le développement des facultés de l'homme*, 2 vols, Muquardt, Brussels, 1835. *A Treatise on Man and the Development of His Faculties* (1842), Scholars Facsimiles and Reprints, Gainsville, Florida, 1962, pp.5, 57–72, 541. See above, pp. 49–50.
63 Percy Boulton, 'On the Physical Development of Children, or, the Bearing of Anthropometry to Hygiene', *Lancet*, (1880 Part 2), pp.610–11.

64 Draper, *Human Physiology*, Preface, p.604.
65 Ibid., p.550.
66 John William Draper, *History of the Intellectual Development of Europe*, 2 volumes, Bell Daldy, 1864, vol. 1, p.v. 'Professor Draper on the Intellectual Development of Europe, considered with reference to the views of Mr Darwin and others, that the Progression of Organisms is determined by Law', *Report of the Thirteenth Meeting of the British Association for the Advancement of Science, 1860,* John Murray, 1861, pp.115–16. See C.U.M. Smith, 'Evolution and the Problem of Mind. Part I: Herbert Spencer', *Journal of the History of Biology*, 51:1 (1982), pp.56–88.
67 Draper, *History of Intellectual Development*, vol. 2, p.388.
68 Combe, *Principles*, pp.9–22.
69 *Lancet*, (1861 Part 1), pp.597–8. *British Medical Journal*, (1864 Part 2), p.714.
70 *Lancet*, (1861 Part 1), pp.597–8.
71 'The Murder of the Innocents', *British Medical Journal*, (1863 Part 2), pp.243–5. British Parliamentary Papers, *First Report of the Commissioners on the Employment of Children and Young Persons in Trades and Manufacturers*, 1863, vol. 18.
72 'Children are, in a very practical sense, the root of the national prosperity. Physically, mentally, and morally, the child-state is the foreshadowing, and the growing and determining condition, of the adult state; the child-character is the outline of the mature character; and the child-life is the harbinger and – more, the constructive and formulating phase, of the life of the adult', *Lancet*, (1879 Part 2), pp.472–3.
73 Size and Weight of English Children; A Letter from Charles Roberts FRCS', *Lancet*, (1875 Part 2), p.755.

5 *The World Turned Within*

1 See Theresa Brennan, *The Interpretation of the Flesh: Freud and Femininity*, Routledge, 1992.
2 As David Bakan found 'background' inadequate to explain the stunning insight that the 'secret' of human existence which the Oedipus complex depicts is sexual in nature. Bakan then asked the question why 'if the scientific background with which Freud was intimately acquainted does not provide us with any cogent clue to the question of the origins of psychoanalysis, what other hypothesis might be advanced?' David Bakan, *Sigmund Freud and the Jewish Mystical Tradition* (1958), Free Association Books, 1990, p.10.
3 Harry Elmer Barnes, *A History of Historical Writing*, Dover, New York, 1963. J.R Hale, *The Evolution of British Historiography. From Bacon to Namier*, Macmillan, 1967. F.M Bernard, 'Natural Growth and

Purposive Development: Vico and Herder', *History and Theory*, 18 (1979), pp.16–36. Philippa Levine, *The Amateur and the Professional. Antiquarians, Historians and Archaeologists in Victorian Britain, 1838–1886*, Cambridge University Press, Cambridge, 1986. Christina Crosby, *The Ends of History. Victorians and 'The Woman Question'*, Routledge, 1991, pp.3–6.

4 'By far the most pervasive paradigm in the nineteenth century is the parallel between the life of the individual and the life-cycle of civilisations. Both were expressions of the deep-seated organicism of the age, and the discovery of the parallel was often the means whereby the individual overcame his alienation and reconciled himself with the world' A. Dwight Culler, *The Victorian Mirror of History*, Yale University Press, New Haven, 1985, p.280.

5 Franco Moretti, *The Way of the World. The Bildungsroman in European Culture*, Verso, 1987, pp.15–73.

6 Ibid., pp.6–7.

7 Crosby, *Ends of History*, pp.69–78.

8 Ibid., pp.2, 9.

9 Ibid., p.9.

10 See above, pp.2–3.

11 Crosby, *Ends of History*, pp.72–3.

12 Peter Brooks, *The Melodramatic Imagination. Balzac, Henry James, Melodrama and the Mode of Excess*, Yale University Press, 1976, p.xiii.

13 Ibid., p.4.

14 Ibid., pp.202, 5.

15 Crosby, *Ends of History*, p.8.

16 Peter Bowler, *The Non-Darwinian Revolution. Reinterpreting a Historical Myth*, Johns Hopkins University Press, Baltimore, Maryland, 1988, pp.4–5, 94–7.

17 Ibid., pp.133–6. Maurice Mandelbaum, *History, and Reason. A Study in Nineteenth Century Thought*, Johns Hopkins University Press, Baltimore, Maryland, 1971, pp.41–138.

18 William Coleman, *Biology in the Nineteenth Century. Problems of Forms, Function and Transformation*, Cambridge University Press, Cambridge, 1977, pp.7–9. For an older account of historians and cultural anthropologists adopting evolutionary structures of explanation, see Harry Elmer Barnes, *A History of Historical Writing*, Dover, New York, 1963, pp.9, 331–5.

19 Coleman, *Biology*, p.9.

20 Stephen Bann, *The Clothing of Clio. A Study of the Representations of History in Nineteenth Britain and France*, Cambridge University Press, Cambridge, 1984.

21 Ibid., p.14. Emphasis in original.

22 Barnes, *A History*, p.245. Leopold von Ranke, *The Secret of World*

History. Selected Writings on the Art and Science of History, ed. Roger Wines, Fordham University Press, New York, 1981, p.58. *Introduction to the History of the Latin and Teutonic Nations, 1494–1514* (1824), trans. P.A. Ashworth, Bell, 1887, p.380, where events are described as happening 'in harmony with their nature'. But this English translation omitted the Preface of 1874 that employed the iconic phrase.

23 Bann, *Clothing of Clio*, pp.15–16.

24 Ibid., p.15.

25 Carl E. Schorske, 'History and the Study of Culture', *New Literary History*, 21:2 (Winter 1990), pp.407–20. Carl E. Schorske, *Fin-de-Siècle Vienna: Politics and Culture*, University of Chicago Press, Chicago, 1979.

26 Charles Langlois and Charles Seignobos, *Introduction to the Study of History*, Duckworth, 1898, pp.302–3. *Introduction aux études historiques* was a manual of historical technique immediately translated from the French and that remained a standard text in higher education, in Britain at least, for the next twenty years.

27 Gillian Beer, *Darwin's Plots. Evolutionary Narrative in Darwin, George Eliot and Nineteenth Century Fiction*, Routledge & Kegan Paul, 1983, p.42. See also Bowler, *Non-Darwinian*, pp.23–4, 26–7.

28 Beer, *Darwin's Plots*, p.43.

29 Ibid., pp.111–12.

30 John Draper, *Human Physiology, Statistical and Dynamical; or the Conditions and Course of the Life of Man* (1856), Harper, New York, 1868, pp.538–51, 602–37; p.550. *History of the Intellectual Development of Europe*, 2 vols, Bell Daldy, 1864, vol. 2, p.388. See Barnes, *A History*, pp.9, 334–5.

31 Draper, *History*, vol. 1, p.17.

32 Hugh Cunningham, *The Children of the Poor. Representations of Childhood since the Seventeenth Century*, Blackwell, Oxford, 1991, pp.123–5.

33 Beer, *Darwin's Plots*, p.119.

34 Frank Sulloway, *Freud. Biologist of the Mind*, Basic Books, New York, 1979, pp.243–51. Cunningham, *Children*, pp.196–7. John R. Morss, *The Biologising of Childhood. Developmental Psychology and the Darwinian Myth*, Lawrence Erlbaum, Hove, 1990, pp.11–23. Charles Darwin, *The Expression of the Emotions in Man and Animals*, Murray, 1873, pp.13, 147–367, *passim*. 'The Biographical Sketch of an Infant', *Mind*, 2 (July 1877), pp.285–94.

35 George Romanes, *Mental Evolution in Man*, Kegan Paul, 1888, p.7. See Sulloway, *Freud*, p.247.

36 Romanes, *Mental Evolution*, p.197.

37 Ibid., p.192.

38 Ibid., p.238.

39 Ibid., p.432.

40 Ibid., p.431.
41 Sulloway, *Freud*, p.247.
42 Ibid., p.247. Sigmund Freud, 'Analysis of a Phobia in a Five-year Old Boy' (1909), in *Standard Addition of the Complete Psychological Works of Sigmund Freud*, vol. 10, Hogarth Press, 1955, pp.3–149.
43 Sulloway, *Freud*, p.245. Sigmund Freud, 'Introductory Lectures on Psycho-analysis (Part III)' (1916–1917), in *Standard Edition of the Complete Psychological Works of Sigmund Freud*, vol. 16, Hogarth Press, 1963, pp.392–411, p.399.
44 Sulloway, *Freud*, p.250; pp.243–51. Morss, *Biologising*, pp.37–49.
45 Sulloway, *Freud*, p.250. Mark James Baldwin, *Mental Development in the Child and the Race*, Macmillan, New York, 1893. Sigmund Freud, *Briefe an Wilhelm Fliess* (Letters to Wilhelm Fliess), *1887–1904*, ed. Jeffrey Masson, Fischer, Frankfurt, 1988, p.299. Letter dated 5 November 1897. See also Steven Kern, 'Freud and the Discovery of Childhood Sexuality', *History of Childhood Quarterly*, 1 (1973), pp.117–41; 'Freud and the Birth of Child Psychiatry', *Journal of the History of the Behavioral Sciences*, 9 (1973), pp.360–8.
46 William Preyer, *The Mind of the Child. Part I. The Senses and the Will* (1882), Appleton, New York, 1890; *The Mind of the Child. Part II. The Development of the Intellect* (1882), Appleton, New York, 1890. James Sully, *Studies of Childhood*, Longmans, 1896. Carl Groos, *The Play of Man* (1899), trans. E.L. Baldwin, Appleton, New York, 1901. Baldwin, *Mental Development*. Sigmund Freud, 'Three Essays on the Theory of Sexuality' (1905), in *Standard Edition of the Complete Psychological Works of Sigmund Freud*, vol. 7, Hogarth Press, 1953, pp.125–245.
47 Preyer, *Mind of the Child*, Volume 1, p.xv. See also Sigmund Freud, 'A Note upon the Mystic Writing Pad' (1925), in *Standard Edition of the Complete Psychological Works of Sigmund Freud*, vol. 19, Hogarth Press, 1961, pp.227–32.
48 Cunningham, *Children*, pp.197–9. See also Carolyn Steedman, *The Tidy House*, Virago, 1982, pp.85–7; p.230, n.5. J.H Muirhead, 'The Founders of Child Study in England', *Paidologist*, 2:2 (July 1900), pp.114–24. John C. Cavanagh, 'Early Developmental Theories: A Brief Review of Attempts to Organise Developmental Data prior to 1925', *Journal of the History of the Behavioral Sciences*, 17 (1981), pp.38–47. Louise N. Wilson, 'Bibliography of Child Study', *Pedagogical Seminary*, 5:4 (1898), pp.541–89. (This journal published an annual bibliography of recent work in child study from 1898 to 1907.) See also William S. Monroe, 'The Status of Child Study in Europe', *Pedagogical Seminary*, 6:3 (1899), pp.372–81. Kate Stevens, 'Child Study in Great Britain', *Pedagogical Seminary*, 13:2 (1906), pp.245–9.
49 See W.B. Drummond, *An Introduction to Child Study*, Arnold, 1907, pp.4, 43–9, where he explains how, over the previous thirty years,

philologists had turned to 'baby linguistics' in expectation of gaining a better understanding of 'the origins of human speech'.

50 James Sully, *Children's Ways. Being Selections from the Author's 'Studies of Childhood'*, Longman, 1897, pp.68–9.

51 Ibid., pp.70–1.

52 Ibid., pp.73–5.

53 Preyer, *Mind of the Child*, vol. 1, pp.107–8, 209–10.

54 Ibid., vol. 2, pp.209–10.

55 Sulloway, *Freud*, p.111. Sigmund Freud, 'Heredity and the Aetiology of the Neuroses' (1896) and 'Further Remarks on the Neuro-Psychoses of Defence' (1896), in *Standard Edition of the Complete Psychological Works of Sigmund Freud*, vol. 3, Hogarth Press, 1962, pp.141–56, pp.157–85.

56 Sulloway, *Freud*, pp.141–56, 159–85.

57 J.M. Masson, *The Assault on Truth: Freud's Suppression of the Seduction Theory* (1984), Penguin, Harmondsworth, 1985. See also Sulloway *Freud*, pp.110–13.

58 Sigmund Freud, 'The Interpretation of Dreams' (1899, 1900), in *Standard Edition of the Complete Psychological Works of Sigmund Freud*, vol. 5, Hogarth Press, 1955, p.620.

59 Sigmund Freud, 'On the Sexual Theories of Children' (1908), and 'Family Romances' (1908), in *Standard Edition of the Complete Psychological Works of Sigmund Freud*, vol. 9, Hogarth Press, 1959, pp.205–26, 235–41.

60 Sigmund Freud, 'Screen Memories' (1899), in *Standard Edition of the Complete Psychological Works of Sigmund Freud*, vol. 3, Hogarth Press, 1962, pp.301–22.

61 Jacqueline Rose, *The Case of Peter Pan, or, the Impossibility of Children's Fiction*, Macmillan, 1985, p.12.

62 Michael S. Roth, *Psychoanalysis as History: Negation and Freedom in Freud*, Cornell University Press, Ithaca, New York, 1987, pp.75–124.

63 Siegfried Bernfeld, 'Freud's Earliest Theories and the School of Helmholtz', *Psychoanalytic Quarterly*, 13 (1944), pp.341–62. Peter Amacher, 'Freud's Neurological Education and Its Influence on Psychoanalytic Theory', *Psychological Issues. Monograph 16* (vol. 4, no.4), International Universities Press, New York, 1965.

64 Ernst Wilhelm von Brücke, *Vorlesungen über Physiologie* (Lectures on Physiology), 2 vols, Braumuller, Vienna, 1874.

65 Bernfeld, 'Freud's Earliest Theories', p.350. Sigmund Freud, 'Psychoanalysis: Freudian School', *Encyclopedia Britannica*, 14th edition, Encyclopaedia Britannica Company, 1929, vol. 18, pp.672–4.

66 This is a quotation of Brücke's famous 'materialist manifesto' of 1842, when he and other young researchers had sworn to 'put into power this truth . . . In those cases which cannot at the time be explained by

these forces, one either has to find the specific way or form of their action by means of the physical mathematical method, or to assume new forces inherent in matter, reducible to the force of attraction and repulsion' (quoted in Sulloway, *Freud*, p.14). Bernfeld, 'Freud's Earliest Theories,' p.348.

67 Sulloway, *Freud*, p.113.

68 Sigmund Freud, 'Project for a Scientific Psychology' (1895), in *Standard Edition of the Complete Psychological Works of Sigmund Freud*, vol. 1, Hogarth Press, 1966, pp.281–97; p.297.

69 Ibid., p.297.

70 Ibid., pp.299–302.

71 Sigmund Freud, 'Beyond the Pleasure Principle' (1920), in *Standard Edition of the Complete Psychological Works of Sigmund Freud*, vol. 18, Hogarth Press, 1950, pp.3–64.

72 Ibid., pp.36, 38.

73 Masson, *Assault on Truth.*

74 Larry Wolff, *Postcards from the End of the World: An Investigation into the Mind of Fin-de-Siècle Vienna*, Collins, 1988.

75 Freud, 'The Interpretation of Dreams', p.620.

76 Sigmund Freud, 'Fragment of an Analysis of a Case of Hysteria' (1905), in *Standard Edition of the Complete Psychological Works of Sigmund Freud*, vol. 7, Hogarth Press, 1953, pp.3–122. 'From the History of an Infantile Neurosis' (1918), in *Standard Edition of the Complete Psychological Works of Sigmund Freud*, vol. 17, Hogarth Press, 1955, pp.1–123.

77 Freud 'Infantile Neurosis', pp.54–6.

78 Roth, *Psychoanalysis*, p.75.

79 Ibid., pp.41, 61.

80 Ibid., p.61.

81 Beer, *Darwin's Plots*, p.108.

82 Ibid., pp.111–12.

83 Draper, *Human Physiology*, p.548.

84 Ibid., p.549.

85 Draper, *History*, vol. 1, pp.13–14.

86 Draper, *Human Physiology*, p.550.

87 Johann Wolfgang von Goethe, *Wilhelm Meister's Years of Apprenticeship*, translated by H.M. Waidson, six volumes, Calder, 1977. References are made in the text to the volume and page of this edition. Mignon rapidly sketches a variety of stances here. See the figures of Horror, Terror and Reproach in Henry Siddons, *Practical Illustrations of Rhetorical Gesture and Action* (1822), Benjamin Blom, New York, 1968. *Practical Illustrations from a Work on the Same Subject by M. Engel*, Phillips, 1807. See Johann Jacob Engel, *Ideen zu einer Mimik* (1785), and Leman Thomas Rede, *The Road to the Stage; or the Performer's Preceptor*, Joseph

Smith, 1827, pp.79–80, 86–7, 93. Also see George Grant, *An Essay on the Science of Acting. By a Veteran Stager*, Cowie & Strange, 1828, pp.120–7, 153–5.

88 See above, p.22.

89 *Briefwechsel zwischen Schiller und Goethe*, 3 vols, Deutsche Bibliothek, Berlin, n.d. Schiller to Goethe, Letter 180, 2 July 1796, trans. Richard Parker. Hereafter *Goethe–Schiller Correspondence*. See Moretti, *Way of the World*, p.47.

90 Moretti, *Way of the World*, pp.6–8.

91 See above, pp.80–81.

6 *Strange Dislocations: Child as Acrobat*

1 For the child and Romanticism see Peter Coveney, *The Image of Childhood. The Individual and Society: a Study of the Theme in English Literature* (published as *Poor Monkey*, 1957), Penguin, Harmondsworth, 1967. Robert Pattison, *The Child Figure in English Literature*, Georgia University Press, Athens, 1978. Reinhard Kuhn, *Corruption in Paradise. The Child in Western Literature*, for Brown University Press by the University of New England, Hanover, Pennsylvania, 1982. Dirk den Hartog, *Dickens and Romantic Psychology. The Self in Time in Nineteenth Century Literature*, Macmillan, Basingstoke, 1987. For autobiography, childhood and the adult self, see Roy Pascal, *Design and Truth in Autobiography*, Routledge & Kegan Paul, 1960. Richard N. Coe, *When the Grass was Taller. Autobiography and the Experience of Childhood*, Yale University Press, New Haven, 1984. For ILP policy on childhood, see Carolyn Steedman, *Childhood, Culture and Class in Britain. Margaret McMillan, 1860–1931*, Virago Press, 1990, pp.62–97.

2 James Kincaid, *Child-loving. The Erotic Child and Victorian Culture*, Routledge, New York, 1992, p.5. See below, pp.165–8 for a discussion of Kincaid's indecent proposals.

3 See above, pp.5–70.

4 *WMA*: references in the text are to Johann Wolfgang von Goethe, *Wilhelm Meister's Years of Apprenticeship*, translated by H.M. Wardson, six volumes, 1977. Volume and page numbers are shown.

5 Johann Wolfgang von Goethe, *Wilhelm Meister's Theatrical Mission*, trans. Gregory H. Page, Heinemann, 1913, p.154.

6 For Goethe's childhood acquaintance with the tightrope and acrobat professions, see Johann Wolfgang von Goethe, *Poetry and Truth From My Own Life* (1811), 2 vols, Bell, 1913, pp.13, 76–7, 80–1.

7 Hughes Le Roux and Jules Garnier, *Acrobats and Mountebanks* (1889), trans. A.P. Morton, Chapman and Hall, 1890, pp.209–75. See also Hermine Demoriane, *The Tightrope Walker*, Secker & Warburg, 1989. Albert A. Hopkins, *Magic. Stage Illusions and Scientific Diversions* (1897),

Benjamin Blom, New York, 1967. Book I, Chapter 5, 'Jugglers and Acrobatic Performances'.

8 John Stokes, '*Aux Funambules*: Acrobatics and Aesthetics', *French Cultural Studies*, 3 (1992), pp.277–98; p.278, p.295. Semiotics replaces aesthetics in a more recent appreciation of the acrobatic art than that of Le Roux and Garnier. See Paul Bouissac, 'Structure and Meaning of Acrobatic Acts', in *Circus and Culture. A Semiotic Approach*, Indiana University Press, Bloomington, 1976, pp.28–51.

9 John Stokes, *In the Nineties*, Harvester Wheatsheaf, Hemel Hempstead, 1992, pp.181, 84–7. Stokes, '*Aux Funambules*', pp.287–90.

10 Henry Mayhew, *London Labour and the London Poor*, Cass, 1967, Volume 3, pp.148–51, 90–4. The interview with the rope-dancer appeared in the weekly parts of *London Labour*, issued in 1851.

11 Ellen Barlee, *Pantomime Waifs. With an Introduction by the Right Honourable the Earl of Shaftesbury*, Partridge, 1884, pp.117–20.

12 Ibid., pp.117, 115.

13 Sir Walter Scott, *Peveril of the Peak* (1820), Adam & Charles Black, Edinburgh, 1883, pp.236–7. However, audiences for 'Fenella or Peveril of the Peak an opera in three acts' (1826) would have learned nothing of it. Here during Act III Fenella, disguised as Zarah the Oriental Princess, leaps through a window twenty feet above the ground to escape the advances of the Duke of Buckingham, with no reference to an acrobatic training or to her body weight, though as she leaps she does casually mention that this is 'the activity which once gained me bread'. 'Fenella or Peveril of the Peak an opera in three acts', British Library, Lord Chamberlain's Collection, Add. Ms 48279, folios 279–566, pp.396–507; p.484. For hungry child acrobats, see also Mayhew, *London Labour*, vol. 3, p.98. *The Era*, 28 March 1852, p.10.

14 Hansard, vol. 282, 20 July–9 August 1883, p.1462. Barlee's book was received as the treatise of a modest and serious social reformer by the *Pall Mall Gazette* (which was to have much occasion to contemplate adults' uses of children in the months to come); her text contrasted with the hyperbole of Shaftesbury's Introduction to it, and his parliamentary utterances on the question. *Pall Mall Gazette*, 14 February 1885, p.5.

15 Hugh Cunningham, *The Children of the Poor. Representations of Childhood since the Seventeenth Century*, Blackwell, Oxford, 1991, pp.51–64. British Parliamentary Papers, *First Report of the Commissioners on the Employment of Children and Young Persons in Trades and Manufactures*, 1863, vol. 18, p.302.

16 For an outline of Shaftesbury's involvement in this legislation, see Geoffrey Finlayson, *The Seventh Earl of Shaftesbury, 1801–1885*, Eyre Methuen, 1981, p.407. See also B.L. Hutchins and A. Harrison, *A*

History of Factory Legislation (1903), Frank Cass, 1966, pp.139–40, 145. Cunningham, *Children*, pp.164–82. Lionel Rose, *The Erosion of Childhood. Child Oppression in Britain 1860–1918*, Routledge, 1991, pp.8–30.

17 Hansard, vol. 212, 21 June–27 July 1872, pp.618–20; p.620.
18 Ibid., 21 June–27 July 1872, pp.1502–3.
19 Hansard, vol. 247, 17 June–9 July 1879, p.137.
20 Frederick Barnard, 'The Dress Rehearsal' (1868), Manchester City Art Gallery.
21 'Juvenile Acrobats', *Lancet* (1883 Part 2), p.244. See also 'Child Acrobats', *British Medical Journal*, (1883 Part 2), p.440. 'Children on the Stage', *Lancet* (1880 Part 1), pp.577–8.
22 Andrew Combe, *The Principles of Physiology Applied to the Preservation of Health and to the Improvement of Physical and Mental Education* (1834), MacLachlan, Edinburgh, 1842, pp.420–1. Combe drew his evidence from work done on boy soldiers recruited in defiance of the laws of physiology. See Henry Marshall, *On the Enlisting, Discharging and Pensioning of Soldiers*, Adam & Charles Black, Edinburgh, 1839.
23 Frederic Keeling, *Child Labour in the United Kingdom*, P.S. King, 1914, pp.11–16.
24 *The Little Acrobat and His Mother*, Religious Tract Society, 1872.
25 Ibid., p.23. 'Heart-rending were the children who had forgotten their names,' writes John Zucchi of Italian street musicians of the 1850s and 1860s. The New York children he describes here had left their home and family at a very young age. John E. Zucchi, *The Little Slaves of the Harp. Italian Child Street Musicians in Nineteenth-Century Paris, London and New York*, McGill–Queens University Press, Montreal and Kingston, 1992, p.57.
26 *Little Acrobat*, pp.23, 8.
27 Ibid., p.20.
28 Sigmund Freud, 'The Uncanny' (1919), in *Standard Edition of the Complete Psychological Works of Sigmund Freud*, vol. 17, Hogarth Press, 1955, pp.217–56; p.240, p.241.
29 Ibid., p.242.
30 Zucchi, *Little Slaves*, pp.144–63, 172–7.
31 Hansard, vol. 337, 17 June–9 July 1889, pp.243–5.
32 Charity Organisation Society [COS], *Report of the Committee of the Charity Organisation Society Appointed to Inquire into the Employment of Italian Children for Medicant and Immoral Purposes*, COS, 1877, p.3.
33 Zucchi, *Little Slaves*, pp.17–41.
34 COS, Report, pp.4–5, 15.
35 Charles Manby Smith, *Curiosities of London Life: or, Phases, Physiological and Social, of the Great Metropolis*, Cash, 1853, pp.1–18.
36 Ibid., pp.15–17.

37 James Greenwood, *In Strange Company. Being the Experience of a Roving Correspondent*, King, 1873, p.72. See also Richard Rowe, *Picked Up in the Streets, or, Struggles for Life amongst the London Poor*, Allen, 1880, pp.176–86. James Greenwood, *Low-Life Deeps. An Account of the Strange Fish to Be Found There*, Chatto & Windus, 1876, pp.109–14. Zucchi, *Little Slaves*, pp.76–110.

38 Greenwood, *In Strange Company*, p.79.

39 Zucchi, *Little Slaves*, pp.39–40 for estimated numbers of Italian children active in street performance.

40 Gertrude Himmelfarb, *The Idea of Poverty. England in the Early Industrial Age*, Faber & Faber, 1984, p.375, quoting Anthony Ashley Cooper, 'The Second Annual Report of the Ragged School Union', *Quarterly Review* 79 (December 1846–March 1847), pp.127–41; p.127, p.128; quoted by Henry Mayhew, *Morning Chronicle*, 19 March 1850.

41 COS, *Report*, pp.4, 30.

42 Judith Walkowitz, *City of Dreadful Delight. Narrative of Sexual Danger in Late-Victorian London*, University of Chicago Press, Chicago, 1992, pp.81–134. Cunningham, *Children*, pp.60–4, pp.74–83. Catherine Gallagher, *The Industrial Reformation of English Fiction. Social Discourse and Narrative Form, 1832–1867*, University of Chicago Press, Chicago, 1985.

43 Hansard, vol. 282, 17 June–9 July 1889, pp.337, 243–5.

44 See Barlee, *Pantomime Waifs*, p.101, where she refers to an account in *The Times* – 'some years ago' – of English children 'sold to an Italian to be trained for stage exhibition'. I have not been able to trace this story. See also the example of 'Alleged Cruelty to Acrobats', *The Era*, 1888, p.15.

45 'You're ours now,' cried Laertes, 'we've bought you.' – 'What did you pay?' the child asked drily – 'A hundred ducats,' replied Laertes; 'if you give them back, you can be free.' – 'That's a lot, I suppose?' the child asked. – 'Oh yes, just you behave properly.' – 'I will be your servant,' she replied. Johann Wolfgang von Goethe, *Wilhelm Meister's Apprenticeship and Travels, Three Volumes in Two* (1839), translated by Thomas Carlyle, Chapman and Hall, 1894, Volume 1, Book II, Chapter iv, p.88.

46 COS, *Report*, p. 31. Zucchi, *Little Slaves*, pp.38–9 for payments in the 1860s.

47 Zucchi, *Little Slaves*, pp.17–41, 172–4.

48 For types of children in melodrama, see Brian Crozier (whose phrase this is), 'Notions of Childhood in the London Theatre, 1880–1905', PhD, Cambridge University, 1981. See his discussion of Sims's cycle of documentary plays, which includes a discussion of the type of Jack Merryweather, pp.93–104.

49 See below, pp.172–3. G.R. Sims and Clement Scott, 'Jack in the Box', British Library, Lord Chamberlain's Collection, Add. Ms 5334.C8,

p.55 (Act II, sc.3). Licence granted 30 July 1885, First performed at the Theatre Royal Brighton, 24 August 1885, and then on provincial tour. *The Era*, 29 August 1885, p.15. *The Times*, 25 August, p.8.

50 'Jack in the Box', p.83 (Act III, sc.3). Ambroise Thomas, *Mignon. Opéra-Comique en trois actes, cinq tableaux. Paroles de Michel Carré & Jules Barbier. Musique de Ambroise Thomas* (Mignon. A Comic Opera in Three Acts, Five Scenes. Words by Michel Carré and Jules Barbier. Music by Ambroise Thomas.) (1866), Calman-Levy, Paris, 1870, pp.5–6 (Act I, sc.2).

51 Marilyn Brown, *Gypsies and Other Bohemians. The Myth of the Artist in Nineteenth Century France*, UMI Research Press, Ann Arbor, Michigan, 1985, pp.28–30.

52 G.R. Sims, 'Master and Man. Play. Four Acts', British Library, Lord Chamberlain's Collection, Add. Ms 53424B, pp.80, 92 (Act IV, sc.1, sc.2). Licence granted 14 March 1889. First performed at the Prince of Wales, Birmingham, 18 March 1889. *The Era*, 23 March 1889, p.10.

53 'Master and Man', p.92 (Act IV, sc.2).

54 Ibid., pp.96, 92 (Act IV, sc.2).

55 Ibid., p.95 (Act IV, sc.2).

56 *The Era*, 23 March 1889, p.10.

57 'Master and Man', pp.98–9 (Act IV, sc.2).

58 British Library, Lord Chamberlain's Collection, Add. Ms 53347.246, 'The Harbour Lights. A New and Original Drama', by G. R. Sims and Henry Pettit, 1885.

59 *The Era*, 29 August 1885, p.15. *The Times*, 25 August, p.8. Walkowitz, *City of Dreadful Delight*, pp.102–20. 'A Mother Seeking a Lost Child', *Lloyd's Weekly Newspaper*, 12 July 1885, p.7.

60 Walkowitz, *City of Dreadful Delight*, pp.125–7.

61 'Circus Children', *Pall Mall Gazette*, 30 March 1885, p.6. See 7 April 1885, p.2, two letters under the heading 'Only Their Playfulness'. See letter published under the title 'The Treatment of Circus Children', 28 March 1885, p.2; 'How Circus Children Are Trained, An Interview with the Proprietor of Ginnett's Circus', 8 April 1885, pp.1–2; 'The Treatment of Circus Children. An Interview With Mr Sanger', 13 April 1885, p.11; 'The Treatment of Circus Children. A Chat With Mr Bimbo', 22 April 1885, p.4; 'The Training of Circus Children. A Show Manager at Home', 28 April 1885, p.2.

62 'The Fairies of the Stage', *Pall Mall Gazette*, 9 February 1885, p.5; 14 February 1885, p.5.

63 Le Roux and Garnier, *Acrobats and Mountebanks*, pp.239–40.

63 Pierre Loti, A *Child's Romance. Translated from the French by Clara Bell*, Kegan Paul, 1891. Coe, *When the Grass Was Taller.*

64 Loti, *A Child's Romance*, p.280.

7 *Children of the Street*

1 For recent accounts of mid-Victorian child workers, see Lionel Rose, *The Erosion of Childhood. Child Oppression in Britain, 1860–1918*, Routledge, 1991, pp.8–79; Hugh Cunningham, *The Children of the Poor. Representations of Childhood since the Seventeenth Century*, Blackwell, Oxford, 1991, pp.164–89; Thomas E. Jordan, *Victorian Childhood. Themes and Variations*, State University of New York Press, Albany, 1987, pp.110–47; James Walvin, *A Child's World. A Social History of English Childhood, 1800–1914*, Penguin, Harmondsworth, 1982, pp.61–78.

2 John Zucchi, *The Little Slaves of the Harp. Italian Child Street Musicians in Nineteenth-Century Paris, London, and New York*, McGill–Queens University Press, Montreal and Kingston, 1992, pp.171–4.

3 Similar powers were available to borough and country police by use of the Town Police Clauses Act. Zucchi, *Little Slaves*, pp.86–8. British Parliamentary Papers, *Report from the Select Committee on Police and Sanitary Regulations*, 1882, vol. 12, p.380. Hansard, vol. 337, 17 June–9 July, 1889. pp.242–3.

4 Carolyn Steedman, *Policing the Victorian Community. The Formation of English Provincial Police Forces, 1856–1880*, Routledge & Kegan Paul, 1984, p.56.

5 Zucchi, *Little Slaves*, pp.6–7.

6 Gertrude Himmelfarb, *The Idea of Poverty. England in the Early Industrial Age*, Faber & Faber, 1984, p.367.

7 Cunningham, *Children*, pp.101–22.

8 Ibid., pp.137–40. Hesba Stretton (Sarah Smith), *Jessica's First Prayer* (1867), Garland, New York, 1976.

9 Claudia Nelson, *Boys Will Be Girls. The Feminine Ethic and British Children's Fiction, 1857–1917*, Rutgers University Press, New Brunswick, 1991. See Cunningham, *Children*, pp.141–2.

10 Martin J.Wiener, *Reconstructing the Criminal. Culture, Law and Policy in England, 1834–1914*, Cambridge University Press, Cambridge, 1990, p.191.

11 James R. Kincaid, *Child-Loving. The Erotic Child and Victorian Culture*, Routledge, 1992, pp.64–5.

12 Michael R. Booth, *English Melodrama*, Herbert Jenkins, 1965, pp.30–2. Brian Crozier, 'Notions of Childhood in the London Theatre, 1880–1905', PhD Cambridge University, 1981, p.70.

13 Henry Mayhew, *Life and Labour and the London Poor*, 4 vols, Griffin Bohn, 1861–2, vol. 1, p.475. See Himmelfarb, *Idea of Poverty*, p.375 on the trajectory of this perception.

14 British Parliamentary Papers, *Report from the Select Committee on the Education of Destitute Children*, 1861, vol. 7, p.10.

15 Mary Sewell, *Our Father's Care. A Ballad*, Jarrold, 1861, p.5.

16 Mayhew, *London Labour*, pp.479, 470–1. Walvin, *A Child's World*, pp.68–9.
17 Walvin, *A Child's World*, p.117, p.151 quoting Jo Manton, *Mary Carpenter and the Children of the Streets*, Heinemann, 1976, p.6. For Shaftesbury's depiction of the London street folk, see p.106 and n.39.
18 Frederic Keeling, *Child Labour in the United Kingdom*, P.S. King, 1914. Rose, *Erosion of Childhood*, pp.8–18.
19 Wiener, *Reconstructing the Criminal*, pp.138–9, 147–8.
20 British Parliamentary Papers, *Third Report of the Royal Commission Appointed to Inquire into the Working of the Elementary Education Acts*, 1887, vol. 30, p.306.
21 George R. Sims, *How the Poor Live With Sixty Illustrations by Frederic Barnard*, Chatto & Windus, 1883. *How the Poor Live and Horrible London*, Chatto & Windus, 1889.
22 Keeling, *Child Labour*, pp.16–26.
23 Ibid., p.18.
24 Benjamin Waugh, 'Street Children', *Contemporary Review*, 53 (January–June 1888), pp.825–35.
25 Hansard, vol. 337, 17 June–9 July 1889, pp.242–3.
26 Henry Mayhew, 'Labour and the Poor. Metropolitan Districts. From Our Special Correspondent. Of the Green Markets of London. Letter 81', *Morning Chronicle*, 5 December 1850, pp.5–6.
27 For earlier discussions of Mayhew's interviews with this child see Carolyn Steedman, *The Tidy House*, Virago, 1982, pp.110–25; *Landscape for a Good Woman*, Virago, 1986, pp.110–31; *Past Tenses. Essays on Writing, Autobiography, and History*, Rivers-Oram, 1992, pp.192–202. The publishing history of Mayhew's *Life and Labour of the London Poor*, in which this interview is recorded, is extremely complex. The publication of the 1851 *Morning Chronicle* inquiry in weekly parts included material that made up Henry Mayhew, *Life and Labour of the London Poor, Volume I, The London Street Folk. Parts, with Answers to Correspondents, Bound*, vol. 1, and parts of vols 2 and 3, George Woodfall, 1851, pp.150–1. Later the same material formed parts of vols 1, 2 and 3 of the four-volume edition of 1861–2. Henry Mayhew, *London Labour and the London Poor*, 4 vols, Griffin Bohn, 1861–2. The edition of 1851 is made up of nos 1–63 of the weekly parts issued by Mayhew. His crucial *Answers to Correspondents* are bound with them in the British Library copy. The only full series of *Answers* extant is bound at the end of the copy of vol. 3 of *London Labour and the London Poor* in the Bibliothèque Nationale, Paris (R.43429). The British Library's series (bound with vol. 1) has several *Answers* missing.
28 Mayhew, *London Labour* [1851] (1861), p.471.
29 Ibid., vol. 2, pp.505–6, vol. 1, p.480.
30 British Parliamentary Papers, *Report* (1861) vol. 7, p.13.

31 E.P. Thompson and Eileen Yeo (eds), *The Unknown Mayhew* (1971), Penguin, Harmondsworth, 1973, p.54.
32 J.B. Johnstone, 'How We Live or London Labour and London Poor. Drama. Three Acts', British Library, Lord Chamberlain's Collection, Add. Ms 52958CC. Licensed 16 March 1856. *The Era*, 30 March 1856.
33 James W. Elphinstone, 'London Labour & London Poor, or Want and Vice A Drama in 2 Acts', British Library, Lord Chamberlain's Collection, Add. Ms 52, 946K, LCP, Licensed 16 March 1854. *The Era*, 19 March 1854, Advertisement: 'Royal Pavilion Theatre, Whitechapel Road . . . On Monday and during the week to commence with a New Local Drama, entitled London Poor . . .'. *The Era*, 2 April 1854, 'Last Week of the Winter Season. Continued Success of "London Labour".'
34 *The Era*, 13 April 1856, p.10. Michael R. Booth, 'The Metropolis on Stage', in H.J. Dyos and Michael Wolff (eds), *The Victorian City. Volume I, Images and Reality*, Routledge & Kegan Paul, 1973, pp.211–24. 'Melodrama and the Working Class', in Carol Hanbery MacKay, *Dramatic Dickens*, Macmillan, 1989, pp.96–109; p.107.
35 *The Era*, 30 March 1856, p.10.
36 Michael R. Booth, *English Melodrama*, Herbert Jenkins, 1965, pp.121–3.
37 Johnstone, 'How We Live', p.15 (Act I, sc.2). Punctuation as in the playscript.
38 Which was not at all how Mayhew behaved. To the lady correspondent donating a sovereign 'to the young in sorrow', he responded with a long protest against the giving of alms, and explained that the money would be handed over to his editor, in order to establish a Loan Office for the poor. Mayhew, *London Labour* (1851), 'No. 10. Answers to Correspondents'.
39 Johnstone, 'How We Live', p.16 (Act I, sc.2). For comments on the relationship of unreality to realism in melodrama celebrating rurality, see Booth, *English Melodrama*, pp.120–1; and 'The Metropolis'.
40 Crozier, *Notions of Childhood*, pp.106–7.
41 Johnstone, 'How We Live', p.15 (Act I, sc.2). 'She frowned like a baby in its sleep when thinking of the answer,' wrote Mayhew of one nice, clean little crossing-sweeper. Mayhew, *London Labour* (1861–2), vol. 2, p.506.
42 William Travers, 'The Watercress Girl. The Original Drama. In Two Acts', British Library, Lord Chamberlain's Collection, Add. Ms 53045T. Licensed 18 October 1865. *The Era*, 15 October 1865. Advertisement: '. . . one of the truly heart-touching, beautiful dramas'. It opened at the City of London on 16 October and ran for seven weeks. *The Era*, 22 October 1865, p.11.
43 Travers, 'Watercress Girl', p.6 (Act I, sc.2). Punctuation as in original.
44 *The Era*, 22 October 1865, p.11.

45 Peter Brooks, *The Melodramatic Imagination. Balzac, Henry James and the Mode of Excess*, Yale University Press, New Haven, 1976, p.48. Martin Meisel, *Realizations. Narrative, Pictorial, and Theatrical Arts in Nineteenth Century England*, Princeton University Press, Princeton, 1983, pp.45–51.

46 Geoffrey B.A. Finlayson, *The Seventh Earl of Shaftesbury, 1801–1885*, Eyre Methuen, 1981, p.543: 'Of all the movements I have ever been connected with . . . I look upon this Watercress Girl Movement as the most successful.' John Pollock, *Shaftesbury. The Poor Man's Earl*, Hodder & Stoughton, 1985, p.159. Ellen Barlee, *Pantomime Waifs*, Partridge, 1884, p.258. Inaugurated in 1866 by Shaftesbury, Clerkenwell Mission extended its work in 1879 when it became John Groom's Crippleage. John Groom, *The Silver Vase, or, The Gathered Posy. With an Introduction by Lady Savory*, Morgan & Scott, 1891; *Mr Groom's Industrial Training Homes . . . The Goal of Charity*, privately printed, 1907, p.5; *Mr Groom's Crippleage and Flower Girls' Mission*, privately printed, 1910, pp.3, 7.

47 Brooks, *Melodramatic Imagination*, p.4 for melodrama speaking the unspeakable.

48 There are now no extant copies of Sarah Fry's *The Little Watercress Sellers* of 1854, though it was reissued by the Presbyterian Committee of Publication of Richmond, Virginia in 1866; references are to this edition.

49 Ibid., p.10.

50 Ibid., p.8.

51 Ibid., pp.9–10. But see Cunningham, *Children*, pp.107–17 on the persistent cry '"Can these be *children*?"'; and Steedman, *The Tidy House*, pp.116–24.

52 Fry, *Little Watercress Sellers*, pp.50–1.

53 Barlee, *Pantomime Waifs*, p.257. Sewell, *Our Father's Care.*

54 Walvin, *A Child's World*, pp.150–1. Steedman, *The Tidy House*, pp.114–15.

55 Sewell, *Our Father's Care*, p.4.

56 Ibid., pp.7, 12, 13.

57 Ibid., p.7.

58 Ibid., pp.19–21, 24. See Nelson, *Boys Will Be Girls*, pp.18–19.

59 Fry, *Little Watercress Sellers*, p.26.

60 See below, pp.159–160. Though this could be a reference not to Blake's 'Little Girl Lost', but to the doleful ballad Bessie sings to the orphan child Jane Eyre. Charlotte Brontë, *Jane Eyre. An Autobiography* (1847), Penguin, Harmondsworth, 1966, p.54.

61 Fry, *Little Watercress Sellers*, p.18.

62 Ibid., p.17.

63 Ibid., pp.10–13.

64 Ibid., p.30.
65 Cunningham, *Children*, pp.119–22.
66 Jordan, *Victorian Childhood*, pp.116–17; Walvin, *A Child's World*, pp.17–21.
67 John Ruskin's observations on this point are highly informative. See John Ruskin, 'Fairyland', from 'The Art of England' (1884), in *The Library Edition of the Works of John Ruskin*, vol. 33, Allen & Unwin, 1908, pp.338–42, 327–49; 'Design in the German School', from 'Ariadne Florentia' (1874) in *Library Edition*, vol. 22, Allen & Unwin, 1906, pp.390–421; 'Humility', from 'Time and Tide' (1867), in *Library Edition*, vol. 17, 1906, pp.405–9. See Carolyn Steedman, *Childhood, Culture and Class in Britain. Margaret McMillan, 1860–1931*, Virago, 1990, pp.64–6.
68 Sewell, *Our Father's Care*, p.14.
69 British Parliamentary Papers, *Report from the Select Committee on the Education of Destitute Children*, 1861, vol. 7, pp.422, 439.
70 John Lucas, 'Hopkins and Symons: Two Views of the City', in John Stokes (ed.), *Fin-de-Siècle, Fin du Globe. Fears and Fantasies of the Late Nineteenth Century*, Macmillan, 1992, pp.52–68; p.65.
71 Arthur Symons, *London. A Book of Aspects*, privately printed, 1909, p.73. These passages were written in the 1890s; see Lucas, 'Hopkins and Symons', pp.65, 68 n.23.
72 Symons, *London*, pp.71, 70, 72.
73 Laurence Binyon, 'The Little Dancers', in *Collected Poems of Laurence Binyon. London Visions. Narrative Poems. Translations*, Macmillan, 1931, p.3.
74 P. Woodham-Smith, 'History of the Froebelian Movement in England', in Evelyn Lawrence (ed.), *Friedrich Froebel and English Education*, Routledge & Kegan Paul, 1952, pp.34–94.
75 Karl Beckson, *Arthur Symons. A Life*, Clarendon, Oxford, 1987, pp.100–12; p.109 for the possible connections between Nora and the ballet dancer 'Lydia'.

8 *Children of the Stage*

1 Michael R. Booth, *The Theatre in the Victorian Age*, Cambridge University Press, Cambridge, 1991, pp.4–11; *Victorian Spectacular Theatre, 1850–1910*, Routledge & Kegan Paul, 1981, pp.60–92. Tracy C. Davis, *Actresses as Working Women. Their Social Identity in Victorian Culture*, Routledge, 1991, p.77.
2 Peter Bailey, 'Introduction: Making Sense of Music Hall', in Peter Bailey (ed.), *Music Hall. The Business of Pleasure*, Open University Press, Milton Keynes, 1986, pp.viii–xxiii.
3 Michael R. Booth, *The Theatre*, pp.4–11. Michael R. Booth, 'The Metropolis on the Stage', in H.J. Dyos and Michael Wolff (eds), *The*

Victorian City. Volume I. Images and Reality, Routledge & Kegan Paul, 1973, pp.211–24; pp.212–13, 224; 'Melodrama and the Working Class', in Carol Hanbery MacKay, *Dramatic Dickens*, Macmillan, 1989, pp.96–109; pp.97–8. Paul Sheridan, *Penny Theatres of Victorian London*, Dennis Dobson, 1981.

4 British Parliamentary Papers, *Third Report of the Royal Commission Appointed to Inquire into the Working of the Elementary Education Acts*, 1887, vol. 30, p.310. John Matthias Weylland, *The Man with the Book; or, The Bible among the People*, William Hunt, 1872, pp.103–6. Eileen Barlee, *Pantomime Waifs*, Partridge, 1884. Tracy C. Davis, 'The Employment of Children in the Victorian Theatre. Training, Exploitation and the Movement for Reform', *New Theatre Quarterly*, 2:60 (1986), pp.117–35. British Parliamentary Papers, *Report from the Select Committee on Theatrical Licences and Regulations*, 1866, vol. 16, pp.188–9; *Report from the Select Committee on Theatres and Places of Entertainment*, 1892, vol. 18.

5 For child stars of the period 1790–1860 and the range of parts available to them, see an interesting comment by George Grant, *An Essay on the Science of Acting. By a Veteran Stager*, Cowie & Strange, 1828, pp.186–9.

6 For an account of a much wider interest in child-display in the 1870s and 1880s, see Brian Crozier, 'Notions of Childhood in the London Theatre, 1880–1905', PhD, Cambridge University, 1981, pp.149–61.

7 Barlee, *Pantomime Waifs*, pp.88–9.

8 British Parliamentary Papers, *Third Report* (1887), vol. 30, p.309; Davis, *Employment of Children*, p.117.

9 Barlee, *Pantomime Waifs*, pp.27–37.

10 For a concise summary of the law relating to the theatrical employment of children, see British Parliamentary Papers, *Third Report* (1887), vol. 30, pp.315–20. Evidence of Charles T. Mitchell, Barrister, Member of the Committee of the National Vigilance Association, Vice-Chairman of the Glasgow School Board.

11 'Theatre Schools' were another way of circumventing the law; see Davis, 'Employment of Children', pp.129–30 for their development and use. See also of details of these schools in British Parliamentary Papers, *Third Report* (1887), vol. 30, pp.315–20.

12 Barlee, *Pantomime Waifs*, pp.27–37.

13 See above, pp.100–3. Hansard, vol. 282, 20 July–9 August 1883, pp.1462–5.

14 Hugh Cunningham, *The Children of the Poor. Representations of Childhood since the Seventeenth Century*, Blackwell, Oxford, 1991, pp.164–89. Evidence of Charles T. Mitchell, British Parliamentary Papers, *Third Report* (1887) vol. 30, pp.315–20. 'Children on the Stage', *Lancet*, (1880 Part 1), pp.577–8.

15 Hansard, vol. 337, 17 June–9 July 1889, pp.20–1.

16 Ibid., pp.32–3.

17 Frederic Keeling, *Child Labour in the United Kingdom*, P.S. King, 1914, pp.xi–xxxii. Brian Simon, *Education and the Labour Movement, 1870–1920*, Lawrence & Wishart, 1965, pp.208–46, 357. Historians of education would agree with Millicent Fawcett, whose words these are: British Parliamentary Papers, *Third Report* (1887), p.306. See Harold Silver, 'Ideology and the Factory Child: Attitudes to Half-time Education', in *Education as History. Interpreting Nineteenth- and Twentieth-Century Education*, Methuen, 1983, pp.35–59. Neil J. Smelser, *Social Paralysis and Social Change. British Working-class Education in the Nineteenth Century*, University of California Press, Berkeley and Los Angeles, 1991, pp.254–95.

18 Millicent Garrett Fawcett, 'The Employment of Children in Theatres', *Contemporary Review*, 56 (July–December 1889), pp.822–9; p.823.

19 Viviana A. Zelizer, *Pricing the Priceless Child. The Changing Social Value of Children*, Basic Books, New York, 1985.

20 For the continued labour of children, well into the twentieth century, see Cunningham, *Children*, pp.174–89. Carolyn Steedman, 'The ILP and Education: The Bradford Charter', in David James, Tony Jowitt and Keith Laybourn (eds), *The Centennial History of the Independent Labour Party*, Ryburn, Halifax, 1992, pp.277–98.

21 The structure of adult feeling delineated by the idea of children being 'priceless' is perfectly described by the psychologist James Sully in his Introduction to *Studies of Childhood*, Longman, 1896, pp.1–24. See particularly p.3: 'The child, while appealing to our admiration and our pity, makes a large and many-voiced appeal also to our sense of laughter in things. It is indeed hard to say whether he is most amusing when setting at naught in his quiet, lordly way, our most extolled views, our ideas of the true and the false, of the proper uses of things . . . or when labouring in his perfectly self-conceived fashion to overtake us and be as experienced and as conventional as ourselves. This ever new play of droll features in childish thought and action forms one of the deepest sources of delight for the modern lover of childhood.'

22 Edith Hogg, 'School Children as Wage Earners', *The Nineteenth Century*, 42 (1897), pp.235–44.

23 Davis, 'Employment of Children' p.126. 'The Fairies of the Stage', *Pall Mall Gazette*, 9 February 1885, p.5.

24 Davis, *Actresses*, pp.32–3. Mrs Jeune, 'Children in Theatres', *English Illustrated Magazine* 1889–90, pp.6–14.

25 Barlee, *Pantomime Waifs*, p.60. This must have been an old story in 1884: legally a child had to be 8 to work in a factory or workshop after 1867 and 10 after 1874. Anyway, after 1878 she would have had to

obtain an educational certificate for full-time unemployment if she were between the ages of 10 and 14.

26 Davis, 'Employment of Children', pp.122–3, 124–6.
27 British Parliamentary Papers, *Third Report* (1887), p.307. Davis, 'Employment of Children', p.122. Fawcett, 'The Employment', p.824.
28 Jeune, 'Children', p.10.
29 Hansard, vol. 337, 17 June–9 July 1889, p.8.
30 Keeling, *Child Labour*, p.12.
31 Claire Tomalin, *The Invisible Woman. The Story of Nelly Ternan and Charles Dickens*, Viking, 1990, p.43.
32 Marcus Tindal, 'Baby Actors', *Pearson's Magazine*, 3 (1897), pp.678–83. A photograph of this 'Baby' accompanies the piece.
33 Weylland, *The Man with the Book*, pp.103–6. Barlee, *Pantomime Waifs*, p.53.
34 British Parliamentary Papers, *Third Report* (1887), vol. 30, p.497.
35 Barlee, *Pantomime Waifs*, pp.2, 14–15.
36 British Parliamentary Papers, *Third Report* (1887), vol. 30, p.306.
37 Ibid., pp.27–37.
38 Ibid., p.77.
39 Ibid., pp.38–9.
40 Hansard, vol. 337, 17 June–9 July 1889, pp.38, 26.
41 Davis, 'Employment of Children', p.131. Keeling, *Child Labour*, p.13.
42 52&53 Vict., c.44, 'An Act for the Prevention of Cruelty, and Better Protection of Children', s.3. 57&58 Vict., c.27, 'An Act to Amend the Law for the Prevention of Cruelty to Children', s.6.
43 Davis, 'Employment of Children', pp.131–3.
44 Hansard, vol. 337, 17 June–9 July 1889, p.8. Booth, 'The Metropolis', p.224; *The Theatre*, pp.1–11.
45 Hansard, vol. 337, 17 June–9 July 1889, p.38.
46 Davis, 'Employment of Children', p.124.
47 James R. Kincaid *Child-loving. The Erotic Child and Victorian Culture*, Routledge, 1992, pp.363–4. See Steedman *The Tidy House*, pp.61–84 for an outline of the origins of domestic child-watching in Britain. See also Ian Bradley, *Visions of Infancy. A Critical Introduction to Child Psychology*, Polity Press, Cambridge, 1989, pp.1–27.
48 Kincaid, *Child-loving*, p.5.
49 Anna Gruetzner Robins, 'Sickert "Painter-in-Ordinary" to the Music-Hall', in Wendy Baron and Richard Shone (eds), *Sickert. Paintings*, Royal Academy of Arts, 1992, pp.13–24. For reproductions of 'Little Dot' see this book.
50 Sara Maitland, *Vesta Tilley*, Virago, 1986, p.16.
51 Claire Tomalin draws on many of these for her discussion of stage childhood, and the psychology of the child performer in *The Invisible Woman*, pp.24–68, *passim*.

52 Gruetzner Robins, 'Sickert', p.16.

53 Dagmar Hoher, 'The Composition of Music Hall Audiences, 1850–1900', in Peter Bailey (ed.), *Music Hall. The Business of Pleasure*, Open University Press, Milton Keynes, 1986, pp.73–92. J.S. Bratton, 'Jenny Hill: Sex and Sexism in Victorian Music Hall', in J.S. Bratton (ed.), *Music Hall: Performance and Style*, Open University Press, Milton Keynes, 1986, pp.92–110.

54 Gruetzner Robins, 'Sickert', p.16.

55 'There are children, many children, who are ruined before they are thirteen; but the crime is one phase of the incest which . . . is inseparable from overcrowding. But the number on the streets is small. Notwithstanding the most lavish offers of money, I completely failed to procure a single prostitute under thirteen. I have been repeatedly promised children under twelve, but they either never appeared or when produced admitted they were over thirteen' ('The Maiden Tribute of Modern Babylon. – III. The Report of Our Secret Commission', *Pall Mall Gazette*, 8 July 1885, pp.1–2). Inquiries earlier in the year had failed to turn up any London prostitute under the age 18. See 'Life Stories from the Streets', and 'The Sacrifice of Women', *Pall Mall Gazette*, 3 March 1885, pp.3–4; 20 March 1885 pp.3–4. Judith Walkowitz, *City of Dreadful Delight. Narratives of Sexual Danger in Late-Victorian London*, University of Chicago Press, Chicago, 1992, pp.81–120.

56 *Pall Mall Gazette*, 6 July, 1885, pp.1–2, 6–7; 7 July 1885, p.1; 8 July 1885, p.1; 10 July 1885, p.1. Walkowitz, *City of Dreadful Delight*, p.102.

57 Walkowitz, *City of Dreadful Delight*, pp.85–6.

58 For questions of composition, see Gruetzner Robins, 'Sickert', and Baron and Shone, *Sickert*, p.74. See also John Stokes, *In the Nineties*, Harvester Wheatsheaf, Hemel Hempstead, 1989, pp.74–6.

59 'Two Views of the "Maiden Tribute." I. – From Saunterer in the Labyrinth', *Pall Mall Gazette*, 18 July 1885, p.2. 'Saunterer' wrote again on 10 August 1885, p.1. See Walkowitz, *City of Dreadful Delight*, p.124. Roller skating was a feature of the entertainments offered at Prince's Hall, and at other West End venues. 'For some time this sport has been very popular in America and thousands of people have been attracted to the different contests which have been got up. The success of this sort of thing has induced the managers of the Aquarium at Westminster to try an entertainment of this kind' ('Roller Skating', *Reynold's Newspaper*, 24 May 1885, p.6).

60 Barlee, *Pantomime Waifs*, pp.30, 68.

61 Ibid., p.69. For the long-established theatrical attraction of the 'Pose Plastique', see Stokes, *In the Nineties*, pp.76–7.

62 For an extremely interesting account of the Jamesian Maisie's knowingness and knowledge, see Peter Brooks, *The Melodramatic*

Imagination. Balzac, Henry James and the Mode of Excess, Yale University Press, New Haven, 1976, pp.165–6.

63 Davis, *Actresses*, p.108.

64 Ibid., p.133.

65 Ibid., p.112.

66 Tracy C. Davis, 'The Spectacle of Absent Costume: Nudity on the Victorian Stage', *New Theatre Quarterly*, 5:20 (1989), pp.321–3; p.323.

67 Albert Smith, *The Natural History of the Ballet Girl*, Bogue, 1847, pp.5, 7.

68 Barlee, *Pantomime Waifs*, pp.53–4.

69 Tomalin, *The Invisible Woman*, pp.64–5.

70 The appearance of nakedness on the stage did not concern Barlee as much as did their actual nakedness in rehearsal, which she carefully noted in the training of acrobat children and the drilling of the pantomime chorus (*Pantomime Waifs*, pp.53, 117).

71 Ibid., pp.70–1. See Maitland, *Vesta Tilley*, pp.114–15, and *passim*.

72 See Crozier, 'Notions of Childhood', p.74.

73 Davis, 'Spectacle', p.325.

74 Smith, *Natural History*, p.7.

75 Ibid., pp.15–17, 91.

76 Ibid., pp.18–19.

77 Ibid., pp.88–9.

78 Leonore Davidoff, 'Class and Gender in Victorian England', in Judith L. Newton, Mary P. Ryan and Judith R. Walkowitz (eds), *Sex and Class in Women's History*, Routledge & Kegan Paul, 1983, pp.17–71. Derek Hudson, *Munby. Man of Two Worlds. The Life and Diaries of Arthur J. Munby, 1828–1910*, Sphere, 1974, pp.248–302, and *passim*. Liz Stanley (ed.), *The Diaries of Hannah Cullwick, Victorian Maidservant*, Virago, 1984.

79 Barlee, *Pantomime Waifs*, p.148. Davis, 'Employment of Children', p.128; *Actresses*, p.63, p.171, n.53. *'Stars.' A Year's Work in the Theatrical Mission*, privately printed, 1892.

80 Crozier, 'Notions of Childhood', p.96.

81 *The Era*, 29 August 1885, p.15.

82 Crozier, 'Notions of Childhood', pp.162–77.

83 Michael R. Booth, *English Melodrama*, Herbert Jenkins, 1965, p.50. Jerome Mitchell, *The Walter Scott Operas. An Analysis of Operas Based on the Works of Sir Walter Scott*, University of Alabama Press, Alabama, 1977, pp.260–70. Jane F. Fulcher, *The Nation's Image. French Grand Opera as Politics and Politicised Art*, Cambridge University Press, Cambridge, 1987, pp.25–31.

84 Isaac Pocock, *Montrose; or the Children of the Mist. A Musical Drama in Three Acts, founded on the Legend of Montrose*, Simpkin & Marshall, 1822, pp.14, 42.

85 Mitchell, *Walter Scott Operas*, p.260. 'Fenella or Peveril of the Peak an opera in three acts', 1826, British Library, Lord Chamberlain's

Collection, Add. Ms 48279, folios 279–566, pp.396–507. Ms. dated 28 September 1826.

86 Ibid., pp.468–9.

87 Edward Fitzball, *Thirty-five Years of a Dramatic Author's Life. In Two Volumes*, Newby, 1859, vol. 1, pp.178–9, 249.

88 Hugh Moss, 'Bootle's Baby. A Comedy Drama in Four Acts', 1888, British Library, Lord Chamberlain's Collection, Add. Ms 53395C. Licensed 8 February 1888. For the place of 'Bootle's Baby' in society London, and its production history, see 'Theatrical Gossip', *The Era*, 18 February 1888, p.8; 12 May 1888, p.14.

89 *The Era*, 12 May 1888, p.14.

90 J.S. Winter, *Mignon's Husband*, F.V. White, 1887, p.11.

91 Original libretto by Jules-Henri Vernoy de Saint-Georges and Jean-François Alfred Bayard. The opera was done into Italian by Carlisto Bassi, and proved much more popular in Britain and the US in that language. *La Figlia del Regimento. A Comic Opera in Two Acts*, Bury, Dublin, 1848.

92 *The Era*, 12 May 1888, p.14. *The Times*, 11 May 1888, p.13. Minnie Terry (b.1882) was the niece of Ellen Terry. See *The Green Room Book and Anglo-American Dramatic Register*, Sealey Clark, 1907, p.349. See Crozier, 'Notions of Childhood', pp.182–98 for her career. He quotes *Theatre*, 1 November 1889, p.272: 'Miss Minnie Terry [exhibits] none of the objectional traits of the "infant phenomenon", but is a sweet lovable child and appears really to mean the words she has to utter in Act II of *A Man's Shadow*: "I am very happy and I always mean to be a good girl".'

93 *The Times*, 11 May 1888, p.13.

9 *Childhood and the Uncanny*

1 Sigmund Freud, 'The Uncanny' (1919), in *Standard Edition of the Complete Psychological Works of Sigmund Freud*, vol. 17, Hogarth Press, 1955, pp.217–56.

2 Ernst Jentsch, 'Zur Psychologie des Unheimlichen', *Psychiatrisch-neurologische Wochenschrift* (On the Psychology of the Uncanny), 8 (1906), pp.195–202.

3 Freud, 'The Uncanny', p.250.

4 Ibid., pp.249–51.

5 In the immediate following passages, references are to Carlyle's translation of *Wilhelm Meister*, simply because for current purposes it seems preferable in style. Johann Wolfgang von Goethe, *Wilhelm Meister's Apprenticeship and Travels. Three Volumes in Two*, translated by Thomas Carlyle (1839), Chapman and Hall, 1894, Volume 1, Book ix, Chapter xiii.

6 Ibid., Carlyle 1, IX, xi. For accounts of children's understanding of

their own littleness, and the importance attached to it in nineteenth-century depictions of childhood, see Carolyn Steedman, 'Maps and Polar Regions', in Steve Pile (ed.), *Mapping the Subject*, Routledge (forthcoming).

7 Johann Wolfgang von Goethe, *Wilhelm Meister's Theatrical Mission*, trans. Gregory A. Page, Heinemann, 1913, p.9.

8 Ibid., pp.9–10.

9 Ibid., p.12.

10 Johann Wolfgang von Goethe, *Poetry and Truth from My Own Life* (1811), two volumes, Bell, 1913, vol. 2, pp.257–8. Georg Witkowski, *Cornelia, die Schwester Goethes* (Cornelia, Goethe's Sister), Rutten & Loening, Frankfurt, 1903.

11 Sigmund Freud, 'A Childhood Recollection from *Dictung und Wahrheit* (1917), in *Standard Edition of the Collected Psychological Works of Sigmund Freud*, vol. 17, Hogarth Press, 1955, pp.145–56. Philipp Sarasin, 'Goethes Mignon. Eine psychoanalytische Studie', *Imago*, 15 (1929), pp.349–99, trans. Richard Parker. For Freud's interest in Mignon, see William McGuire (ed.), *The Freud–Jung Letters*, Hogarth Press/and Routledge & Kegan Paul, 1974, p.388. Freud to Jung, 22 January 1911. 'I have long taken an interest in Mignon . . .' he wrote here. In the same year he used Mignon and one of her songs in order to describe a principle of wish-fulfilment, that 'in the life beyond . . . we shall at last be free from the differences between the sexes'. He then quoted from book 8, chapter 2 of Goethe's text of *Wilhelm Meister*, translated by Strachey as 'And those calm shining sons of morn/They ask not who is maid or boy'. (Wardson translates this as 'For beings in their heavenly shape/Are unaware of male or female': Johann Wolfgang von Goethe, *Wilhelm Meister's Years of Apprenticeship*, translated by H.M Waidson, Calder 1977, volume III, p.83.) Sigmund Freud, 'Psychoanalytic Notes on an Autobiographical Account of a Case of Paranoia' (1911), in *Standard Edition of the Complete Psychological Works of Sigmund Freud*, vol. 12, Hogarth Press, 1958, pp.3–82; p.29.

12 Paul Julius Moebius, *Goethe*, 2 vols, Barth, Leipzig, 1903.

13 Sarasin, 'Goethes Mignon', pp.374–5, 390.

14 K.R. Eissler, *Goethe. A Psycho-analytic Study, 1775–1786*, 2 vols, Wayne State University Press, Detroit, 1963, vol. 2, pp.757, 756, 764–5.

15 Ibid., pp.759–63.

16 Nicholas Boyle, *Goethe. The Poet and the Age. Volume 1. The Poetry of Desire*, Clarendon, Oxford, 1991, pp.53, 294–6 for the relationship between Cornelia and Wolfgang, in childhood and after.

17 Ibid., pp.352–53.

18 Ibid., p.396. Sigmund Freud, 'Creative Writers and Day-dreaming' (1908), in *Standard Edition of the Complete Psychological Works of Sigmund Freud*, vol. 9, Hogarth Press, 1959, pp.141–66.

19 Sarasin, 'Goethes Mignon', p.398. For the dream sequence, *WMA* III:10–11.
20 Otto Fenichel, 'The Symbolic Equation: Girl = Phallus', *Psychoanalytic Quarterly*, 18:3 (1949), pp.303–24.
21 Ibid., p.310.
22 Ibid., pp.310–11.
23 Ibid., p.313.
24 Ibid., p.322.
25 Fenichel's alignment of Mignon with a persistent motif of fairy-tale and legend adds some depth to my speculation about Sarah Fielding's Mignon, who came into being in the year of Goethe's birth. See above p.40 and Sarah Fielding (1749), *The Governess, or, The Little Female Academy*, edited and with an Introduction by Jill E. Grey, Oxford University Press, 1968. See the Introduction for details of German editions. For Goethe's childhood reading, see Johann Wolfgang von Goethe, *Poetry and Truth from My Own Life* (1811), 2 vols, Bell, 1913, vol. 1, pp.23–5.
26 Hellmut Ammerlahn, 'Wilhelm Meisters Mignon. Ein offenbares Ratsel' (Wilheim Meister's Mignon. An Evident Riddle), *Deutsche Vierteljahrsschrift*, 42:1 (1968), pp.89–116, trans. Richard Parker.
27 William Gilby, 'The Structural Significance of Mignon in *Wilhelm Meisters Lehrjahre*', *Seminar*, 16:3 (1980), pp.136–50.
28 Heinrich von Kleist, 'On the Marionette Theatre' (1810), trans. Roman Paska, in Michel Feher (ed.), *Fragments for a History of the Human Body. Part One*, Zone, New York, 1989, pp.415–20. See also Idris Parry, *Hand to Mouth*, Carcanet, Manchester, 1981, pp.9–18.
29 Frank Kermode, *The Romantic Image*, Routledge & Kegan Paul, 1957, pp.48, 58.
30 Frank Kermode, *The Sense of an Ending*, Oxford University Press, New York, 1967, pp.11–12.
31 Angela Carter, *Nights at the Circus*, Chatto & Windus, 1984. Page numbers in the text refer to this edition.
32 Carter herself claimed Mignon's origin in Alban Berg's opera *Wozzeck* of 1925. John Haffenden, *Novelists in Interview*, Methuen, 1985, p.82. The libretto of *Wozzeck* however quite clearly shows Berg's child to be a boy. George Perle, *The Operas of Alban Berg. Volume One/Wozzeck*, University of California Press, 1980.
33 Freud, 'The Uncanny', p.245.
34 William Blake, 'The Little Girl Found', in *Songs of Innocence and Experience* (1789, 1794), Hart-Davis, 1967, Plates 34, 35.

10 *The Child-figure and the Melodramatic Imagination*

1 Philipp Sarasin, 'Goethes Mignon. Eine psychoanalytische Studie', *Imago*, 15 (1929), pp.349–99, 353 trans. Richard Parker. See also Gies

Hatch, 'Mignon: Goethe's Study of Affectional Frustration in Childhood', in Alexej Ugrinsky (ed.), *Goethe in the Twentieth Century*, Greenwood Press, New York, 1987, pp.133–5; p.137, n.4.

2 Harlan Lane, *The Wild Boy of Aveyron*, Paladin, St Albans, 1979, pp.6–29. The literature on the Wild Boy is very extensive. See Roger Shattuck, *The Forbidden Experiment. The Story of the Wild Boy of Aveyron*, Secker & Warburg, 1980. Much interest was engendered by François Truffaut's film *L'Enfant sauvage* of 1969, in which he also played Jean Itard. See Lucien Malson, *Les Enfants sauvages*, Union Générale d'Editions, Paris, 1964. When translated into English, the book contained Itard's 'Of the First Development of the Young Savage of Aveyron' (1801), and 'Report on the Progress of Victor of Aveyron' (1807), and the cover notes claimed it as 'From the film "L'enfant Sauvage" by Truffaut'. Lucien Malson, *Wolf Children*, Jean Itard, *The Wild Boy of Aveyron*, trans. Edmund Fawcett, Peter Ayrton and Joan White, New Left Books, 1972.

3 Lane, *The Wild Boy*, pp.99–165.

4 Ibid., p.163.

5 Quoted ibid., pp.163–4. J.E. Esquirol, *Des Maladies mentales* (A Treatise on Mental Disorders), Ballière, Paris, 1838, pp.374–5.

6 Lane, *The Wild Boy*, pp.176–9. Bruno Bettelheim, *The Empty Fortress. Infantile Autism and the Birth of the Self*, Free Press, New York, 1967, pp.371–2. F. Brauner and A. Brauner, 'Le "sauvage" psychotique de l'Aveyron' (The Psychotic 'Wild' Boy of Aveyron), *Tribune de l'enfance*, 7:61 (1969), pp.41–50.

7 Reinhard Kuhn, *Corruption in Paradise. The Child in Western Literature*, Brown University Press for the University Press of New England, Hanover, Pennsylvania, 1982, pp.60–5.

8 Peter Brooks, *The Melodramatic Imagination. Balzac, Henry James, Melodrama, and the Mode of Excess*, Yale University Press, New Haven 1976, p.xiii, p.202. And see above, pp.2–3.

9 Brooks, *Melodramatic Imagination*, pp.55–66, 75.

10 Ibid., pp.75–80.

11 'Ask me not to speak, but leave me silent/For my secret is a duty for me', according to Waidson (*WMA* III:134).

12 *The Times Literary Supplement*, 24 July 1992, pp.7–8.

13 James R. Kincaid, *Child-loving. The Erotic Child and Victorian Culture*, Routledge, New York and London, 1992, p.187.

14 Ibid., pp.375, 6.

15 Ibid., p.381.

16 Ibid., p.25.

17 Ibid., p.386.

18 Ibid., p.204.

19 Ibid., p.190.

20 See above pp.106, 139–40. See Judith R. Walkowitz, *City of Dreadful Delight. Narratives of Sexual Danger in Late-Victorian London*, University of Chicago Press, Chicago, 1992, pp.81–134.
21 Ibid., pp.85–6.
22 Peter Brooks, *The Melodramatic Imagination*, p.34.
23 Otto Fenichel, 'The Symbolic Equation: Girl = Phallus', *Psychoanalytic Quarterly* 18:3 (1949), pp.303–24; p.313.
24 Paul Connerton, *How Societies Remember*, Cambridge University Press, Cambridge, 1989, pp.72–104.
25 Ibid., pp.94–5.
26 Michael S. Roth, *Psycho-analysis as History. Negation and Freedom in Freud*, Cornell University Press, Ithaca, New York, 1987, p.79. Jean Laplanche, *Life and Death in Psycho-analysis*, trans. Jeffrey Mehlman, Johns Hopkins University Press, Baltimore, Maryland, 1976, pp.19–20.
27 T.G.A. Nelson, 'The Child in Augustan Farce and Comedy', *The Eighteenth Century. Theory and Interpretation*, 30:1 (Spring 1989), pp.23–44; p.27. Norman O. Brown, *Life against Death. The Psychoanalytical Meaning of History*, Routledge & Kegan Paul, 1959, pp.107–8. Frederic Nietzsche, *Thus Spoke Zarathustra* (1891–2) in *The Portable Nietzsche*, ed. Walter Kaufman, Chatto, 1971, p.434.
28 Richard Sennett, *The Fall of Public Man*, Cambridge University Press, Cambridge, 1977, pp.16–24, 34–5.
29 G.R. Sims and Clement Scott, 'Jack in the Box', British Library, Lord Chamberlain's Collection, Add. Ms 5334.C8, p.55 (Act II, sc.3).
30 Mayhew, *Morning Chronicle*, 5 December 1850, pp.5–6.
31 Henry Mayhew, *London Labour and the London Poor*, 4 vols, 1861–2, Griffin Bohn, 1861, vol. 1, pp.151–2.
32 Margaret McMillan, *The Camp School*, Allen & Unwin, 1917, pp.82–3.
33 British Parliamentary Papers, *First Report of Her Majesty's Commissioners for Inquiring into the Housing of the Working Classes*, 1884–5, vol. 30, pp.167–77; p.172.

Bibliography

1. Published Sources

(The place of publication is London, unless otherwise indicated.)

Albani, Emma, *Forty Years of Song*, Mills & Boon, 1911

Albury, W.R. 'Experiment and Explanation in the Physiology of Bichat and Magendie,' *Studies in the History of Biology*, 1 (1977), pp.47–131

Allen, Garland E., *Life Sciences in the Twentieth Century*, Cambridge University Press, Cambridge, 1978

Amacher, Peter, 'Freud's Neurological Education and Its Influence on Psychoanalytic Theory', *Psychological Issues. Monograph 16* (vol. 4, no.4), International Universities Press, New York, 1965

Ammerlahn, Hellmut, 'Wilhelm Meisters Mignon. Ein offenbares Rätsel' (Wilheim Meister's Mignon. An Evident Riddle), *Deutsche Vierteljahrsschrift*, 42:1 (1968), pp.89–116

Anon., *Letters to a Mother on the Watchful Care of Her Infant*, Seeley & Burnside, 1831

Anon., 'Review of J.M Schleiden, *The Plant; a Biography. In a Series of Popular Lectures.* Translated by Arthur Henfrey, London, 1848', *British and Foreign Medico-Chirurgical Review*, 2 (October 1848), pp.368–82

Anon., 'Coleridge and Freke on Life. Review of *Hints Towards the Formation of a More Comprehensive Theory of Life.* By S.T. Coleridge., Edited by Seth Watson, London, 1848', *British and Foreign Medico-Chirurgical Review*, 3 (January 1849), pp.194–8

Anon., 'Dr Carpenter's Principles of Human Physiology', *British and Foreign Medico-Chirurgical Review*, 8 (October 1851), pp.509–25

Anon., 'Physical Physiology', *British and Foreign Medico-Chirurgical Review*, 19 (April 1857), pp.261–74

Anon., *Mignon. A Tale. Translated from the French*, P. O'Shea, New York, 1868

Arber, Agnes, 'Goethe's Botany. The Metamorphosis of Plants (1790) and Tobler's Ode to Nature (1782)', *Chronica Botanica*, 10:2 (1946), pp.63–126

Ariès, Philippe, *Centuries of Childhood* (1960), Penguin, Harmondsworth, 1973

Ashplant, Timothy and Wilson, Adrian, 'Present-Centred History and the Problem of Historical Knowledge', *The Historical Journal*, 31:2 (1988), pp.253–74

Baer, Karl Ernst von, *Über die Entwickelungsgeschichte der Thiere* (On the History of the Development of Animals), Borntrager, Königsberg, 1828

Bailey, Peter, 'Introduction: Making Sense of Music Hall', in Peter Bailey (ed.), *Music Hall. The Business of Pleasure*, Open University Press, Milton Keynes, 1986, pp.viii–xxiii

Bakan, David, *Sigmund Freud and the Jewish Mystical Tradition* (1958), Free Association Books, 1990

Baldwin, Mark James, *Mental Development in the Child and the Race*, Macmillan, New York, 1893

Banier, Abbé Antoine, *Mythology and Fables of the Ancients. Translated from the French*, 4 vols, Andrew Millar, Edinburgh, 1739–40

Bann, Stephen, *The Clothing of Clio. A Study of the Representations of History in Nineteenth-Century Britain and France*, Cambridge University Press, Cambridge, 1984

Barlee, Ellen, *Pantomime Waifs. With an Introduction by the Right Honourable the Earl of Shaftesbury*, Partridge, 1884

Barnes, Harry Elmer, *A History of Historical Writing*, Dover, New York, 1963

Beckson, Karl, *Arthur Symons. A Life*, Clarendon, Oxford, 1987

Beer, Gillian, *Darwin's Plots. Evolutionary Narrative in Darwin, George Eliot and Nineteenth Century Fiction*, Routledge & Kegan Paul, 1983

Benton, E., 'Vitalism in Nineteenth Century Scientific Thought. A Typology and Reassessment', *Studies in the History and Philosophy of Science*, 5:1 (1974–5), pp.17–48

Bernard, F.M., 'Natural Growth and Purposive Development: Vico and Herder', *History and Theory*, 18 (1979), pp.16–36

Bernfeld, Siegfried, 'Freud's Earliest Theories and the School of Helmholtz', *Psychoanalytic Quarterly*, 13 (1944), pp.341–62

Bettelheim, Bruno, *The Empty Fortress. Infantile Autism and the Birth of the Self*, Free Press, New York, 1967

Bichat, François, *Anatomie générale, appliqué à la physiologie et á la médicine* (1801), translated as *General Anatomy applied to Physiology and the Practice of Medicine*, by Constant Coffin, and privately printed, 2 vols, 1824

Binyon, Laurence, 'The Little Dancers', in *Collected Poems of Laurence Binyon. London Visions. Narrative Poems. Translations*, Macmillan, 1931

Black, Cornelius, *Letters on the More Evident Changes Which the Body Undergoes, and, The Management of Health in Infancy and Adult Age*, Whittaker, 1846

Blake, William, 'Little Girl Found', in *Songs of Innocence and Experience* [1789, 1794], Hart-Davis, 1967

Bohm, Arnd, '"O Vater, lass uns ziehn!": A Mythological Background to "Mignon's Italian Song",' *MLN* (*Modern Language Notes*), 100:3 (April 1985), pp.651–9

Booth, Michael R., *English Melodrama*, Herbert Jenkins, 1965

Booth, Michael R., 'The Metropolis on the Stage', in H.J. Dyos and Michael Wolff, *The Victorian City. Volume I. Images and Reality*, Routledge & Kegan Paul, 1973, pp.211–24

Booth, Michael R., *Victorian Spectacular Theatre*, 1850–1910, Routledge & Kegan Paul, 1981

Booth, Michael R., 'Melodrama and the Working Class', in Carol Hanbery MacKay, *Dramatic Dickens*, Macmillan, 1989, pp.96–109

Booth, Michael R., *The Theatre in the Victorian Age*, Cambridge University Press, Cambridge, 1991

Bouchut, M.E., *Treatise on the Diseases of Children and Infants at the Breast, including the Hygiene and Physical Education of Young Children. Translated from the French of . . . With Notes and Additions by Peter Hinkes Bird*, John Churchill, 1855

Bouissac, Paul, 'Structure and Meaning of Acrobatic Acts', in *Circus and Culture. A Semiotic Approach*, Indiana University Press, Bloomington, 1976, pp.28–51

Boulton, Percy, 'On the Physical Development of Children or the Bearing of Anthropometry to Hygiene', *Lancet*, (1880 Part 2), pp.610–11

Bowler, Peter J., *The Non-Darwinian Revolution. Reinterpreting a Historical Myth*, Johns Hopkins University Press, Baltimore, Maryland, 1988

Boyd, James, *Goethe's Knowledge of English Literature*, Clarendon, Oxford, 1932

Boyle, Nicholas, *Goethe. The Poet and His Age. Volume I. The Poetry of Desire (1749–1790)*, Clarendon , Oxford, 1991

Bradley, Ben S., *Visions of Infancy. A Critical Introduction to Child Psychology*, Polity Press, Cambridge, 1989

Braidwood, P.M., *The Domestic Management of Children*, Smith Elder, 1874.

Bratton, J.S., 'Jenny Hill: Sex and Sexism in Victorian Musica Hall', in J.S Bratton (ed.), *Music Hall: Performance and Style*, Open University Press, Milton Keynes, 1986, pp.92–110

Brauner F. and Brauner, A., 'Le "sauvage" psychotique de l'Aveyron' (The Psychotic 'wild' child of Aveyron), *Tribune de l'enfance*, 7:61 (1969), pp.41–50

Brennan, Theresa, *The Interpretation of the Flesh: Freud and Femininity*, Routledge, 1992

British Parliamentary Papers, *Report from the Select Committee on the Education of Destitute Children*, 1861, vol. 7

British Parliamentary Papers, *First Report of the Commissioners on the Employment of Children and Young Persons in Trades and Manufacturers*, 1863, vol. 18

British Parliamentary Papers, *Report from the Select Committee on Theatrical Licences and Regulations*, 1866, vol. 16

British Parliamentary Papers, *Report from the Select Committee on Police and Sanitary Regulations*, 1882, vol. 12

British Parliamentary Papers, *First Report of Her Majesty's Commissioners for Inquiring into the Housing of the Working Classes*, 1884–5, vol. 30

British Parliamentary Papers, *Third Report of the Royal Commission Appointed to Inquire into the Working of the Elementary Education Acts*, 1887, vol. 30

British Parliamentary Papers, *Report from the Select Committee on the Infant Life Protection Bill*, 1890, vol. 13, p.694

British Parliamentary Papers, *Report from the Select Committee on Theatres and Places of Entertainment*, 1892, vol. 18

Brontë, Charlotte, *Jane Eyre* (1847), Penguin, Harmondsworth, 1966

Brooks, Peter, *The Melodramatic Imagination. Balzac, Henry James, Melodrama and the Mode of Excess*, Yale University Press, New Haven, 1976

Brown, Marilyn R., *Gypsies and Other Bohemians. The Myth of the Artist in Nineteenth Century France*, UMI Research Press, Ann Arbor, Michigan, 1985

Brown, Norman O., *Life against Death. The Psychoanalytical Meaning of History*, Routledge & Kegan Paul, 1959

Browning, Robert M., *Selections from Goethe's Letters to Frau von Stein. 1776–1789*, Camden House, Columbia, 1990

Brücke, Ernst Wilhelm von, *Vorlesungen über Physiologie* (Lectures on Physiology), 2 volumes, Braumuller, Vienna, 1874

Bruford, W.H., *Culture and Society in Classical Weimar. 1775–1806*, Cambridge University Press, Cambridge, 1962

Bryant, Thomas, 'Lettsomian Lectures on the Surgical Diseases of Children', *British Medical Journal* (1863 Part 1), pp.287–8

Cannon, Walter F., 'History in Depth: The Early Victorian Period', *History and Science*, 3 (1964), pp.20–38

Carpenter, William B., *Principles of Human Physiology, General and Comparative*, 5th edition, John Churchill, 1855. (Originally published as *Principles of General and Comparative Physiology*, 1839)

Carré, Michel and Barbier, Jules, *Mignon. Opéra Comique. Paroles de Michel Carré et Jules Barbier. Musique de Ambroise Thomas* (Mignon, A Comic Opera. Words by Michel Carré and Jules Barbier. Music by Ambroise Thomas) (1866), Calmann-Levy, Paris, 1870

Carter, Angela, *Nights at the Circus*, Chatto & Windus, 1984

Cavanagh, John C., 'Early Developmental Theories: A Brief Review of Attempts to Organise Developmental Data prior to 1925', *Journal of the History of the Behavioral Sciences*, 17 (1981), pp.38–47

Charity Organisation Society, *Report of the Committee of the Charity Organisation Society Appointed to Inquire into the Employment of Italian Children for Medicant and Immoral Purposes*, COS, 1877

Chartier, Roger (ed.), *The Culture of Print. Power and the Uses of Print in Early Modern Europe*, Polity Press, Cambridge, 1989

Churchill, Fleetwood, *Diseases of Children*, Hodges & Smith, Dublin, 1850.

Coe, Richard N., *When the Grass was Taller. Autobiography and the Experience of Childhood*, Yale University Press, New Haven, 1984

Coleman, William, *Biology in the Nineteenth Century. Problems of Form, Function and Transformation*, Cambridge University Press, Cambridge, 1977

Combe, Andrew, *Principles of Physiology Applied to the Preservation of Health and to the Improvement of Physical and Medical Education* (1834), MacLachlan, Edinburgh, 1842

Combe, Andrew, *A Treatise on the Physiological and Moral Management of Infancy*, MacLachlan, Stewart, Edinburgh, 1840

Connerton, Paul, *How Societies Remember*, Cambridge University Press, Cambridge, 1989

Conquest, John Tricker, *Letters to a Mother on the Management of Herself and Her Children in Health and Disease*, Longman, 1848

Cooper, Anthony Ashley, 'The Second Annual Report of the Ragged School Union', *Quarterly Review* 79 (December 1846–March 1847), pp.127–41

Cory, Edward Augustus, *The Physical and Medical Management of Children, Adapted for General Perusal* (1834), Draper, 1844

Coveney, Peter, *The Image of Childhood. The Individual and Society: A Study of the Theme in English Literature* (originally published as *Poor Monkey*, 1957), Penguin, Harmondsworth, 1967

Crosby, Christina, *The Ends of History. Victorians and 'The Woman Question'*, Routledge, 1991

Cross, Stephen J., 'John Hunter, the Animal Oeconomy and Late Eighteenth Century Physiological Discourse', *Studies in the History of Biology*, 5 (1981), pp.1–110

Culler, A. Dwight, *The Victorian Mirror of History*, Yale University Press, New Haven, 1985

Cunningham, Hugh, *The Children of the Poor. Representations of Childhood since the Seventeenth Century*, Blackwell, Oxford, 1991

Darwin, Charles, *The Expression of the Emotions in Man and Animals*, Murray, 1873

Darwin, Charles, 'The Biographical Sketch of an Infant', *Mind*, 2 (July 1877), pp.285–94

Darwin, Erasmus, *The Temple of Nature, or The Origin of Society* (1803), in Donald A. Reiman (ed.), *The Golden Age. The Temple of Nature*, Garland, New York, 1978

Davidoff, Leonore, 'Mastered for Life: Servant and Wife in Victorian and Edwardian England', *Journal of Social History*, 7:4 (1974), pp.406–28

Davidoff, Leonore, 'Class and Gender in Victorian England', in Judith L. Newton, Mary P. Ryan and Judy R. Walkowitz, *Sex and Class in Women's History*, Routledge & Kegan Paul, 1983, pp.17–71

Davie, Donald, 'Personification', *Essays in Criticism*, 31:2 (April 1981), pp.91–104

Davies, Henry, *Dr Underwood's Treatise on the Diseases of Children: with Directions for the Management of Infants*, John Churchill, 1846

Davis, Tracy C., 'The Employment of Children in the Victorian Theatre. Training, Exploitation and the Movement for Reform', *New*

Theatre Quarterly, 2:60 (1986), pp.117–35

Davis, Tracy C., 'The Spectacle of Absent Costume. Nudity on the Victorian Stage', *New Theatre Quarterly*, 5:20 (1989), pp.321–47

Davis, Tracy C., *Actresses as Working Women. Their Social Identity in Victorian Culture*, Routledge, 1991

Davy, Humphrey, *Consolations in Travel, or, The Last days of a Philosopher*, John Murray, 1830

Delaporte, François, *Nature's Second Kingdom. Explorations of Vegetality in the Eighteenth Century*, trans. Arthur Goldhammer, MIT Press, Cambridge, Mass., 1982

Demoriane, Hermine, *The Tightrope Walker*, Secker & Warburg, 1989

De Staël-Holstein, Ann Louise Germaine, *Germany. Translated from the French. In Three Volumes* (1810), John Murray, 1813

Dick, Robert, *Diet and Regimen, Physical, Intellectual, Moral, as Means in the Cure and Prevention of Disease*, Symington, Glasgow, 1838

Dobson, Austin, *Samuel Richardson*, Macmillan, 1902

Donaldson, Ian, *The Rapes of Lucretia: A Myth and Its Transformations*, Clarendon, Oxford, 1982

Doody, Margaret Ann, *A Natural Passion. A Study of the Novels of Samuel Richardson*, Clarendon , Oxford, 1974

Draper, John William, *Human Physiology, Statistical and Dynamical; or the Conditions and Course of the Life of Man* (1856), Harper, New York, 1868.

Draper, John William, *History of the Intellectual Development of Europe*, 2 vols, Bell Daldy, 1864

Drummond, Henry, *Lowell Lectures on the Ascent of Man*, Hodder & Stoughton, 1894

Drummond, W.B., *An Introduction to Child Study*, Arnold, 1907

Duhomme, Frédéric et de Troisements, Piel, *Le Dernier jour de Mignon. Drame en un acte, en vers. Répresenté pour la première fois, à Paris, sur le theâtre de la Porte-St-Martin, le 19 avril 1874* (Mignon's Last Day. A Verse Drama in one Act. Staged for the first time at the Porte-St-Martin Theatre on 19 April 1874), Barbré, Paris, 1874

Du Maurier, George, *Trilby. A Novel*, Osgood McIlvaine, 1895

Eagleton, Terry, *The Rape of Clarissa*, Blackwell, Oxford, 1982

Eissler, K.R., *Goethe. A Psycho-analytic Study, 1775–1786*, 2 vols, Wayne State University Press, Detroit, 1963

Encyclopédie, ou Dictionnaire raisonné des sciences, des arts et des métiers, Tome Dixième [vol.10], Neufchastel, 1765

Eng, Erling, 'Thomas Henry Huxley's Understanding of Evolution', *History of Science*, 16 (1978), pp.291–303

Esquirol, J.E., *Des Maladies mentales*, Ballière (A Treatise on Mental Disorders), Paris, 1838

Ewals, Leo, *Ary Scheffer, Sa Vie et son oeuvre* (Ary Scheffer, His Life and Work), s.l, s.n, Nijmegen, 1987

Fawcett, Millicent Garrett, 'The Employment of Children in Theatres', *Contemporary Review*, 56 (July–December 1889), pp.822–9

Fénelon, Salignac de la Mothe, *Dialogues of the Dead*, D. Browne, 1735

Fenichel, Otto, 'The Symbolic Equation: Girl = Phallus', *Psychoanalytic Quarterly*, 18:3 (1949), pp.303–24

Fertig, Ludwig, *Johann Wolfgang von Goethe, der Mentor*, Wissenschaftliche Buchgesellschaft, Darmstadt, 1991

Fielding, Sarah, *The Governess, or, the Little Female Academy* (1749), Women's Press, 1987

Figlio, Karl M., 'The Metaphor of Organisation. An Historical Perspective on the Bio-Medical Sciences of the Early Nineteenth Century', *History of Science*, 14 (1976), pp.17–53

Finlayson, Geoffrey, *The Seventh Earl of Shaftesbury, 1801–1885*, Eyre Methuen, 1981

Fitzball, Edward, *Thirty-five Years of a Dramatic Author's Life. In Two Volumes*, Newby, 1859

Flashar, Dorothea, *Bedeutung, Entwicklung und literarische Nachwirkung von Goethes Mignongestalt* (Significance, Development and Literary After-effects of Goethe's Mignon figure) , E. Ebering, Berlin, 1929

Forrester, Mrs, *Mignon*, 3 volumes, Hurst & Blackett, 1877

Foucault, Michel, *The Order of Things. An Archaeology of the Human Sciences*, Tavistock, translated by A.M. Sheridan Smith, 1970

Foucault, Michel, *The Archaeology of Knowledge*, translated by A.M. Sheridan Smith, Harper & Row, New York, 1972

Foucault, Michel, *The Care of the Self. Volume 3. The History of Sexuality* (1984), trans. Robert Hurley, Allen Lane, Harmondsworth, 1988

Freeman, Mark, *Rewriting the Self. History, Memory, Narrative*, Routledge, 1993

Freud, Sigmund, 'Project for a Scientific Psychology' (1895), in *Standard Edition of the Complete Psychological Works of Sigmund Freud*, vol. 1, Hogarth Press, 1966, pp.281–397

Freud, Sigmund, 'Heredity and the Aetiology of the Neuroses' (1896) and 'Further Remarks on the Neuro-Psychoses of Defence' (1896), in *Standard Edition of the Complete Psychological Works of Sigmund Freud*, vol. 3, Hogarth Press, 1962, pp.141–56; pp. 157–85

Freud, Sigmund, 'Screen Memories' (1899), in *Standard Edition of the Complete Psychological Works of Sigmund Freud*, vol. 3, Hogarth Press, 1962, pp.301–22

Freud, Sigmund, 'The Interpretation of Dreams' (1899, 1900), in *Standard Edition of the Complete Psychological Works of Sigmund Freud*, volumes 4–5, Hogarth Press, 1955

Freud, Sigmund, 'Three Essays on the Theory of Sexuality' (1905), in *Standard Edition of the Complete Psychological Works of Sigmund Freud*, vol. 7, Hogarth Press, 1953, pp.125–245

Freud, Sigmund, 'Fragment of an Analysis of a Case of Hysteria' (1905), in *Standard Edition of the Complete Psychological Works of Sigmund Freud*, vol. 7, Hogarth Press, 1953, pp.3–122

Freud, Sigmund, 'Creative Writers and Day-dreaming' (1908), in *Standard Edition of the Complete Psychological Works of Sigmund Freud*, vol. 9, Hogarth Press, 1959, pp.141–66

Freud, Sigmund, 'On the Sexual Theories of Children' (1908) and 'Family Romances', (1908), in *Standard Edition of the Complete Psychological Works of Sigmund Freud*, vol. 9, Hogarth Press, 1959, pp.205–26; pp.235–41

Freud, Sigmund, 'Analysis of a Phobia in a Five-year Old Boy' (1909), in *Standard Addition of the Complete Psychological Works of Sigmund Freud*, vol. 10, Hogarth Press, 1955, pp.3–149

Freud, Sigmund, 'Psycho-analytic Notes on an Autobiographical Account of a Case of Paranoia' (1911), in *Standard Edition of the Complete Psychological Works of Sigmund Freud*, vol. 12, Hogarth Press, 1958, pp.3–82

Freud, Sigmund, 'Introductory Lectures on Psycho-analysis (Part III),' (1916–1917) in *Standard Edition of the Complete Psychological Works of Sigmund Freud*, vol. 16, Hogarth Press, 1963, pp.392–411

Freud, Sigmund, 'A Childhood Recollection from *Dichtung und Wahrheit*' (1917), in *Standard Edition of the Collected Psychological Works of Sigmund Freud*, vol. 17, Hogarth Press, 1955, pp.145–56

Freud, Sigmund, 'From the History of an Infantile Neurosis' (1918), in *Standard Edition of the Complete Psychological Works of Sigmund Freud*, vol. 17, Hogarth Press, 1955, pp.1–123

Freud, Sigmund, 'The Uncanny' (1919), in *Standard Edition of the Collected Works*, vol. 17, Hogarth Press, 1955, pp.217–56

Freud, Sigmund, 'Beyond the Pleasure Principle' (1920), in *Standard Edition of the Complete Psychological Works of Sigmund Freud*, vol. 18, Hogarth Press, 1950, pp.3–64

Freud, Sigmund, 'A Note Upon the Mystic Writing Pad' (1925), in *Standard Edition of the Complete Psychological Works of Sigmund Freud*, vol. 19, Hogarth Press, 1961, pp.227–32

Freud, Sigmund, 'Psycho-analysis: Freudian School', *Encyclopaedia Britannica*, 14th edition, Volume 18, Encyclopaedia Britannica Co. 1929, pp.672–4

Freud, Sigmund, *Briefe an Wilhelm Fliess* (Letters to Wilhelm Fliess), *1887–1904*, ed. Jeffrey Masson, Fischer, Frankfurt, 1988

Friedenthal, Richard, *Goethe. His Life and Times*, Weidenfeld & Nicolson, 1965

Fry, Sarah, *The Little Watercress Sellers* (1854), Presbyterian Committee of Publication of Richmond, Virginia, 1866

Fulcher, Jane F., *The Nation's Image. French Grand Opera as Politics and Politicised Art*, Cambridge University Press, Cambridge, 1987

Gallagher, Catherine, *The Industrial Reformation of English Fiction. Social Discourse and Narrative, 1831–1867*, University of Chicago Press, Chicago, 1985

Gaskell, Elizabeth Cleghorn, *My Diary*, ed. Clement Shorter, privately printed, San Francisco, 1923

Gautier, Théophile, 'Ary Scheffer', *L'Artiste*, 20 June 1858, p.99

Geison, Gerald L., *Michael Foster and the Cambridge School of Physiology*, Princeton University Press, Princeton, 1978

Gélis, Jacques, *History of Childbirth. Fertility, Pregnancy and Birth in Early Modern Europe*, trans. Rosemary Morris, Polity Press, Cambridge, 1991

Gilby, William, 'The Structural Significance of Mignon in *Wilhelm Meister*, *Seminar*, 16:3 (1980), pp.136–50

Goethe, Johann Wolfgang von, *Dichtung und Wahrheit* (Poetry and Truth) (1813), Part Three, in vol. 28 of the *Sophienausgabe* edn, 133 vols in 143, Boehlau, Weimar, 1887–1919

Goethe, Johann Wolfgang von, *Poetry and Truth From My Own Life* (1811), 2 vols, Bell, 1913

Goethe, Johann Wolfgang von, *Wilhelm Meister's Apprenticeship and Travels. Three Volumes in Two*, translated by Thomas Carlyle (1839), Chapman and Hall, 1894

Goethe, Johann Wolfgang von, *Wilhelm Meister's Theatrical Mission*, trans. Gregory A. Page, Heinemann, 1913

Goethe, Johann Wolfgang von, *Gedenkausgabe der Werke, Briefe und Gespräche* (Memorial Edition of Goethe's work. Letters and Conversations.), ed. Ernst Beutler, Artemis, Zurich, 1948

Goethe, Johann Wolfgang von, *Wilhelm Meister's Years of Apprenticeship*, trans. H.M. Waidson, 6 vols, Calder, 1977

Goethe, Johann Wolfgang von, *Italian Journey, 1786–1788*, trans. W.H. Auden and Elizabeth Mayer, (1962), North Point Press, San Francisco, 1982

Goethe, Johann Wolfgang von, *Briefwechsel zwischen Schiller und Goethe* (Schiller-Goethe Correspondence), ed. Heinz Amerlung, 3 vols, Deutsche Bibliothek, Berlin, n.d

Golden, Morris, 'Public Context and Imagining Self in *Pamela* and *Shamela*', *English Literary History*, 53:2 (1986), pp.311–29

Goodfield-Toulmin, June, 'Some Aspects of English Physiology, 1780–1940', *Journal of the History of Biology*, 2 (1969), pp.283–320

Grant, George, *An Essay on the Science of Acting. By a Veteran Stager*, Cowie & Strange, 1828

Greenwood, James, *In Strange Company. Being the Experience of a Roving Correspondent*, King, 1873

Greenwood, James, *Low-Life Deeps. An Account of the Strange Fish to Be Found There*, Chatto & Windus, 1876

Grey, Jill E., Introduction to Sarah Fielding, *The Governess or The Little*

Female Academy (ed. Jill E. Grey), Oxford University Press, Oxford, 1968.

Groom, John, *The Silver Vase, or, The Gathered Posy. With an Introduction by Lady Savory*, Morgan & Scott, 1891

Groom, John, *Mr Groom's Industrial Training Homes . . . The Goal of Charity*, privately printed, 1907

Groom, John, *Mr Groom's Crippleage and Flower Girls' Mission*, privately printed, 1910

Groos, Carl, *The Play of Man* (1899), trans. E.L Baldwin, Appleton, New York, 1901

Grote Mrs (Harriet Grote, née Lewin), *Memoir of the Life of Ary Scheffer*, John Murray, 1860

Haffenden, John, *Novelists in Interview*, Methuen, 1985

Hale, J.R., *The Evolution of British Historiography. From Bacon to Namier*, Macmillan, 1967

Harris, Jocelyn, *Samuel Richardson*, Cambridge University Press, Cambridge, 1987

Hartog, Dirk den, *Dickens and Romantic Psychology. The Self in Time in Nineteenth Century Literature*, Macmillan, Basingstoke, 1987

Harvey, A.D., *Literature into History*, Macmillan, 1978

Hatch, Mary Gies, 'Mignon: Goethe's Study of Affectional Frustration in Childhood', in Alexej Ugrinsky, (ed.), *Goethe in the Twentieth Century*, Greenwood Press, New York, 1987, pp.133–8

Hess, A., 'On the Necessity of Practical Instruction in the Treatment of Diseases in Children', *Lancet* (1849 Part 1), pp.341–2

Himmelfarb, Gertrude, *The Idea of Poverty. England in the Early Industrial Age*, Faber & Faber, 1984

Hoffmeister, Gerhart (ed.), *Goethes Mignon und ihre Schwestern in Literatur, Psychologie und Kunst* (Goethe's Mignon and her Sisters in Literature, Psychology and Art), Lang, Frankfurt, forthcoming

Hogg, Charles, *On the Management of Infancy. With Remarks on the Influence of Diet and Regimen*, John Churchill, 1849

Hogg, Edith, 'School Children as Wage Earners', *The Nineteenth Century*, 42 (1897), pp.235–44

Hoher, Dagmar, 'The Composition of Music Hall Audiences, 1850–1900', in Peter Bailey (ed.), *Music Hall. The Business of Pleasure*, Open University Press, Milton Keynes, 1986, pp.73–92

Hopkins, Albert A., *Magic. Stage Illusions and Scientific Diversions* (1897), Benjamin Blom, New York, 1967

Hudson, Derek, *Munby. Man of Two Worlds. The Life and Diaries of Arthur J. Munby, 1828–1910*, Sphere, 1974

Huizinga, Johann, *The Waning of the Middle Ages* (1924), Arnold, 1970

Hunter, John H., *The Works of John Hunter*, ed. J.F. Palmer, 4 vols, Longman, 1835–7

Hutchins B.L. and Harrison, A., *A History of Factory Legislation* (1903), Frank Cass, 1966

Huxley, T. H. 'The Cell-Theory,' *British and Foreign Medico-Chirurgical Review*, 12 (October 1853), pp.15–243

Jackson, John Hughlings, 'On Some Implications of the Dissolution of the Nervous System', *Medical Press and Circular*, (1883 Part 2), pp.64, 84; (1884 Part 2),pp.411, 433

Jackson, John Hughlings, 'Croonian Lectures on the Evolution and Dissolution of the Nervous System', *British Medical Journal*, (1884 Part 1), pp.591, 660, 703

Jacyna, L.S., 'John Goodsir and the Making of Cellular Reality', *Journal of the History of Biology*, 16:1 (1983), pp.75–99

Jacyna, L.S., 'The Romantic Programme and the Reception of Cell Theory in Britain', *Journal of the History of Biology*, 17:1 (1984), pp.13–48

Jacyna L.S., 'Romantic Thought and the Origins of Cell Theory', in Andrew Cunningham and Nicholas Jardine (eds), *Romanticism and the Sciences*, Cambridge University Press, Cambridge, 1991, pp.161–8

Jadelot, J. Jules, *Quelques considérations sur la physiologie et la pathologie de l'enfance* (Some Thoughts on the Physiology and Pathology of Infancy) in *Collections des Thèses soutenues à la Faculté de Médicine de Paris* (Theses defended at the Faculty of Medicine, Paris), Tome Huitième [vol. 8]; thèse 240, Didot, Paris, 1835

Jameson, Thomas, *Essays on the Changes of the Human Body, at Its Different Ages; the Diseases to Which It is Predisposed in each Period of Life: and the Physiological Principles of Its Longevity*, Longman, 1811

Jentsch, Ernst, 'Zur Psychologie des Unheimlichen' (On the Psychology of the Uncanny), *Psychiatrisch-neurologische Wochenschrift*, 8 (1906), pp.195–202

Jeune, Mrs, 'Children in Theatres', *English Illustrated Magazine*, 1889–90, pp.6–14

John, V. *Quetelet bei Goethe* (Quetelet in Goethe), Fischer, Jena, 1898

Jordan, Thomas E., *Victorian Childhood. Themes and Variations*, State University of New York Press, Albany, 1987, pp. 110–47

Keeling, Frederic, *Child Labour in the United Kingdom*, P.S. King, 1914

Kermode, Frank, *The Romantic Image*, Routledge & Kegan Paul, 1957

Kermode, Frank, *The Sense of an Ending*, Oxford University Press, New York, 1967

Kern, Steven, 'Freud and the Discovery of Childhood Sexuality', *History of Childhood Quarterly*, 1 (1973), pp.117–41

Kern, Steven, 'Freud and the Birth of Child Psychiatry', *Journal of the History of the Behavioral Sciences*, 9 (1973), pp.360–8

Kincaid, James R. *Child-loving. The Erotic Child and Victorian Culture*, Routledge, New York and London, 1992

Kleist, Heinrich von, 'On the Marionette Theatre' (1810), trans. Roman

Paska, in Michel Feher (ed.), *Fragments for a History of the Human Body. Part One*, Zone, New York, 1989, pp.415–20

Knapp, Steven, *Personification and the Sublime. Milton to Coleridge*, Harvard University Press, Cambridge, Mass., 1985

Knight, D.M., 'The Physical Sciences and the Romantic Movement', *History of Science*, 9 (1970), pp.54–75

König, Julia, '*Das Leben im Kunstwerk: Studien zu Goethes Mignon und ihrer Rezeption*' (Life in the Work of Art. Studies on Goethe's Mignon and her Reception), Lang, Berlin, 1991

Kuhn, Reinhard, *Corruption in Paradise. The Child in Western Literature*, Brown University Press/the University Press of New England, Hanover, Pennsylvania, 1982

Lachmann, Fritz R., 'Goethes Mignon', *Germanisch-Romanische Monatsschrift*, 15 (1927), pp.103–5

Lane, Harlan, *The Wild Boy of Aveyron*, Paladin, St Albans, 1979

Langlois, Charles and Seignobos, Charles, *Introduction to the Study of History*, Duckworth, 1898

Laplanche, Jean, *Life and Death in Psycho-analysis*, trans. Jeffrey Mehlman, Johns Hopkins University Press, Baltimore, Maryland, 1976

Lenoir, Timothy, 'Generational Factors in the Origin of Romantische Naturphilosophie', *Journal of the History of Biology*, 11:1 (1978), pp.57–110

Lenoir, Timothy, 'Teleology without Regrets. The Transformation of Physiology in Germany, 1790–1847', *Studies in the History and Philosophy of Science*, 12:4 (1981), pp.293–354

Lenoir, Timothy, *The Strategy of Life. Teleology and Mechanism in Nineteenth Century German Biology*, Reidel, Dordrecht, 1982

Le Roux, Hughes and Garnier, Jules, *Acrobats and Mountebanks* (1889), trans. A.P. Morton, Chapman and Hall, 1890

Levine, Philippa, *The Amateur and the Professional. Antiquarians, Historians and Archaeologists in Victorian Britain, 1838–1886*, Cambridge University Press, Cambridge, 1986

Lewes, George Henry, *The Life and Works of Goethe* (1858), Dent, 1908

Lewes, George Henry, *Sea-side Studies at Ilfracombe, Tenby, the Scilly Isles and Jersey*, Blackwood, Edinburgh, 1858

Lewes, George Henry, *The Physiology of Common Life*, 2 vols, Blackwood, Edinburgh, 1859–60

Lewes, George Henry, *Female Characters of Goethe, from the Original Drawings of William Kaulbach. With Explanatory Text by G.H. Lewes*, Frederick Buckmann, 1872

Locke, John, *Some Thoughts Concerning Education* (1693), ed. J.W. and Jean S. Yolton, Clarendon, Oxford, 1989

Loti, Pierre, *A Child's Romance. Translated from the French by Clara Bell*, Kegan Paul, 1891

Lucás, John, 'Hopkins and Symons: Two Views of the City', in John Stokes (ed.), *Fin-de-Siècle, Fin du Globe. Fears and Fantasies of the Late Nineteenth Century*, Macmillan, 1992, pp.52–68

Ludwig, Emil, *Goethe. The History of a Man*, 2 vols, Putnam, 1928

Lukacs, Georg, *Goethe and His Age*, Merlin, 1968

McGuire, William (ed.), *The Freud–Jung Letters*, Hogarth Press/Routledge & Kegan Paul, 1974

McMillan, Margaret, *The Camp School*, Allen & Unwin, 1917

Magner, Lois N., *A History of the Life Sciences*, Dekker, New York, 1979

Maitland, Sara, *Vesta Tilley*, Virago, 1986

Malson, Lucien, *Les Enfants sauvages* (Wild Children), Union Générale d'Editions, Paris, 1964

Malson, Lucien, *Wolf Children*, and Jean Itard, *The Wild Boy of Aveyron*, trans. Edmund Fawcett, Peter Ayrton and Joan White, New Left Books, 1972

Mandelbaum, Maurice, *History and Reason. A Study in Nineteenth Century Thought*, Johns Hopkins University Press, Baltimore, Maryland, 1971

Manier, Edward, 'History, Philosophy and Sociology of Biology. A Family Romance', *Studies in the History and Philosophy of Science*, 11:1 (1980), pp.1–24

Manton, Jo, *Mary Carpenter and the Children of the Streets*, Heinemann, 1976.

Marshall, Henry, *On the Enlisting, Discharging and Pensioning of Soldiers*, Adam & Charles Black, Edinburgh, 1839

Masson, J.M., *The Assault on Truth: Freud's Suppression of the Seduction Theory*, Penguin, Harmondsworth, 1985

Mayhew, Henry, 'Labour and the Poor. Metropolitan Districts. From Our Special Correspondent. Of the Green Markets of London. Letter 81', *Morning Chronicle*, 5 December 1850, pp.5–6

Mayhew, Henry, *Life and Labour of the London Poor*, vol. 1, and parts of vols 2 and 3, George Woodfall, 1851

Mayhew, Henry, *London Labour and the London Poor*, 4 vols, Griffin Bohn, 1861–2

Meisel, Martin, *Realizations. Narrative, Pictorial, and Theatrical Arts in Nineteenth Century England*, Princeton University Press, Princeton, 1983

Mendelsohn, Everett, 'The Biological Sciences in the Nineteenth Century. Some Problems and Sources', *History of Science*, 3 (1964), pp.39–59

Middleton, Christopher (ed.), *Johann Wolfgang von Goethe. Selected Poems*, Suhrkamp/Insel, Boston, 1983

Miller, J. Hills, *Versions of Pygmalion*, Harvard University Press, Cambridge, Mass., 1990

Mitchell, Jerome, *The Walter Scott Operas. An Analysis of Operas Based on the Work of Sir Walter Scott*, University of Alabama, Alabama, 1977

Moebius, Paul Julius, *Goethe*, 2 volumes, Barth, Leipzig, 1903

Monroe, William S., 'The Status of Child Study in Europe', *Pedagogical Seminary*, 6:3 (1899), pp.372–81

Moravia, Sergio, 'The Enlightenment and the Sciences of Man', *History of Science*, 18 (1980), pp.247–68

Moretti, Franco, 'Kindergarten', in *Signs Taken for Wonders*, Verso, 1983, pp.157–81

Moretti, Franco, *The Way of the World. The Bildungsroman in European Culture*, Verso, 1987

Morss, John R. *The Biologising of Childhood. Developmental Psychology and the Darwinian Myth*, Lawrence Erlbaum, Hove, 1990

Muecke, D.C., 'Beauty and Mr. B.', *Studies in English Literature*, 7 (1967), pp.467–74

Muir, Percy, *English Children's Books, 1600–1900*, Batsford, 1954

Muirhead, J.H., 'The Founders of Child Study in England', *Paidologist*, 2:2 (July 1900), pp.114–24

Neff, Emery, *The Poetry of History. The Contribution of Literature and Literary Scholarship to the Writing of History Since Voltaire*, Columbia University Press, New York, 1947

Nelson, Claudia, *Boys Will Be Girls. The Feminine Ethic and British Children's Fiction, 1857–1917*, Rutgers University Press, New Brunswick, 1991

Nelson, T.G.A., 'The Child in Augustan Farce and Comedy', *The Eighteenth Century. Theory and Interpretation*, 30:1 (Spring 1989), pp.23–44

Neubauer, John, *The Fin-de-Siècle Culture of Adolescence*, Yale University Press, New Haven, 1992

Nietzsche, Frederich, *Thus Spoke Zarathustra* (1891–2) in Walter Kaufman (ed.), *The Portable Nietzsche*, Chatto, 1971

Parry, Idris, *Hand to Mouth*, Carcanet, Manchester, 1981

Pascal, Roy, *Design and Truth in Autobiography*, Routledge & Kegan Paul, 1960

Pattison, Robert, *The Child Figure in English Literature*, University of Georgia Press, Athens, 1978

Payne, John Howard, *Clari; or, The Maid of Milan. An Opera in Two Acts* (1923), Cumberland's British Theatre, 1829

Pearce, A.L., *An Essay on Children, and the Disease Designated Mesenteric Obstruction, Atrophy or Marasmus. Adapted Partly for Parents*, privately printed, 1838

Pereira, Jonathan, *A Treatise on Food and Diet*, Longman, 1843

Perle, George, *The Operas of Alban Berg. Volume One/Wozzeck*, University of California Press, 1980

Pocock, Isaac, *Montrose: or the Children of the Mist. A Musical Drama in Three Acts, founded on the Legend of Montrose*, Simpkin & Marshall, 1822

Pollock, John, *Shaftesbury. The Poor Man's Earl*, Hodder & Stoughton, 1985

Popham, William Home, *Nursery Guide, or, Practical Hints on the Diseases and Management of Children*, Simpkin, Marshall, 1847

Prawer, S.S., 'Mignon's Revenge: a Study of Mörike's *Maler Nölten*', *English Goethe Society, Publications*, New Series, 25 (1955–6), pp.63–85

Preyer, William, *The Mind of the Child. Part I. The Senses and the Will* (1882), Appleton, New York, 1890

Preyer, William, *The Mind of the Child. Part II. The Development of the Intellect* (1882), Appleton, New York, 1890

Quetelet, Lambert J., *Physique social. Essai sur le developpement des facultés de l'homme*, 2 vols, Muquardt, Brussels, 1835

Quetelet, Lambert J., *A Treatise on Man and the Development of His Faculties* (1842), Scholars Facsimiles and Reprints, Gainsville, Florida, 1962

Ranke, Leopold von, *Introduction to the History of the Latin and Teutonic Nations, 1494–1514* (1824), trans. P.A. Ashworth, Bell, 1887

Ranke, Leopold von, *The Secret of World History. Selected Writings on the Art and Science of History*, ed. Roger Wines, Fordham University Press, New York, 1981

Raverat, Gwen, *Period Piece. A Cambridge Childhood* (1941), Faber & Faber, 1962

Rede, Leman Thomas, *The Road to the Stage; or the Performer's Preceptor*, Joseph Smith, 1827

Reed, T.J. *Goethe*, Oxford University Press, Oxford, 1984

Rees, Henry, *Popular Directions to Parents on the Management of Children in Health and Disease*, Sherwood, Gilbert & Piper, 1829

Reid, Thomas, *Essays on the Intellectual Powers of Man* (1785), in Sir William Hamilton (ed.), *The Works of Thomas Reid*, 2 vols, MacLachlan & Stewart, Edinburgh, 1846–63

Religious Tract Society, *The Little Acrobat and His Mother*, Religious Tract Society, 1872

Richards, Evelleen, '"Metaphorical Mystifications": the Romantic Gestation of Nature in British Biology', in Andrew Cunningham and Nicholas Jardine (eds), *Romanticism and the Sciences*, Cambridge University Press, Cambridge, 1990, pp.130–43

Richardsonia XII. Pamela: Four Versions, 1741–1746, by Dance, Clifford, Edge and Goldoni, Garland, New York, 1976

Riese, Walther, 'Goethe's Conception of Evolution and its Survival in Medical Thought,' *Bulletin of the History of Medicine*, 23 (1949), pp.546–53

Riley, Denise, *'Am I That Name?' Feminism and the Category of 'Woman' in History*, Macmillan, 1988

Rilke, Rainer Maria, *Duino Elegies*, trans. J.B. Leishman and Stephen Spender, Hogarth Press, 1963

Robins, Anna Gruetzner, 'Sickert "Painter-in-Ordinary" to the Music-Hall,' in Wendy Baron and Richard Shone (eds), *Sickert. Paintings*, Royal Academy of Arts, 1992, pp.13–24

Romanes, George, *Mental Evolution in Man*, Kegan Paul, 1888

Rosaldo, Michelle Z., 'Towards an Anthropology of Self and Feeling', in Richard A. Shweder and Robert A. LeVine (eds), *Culture Theory. Essays on Mind, Self and Emotion*, Cambridge University Press, Cambridge, 1984, pp.137–57

Rose, Jacqueline, *The Case of Peter Pan, or, the Impossibility of Children's Fiction*, Macmillan, 1985

Rose, Lionel, *The Erosion of Childhood. Child Oppression in Britain 1860–1918*, Routledge, 1991

Rosenbaum, Richard, 'Mignons Urbild' (Mignon's Original), *Deutsche Literatur-Zeitung*, 7 November 1896

Rosenbaum, Richard, 'Mignons Urbild' (Mignon's Original), *Chronik des Wiener Goethe-Vereins*, 11, 10 March 1897, pp.5–6

Rosenbaum, Richard, 'Mignons Herkunft' (Mignon's Origin), *Archiv für das Studium der neueren Sprachen und Literaturen*, 100 (1898), pp.1–22

Rosenblum, Robert, *The Romantic Child. From Runge to Sendak*, Thames & Hudson, 1988

Roth, Michael S., *Psychoanalysis as History: Negation and Freedom in Freud*, Cornell University Press, Ithaca, New York, 1987

Rowe, Richard, *Picked up in the Streets, or, Struggles for Life amongst the London Poor*, Allen, 1880

Royle, Edward, *Victorian Infidels. The Origins of the British Secularist Movement, 1791–1866*, Manchester University Press, Manchester, 1974

Royle, Edward, *Radicals, Secularists and Republicans. Popular Freethought in Britain, 1866–1915*, Manchester University Press, Manchester, 1980

Ruskin, John, 'Humility', in 'Time and Tide' (1867), *The Library Edition of the Works of John Ruskin*, vol. 17, 1906, pp.405–9

Ruskin, John, 'Design in the German School', in 'Ariadne Florentia' (1874), *The Library Edition of the Works of John Ruskin*, vol. 22, Allen & Unwin, 1906, pp.390–421

Ruskin, John, 'Fairyland', in 'The Art of England' (1884), *The Library Edition of the Works of John Ruskin*, vol. 33, Allen & Unwin, 1908, pp.327–49

Saint-Hilaire, Geoffroy, *Histoire générale et particulière des anomalies de l'organisation chez l'homme et les animaux* (A General and Specific Account of Organizational Irregularities in Man and Animals), 3 vols, Ballière, Paris, 1832–7

Sanders C.R. and Fielding K.J. (eds), *The Collected Letters of Thomas and Jane Welsh Carlyle*, 7 vols, Duke University Press, Durham, North Carolina, 1970–7

Sarasin, Philipp, 'Goethes Mignon. Eine psychoanalytische Studie', (Goethe's Mignon. A psychoanalytic Study) *Imago*, 15 (1929), pp.349–99

Saussure, Mme Necker de, *Progressive Education; or, Considerations on the Course of Life* (1828–32), Longman, 1839

Schiller, J., 'Physiology's Struggle for Independence in the First Half of the Nineteenth Century', *History of Science*, 7 (1968), pp.64–89

Schleiden, J.M., *Principles of Scientific Botany, or, Botany as an Inductive Science*, trans. Edwin Lankester, Longman, 1849

Schorske, Carl E., *Fin-de-Siècle Vienna: Politics and Culture*, University of Chicago Press, Chicago, 1979

Schorske, Carl E., 'History and the Study of Culture', *New Literary History*, 21:2 (Winter 1990), pp.407–20

Schwann, Theodore, *Microscopical Researches into the Accordance of the Structure and Growth of Animals and Plants* (1839), trans. Henry Smith, Sydenham Society, 1847

Scott, Clement and Howard, Cecil, *The Life and Reminiscences of E.L. Blanchard, with Notes from the Diary of Wm. Blanchard, in Two Volumes*, Hutchinson, 1891

Scott, Sir Walter, *A Legend of Montrose* (1819), Adam & Charles Black, Edinburgh, 1883

Scott, Sir Walter, *Peveril of the Peak* (1820), Adam & Charles Black, Edinburgh, 1883

Sennett, Richard, *The Fall of Public Man*, Cambridge University Press, Cambridge, 1977

Sewell, Mary, *Our Father's Care. A Ballad*, Jarrold, 1861

Sewell, William H., 'Review of Joan Wallach Scott, *Gender and the Politics of History*', *History and Theory*, 29:1 (1990), pp.71–82

Siddons, Henry, *Practical Illustrations of Rhetorical Gesture and Action* (1822), Benjamin Blom, New York, 1968

Silver, Harold, 'Ideology and the Factory Child: Attitudes to Half-time Education', in *Education as History. Interpreting Nineteenth- and Twentieth-Century Education*, Methuen, 1983

Simon, Brian, *Education and the Labour Movement, 1870–1920*, Lawrence & Wishart, 1965

Sims, George R., *How the Poor Live With Sixty Illustrations by Frederic Barnard*, Chatto & Windus, 1883

Sims, George R., *How the Poor Live and Horrible London*, Chatto & Windus, 1889

Shattuck, Roger, *The Forbidden Experiment. The Story of the Wild Boy of Aveyron*, Secker & Warburg, 1980

Sheridan, Paul, *Penny Theatres of Victorian London*, Dennis Dobson, 1981

Smelser, Neil J., *Social Paralysis and Social Change. British Working-class Education in the Nineteenth Century*, University of California Press, Berkeley and Los Angeles, 1991

Smiles, Samuel, *Physical Education; or, the Nurture and Management of Children, Founded on the Study of their Nature and Constitution*, Oliver & Boyd, Edinburgh, 1838

Smith, Albert, *The Natural History of the Ballet Girl*, Bogue, 1847

Smith, Charles Manby, *Curiosities of London Life: or, Phases, Physiological and Social, of the Great Metropolis*, Cash, 1853

Smith, C.U.M., 'Evolution and the Problem of Mind. Part I. Herbert Spencer', *Journal of the History of Biology*, 51:1 (1982), pp.56–88

Smith, C.U.M. 'Evolution and the Problem of Mind. Part II. John Hughlings Jackson', *Journal of the History of Biology*, 15:2 (1982), pp.241–62

Stanley, Liz (ed.), *The Diaries of Hannah Cullwick, Victorian Maidservant*, Virago, 1984

Steedman, Carolyn, *The Tidy House*, Virago, 1982

Steedman, Carolyn, *Policing the Victorian Community. The Formation of English Provincial Police Forces, 1856–1880*, Routledge & Kegan Paul, 1984

Steedman, Carolyn, *Landscape for a Good Woman*, Virago, 1986

Steedman, Carolyn, *Childhood, Culture and Class in Britain. Margaret McMillan, 1860–1931*, Virago, 1990

Steedman, Carolyn, *Past Tenses. Essays on Writing, Autobiography and History*, Rivers-Oram, 1992

Stengal, E.A., 'Hughlings Jackson's Influence on Psychiatry', *British Journal of Psychiatry*, 109 (1963), pp.348–55

Stevens, Kate, 'Child Study in Great Britain', *Pedagogical Seminary*, 13:2 (1906), pp.245–9

Stokes, John, *In the Nineties*, Harvester Wheatsheaf, Hemel Hempstead, 1992

Stokes, John, '*Aux Funambules*: Acrobatics and Aesthetics', *French Cultural Studies*, 3 (1992), pp.277–98

Stretton, Hesba (Sarah Smith), *Jessica's First Prayer* (1867), Garland, New York, 1976

Struve, Christian Augustus, *A Familiar View of the Domestic Education of Children. Translated from the German. To Which Are Prefaced Three Introductory Lectures on the Same Subject by A.F.M. Willich* (1800), Murray & Highley, 1812

Sulloway, Frank, *Freud. Biologist of the Mind*, Basic Books, New York, 1979.

Sully, James, *Studies of Childhood*, Longman, 1896

Sully, James, *Children's Ways. Being Selections from the Author's 'Studies of Childhood'*, Longman, 1897

Symons, Arthur, *London. A Book of Aspects*, privately printed, 1909

Symons, Arthur, *Poems by Arthur Symons*, vol. 1, John Lane, New York, 1911

Tanner, J.M., *A History of the Study of Human Growth*, Cambridge University Press, Cambridge, 1981

Taylor, Charles, *Sources of the Self. The Making of Modern Identity*, Cambridge University Press, Cambridge, 1989

Temkin, Oswei, *The Double Face of Janus and Other Essays in the History of Medicine*, Johns Hopkins University Press, Baltimore, Maryland, 1977

Thomas, Ambroise, *Mignon. Opéra-Comique en trois actes, cinq tableaux. Paroles de Michel Carré & Jules Barbier. Musique de Ambroise Thomas*

(Mignon. A Comic Opera in Three Acts, Five Scenes. Words by Michel Carré and Jules Barbier. Music by Ambroise Thomas) (1866), Calman-Levy, Paris, 1870

Thompson, E.P. and Yeo, Eileen (eds), *The Unknown Mayhew* (1971), Penguin, Harmondsworth, 1973

Tindal, Marcus, 'Baby Actors', *Pearson's Magazine*, 3 (1897), pp.678–83

Tomalin, Claire, *The Invisible Woman. The Story of Nelly Ternan and Charles Dickens*, Viking, 1990

Tuggle, Robert R., *The Golden Age of Opera*, Holt Reinhart & Winston, New York, 1983

Tunner, Erika, '"L'Esprit de Mignon": Bilder von der Klassik bis zur Gegenwart' (Images from Classicism to the Present), *Goethe-Jahrbuch*, 106 (1989), pp.11–21

Uglow, Jenny, *Elizabeth Gaskell. A Habit of Stories*, Faber & Faber, 1993

Valentin, G., *Handbuch der Entwickelungsgeschichte des Menschen* (Guide to the History of the Development of Human Beings), Rucker, Berlin, 1835

Vincent, David, *Literacy and Popular Culture*, Cambridge University Press, Cambridge, 1989

Virchow, Rudolph Ludwig Carl, *Cellular Pathology as based upon Physiological and Pathological Histology* (1859), trans. F. Chance, John Churchill, 1860

Wagner, Walter, 'Goethes Mignon', *Germanisch-Romanische Monatsschrift*, 21 (1933), pp.401–15

Walkowitz, Judith, *City of Dreadful Delight. Narrative of Sexual Danger in Late-Victorian London*, University of Chicago Press, Chicago, 1992

Walvin, James, *A Child's World. A Social History of English Childhood, 1800–1914*, Penguin, Harmondsworth, 1982

Warner, Marina, *Joan of Arc: The Image of Female Heroism*, Weidenfeld and Nicolson, 1981

Waugh, Benjamin, 'Street Children', *Contemporary Review*, 53 (January–June 1888), pp.825–35

Weylland, John Matthias, *The Man With the Book; or, The Bible among the People*, William Hunt, 1872

Wiener, Martin J., *Reconstructing the Criminal. Culture, Law and Policy in England, 1834–1914*, Cambridge University Press, Cambridge, 1990.

Williams, L. Pearce, 'The Physical Sciences in the First Half of the Nineteenth Century. Problems and Sources', *History of Science*, 1 (1962), pp.1–15

Wilson, Adrian, 'The Infancy of the History of Childhood: An Appraisal of Philippe Ariès', *History and Theory*, 19 (1980), pp.132–53

Wilson, Louise N., 'Bibliography of Child Study', *Pedagogical Seminary*, 5:4 (1898), pp.541–89

Winter, J.S. *Bootle's Baby. A Story of the Scarlet Lancers*, Frederic Warne, 1885

Winter, John Strange, *Mignon's Secret*, F.V. White, 1886

Winter, John Strange, *Mignon's Husband*, F.V. White, 1887

Wittkowski, Georg, *Cornelia, die Schwester Goethe* (Cornelia, Goethe's Sister), Rutten Loening, Frankfurt, 1903

Wolff, Eugen, *Mignon. Ein Beitrag zur Geschichte des Wilhelm Meister* (A Contribution to the History of the Development of Human Beings), C.H Beck, Munich, 1909

Wolff, Larry, *Postcards from the End of the World: An Investigation into the Mind of Fin-de-Siècle Vienna*, Collins, 1988

Woodham-Smith, P., 'History of the Froebelain Movement in England', in Evelyn Lawrence (ed.), *Friedrich Froebel and English Education*, Routledge & Kegan Paul, 1952, pp.34–94

Young, Robert M. 'Darwin's Metaphor: Does Nature Select?', *Monist*, 55 (1971), pp.442–503

Zelizer, Viviana A., *Pricing the Priceless Child. The Changing Social Value of Children*, Basic Books, New York, 1985

Zucchi, John E., *The Little Slaves of the Harp. Italian Child Street Musicians in Nineteenth-Century Paris, London and New York*, McGill–Queens University Press, Montreal and Kingston, 1992

2. *Unpublished Sources*

Coleridge, Sara 'Diary of Her Children's Early Years, 1830–1838', Humanities Research Centre, University of Texas at Austin

Crozier, Brian, 'Notions of Childhood in the London Theatre, 1880–1905', PhD, Cambridge University, 1981

Elphinstone, James W., 'London Labour & London Poor, or Want and Vice A Drama in 2 Acts', 1854, British Library, Lord Chamberlain's Collection, Add. Ms 52, 946K

'Fenella or Peveril of the Peak an opera in three acts', 1826, British Library, Lord Chamberlain's Collection, 1826, Add Ms 48279, folios 279–566, pp.396–507

Johnstone, J.B., 'How We Live or London Labour and London Poor. Drama. Three Acts', 1856, British Library, Lord Chamberlain's Collection, Add. Ms 52958CC

Merivale, Herman, 'The Lord of the Manor. A Drama in Three Acts. Founded Upon Goethe's *Wilhelm Meister*', 1879, British Library, Lord Chamberlain's Collection. Add. Ms 532230

Morton, F. Leslie, 'Mignon. The One-Act Operatic Comi-tragique Burlesque, or, The Egg-dancer's Pet and the Artful Coquette', 1886 British Library, Lord Chamberlain's Collection, Add. Ms 53357K

Moss, Hugh, 'Bootle's Baby. A Comedy Drama in Four Acts', 1888, British Library, Lord Chamberlain's Collection, Add. Ms 53395C

Sims, G.R., 'Master and Man. Play. Four Acts', 1889, British Library, Lord Chamberlain's Collection, Add. Ms 53424B

Sims, G.R. and Pettit, Henry, 'The Harbour Lights. A New and Original

Drama', 1885, British Library, Lord Chamberlain's Collection, Add. Ms 53347.246

Sims, G.R. and Scott, Clement, 'Jack in the Box', 1885, British Library, Lord Chamberlain's Collection, Add. Ms 5334C8

Sharples, Ellen, 'Diaries, 1803–1832', City of Bristol Museum and Art Gallery

Stanley, Catherine, of Alderley, 'Journal of Her Four Children', 1811–1819, Cheshire Record Office, DSA 75

Travers, William, 'The Watercress Girl. The Original Drama. In Two Acts', 1865, British Library, Lord Chamberlain's Collection, Add. Ms 53045T

Williams, Thomas J., 'Mignon. Opera in Three Acts. English Translation by Thomas J. Williams', 1870, British Library, Lord Chamberlain's Collection, Add. Ms 53086

Index

Also by Carolyn Steedman

CHILDHOOD, CULTURE AND CLASS IN BRITAIN
MARGARET McMILLAN, 1860–1931

Taking Margaret McMillan's life and work as a starting point, *Childhood, Culture and Class in Britain* illuminates a profound transformation in Western sensibility, and looks at the psychological and political fate of this woman who gave up her life 'for the children'.

In this richly informative and widely researched book, Carolyn Steedman describes and explores the ways in which children – especially working-class children – became symbols of social hope for a better future at the end of the nineteenth century. McMillan, on the national executive of the Independent Labour Party and a charismatic socialist propagandist, played a key role in a new development in late-nineteenth-century socialism. Her writing and her political action on behalf of the children of Bradford and London formed Labour Party policy on childhood, the family and the state. More than just an account of one woman's life, this book considers major shifts in turn-of-the-century British social life.

THE TIDY HOUSE

'. . . very interesting and heartening. Seeing the problems and rewards of children's perceptions and writings that close is a great help to understanding a much wider and more persistent process' – Raymond Williams

Three working class eight-year-old girls write a story, 'The Tidy House'. It is about the house they will live in one day, the streets of their own decaying urban estate, about love and motherhood and the pattern of life they expect to inherit. The children in the story are themselves as they believe their parents see them – longed for, yet because of poverty, also sources of irritation and resentment.

In analysing this fascinating document, the author uses her remarkable perceptions of children's writing and their expectations of the world, as well as literature, linguistics, theories of education and history, to reach her highly original and controversial conclusions on how children confront the way things are and imagine the way things might be.

LANDSCAPE FOR A GOOD WOMAN
A Story of Two Lives

'A brave disciplined book about longing: not sexual longing as such but the endless longing of the underprivileged that history (and life) be different from what it has been and what it still is' – *John Berger*

There are lives, real lives, and there are the theories that explain them. *Landscape for a Good Woman* is partly autobiographical, taking a mother and her daughter, two working-class childhoods (Burnley in the 1920s, South London in the 1950s) and trying to find a place for their stories in history and politics, in psychoanalysis and feminism. What happens to cultural criticism when you confront it with working-class women and little girls? What happens when psychoanalysis is asked to look at women who don't possess the wish for a child? And what happens to theories of patriarchy when autobiography deals with a working-class father who isn't important in the world outside the household? This book is about the centrality of some stories and the marginality of others, and about the stories we tell ourselves to explain our lives.

Also of interest from Virago

BECOMING A WOMAN
And Other Essays in 19th and 20th Century Feminist History

Sally Alexander

Sally Alexander, one of Britian's most reputed feminist historians, has selected from her essays and papers of the past two decades. Writings on women and work in nineteenth-century London; feminism and social movements in Victorian England; subjectivity, memory and psychoanalysis; generation and history writing, all demonstrate the depth of her concern with the historical temporalities and imagery of feminism and sexual difference. Also charted and reflected here are the developments within feminism and feminist historiography, whether it be in the very immediate detailing of the 1970s Nightcleaners' campaign or in the wonderfully insightful account of becoming a woman in 1920s and '30s London. These exemplary papers offer us both a fascinating exploration of different historical moments and of the process of history writing itself.

CITY OF DREADFUL DELIGHT
Narratives of Sexual Danger in Late-Victorian London

Judith Walkowitz

'This remarkably polished, lucidly argued work is innovative cultural history at its best. It is one of the most sophisticated and thorough historical treatments of issues that are of widespread interest, among them sexual conflict and violence against women' – Martha Vicinus

Late-Victorian London, city of dreadful delight with new pleasures where amongst the mingling of high and low life women of every class asserted their presence in the public domain. It was a city of sexual repression, scandal and danger with Stead's famous exposé of child prostitution and the tabloid sensationalism of the Ripper murders in 1888. In this brilliantly illuminating study, Judith Walkowitz shows how these narratives played out complex dramas of power, politics and sexuality, and how they influenced the language of politics, journalism and fiction. What were the consequences for women in these accounts of class anxiety and gender conflict?

SEXUAL ANARCHY
Gender and Culture at the *Fin de Siècle*

Elaine Showalter

'A triumph . . . gleams with wit and wry insight' –
New Statesman & Society

'Sexual anarchy' – dire predictions, disasters, apocalypse – became the hallmark of the closing decades of the nineteenth century. The New Woman and the Odd Woman threatened male identity and self-esteem; the emergence of feminism and homosexuality meant the redefining of masculinity and femininity. This is the terrain which Elaine Showalter explores with such consummate originality and wit.

Looking at parallels between the ends of the nineteenth and twentieth centuries and their representations in literature, art and film, she ranges over the trial of Oscar Wilde, public furore over prostitution and syphilis, and in our own time, moral outrage over the breakdown of the family, abortion rights, AIDS. High and low culture – from male quest romances to contemporary male bonding movies (*Heart of Darkness* reworked into *Apocalypse Now*), Freud to *Fatal Attraction* – all are part of this scholarly and entertaining study of the *fin de siècle*.

HEARTS UNDEFEATED
Women's Writing of the Second World War

Edited by Jenny Hartley

Barbara Cartland, Clementine Churchill, Gracie Fields, Virginia Woolf, a Soho street-sweeper and an air-raid warden all wrote superbly about the Second World War. In articles, journals, memoirs and wartime editions of long-vanished books, they recorded their experiences of and responses to the new and disjointed world of evacuees, the Blitz, the WRENS, gas masks, the War Office and rationing.

Featuring well over a hundred women, from well-known writers such as Elizabeth Bowen, Rosamond Lehmann, Freya Stark and Beatrice Webb, to canteen workers and clippies who had never picked up a pen before, this fascinating collection unites their work for the first time. Ranging from lighter accounts of austerity – the struggle for an onion, endless queues and shorter hemlines – to a chilling description of the 1938 Nuremberg Rally and Martha Gellhorn's devastating report of Dachau in 1945, it is an invaluable portrait of the war years, as seen through women's eyes.